For Greg,

With gratitude for moments of company and abiding friendship.

Love,
Bill

RHETORIC AND PLURALISM

RHETORIC AND PLURALISM

Legacies of Wayne Booth

Edited by

Frederick J. Antczak

Ohio State University Press
Columbus

Copyright © 1995 by the Ohio State University Press.
All rights reserved.

Library of Congress Cataloging-in-Publication Data
Rhetoric and pluralism : legacies of Wayne Booth / edited by
Frederick J. Antczak.
   p. cm.
Includes bibliographical references and index.
ISBN 0-8142-0642-5. — ISBN 0-8142-0643-3 (pbk.)
   1. Booth, Wayne C.—Influence.   2. Literature and morals.
3. Rhetoric.   4. Pluralism (Social sciences) in literature.
I. Antczak, Frederick J., 1952–   .
PN75.B62R44   1994
801'.3—dc20   94-26358
                                                                  CIP

Text and jacket design by Nighthawk Design.
Type set in Granjon by Tseng Information Systems, Durham, NC.
Printed by Bookcrafters, Chelsea, MI.

The paper in this book meets the guidelines for permanence and durability of the Committee on Production Guidelines for Book Longevity of the Council on Library Resources.

9 8 7 6 5 4 3 2 1

CONTENTS

Acknowledgments — ix

Short Titles — xi

Introduction — 1

Part 1: Situating Booth

1. Teaching the Topics: Character, Rhetoric, and Liberal Education — 19
   WALTER JOST

2. Cultural Literacy: Concepts and Information — 40
   FRANCIS-NOËL THOMAS

Part 2: Ethics and Fictions

3. Wayne Booth and the Ethics of Fiction — 59
   MONICA JOHNSTONE

4. Elie Wiesel and the Ethics of Fiction — 71
   SUSAN E. SHAPIRO

5. Booth, Bakhtin, and the Culture of Criticism — 88
   DON H. BIALOSTOSKY

6. From Pluralism to Heteroglossia: Wayne Booth and the Pragmatics of Critical Reviewing — 104
   DAVID RICHTER

Part 3: Rhetoric and Politics

7. Pluralism, Politics, and the Evaluation of Criticism — 119
   JAMES PHELAN

8. Wayne Booth and the Politics of Ethics 135
BARBARA FOLEY

9. Learning to Read Martin Luther King's "Pilgrimage to Nonviolence": Wayne Booth, Character, and the Ethical Criticism of Public Address 153
FREDERICK J. ANTCZAK

Part 4: Booth across Disciplines

10. "Three Times out of Five Something Happens": James M. Cain and the Ethics of Music 167
PETER J. RABINOWITZ

11. Keeping the Company of Sophisters, Economists, and Calculators 187
DONALD N. MCCLOSKEY

12. Saying What Goes without Saying: The Rhetoric of Bacon's *Essays* 211
EUGENE GARVER

Part 5: Booth, Assent, and Argument

13. Wayne Booth and the Ethics of Argument 239
PATSY CALLAGHAN AND ANN DOBYNS

14. The Logic and Rhetoric of Systematic Assent 253
ALAN BRINTON

15. Rhetoric without Sophistry: Wayne Booth and the Rhetoric of Inquiry 266
JAMES B. MCOMBER

Afterword: Let Us All Mount Our Good Chargers, Whatever Their Names, and Gallop Off Joyfully in All Directions, a Mysteriously United Company Serving the Empress of All the Sciences, Rhetoric 279
WAYNE BOOTH

Bibliography: Wayne C. Booth COMPILED BY LEE ARTZ	309
Contributors	323
Index	327

ACKNOWLEDGMENTS

IT IS ONLY APPROPRIATE in a volume on Booth to acknowledge the community of discourse and assent which made it possible. This volume could only have come together with the support of a great number of people, including first the contributors whose patient responses to my inquiries and proddings make this a better and more coherent collection than my succession of master plans could ever have made it. Some of the editorial work and the revision of my essay were done during my participation in the Iowa Scholars' Workshop on Political Argumentation; thanks especially to John Nelson who directed it, to the Speech Communication Association and the National Endowment for the Humanities who helped pay for it, to the Project on the Rhetoric of Inquiry whose good officers ran it, and to my colleagues Mary Stuckey, Kenneth Cmiel, Ira Strauber, Robert Hariman, Frank Beer, William Lewis, Marianne Constable, G. R. Boynton, C. Edward Arrington, James Throgmorton, Teri Shearer, and Kathleen Farrell for making it so productive.

Thanks to James Aune, Thomas Benson, Donald McCloskey, David Tracy, and James Boyd White for early suggestions, and to Stephen Browne for taking a look at yet-unfinished drafts. Lee Artz was extraordinarily helpful and resourceful in helping to bring the project to completion; Peter Givler, director of the Ohio State University Press, has been most patient, and I have learned much from the anonymous reviewer he provided. Along the way I have also benefited directly from the suggestions, support, and friendship of Ben Attias, Kendall Bartsch, Bonnie Bender, Barbara Biesecker, William Brandt, David Cheshier, James Childress, Gary Comstock, Celeste Condit, Carol Corbin, Diane Crosby, Tim Crosby, Fernando Delgado, Marcia Dixson, Michael Dreher, Joseph Evans, John Gage, Edward Goerner, Susan E. George, Karen Joy Greenberg, James Grober, Bruce Gronbeck, John Hammerback, Carl Hartman, Lynn Hartman, Deborah Hauser, Allison Heffern, Michael Heffern, Michael Hogan, Judy Hunter, Diane Irvine, Michael Howard Irvine, Lorrie Jackson, Michael Janas, Geoffrey Klinger, Patrick Lewis, Deb Loss, Nancy Lowenberg, Randy Lowenberg, John Lyne, Edward Martin, Michael McGee, James McOmber, Kate Neckerman, Bill Nicholson, Janice Norton, Donovan Ochs, Takis Poulakos, Arthur Quinn, Mary Rohlfing, Warren Sandmann, Randall Schluter, Edith Siemers, Charles O. Smith, Celinda K. Stevens, John Sullivan, Jane Taylor, Sue Tjardes, Mary Trachsel, Doug Trank, Robert Vacca, Charles Wegener, and David Zarefsky.

Special thanks go to Deborah Hughes and Phyllis Booth, and of course to Wayne Booth, for his inspiration, his humor (some puns excepted) and the ethical quality of his intellectual engagement. I am also obligated, in the end, to Booth's teachers—R. S. Crane, Richard McKeon, and Elder Olson, but also P. A. Christensen, Karl Young, Luther Giddings, and the rest. For their student has lived out, with a generosity resonant in these pages, a fundamental ethic of the life of learning: that the most important obligations one incurs to one's teachers are not so much reciprocal, but transitive.

SHORT TITLES

Full publication information for the works by Wayne Booth listed here can be found in the Bibliography at the end of the volume.

Company	*The Company We Keep: An Ethics of Fiction*
Critical Understanding	*Critical Understanding: The Powers and Limits of Pluralism*
"Ethical Criticism"	"Why Ethical Criticism Fell on Hard Times"
"Freedom of Interpretation"	"Freedom of Interpretation: Bakhtin and the Challenge of Feminist Criticism"
"George Eliot"	" 'The Way I Loved George Eliot': Friendship with Books a Neglected Critical Metaphor"
Irony	*A Rhetoric of Irony*
"Kenneth Burke"	"Kenneth Burke's Way of Knowing"
Modern Dogma	*Modern Dogma and the Rhetoric of Assent*
Now Don't Try to Reason	*Now Don't Try to Reason with Me: Essays and Ironies for a Credulous Age*
Reader	*The Harper and Row Reader: Liberal Education Through Reading and Writing* (with Marshall W. Gregory)
"Revival"	"The Revival of Rhetoric"
Rhetoric	*The Harper and Row Rhetoric: Writing as Thinking, Thinking as Writing* (with Marshall W. Gregory)

"*Rhetoric* and Poetics"	"*The Rhetoric of Fiction* and the Poetics of Fictions"
Rhetoric of Fiction	*The Rhetoric of Fiction*
"Three Functions"	"Three Functions of Reviewing at the Present Time"
Vocation	*The Vocation of a Teacher: Rhetorical Occasions, 1967–1988*

INTRODUCTION

After all is said and done, it is the human aspect that lasts the longest. The scholar, thinker, teacher is merged at last in the human being, the man is the ultimate and everlasting value.

WILLIAM JAMES

THE ENTRY ON Wayne Booth in the *Dictionary of Literary Biography* is full of richly deserved praise. But one can't read it without noting that there's something unusual about it, or perhaps about Booth. The praise is of two kinds, one much rarer in typical assessments of scholarly careers than the other. The first kind of praise, however deeply felt and however impressively true, takes forms that we are used to seeing in reference to prolific and influential authors. This perhaps unavoidably resonates when we hear that "[t]he impressive variety and consistent force of Booth's work have earned him one of the broadest audiences of any twentieth-century critic, and have made him one of the most important voices in American criticism over the past twenty-five years" (51); and "the work is stunning in its range, remarkable in its lucidity, ambitious in its conception and impressive in its execution" (66).

It is clear that these claims for the originality and force of Booth's contributions are as far from perfunctory as they are from dismissive; they are sincere high praise. But in a day when so crowded a curriculum vitae would usually be thought sufficient to chronicle a professional life, Booth somehow proves more complicated, more elusive. He is a scholar whose measure cannot adequately be kenned simply in terms of the arguments he has advanced and the points he has made; it must also be seen in the kinds of activities and intellectual life in which he has engaged people: Booth *is* "that rare critic whom others read for both his company and his conclusions" (51).

His recent release of two widely acclaimed books, *The Company We Keep: An Ethics of Fiction* and *The Vocation of a Teacher: Rhetorical Occasions 1967–1988,* may have brought Booth to the attention of still more audiences. Certainly the kinds of questions he has over the course of his writing equipped his readers to explore seem of increasing interest in a variety of areas. Booth himself has entered a new stage of his career, taking emeritus status. So the time seems particularly right for reflecting on the reach and the distinctive character of his contributions, not as a retrospective but as a challenge to him for the "conclusions" that come next. But an adequate response to Wayne Booth must also find a way to reflect in appropriate terms the profit and pleasure of his company.

Although in retrospect Booth's work seems strikingly coherent, his life did not unfold in so straight a line. The first surprise was that he engaged in such academic work at all. Wayne Clayson Booth was born in American Fork, Utah, on February 22, 1921. In school he came under the influence of a teacher named Luther Giddings, and went off to college at Brigham Young University with a clear academic aspiration: to become a chemical engineer. But at BYU, his experience with two more excellent teachers, Karl Young and P. A. Christensen, turned his interests to the study of English. After earning his B.A. in 1944 and serving in the U.S. Army, Booth returned to Chicago—the site of his Mormon mission—for graduate school. At the University of Chicago, he earned an M.A. in 1947 and a Ph.D. in 1950 working with Ronald S. Crane, Elder Olson, Richard McKeon, and other members of the "Chicago school" of criticism.

At Brigham Young, Booth had begun to envision a career teaching literature to undergraduates in liberal arts colleges. And for a while, things turned out as he planned. Booth served as an assistant professor of English at Haverford College (1950–53) and then as professor and chair of English at Earlham College until the appearance of his first book, *The Rhetoric of Fiction*. After its publication in 1961, Booth accepted the George M. Pullman Chair in English at the University of Chicago.

It would have been difficult for the boy growing up in Utah, or even the graduate student in Chicago, to have envisioned a more heralded publishing debut, or as widely honored a career. *The Rhetoric of Fiction* won an unusual combination of honors: from Phi Beta Kappa, the Christian Gauss Award; from the National Council of Teachers, the David H. Russell Award. Booth held two Guggenheim fellowships (1956–57 and 1969–70). In 1970 he was named Distinguished Service Professor at the University of Chicago, and the subsequent year won the Quantrell Prize for Undergraduate Teaching, a striking combination. In 1972 he was named a Fellow of the American Academy of Arts and Sciences. He conducted the Christian Gauss seminars at Princeton University in 1974, held a National Endowment for the Humanities in 1975-76, and was Phi Beta Kappa Visiting Scholar in 1977-78. In 1979 he delivered the Beckman Lectures at the University of California at Berkeley, where he was also visiting professor of English, and that summer spent a term as professor at the University of California at Irvine's School of Criticism and Theory. In 1981-82 he held a Fellowship from the Rockefeller Foundation. He has been awarded several honorary doctorates, as well as the Distinguished Alumni Award from Brigham Young University.

Booth has served his academic communities in a variety of administrative roles. He was dean of the College at Chicago during the turbulent years of 1964 to 1969. He chaired the Committee on Ideas and Methods from 1972 until 1975 and served three terms as chair of the Board of University Publications (1974-75, 1979-80, 1984-85). He assisted Sheldon Sacks in launching the journal *Critical Inquiry,* served as coeditor until 1985, and was subsequently on its editorial board. Booth also served on the editorial boards of *Novel, Philosophy and Literature, Philosophy and Rhetoric, Rhetorica,* and *Scholia Satyrica.* But his service has not only been local. From 1952 to 1956 he served on the National Executive Committee of the College Conference on Composition and Communication, and from 1967 to 1970 on the Commission on Literature of the National Council of Teachers of English. He served on the executive council of the Modern Language Association of America from 1973 to 1976, as second vice president in 1980, first vice president in 1981, and in 1982 as president of the MLA.

In retrospective narration, the arc of this remarkable career seems a smooth line. But as Gary Comstock has observed (253), *The Rhetoric of Fiction* was an act of intellectual independence; it was not only a confirmation of his intellectual inheritance, but an act of self-criticism that shaped his subsequent work by engaging him in the development of distinct notions of pluralism and, more basically, of rhetoric as the historical synthesis that would ground and drive his inquiries.

The Chicago school critics under whom Booth trained had resisted the trend of their day to biographical study, and had insistently called attention back to the text. Their characteristic neo-Aristotelian focus was on the craft with which problems are solved and purposes achieved in the text. A great deal of this respect for the text has obviously stayed with Booth, although his sense of "the text" as a problematic term has developed into something more sophisticated than at least some of his critics have noticed. But what Booth did in *The Rhetoric of Fiction* went beyond Chicago school concerns, and consequently did much to revive in literary studies the ancient tradition of rhetoric. Booth sought to examine then-popular dogmas about narrative technique—for example, that showing is always "better" than telling, or that good audiences must remain neutral emotionally, or that art ignores the audience. The problem he saw with such dogmas was that they judge literary technique in a kind of vacuum, apart from the contribution it makes to a work's specific fictive purposes. While Booth clearly never abandoned the Chicago school respect for the text, in order to pursue the issues he thought to be of interest he moved beyond its prevailing approaches, assumptions, issues, and arguments.

In this book, Booth adopted a perspective on texts that has stayed with him throughout his work—an ethical perspective, in that he envisioned literary texts as scenes of human activity and relation, of interaction between people. Booth discussed them not as freestanding aesthetic structures or as eruptions of authors' bent childhoods, but as rhetorical acts: authors shaping readers into the audiences envisioned while writing, readers attempting to join those implied audiences. Already the pluralizer, Booth sought to multiply the considerations in terms of which critics might describe narrators to include such concerns as degree of dramatization, of self-consciousness, of involvement in the action, and even of the distance from the author's views. This allowed him to make distinctions that, as James Phelan observes, "have become so much a part of the vocabulary of narrative theory that they are commonly used with attribution" (56): the distinction between the implied author and the narrator, and distinctions among variously reliable and unreliable narrators.

The book also pushed him into lines of thought and discourse in which he still remains productively engaged. Booth closed the first edition of *The Rhetoric of Fiction* with an extensive discussion of the ethical risks and gains of certain sorts of narration. His chapter on "The Morality of Impersonal Narration" drew fire from those who read Booth as flatly condemning all impersonal narration, even though he had continued to discuss techniques in terms of particular purposes. Booth himself has acknowledged both that this chapter was in some interesting sense a failure, and that the roles our moral judgments play in reading are more complicated than he had first represented them; in the second edition of the book he attempted with some success (and still more controversy) to address those complications.

Much of his subsequent work shows the influence of what he learned in these controversies. But even at this stage, ethical concerns were fundamentally connected with Booth's project of envisioning fictive discourse as rhetorical: Gary Comstock even contends that *The Rhetoric of Fiction*'s greatest contribution may be its insistence that the choice of narrative effects inescapably involves moral choices about the relation of author and reader and the way they may share meaning.

That relation formed the backdrop of *A Rhetoric of Irony,* Booth's inquiry into perhaps a most elusive kind of sharing of meaning. Again, Booth saw irony as a kind of interaction between people. Booth's now-familiar distinction of stable and unstable irony depends on the extent to which any given "reading" of an irony may be subverted further in a way that brings both reader and author along: stable irony is intended, covert, fixed in where interpretation is to stop, and finite in application. Of course any irony can be destabilized if its author's intended meaning and relation to the reader are ignored, but there are benefits that arise from anchoring inquiry in this relation. Booth was able to do a variety of things with irony that no one had done quite so well before; to distinguish irony from other figurings of language that require readers to go beyond literal meaning, to explore the extraordinary literary "knowledge" that irony can afford, to explicate the clues to that knowledge, to analyze distinct levels of evaluating irony, and even to identify handicaps of character that might prevent readers from forming such a relation.

Booth's persistent emphasis on reasonable and arguable judgments illuminates another aspect of his conception of rhetoric, while it displayed his uncommon intellectual range. *A Rhetoric of Irony* was widely recognized as a distinguished book of literary criticism and, to some extent at least, theory. *Modern Dogma and the Rhetoric of Assent* was rather a philosophy of rhetoric. Here Booth took up the problem of subjectivity where *The Rhetoric of Fiction* left it, by putting into question modernism's antirhetorical split of fact and value. Some commentators have speculated about the extent to which his own experience as dean of a college in a tumultuous time is recapitulated in the two camps he describes, "irrationalists" and "scientismists." If so, he behaved as he did in his deanship, still refusing simply to pick a side; arguing that facts and values cannot be split, Booth questioned the modernist dogmas of both scientismists and irrationalists, and offered some alternative ways of proceeding.

His "warrants of assent" depend on a new picture of the thing we change when we change minds: the human mind, the human self as a "field of selves." Our hold on "truths"—be they truths of the wildest heart or truths of the coldest laboratory—is always social, always made in symbolic exchange, always refined in the process of sharing values and facts. James Phelan explains (62) why this emphasis on the social is a key move for Booth's commitment to pluralism, as well as to his interdisciplinary bent: it implies that "there can be no one supreme logic against which all assertions must be tested," and that we must recognize many valid logics, a plurality of domains of knowing.

Modern Dogma was an attempt to found and enact a peaceable, pluralistic community of those readers whose essential assent was an assent to rhetoric—to the pursuit of good reasons together. But in the 1960s and 1970s, Booth saw that his own profession had been riven by increasingly virulent "logomachy," critical warfare. His next book, *Critical Understanding: The Powers and Limits of Pluralism,* developed the pluralistic insights of the rhetoric of assent in a way that applied to critical pluralism.

Critical Understanding takes up issues that needed to be addressed for Booth to extend, and even defend, the conclusions of *The Rhetoric of Fiction,* so in some ways its place in Booth's career is easy to fix retrospectively. Yet in important ways it was a surprise because of the ethically extraordinary turn it took. The opening chapter, expectably, posed the comprehensive philosophical questions that confront such arguments: Is pluralism ever really genuine, or does it always ultimately cloak a deeper monism or lapse into relativism? How might one argue that the meaning of a work might be made determinate in different ways? In what pluralisms is there a chance for these different ways to be reconciled in a critical coexistence, and how in turn might different pluralisms be related to each other?

To answer, Booth discussed in extensive detail three different pluralists: R. S. Crane, Kenneth Burke, and M. H. Abrams. These discussions led Booth to articulate two principles of his own pluralism: that there is no one true definition of the text, but rather something like five major approaches to texts, each of which admits of further variations; and, nevertheless, there are ways in which one can share, test, and try to improve a particular interpretation. The explanation must have its own logic or "coherence"; it must treat accurately with the world outside of itself, which Booth called "correspondence"; and it must show "comprehensiveness," accounting for all the textual features its own principles implicate and all those identified in the object by other modes.

At this point, a reader might expect Booth to use conclusions from these "case studies" to somehow resolve the philosophical questions he raised. Here instead arose the surprise: even though he would not abandon his commitment to pluralism, Booth's next move was to point out his own inability to carve out a ground from which to argue for it, since none of the three pluralisms adequately passed these three tests.

The measure of a mind often is apparent in what it does after it confronts an interesting failure; so it has been consistently with Booth. The self-avowed "failure" of the last chapter of *The Rhetoric of Fiction,* for example, spawned the whole line of ethical thinking about discourse that would so productively occupy Booth for twenty-five years, to culminate (so far) in *The Company We Keep.* Within *Critical Understanding,* this failure forced Booth to articulate his own privileged assumption, that pluralism is so important a good for criticism that no arguments nor argumentative failures can overturn it. What had to be overturned is the book's apparent purpose, to work out a justification for pluralism on the philosophical level of a *Modern Dogma.* Booth instead took a pragmatic turn: the critical community must be dedicated to the advancement of three inseparable ends that are, when push comes to shove, more important than comprehensive truth: *vitality,* the end of cultivating rather than stilling further discourse; *justice,* which calls each critic to apply a consistent standard; and *understanding,* the capacity to set aside even the strongest convictions and deepest presumptions long enough to enter another's critical framework and mind, to take in another self in a continually enriching field of selves.

Booth then worked out the implications of a pluralism based on vitality, justice, and understanding, a pluralism for which truth is less important than the way of life critics create for themselves and each other when they talk. A pursuit of truth that violates these values in its interactions—with literary authors or with other critics—is for practical purposes an ethical contradiction, in that it subverts the community of discourse in which it seeks to claim or carve a place. A cultivation of vitality, justice, and understanding that falls short of the whole truth will nonetheless enhance the critical community and the possibilities of the lives we can live together in it.

In addition to editing *The Knowledge Most Worth Having,* Booth subsequently published collections of his own essays and occasional addresses, *Now Don't Try to Reason with Me: Essays and Ironies for a Credulous Age* and *The Vocation of a Teacher: Rhetorical Occasions, 1967–1988.* The seriousness with which Booth has always taken teaching is reflected and refracted in the occasional pieces he produced all along and collected in these works. The variety of those occasions, the inventiveness and flexibility in perspectives, and the gentle irony that make those books cohere grace all his work. But perhaps because of their subject matter, those books have not received much attention. In a scholarly generation not noted for such concern, no retrospective on Booth can afford to understate how seriously he has always taken his teaching; nowhere is this seriousness more variously, resourcefully, convincingly, and even buoyantly represented than in these works. Most recently, he has chosen from his own compendious reading a poignant and bracing anthology of selections on *The Art of Growing Older*.

Among his most widely noted books is *The Company We Keep*. Thomas Conley points out that Booth shares the conviction that literature is equipment for living with contemporary political critics, both Marxist and feminist. But characteristically, "Booth's ethical criticism is based not on universals but on particulars, not on theoretical demystifications but on our experience of literature" (162). In coining the critical concept of *coduction,* Booth opens a way to address ethical problems left untouched, it seems, by the traditional categories of logic. Criticism neither follows deductively from premises held above the fray nor does it arise inductively from a series of all-authoritative instances, but emerges "coductively," in comparing one's experience with other more or less qualified observers in acts of reading that are always "reciprocal and responsive," part of a "continuing conversation."

Ethical conversation about narrative texts is worth pursuing, Booth argues, because narratives embody norms that may be accepted, rejected, tolerated, negotiated; because evaluations of a narrative can be rational if they are based on accurate descriptions of a narrative's power to elicit responses; because the inevitable diversity in ethical judgments does not by itself undercut the legitimacy of such judgment; and (in a move reminiscent of *Modern Dogma*) because in practice we live as if some judgments qualify as shared knowledge.

If we regard narratives, as some contemporary critics do, under the metaphors of games or puzzles, ethical criticism seems inappropriate. But Booth provides an alternative metaphor: texts may be seen as acts of personal relation; implied authors claim to be not just companions but friends. So instead of asking what future effects a story will have on a reader, Booth wants to discern the kind and quality of company it offers while the reader is engaged with it. Booth uses the rhetorical tradition to set up criteria for friendship that can be applied to the evaluation of literature. Then he applies them, with some surprising results, to some of his own favorites: Rabelais, Austin, Lawrence, and Twain. In fact, Booth introduces this project with the story of a decades-old controversy about teaching Twain's *Huckleberry Finn*. The objections that Booth once discounted, he now takes more seriously; characteristically, he has learned from the discourse in which he has engaged, has been changed by it, though not in the ways that any of his interlocutors might have foreseen. And in this insight as well as any might be captured part of Booth's intellectual and ethical legacy.

In our day's academic bestiary we are more than familiar with Old Boars who have closed their minds, or at least their ears. Booth surely was in a sufficiently cushy position to have done that, to have defended himself, as some contemporaries have, behind a palisade of academic honor and power. Instead, he has been persistently hard on himself in print, not for the sake of public penitence but to push his own thought further in original ways. In *The Rhetoric of Fiction* he criticized the assumptions that might have been his professional gravy train, and pushed himself beyond them. In *The Vocation of a Teacher* he mocks the sexism in an earlier essay with "Is There Any Knowledge a Woman Must Have?" And the whole introduction to *Company* depends on Booth's having continued to think about Paul Moses's objection to *Huckleberry Finn,* thought that leads him not to Moses's position but to one more fully his own.

Booth has taken a certain amount of flak for this bothersome habit of continuing to think from those who wish him to champion Determinate Meaning in Texts, who see him as having recanted what he knows or, at least, knew. It is true that he has continued to reshape certain of his conclusions. But he has done so not as a literary Galileo, bent to the corrupt papacy of the politically correct, but (what some might find more subversive) because he has listened, learned, and changed his mind. Booth talks in *The Vocation of a Teacher* about teaching by modeling; what he has modeled in his writing about good reasons is the capacity to change his mind in response to good reasons. To an extraordinary extent, Wayne Booth has been living in his critical discourse the kind of critical life that he has been writing about. By the way he has "taken in"—although I'm sure he'd tell me to use that phrase advisedly and with due irony in this context—other selves into his field of selves, he has not only practiced what he's preached; he has "preached" it in an even more persuasive way in the quality of his intellectual company, and in the critical life in which he has engaged others.

This volume is evidence of just how true and how high a compliment that is. A few of the authors included here have been students in Booth's classrooms. But in pursuing their own very diverse projects, all have found it important to keep his company in reading, and each in distinctive ways and degrees has clearly been shaped in that interrelation. Each—whether investigating logic or literary criticism, Bakhtin or Bacon, economics or music—shows at least this much of his influence: each genuinely and rigorously engages Booth's work and grapples seriously with Booth's evolving notions of rhetoric and pluralism; each, however, extends his work in a productive new direction. Reflecting on what Booth brings to their areas of inquiry, each responds with the "yes, but . . ." that Booth regards as the most welcome of critical responses; striving to understand and to do justice to his work while vitalizing the critical conversation further, in an intriguing variety of directions.

First come two chapters that attempt to resituate Booth, both within contemporary controversies and within the life experiences and roles where such controversies matter most for human character.

Booth has taken on several roles in his illustrious career, most intriguingly the simultaneous roles of generalist and specialist in rhetoric. Walter Jost looks for a way to integrate the roles without demoting or denigrating either one. He finds it in a discussion of the formal and special topics of rhetoric, and the argument that Booth makes about them: that the duty of liberal education is to provide a base on which specialties might be built without losing sight of the foundations on which they rest. Jost finds in this approach to considering specifics while attending to the whole an essential characteristic of Booth's life, beliefs, and work.

One peculiar aspect of that work is the distinctive continuity—in which Booth takes great pleasure—between what Booth has done and what teachers of elementary literacy, grade school teachers of reading and writing, do. Francis-Noël Thomas enlists Booth's continuity with those who are on the front lines of teaching to make a revealing critique of current dogmas about literacy. To say more risks giving away too much, but Thomas's argument is a most ingenious, and perhaps *the* most devastating, contribution to our ongoing discussions about "core" knowledge—and as such is a meaningful mobilization of (and tribute to) Booth's specific excellences as a teacher.

Booth's work as a literary critic shapes the second section. These chapters focus what the authors take to be Booth's key ethical questions on literature and the criticism of literature. Monica Johnstone takes up two related topics: the first to explicate Booth's version of ethics as heuristic, the second to demonstrate what his ethics offers that other explicitly ethical rhetoricians do not. While two more prescriptive approaches fail in application to Jean Genet's *Querelle,* she shows how Booth's more descriptive criticism makes conversation possible even among critics of differing disciplinary commitments who are bound into community by their very activity as critics.

Susan Shapiro examines an intriguing limit case—a case involving the breakdown of narrative community and even the possibilities of discourse—in reading Elie Wiesel's "true fiction" on the Holocaust through Booth. Shapiro sees Wiesel confronting a dilemma: How could Wiesel narrate such an event—seemingly the end of all history and God's presence in history—as stories, accounts that have beginnings, middles, and ends? Yet how could he remain silent, and fail to witness? What seemed to be demanded was no less an enactment, in fiction, of some sort of "postcovenantal religious praxis." Shapiro uses Booth to explicate how Wiesel found the authenticating possibilities of true fiction risked in friendship.

Don Bialostosky examines Booth's revision of his notions of rhetoric in light of Mikhail Bakhtin's works on Dostoevsky and on feminist criticism. Bialostosky characterizes Booth as shifting from a monologic Chicago school perspective toward Bakhtin's dialogic perspective, demonstrating how rhetoric and dialogics have a symbiotic relation worth further analysis. But Bialostosky also argues that Booth, in his response to Bakhtin, effectively shifts the grounds of argument from technical attacks to something like moral differences, confronting directly the problem of evaluating the number of critical voices implied by pluralism, given that neither rhetorical nor dialectical means can fully answer all critical objections.

David Richter examines the evolution in Booth's sense of pluralism—a critical approach that grew and deepened from originally championing instrumental pluralism to revealing an inherent weakness in it, its peculiar and distorting reliance on aligning critical methods as competing rather than as complementary. Richter notes how Booth's move from instrumental pluralism to a pragmatic scheme embroils him in the debate over textual meaning: can Booth reasonably search for inherent meanings in a text—the values of vitality, justice, and understanding—while at the same time not limiting the meaning of the text to the inherent, the predetermined? Although Booth has not yet offered a full solution for this problem, Richter notes a sense in which Booth's emphasis on the social and practical aspect of criticism has enabled him to elude it.

As a University of Chicago dean during the tumultuous 1960s and as the president of MLA and a national figure during difficult times for literary study, Booth has surely had a public life. But Booth's greater public significance may lie in the implications of his writing. Part 3 pushes Booth further on various aspects of the politics of his work. James Phelan probes Booth's conception of pluralism by elaborating its connection with politics. By examining Gilbert and Gubar's work in feminist criticism and their critique by Toril Moi, Phelan suggests that committed pluralists do indeed have standards by which they judge critics, standards by which he can show how Moi's arguments fail, and how Gilbert and Gubar also fall short. Phelan notes the political implications of his choice of texts, which allow him to conclude "though there is no getting outside of politics, there is also no good reason to treat discourse only as political."

Barbara Foley nonetheless wishes for the connections between Booth's work and politics to be stronger. *The Company We Keep* has evoked in several quarters a similar kind of critique—that the book is apolitical to a fault. Since Booth himself comments extensively in response to Foley's essay, suffice it to say that it is a resourceful and rousing challenge to Booth's choice of putting ethics before politics.

In my own chapter, on Martin Luther King, Jr.'s rhetoric of nonviolence, I may be offering a partial response to Foley's criticisms. I argue for an inherently political (if as yet not fully explicated) strain in Booth's ethical approach to rhetoric, and explore its character by using it to open up aspects of a particular text that is wonderfully problematic, both ethically and politically.

Booth's "interdisciplinarity" provides the unifying (or, perhaps the plurifying) theme for part 4, where his influence is stretched from music to economics to philosophy. First, Peter Rabinowitz imports Boothian insights into the musical variant of the rhetorical situation. He constructs at least the foundations of a theoretical framework for understanding how people derive spiritual and emotional messages—essential material for ethical stances and systems—from music. Rabinowitz shows us how to seek such messages not "in the music itself" but in the listener's attributions, made via recollections and interpolations of life experience, to which Booth gives him an original and interesting angle of access.

Few disciplinary worlds are more apparently different from Booth's, if Donald McCloskey is to be believed, than economics, which sustains a kind of academic tradition of divorcing itself from ethics. Nonetheless, McCloskey insists that "modern economics would do well to recognize its Aristotelian *ethos*"; he points to important ways that a Boothian pluralism can speak ethically to economics, and even to a few reciprocal ways in which economics is needed to teach students of literature "a thing or two about ethics." The economist who can make the realization that she is, after all, "a teller of tales" a part of everyday practice will become more valuable company to keep, and thus can teach us more interesting senses of valuable company.

Eugene Garver brings Booth's perspective to a kind of discourse he charges Booth with having scanted, at least in *The Rhetoric of Fiction* (a charge of selectivity to which Booth will choose to respond): discourse in which neither the author nor the reader is abstracted—at least quite so fully as in fiction—from specific political and ethical context. Garver shows how this may be true of discourse that is didactic by design. In this, Garver takes on an interesting burden, for we have all read dreary species of the bludgeoningly didactic kind. And in many instances of this kind of discourse, the purpose of which is to teach, we have seen authors seeking actually to reduce the moral activity of the reader. But for Garver, the genre need not be so bankrupt; he sees in Francis Bacon an intriguing alternative, and uses concepts from Booth to make it accessible, and to allow us to explore how reading didactic discourse can make us better people.

Part 5 explores the problematic and promising relation among assent, ethics, and pluralism. Patsy Callaghan and Ann Dobyns explore that relation as it arises in teaching ethical argument. They place argument at "the theoretical heart of the ethical pursuit," in that region of contingency between the unbending certainties of "hard fact" and the easy relativism of "soft faith" where characters are made. They explicate provocative implications for the purpose and status of the basic course in composition. Booth's notion of assent emerges from their analysis as a prime resource for retheorizing critical thinking for this essential component of education.

Alan Brinton approaches Booth's notions of systematic assent from an analytic tradition, and raises challenging questions about the nature of systematicity. He argues both that Booth's foils in *Modern Dogma*, especially Descartes and Russell, were not as systematically dubious as he characterizes them, and that a truly systematic assent—endorsing the diametric opposite of these foils—would confine Booth to the same intellectually barren ground that rejecting all propositions would. If Brinton can hang Booth on this hook, then systematic assent turns out neither a method of assent, nor systematic. Rather, it would be revealed as an ethically conservative method, favoring established beliefs and relying on authorities for matters of belief—not a systematic assent, but a system of presumptions and burdens, ironically like the program put forth by Bertrand Russell.

James McOmber regards Booth as in pursuit of a rhetoric of inquiry that is also an ethic of inquiry, urging and enabling persuaders "to attend carefully to the kinds of persons they make of themselves and their followers as they inquire together." McOmber explores the special connections Booth has forged between argument and character in our pluralistic context, and assesses the value of such connections for the life of the mind and the possibilities of continuing discourse.

Of course it would be an impoverished version of "pluralism" that read it as a mandate for Booth to just stand up and take hit after hit. In the afterword, Booth reflects on these essays and their relative reasonableness; the understanding and the force with which he does so is itself instructive of how he has characteristically engaged in critical discourse. For while Booth has, throughout his career, been willing to correct himself, admit failure, and learn, he has also engaged in strenuous debates with his critics, as much in this volume as elsewhere, and has devastated many of the attacks made upon him. Booth again makes clear that pluralism entails not an uncritical passive acceptance, but a greater responsibility to argue actively (see, for example, the second edition of *The Rhetoric of Fiction*); he continues to teach us here in the critical and ethical qualities with which he makes his counterarguments.

I find consolation in the belief that this book is not the last we will be hearing about, or from, Wayne Booth. This eases my apprehension that full perfect justice has not yet been done to all sides of him—say, to Booth the ironist (has one of our authors missed the irony in Booth's call for "inventionics or arrangementistics"?); to Booth, the still-aspiring cellist; or to the Booth whose attention, teasing, and practical jokes convinced at least one dubious graduate student of the humanity of the scholarly life, and thus almost singlehandedly kept him in it. After all is said and done, it may be this human aspect that is most elusive. Yet the merger of scholar, thinker, and teacher into the human being is perhaps the ultimate realization of value that makes all the rest of his virtues and insights so enduring and persuasive.

Bibliography

Comstock, Gary. "Wayne Booth, Pluralist." *Religious Studies Review* 10.3 (1984): 252–57.
Conley, Thomas. "Booth's *Company* and the Rhetoric We Keep." *Rhetorica* 3.2 (1990): 161–74.
Phelan, James. "Wayne C. Booth." *Dictionary of Literary Biography.* Vol. 67, "Modern American Critics Since 1965." Ed. Gregory S. Jay. Detroit: Gale, 1988. 49–66.

I

Situating Booth

1

Teaching the Topics: Character, Rhetoric, and Liberal Education

WALTER JOST

Betwixt genius and dilligence there is very little room left for art.
CICERO, DE ORATORE, 2.35

TOWARD A UNIFIED FIELD THEORY

CONSIDER HOW, AT first glance (and for some time thereafter), Wayne Booth impresses one not so much as a single Booth than as a complex field of Booths: teacher, dean, member of university and national seminars-colloquia-committees uncountable, MLA president, visiting lecturer, author of works on fiction, criticism, film, education, irony, rhetoric, ethics, religion, teaching. . . .[1] In a recent address Booth calls himself a rhetorician, and in a recent book a generalist: a closer look will reveal to the initiate that for Booth these mean the same thing, but a set of questions will have occurred to the longtime Booth reader well before this: Is there a center to this widening (or at least fluctuating) gyre, is there some doctrine, activity, character, that pulls these pursuits together? Is calling oneself a generalist only an unsuccessful dodge of the more obviously demeaning label "dilettante" (however brilliant this

---

A slightly different version of this essay appeared in *Rhetoric Society Quarterly*, 21 (Winter 1991), 1–16.

dilettantism may be)? Or is there a unified field theory to account for these many Wayne Booths?

Such a unified center does exist, I believe, though my aim in this chapter is not personal praise. Instead, I am interested in arguing that Booth's version of rhetorical generalism is relevant to understanding—Booth, to be sure; in my view an essential perspective on Booth—but, more importantly, to understanding the very enterprise of rhetoric itself, as a dynamic, changing basis for liberal education—an education precisely to a specific, coherent, intellectual and moral character.[2] Booth has never been content with whatever ethical order or identity he may have managed for himself (as real-life author or act-er) over forty-odd years of multiform activity. Explicitly in most of his writings, more or less implicitly in the rest, Booth has not only written about rhetorical education, he has urged it on his readers (and exemplified it in doing so) as an ideal that will organize us—both our own individual characters, and the collective character of the communities we share. My question about Booth, then, is at the same time a question about the unity of rhetoric, ethics, and education: Just what is the unified activity of a rhetorician (qua generalist) such that we should attempt to fashion ourselves, our communities, and this very fashioning itself, in accord with it? My emphasis, it will be clear, is not on Booth the man or "Booth" the implied author, much less on anything like a real "theory" (certainly as metaphorical a concept here as "center" and "gyre"), but on the rhetorical activity of educating to a "rhetoric" that can be named and identified and studied in performance, but not frozen in historical time or place.

An inquiry that would begin to do justice to these themes would range further and penetrate deeper than the limits of this chapter allow, but within these limits I seek to offer some insights into these related matters. My thesis is simple but works on two levels: first, character, rhetoric, and the cultivation of these in liberal education constitute the very center of Booth's concerns—both the subject of his writings, and the activity exemplified in those writings and in his other activities—and I am concerned on this level with the coherence of the two together. Second, and more broadly, I believe that we can all gain a coherent and compelling view of what liberal education should be, precisely through an understanding of what a rhetorical character should be. I might set up my argument more clearly by dispatching (if not disproving) a few common misconceptions.

First, as Aristotle (and the subsequent tradition in which the likes of Cicero, Vico, Newman, and Booth stand) makes clear, rhetoric is not a principled inquiry into a determinate subject matter, but rather a "faculty" or "power" or (loosely, as in Cicero) an "art" or method. This power or method in turn, however, is to be equated with neither those interminable, barren lists of tropes, or commonplaces, or rules, or argument-types, that rhetoricians have regularly accumulated in the past, nor again with those "good reasons" or "warrantable assents" that theorists (like Booth, partly following Dewey) have rightly championed against various positivisms in our own time. Booth's stress on "good reasons" has been right, no doubt, given the dogmas he was trying to remove, but throughout his works implicitly, and explicitly in *The Vocation of a Teacher* (1988), Booth reminds us that rhetoric involves not only proof or judgment, but discovery or *inventio*. In diverting our attention from judgment to invention, I am suggesting that earlier campaigns in the rhetoric war, particularly those fought to establish the nonfoundationalist nature of reason (excellently chronicled by Richard Bernstein, among others[3]), are now widely seen to have been successful. On the other hand, we have not yet begun to fight for the changes in education our earlier gains require if they are not to be wasted. More than twenty-five years ago, in "The Revival of Rhetoric" (1965), Booth had observed (not entirely tongue-in-cheek): "I find it interesting . . . that with all our modern passion for inventing new studies with proper labels we do not even have words in our language for the sciences of invention and arrangement. . . . [S]urely it is time for someone to make himself a professor of inventionics or arrangementistics . . ." (42). For Booth, as for Aristotle and Cicero, rhetoric involves inquiry as well as proof; and for Booth and Cicero, Vico and Vives, Newman, Kierkegaard, and Kenneth Burke, rhetoric comprises the building of character, community, and truth by cultivating the ability to discover warrantable assents in all areas of knowledge (or, across the curriculum), because all knowledge is more or less rhetorical, more or less bound up with the interests, values, beliefs, expectations, and the like of inquirers.

From this perspective, secondly, we can conceive of liberal education, after Booth himself, not so much in the first instance as a doctrine, a "knowledge most worth having," than as a method, a knowing most worth *doing,* that shares with rhetoric three characteristics: first, it concerns all areas of knowledge, not a single determinate subject matter; second, it is mediated (in varying degrees) by the "whole person"; and third, it involves a critical inquiry or invention not reducible to algorithmic methods—it involves a rhetorical power of discovering, as Booth says, what really warrants our assent (not only within a stable framework of truths, as in Aristotle, but also among competing frameworks or paradigms). To be sure, this view of liberal education as rhetorical is not unique to Booth, nor is it free of tension with several contrary currents in his thought. Still, it is a view in eclipse in recent discussions of liberal education, though there are stirrings on the right and the left respecting rhetoric and education.[4] But it has been little observed and less remarked that Booth illuminates this matter in rich detail in both his discussion and his critical practice, and for the remainder of this chapter I pursue his type of rhetoric of liberal education, in part by reference to his works, but first by picking up a discussion among rhetoricians over what I take to be the heart of rhetorical invention (and thus liberal education): the role of rhetorical topics (*topoi*) in teaching and inquiry.

PLACING THE TOPICS

The history of the topics is notoriously slippery (as is well known, the term has a dozen or more meanings and applications) but we might try to simplify: *topics* are "places" the rhetor turns to—or, less metaphorically, ideas, terms, formulas, phrases, propositions, argument forms, and so on that the rhetor turns to—to discover what to say on a given matter. Topics as determinate formulas of one sort or another, what Bacon called "promptuary devices" and others "commonplaces," ranging from a memorized word or line to entire prefabricated passages, are of no concern here since they are peculiarly nonrhetorical (fixed and determinate when the supposition of rhetoric is the opposite). What is of interest are those topics that are more or less indeterminate verbal resources useful for discovering (or "inventing") what is relevant, arguable, persuasive in a given case (let us call them *inventional* topics). The inventional topics belong to rhetoric as an intellectual faculty oriented to "action" (to practical effect, to nonexpert audiences or expert audiences considering nonexpert aspects of their expertise, and to the "practical" generally), and to "indeterminacy" (the concrete and contingent nature of rhetorical issues).[5] But how, more specifically, are topics to function, and how is the teaching of topics to proceed? To answer these questions we need to do two things: first, by an act of (topical) "placement," in Kenneth Burke's terms, we need to identify how topics have been understood historically; and secondly, by a further act of placement, we need to turn to specific examples (the exemplary work of Wayne Booth), to the *application* of an otherwise abstract knowledge of rhetoric, to appreciate that *only* such concrete knowledge of topics can provide what has long been understood to be genuine liberal education.

The most comprehensive schema in the literature on topics distinguishes between *material* and *formal*, that is, topics that express or generate substantive issues and warrants of various sorts, and those that provide only the "forms" of arguments.[6] Aristotle is a case in point (Cicero, Quintilian, and later theorists would do as well): the twenty-eight inferential "forms" (the *topoi enthumematon*) listed in Book II of the *Rhetoric*, arguments from definition, cause, sign, similarity, circumstance, and so on (which have never ceased to reappear in one guise or another in textbooks on composition, speech, rhetoric, and criticism) are formal topics. Material topics (in Aristotle at least) are of two types: the *koina* or "the commons" applicable to all subjects (more/less, possible/impossible, past/future fact, and the premises that derive from these headings); and the *eide* or "special topics" belonging to specific substantive areas. To be sure, the distinction between material and formal topics is relative: formal topics seek to help generate material but are themselves empty, and material topics naturally have some formal dimension to them, inferential or otherwise, though their utility is substantive, not formal.

Of the material topics there are several types or forms that can be found in Aristotle, Cicero, and other theorists: in particular, special topics (though common also) can be (1) general substantive headings or categories of knowledge (in Cicero "act" and "person," or again the *utile* and *honestas;* in Aristotle "ways and means," "imports and exports," "motives," "laws"); or substantive concepts (and groups of concepts), or indeed verbal structures of any sort (a law case, a character in a narrative, a narrative itself, an image), whose meaning is to be (re-)negotiated in a given case; (2) propositions used as major premises in arguments (vid. *Rhetoric*, Book I, 5–15); and (3) background information—assumptions, truths, and so on—that the rhetor can use to generate arguments of various sorts based on such information (e.g., Aristotle's analyses of the emotions in *Rhetoric*, Book II). With respect to the greater importance of special as compared to common topics, John Henry Newman observed, "To say nothing else, common-places are but blunt weapons, whereas it is particular topics that penetrate and reach their marks" (338). And Bacon was equally impressed by the special *topoi:* ". . . *topics* are of two sorts, general and special. The general we have spoken to; but the particular hath been touched by some, but *rejected generally as inartificial and variable*. But . . . I do receive particular topics, (that is, places or directions of invention and inquiry in every particular knowledge,) as *things of great use,* being mixtures of logic with the matter of sciences. . ." (129, emphasis added). (But this acceptance by Bacon of the special topics is historically untypical.)

Finally, all such categories, concepts, propositions, and information can be explicit or implicit in a given text.

Something like this scheme covers the rhetorical topics, so that we are in a position to inquire more closely into how topics are to function realistically in teaching, inquiry, and criticism. We know how they typically have functioned. Some years ago Professor Carolyn Miller expressed consternation over what she argued has been the repeated loss of the special topics in the teaching of rhetoric (she meant, I believe, all material topics, common or special, but particularly the special topics), and the habitual turn to the formal or "inferential" topics.[7] Miller rightly saw that the history of rhetorical pedagogy and theory has favored inferential or formal topics, in great part because, unlike material topics, formal topics can be easily itemized, circumscribed, and transmitted, as Bacon himself had observed, "But leaving the humour which hath reigned too much in the schools, which is, to be fairly subtle in a few things which are within their command, and to reject the rest" (129). As Miller writes: ". . . the inferential perspective is clearly advantageous to the teacher—it provides convenience, coherence, and limitations; it permits isolation [from the topics' original context] and elaboration. The materialist perspective, in contrast, emphasizes the diversity and complexity of rhetorical practice" (65). In other words, what we gain in the turn from material topics to formal topics is a (sometimes dubious) systematic coherence at the risk of forfeiting reality and informed judgment.

Miller's response to this problem, with which I concur, is to call for the rejuvenation of the special (material) topics, those drawn from specific areas or disciplines, in rhetorical study and education, and she proceeds to offer a triad of topical headings as a new typology for special topics.[8] Her typology is perfectly reasonable, but it could, one imagines, easily degenerate into the rhetorician's characteristic move toward systemizing that she rightly fears. The problem here is that we cannot really rejuvenate the material topics unless we appreciate the goal of rhetorical education; too often in the past the use and teaching of topics have been cut off from what rhetoric might practically be and what organizational structure our knowledge and teaching might plausibly take. In fact I think it quite probable that the very "places" where rhetoricians have looked to understand both topics and rhetoric, namely the standard theories of rhetoric from Aristotle and Cicero onwards, have blinded us in two ways: (1) the previous historical contexts that gave rise to these theories of rhetoric and topics may have occluded our view of the new conditions under which we might now more realistically understand topics; and (2) the theoretical remove at which such general inquiries into topics have been conducted has led us to deflect ourselves inadvertently from a more realistic, practical, rhetorical grasp of what topics might be and do. An "objective" or theoretical knowledge of topics is necessary but insufficient for grasping such practical devices.

The task, then, is not to dismiss rhetorical history or theory, but to read both in the light of present (and past) realities of rhetorical practice, the structure and aims of liberal education, and the practice of teaching. That practical turn in my title—teaching the topics—may appear to some to threaten to make elementary (to juvenilize) this aspect of the philosophy and theory of rhetoric, rather in the way Miller has rightly argued it has in the past, but my argument here is that this need not occur. In the thought and practice of Wayne Booth, I believe, we find a model of practical sensitivity to the special topics often lacking in "general" rhetorics, and it is to this thought and practice, now itself understood as a material or "special" rhetoric, that I wish to turn.

REINVENTING THE MATERIAL TOPICS

From the beginning of his career, Booth has ventured characterizations and definitions of rhetoric, which we might simply summarize thus: *rhetoric* is the faculty and art of producing and appraising what really warrants our assent. This is simple enough, though far reaching in its scope and depth. It is grounded on the premise that all knowledge is mediated in some degree by the "horizons" or "paradigms" or "fiduciary frameworks" in which we necessarily move and have our being. Of course, some problems are more determinate than others, but, when we face those problems we agree can or should be treated more or less "objectively," as recurrencies susceptible to determinate methods, our initial recognition that such problems need to be so treated (given our purposes) depends on our ability to encounter them *first as indeterminacies,* within contexts that admit of more and less, possible and impossible—that is, within rhetorical contexts of interpretation, emphasis, valuing. A datum or problem can only first be recognized as amenable to more or less determinate or "objective" treatment against the full range of possibilities as to its existence and meaning, and this requires its interpretation by the "whole person" using the full range of his or her powers and resources—cognitive, emotional, ethical, and so on.

Moreover, the more our questions about a problem implicate our total ways of life, the more rhetoric is involved. And when the whole of life and knowledge becomes the object of our inquiry, as it does in all accounts of liberal education, rhetoric is maximally involved; indeed, the challenge of education is just that of producing a "whole" person—and, by extension, a *uni*versity (not a multiversity), a community, a culture (the diversity intrinsic to such "wholes" notwithstanding).[9] On this view, liberal education is the cultivation of our ability to discriminate what is indeterminate, to produce warrants for assent, and to appraise those warrants and the warrants offered to us by others.

The way we achieve such cultivation, Booth has said explicitly and repeatedly, is "to find new topics, new shared places from which any given rhetorical community can move, trusting to various degrees of warranting in the search for liveable truths, not certainties" (*Vocation* 126); also, "In the ancient terminology of rhetoricians, we seek to discover the topics, the topoi, the places or locations on which, or *in* which, a shared inquiry can take place" (*Vocation* 108). Such topics are not abstract lists of inferential forms to be memorized; they are rather substantive resources for inquiry into the concrete. But what is meant here by topics, how can they be taught, and how exactly will they function such that we shall indeed cultivate abilities of discrimination and judgment, and not merely replicate commonplaces and diffuse all sense of unity and structure?

In one of his footnoted asides in *Modern Dogma,* Booth again has recourse to rhetoric and topics to explain what he is up to, although a little reflection will show that these remarks apply to all of his work: "Those who know classical rhetoric will be aware that I am experimenting with the old notion of the topoi, those . . . shared 'standpoints' where good arguments can be found because in them men did in fact discover warrantable beliefs" (111n18). Booth is right about his "experimenting" here, because the collection (as he calls it) of *topoi* that he offers us differs from traditional lists in at least two ways: first, Booth offers special topics, not vague common or formal topics, so that he ends up with no "list" at all but a "collection," enormously wide ranging and therefore difficult to formalize; and second, the special topics he offers, while they include the standard value propositions and headings, include also any and all verbal (and presumably nonverbal) artifacts capable of providing warrants for claims. Booth lists "stories as reasons," for example, "art as the changing of minds," and the first principles of specific disciplines, discussing many of the specific topics that come under such matters. Not since Cicero (or, not since Richard McKeon and Kenneth Burke) has anyone recommended so sweeping a topical philosophy. As Cicero has Crassus state it in *De oratore,* "the real power of eloquence is such, that it embraces the origin, the influence, the changes of all things in the world, all virtues, duties, and all nature, so far as it affects the manners, minds, and lives of mankind" (213).

The manners, minds, and lives of mankind: Cicero's qualification (such as it is) of the kind of knowledge rhetoric embraces points to just that indeterminacy of the real and the known central to Booth. But we must not misconceive how the rhetorician is to go about this virtual "knowing all things," as both Cicero and Booth urge. In the *De oratore* (2.39–40), Cicero explicitly adverts to the formal topics as useful devices for the rhetor, but it is equally clear that such *topoi* are easily memorized and applied, hence not central to his problem. What is of far greater concern to Cicero, as to Booth, is the orator's more or less systematic exposure to "all things." Cicero, it is true, does not call these complex and various matters *topoi,*[10] but clearly they function as material, special topics—ideas, terms, distinctions, value propositions in all fields, literary works, histories, the civil law, "all antiquity" (1.35)—not as determinate and fixed facts and truths, but as more or less negotiable, interpretable possibilities for argument—"general principles" (2.17) used as places to argue on both sides of a question (1.34).[11] This, I take it, is what Booth himself has in mind:

> ... what would happen if you probed and found what assumptions your own intellectual convictions *really rest on,* then tested them against other people's assumptions, and finally concluded with more or less confidence....
>
> The collection of topoi from which such principles come would have become an organon, always to some degree sifting and uncertain, but reliable in discovering not only what you yourself believe but what you *should* believe....
>
> Instead of making an a priori list of topics at a high level of generality, as those who revive classical rhetoric sometimes do, I shall pursue the consequences of this notion [of special topics] inductively.... (*Modern Dogma* 111n18)

This inductive turn to special topics is what makes Cicero's and Booth's approaches to rhetorical invention in all of their works mature ones. In the abstract, topics lose touch with what gives them purpose; to approach topics inductively—by examples, by entering concrete cases—renders rhetoric realistically complex, demanding, and sophisticated.[12]

Admonished myself here to practice what is preached, I propose to examine a quite simple yet telling example of Booth's own topical theory and practice, as a way of making my argument more concrete.

In the first chapter of *A Rhetoric of Irony,* Booth attempts (among other things) simply to locate his subject matter (note that for Booth this is preeminently a rhetorical task, as "irony" is understood to be, not fixed and given, but a contestable and negotiable concept, properly approached by way of rhetorical topics). He then explains how one type of irony (stable irony) is recognized, and subsumes the interpretation of irony under the rubric "knowledge," all the while urging quietly that irony is particularly worthy of such pains as he is taking, distinguishing it from puns, allegory and fable, satire, and so on.

But note what happens next, in the beginning of chapter 2. Aware of the limits of abstract explanation, our rhetorician has recourse to a metaphor to illuminate the interpretation of irony—one trope to clarify another. Stable irony, Booth says, entails a "reconstruction" of our beliefs and values, our "dwelling places," one in which we experience a move or climb to a new level of understanding (33–37). Now, when I say that Booth turns to the metaphor of building (or rebuilding) to clarify or illuminate irony, I really have in mind a far more complex rhetorical transaction (or reconstruction) than might otherwise be noted. Consider the following:

1. Along with his argument and claims about irony in chapter 1, Booth's metaphor of reconstruction directs attention to facts about irony and its interpretation, its use by speakers to transform their audiences, which together are intended to *qualify* irony as a source of knowledge. Now, this is itself the use of rhetorical argument (in part by way of metaphor) to reconstitute what had been considered a mere trope and turn it into a topic, a source of arguments. (And characteristically, Booth himself is explicit about this linkage with topics; see p. 34).
2. The metaphor, moreover, requires on the reader's part a reconstruction of meaning similar to the interpretation of any stable irony. Said otherwise, here the metaphor too is not only a trope but a topic. Like stable irony, it engages and reconstitutes both the meaning of

metaphor and of irony, as well as the audience taking it in. Like irony, it requires that we "dwell" in its implications about dwelling, inhabiting "places" that we find livable or not, comfortable or not, *true* or not, so that if we come to accept this place as acceptable, our world (and its inhabitants) is reconstructed as a place where irony and metaphor do in fact reconstruct.[13]

3. The grasp and appreciation of the metaphor involves (at least in principle) all the "powers and resources" the *reader-as-generalist* has at hand. That is, only if the reader can actively imagine houses or other dwellings, has a sense for private rooms and public rooms and the values they imply, knows something (but not necessarily much) about interior wall frames and exterior sheet-rock, about foundations and so on—only then can the reader follow Booth in what he makes of his metaphor.[14] We cannot grasp the arguments and claims the metaphor suggests without implicitly relying on a range of beliefs, values, and experiences; such an ability (even if not deeply called into play by any given metaphor) requires just that broad "universal" knowledge of the "manners, minds, and lives of mankind" that Cicero promoted. Like irony, our rhetorician's metaphor invites discrimination and judgment.

4. The metaphor of reconstruction points back to the "four steps" of reconstructing ironic meaning that Booth outlines in chapter 1. Together, the discursive "steps," along with the metaphor, exemplify how material topics (i.e., the steps and the metaphor themselves) function as both *list* and *skill:* alone, the list of the four steps of interpretation could easily become abstract and mechanical; made concrete in the metaphor and in subsequent examples, the topics activate interpretive skills that a list alone cannot touch.

5. The metaphor is intended to persuade in an extended sense of the word (extended in the way that irony-as-*topos* extends the classical sense of *topos*): like irony, it initiates an intellectual dance whose truth-values are proved (or disproved) in the dancing. Such a "dance" for Booth is community oriented in the way persuasion often is not.

6. Irony as reconstruction also seeks community. The point of Booth's reconstituting it as *topos* is partly to indicate how irony creates a complex dwelling-together not appreciated before. Thus the rhetorician finds new common ground.

It would not be in the least difficult to apply these six lessons to any other of Booth's works. *The Rhetoric of Fiction* (1961) (to cite but one), notwithstanding its concession to the mimetic–didactic dichotomy, reconstituted the *topos* of fiction itself as the rhetorical practice of an implied author seeking to shape the response of implied readers. More rhetorically still (to cite another), *The Company We Keep: An Ethics of Fiction* (1989) is also a "rhetoric," this time of fiction's ability to reconstitute ethically (and politically) both character and community—themes only implicit in the *Rhetoric of Fiction*. Indeed, in many ways *Company* summarizes Booth's conception of rhetorical education: reading any sort of narrative (reading anything) requires that we draw on and make more or less subtle and comprehensive connections among values, ideas, emotions, beliefs, historical contexts, historical and other kinds of narrative, and so on, in order to cultivate our ability to know. This is quite along the lines of what MacIntyre, Hauerwas, and Charles Taylor call for in ethics,[15] and what Gerald Graff, in *Professing Literature,* calls for in the contemporary teaching of English (and, presumably, all liberal studies): in Cicero's language, the placing of the "origin, the influence, the changes of all things in the world, all virtues, duties, and all nature" as these are manifested in literature, in the context of the "manners, minds, and lives of mankind."

To take this a step further, Graff also recommends a more honest airing of our interpretive disputes and the conflicts among interpretive modes, and here too Booth's *Critical Understanding: The Powers and Limits of Pluralism* (1979) uses rhetoric to adjudicate paradigm disputes among critics. That is, while adhering to rhetoric, the rhetorician above all will be sensitive to different and even opposing critical paradigms precisely by recognizing how they cultivate the lives of mankind. Unable to fit them all under a monistic critical umbrella, Booth does not forswear the goal of "truth," as is sometimes claimed, but operationally maximizes the rhetorical community of criticism, redefining it as a place not for aimless killing but for inquiry (under controlled conditions) for as inductively adequate a community of inquirers as we can get. Here theoretical incommensurability of paradigms is subordinated to a practical (and analogical) compatibility built on open-ended, indeed topical, criteria of adequacy: univocity of statements about truth in criticism takes second place to the critical inquiry about such statements.

POLYTOPIA

It might be useful to summarize Booth's approach to material topics. First, topics involve a holistic thought of various sorts—the unity of the knower as a "whole person," of the knower and the known, and of the known as a universe (or pluri-verse whose unity we know, however, only asymptotically). For Booth, topical rhetorical thought is connective and comprehensive, as in Cicero, such that all specialist advancement of learning is controlled by an equally indispensable generalist comprehension of what is learned.

Second, such generalism need not contradict (though it will almost certainly exist in tension with) specialism, because specialism both presupposes generalism—topical connectiveness—and is also able to make use of generalism itself. This point can be made clearer by considering in some detail one of Booth's most succinct treatments of this question.

In his Ryerson Lecture for 1987 presented to the University of Chicago, entitled (significantly) "The Idea of a *Uni*versity as Seen by a Rhetorician" (1987) (rpt. in *Vocation* 309–34), Booth asks how those in institutions of higher learning, threatened on all sides as they are by forces of specialization and departmentalization, manage to communicate with each other, formulate and undertake common enterprises, discuss their activities, conduct the business of the place—hiring and firing and promoting and planning—in short, how they manage to be a *uni*versity rather than a *multi*versity. This is, of course, much the same question, in different guise, that Booth asks in *Critical Understanding*: how do/can critics of radically different stripes talk to each other in a common enterprise of criticism? It is also the question (the same special topic) with which I began, namely, what identity, what integrated self, does so diverse a generalist as Booth offer us?

Booth sketches out in this lecture a characteristically rhetorical response to this problem facing the university, when he locates three overlapping sets of special *topoi* by means of which the members of a university community earn their unity and get their collective work done. First, there are those shared facts and assumptions within a given field of expertise by means of which specialists talk to each other about their field and their individual work. Second, the members of a university community (or of any community, for that matter) share many values, beliefs, expectations, experiences, and so on that they can call on to assess character, in hiring and firing for example, or to judge actions. And third, there are those not-quite-so-general values and beliefs of the academic community in particular, about whether another academic sounds intelligent, has mastered the tricks of the trade, argues well, and so on. Quoting Polanyi, Booth asserts that all of us live in complex and overlapping fiduciary structures or webs of beliefs of the kind just mentioned, and that that is how we get our work done, through a rhetorical or topical invention that seeks "good reasons" for assent.

To rhetoricians at least this is perhaps obvious enough regarding how the university gets its more quotidian business accomplished. But Booth goes further and suggests that it is also by locating rhetorical *topoi* that specialists *within* the disciplines can themselves make connections within and among (not just outside of) their disparate specialties, specialties of which no single individual can hope to master even one, let alone six or a dozen or a score. Note that Booth's suggestion about the centrality of topical generalism is consonant with their being specializations and specialists: himself a specialist speaking in this address as a generalist to a group of specialists, it is not surprising that Booth directs his discussion here to how specialists as such can contribute to the making of community through topics. But note also that topical inventiveness is a power, and a kind of character, that belongs first to the rhetorician-as-generalist, and only secondarily to the specialist, who uses this power both to contact what is indeterminate in her field, as well as to make new connections with realities (and people) outside of the field. In other words, despite Booth's rhetorical adaptation here to an audience of specialists, liberal education through the rhetorical arts of topical inquiry and persuasive proof privileges, not a specialist's expertise, but the generalist's orientation to all of reality, since such education concerns finding good reasons for beliefs in any field. Thus, to educate liberally is to enfranchise to the arts of invention and judgment across disciplines, with the aim of producing reasonable assents.

In a (again not entirely tongue-in-cheek) sketch of an ideal University of Polytopia, Booth explicitly situates what he calls rhetorical "curiosity," this topical inventiveness within and across subject matter specialisms, at the very center, not only of liberal education, but even of the research university itself. The practice of the three rhetorics mentioned, and the study of these rhetorics, what Booth calls *rhetorology,* would promote a "polytopicality" that would stimulate original research, insure its communicability, and generate that orientation towards the whole of knowledge and of community that makes for a shared universe of value, aim, and action. Here there exists no split between the "two cultures," or between specialism and generalism: the generalism to which one is habituated or enfranchised in the college of a university provides the basis for just that more focused inventiveness that the specialist himself needs and uses to seek novelty and to communicate to others. In the University of Polytopia, as Booth indicates elsewhere, the work of the rhetorologist "is precisely to pursue the comparative worth of different warrants in different persuasive enterprises, and to invent—or if you prefer, discover—improved ways for minds to meet within disciplines and among seemingly different or conflicting disciplines" (*Vocation* 126).[16]

To be sure, such a position is not without its dangers. In an article entitled "Modern Sophistic and the Unity of Rhetoric," Michael C. Leff has argued that one of the dangers in imperializing rhetoric across the disciplines (in the way that Booth has done) is that we may miss the special kinds of rhetoric that the specialist sciences practice, if we only speak—in our quest for hunting out the "rhetoric of" these sciences—of rhetoric as a matter of civic discourse, that is, of talk directed to an uninitiated public. I should think, however, that Booth's focus on the topics, including topics as first principles of subject matters, manages to avoid this danger, for it allows us to see that the constitution of "communities" is not bound by one model of community (or "public"), that the use of different sets of *topoi* allows us to create different types of community, specialized or generalized. By the same token, however, we can never lose the concept of community if we stay focused on topics, in the way that it has often been lost in our blind pursuit of specializations and individualisms among both humanists and scientists. Whether it is structuralists seeking a closed system of signs, or deconstructionists elevating the play of the trace, or physicists or sociologists pledging allegiance to something called scientific method, the topic as a locus of relatively indeterminate meanings, as a fluid, potential connection to other meanings, and as a first principle that can ground all further inquiry and appraisal, is the sort of device that, when inventively used, is able to conserve tradition while allowing for new connections to new meanings—and thus to new communities.

PRACTICAL APPLICATIONS

If all discourse is more or less rhetorical, as Booth and others argue, then rhetorical topics are useful to specialists within a discipline, to specialists trying to link their disciplines with others, and to specialists and generalists linking disciplines with larger ethical, political, and other concerns. Booth's contribution is to have argued, and exemplified in his own writings, that rhetorical topics are the means for building community within and among different specialties, and indeed that liberal education is best when it trains its students to function first as generalists who can connect fields by constituting indeterminate issues within larger ethical, political, and other contexts, and then as specialists-qua-generalists within fields who can create new areas for inquiry and proof. The character of the rhetorician, then, is first and foremost that of the generalist who learns to use the field-variant *topoi* of the different disciplines to achieve (always limited) views of the whole of an always shifting reality. Education to such a character means providing students with controlled opportunities to address indeterminate and ambiguous problems that require, from the student's own changing and developing knowledge and experience, the deployment of ideas (topics) that promise to constitute an issue adequately, disclose its circumstances for apprehension and understanding, interpret its meanings, and assess its value and truth. For Booth, of course, it is the great texts of our tradition and indeed potentially of all traditions (whose canons are themselves always undergoing topical negotiation—Arnold's "best that has been thought and said" understood topically rather than dogmatically) that most fully provide such opportunities.

To bring that about, how will the teaching of topics occur?

First, it should be clear by now that the "general rhetorics," as they might be called, of Aristotle, Cicero, Quintilian, Hermogenes, Ramus, and the like, cannot teach special topics, which are, I have argued, the very stock-in-trade of the rhetorician's (or rhetorologist's) art. In fact, when it comes to topics (though not necessarily to other rhetorical matters—argument forms, style, genres of discourse, and the rest), it is doubtful that the term *art* applies in any very useful way at all, because special topics slip through such general categories, and their number and types preclude any helpful comments at so general a level. I believe this is what Aristotle had in mind in the lost *Gryllus,* where he is alleged to have said that rhetoric is not an art; or what Cicero himself had in mind when he had Antonius in the *De oratore* declare, "Betwixt genius and dilligence there is very little room left for art," and when he prescribed broad liberal learning as the best training for the orator.[17] It is what Quintilian meant when he referred to topics as more a *skill* than a list—a power or faculty of adapting to specific cases rather than any list to be memorized[18]—and what Miller intended when she said that the special topics exist in an unstable relationship to the rest of Aristotle's *Rhetoric* (64–65). It is what Booth is up to in *Modern Dogma* when he forswears an "a priori list of topics at a high level of generality," and what he *does* in all of his writings, where he works out what ought to be called "special rhetorics" on a variety of problems.[19]

This is not to suggest that we can or should dispose of lists of topics, or even lists of general topics. We ought not to stop teaching the general rhetorics of Aristotle, Cicero, Quintilian, and so on, nor try to imagine a composition teacher teaching invention, or a Wayne Booth writing a rhetoric of irony, without either one's having recourse to lists, schemas, grids, "steps of interpretation," and the like. The problem is not schemas per se, but our failure to recognize that rhetoric really lives only at the level of concrete examples, cases, problems—unstably, as it were, between pure theory and determinate fact. Learning rhetoric must be "inductive," and when it becomes so even the history of rhetorical theory will look quite different, focused as much (if not more) on special rhetorics in various fields. This turn to special rhetorics in the name of rhetorical generalism may appear paradoxical, but it rather underscores the entire point: the generalist herself needs specific matter to connect if she is to escape mere dilettantism (however brilliant).

Second, it is another of Booth's contributions to the contemporary discussion of rhetoric and liberal education to point out that much of what we do in the curriculum is *already* rhetorical, whether flown under the banner of Rhetoric or not: "You can see immediately that there are a lot of rhetorologists around, travelling under other names" (*Vocation* 125); also, "I hasten to add that it is an art that need not be taught under the title of 'rhetoric.' I cannot think of any course in which some contribution to its mastery could not be made . . ." (*Vocation* 117).

Yet the problem remains that the rhetorical nature of most courses goes unthematized, if not totally unrecognized, so that we need in the undergraduate curriculum at least both to recognize and to dwell on the negotiated nature of subject matters and their canons, and the means of such negotiation—material topics (and tropes), and persuasive warrants. In the rhetoric major itself (in those too few places where it exists), we need courses that thematize invention, whose goal it is to study inquiry and to cultivate the effectiveness of would-be inquirers. Such courses can take at least two forms: (1) courses that trace the history of negotiation of some special topic or network of topics (e.g., the growth of some concept in common law), focusing, as Gerald Graff and Thomas Sloane have recommended, on the rhetorical contest to view it in one way or another; and (2) courses that identify rhetorical "arts," what I have called special rhetorics operative in fields not obviously rhetorical—history, theology, philosophy, psychology, and so on—focusing on the articulation of topics and their use in specific cases. *The Federalist Papers* or *The Constitution of the United States,* Machiavelli's *The Prince* or More's *Utopia,* Bacon's or Johnson's essays, Buber's

I and Thou or Carl Rogers's *On Becoming a Person,* Newman's *Tracts for the Times* or Coleridge's *Aids to Reflection,* Cicero's *De officiis* or Kierkegaard's *Concluding Unscientific Postscript*—these and innumerable other works can be profitably approached as special "rhetorics" that require and develop inventional powers while they exhibit the indefinite range of rhetorical thought. As rhetoricians we must not be afraid to blur genres, as Geertz has put it, or to treat alike both "texts and lumps," in Rorty's phrase—or, as Booth has it, to "pursue the comparative worth of different warrants in different persuasive enterprises" (*Vocation* 126).

Lastly, lest the infinite range of special topics alluded to above threaten to create a crisis of coherence for the rhetorician, indeed an identity crisis of the sort that I earlier suggested seemed to threaten Wayne Booth, we need to bear in mind Booth's own focus on "community." It is true, as Booth allows, that there are innumerable communities, each as generalized or as specialized as the *topoi* that constitute them. But the ongoing struggle of the community of communities, the place of places that offers a topical center from which further rhetorical studies can radiate, is that ethical–political community, that company we keep, in which all human beings live and have their being. The topical study of "civil discourse" broadly conceived can provide that center where rhetoric itself is maximized, as Aristotle, Cicero, and the Renaissance humanists understood, and it can provide the common ground (of consensus as well as conflict) that can integrate liberal learning. Wayne Booth's contribution to the study of such discourse has been to demonstrate in his own inquiries how special topics can be used to discover new meanings and to renovate traditional values.

Notes

1. For an account of Booth's career and writings, see James Phelan, "Wayne C. Booth," in *Dictionary of Literary Biography,* vol. 67, *Modern American Critics Since 1965,* ed. Gregory S. Jay (Detroit: Gale, 1988), pp 49–66.

2. It is not my intention to collapse ethics and rhetoric here, but to indicate that the *phronimos* is the rhetorical ideal. For pertinent works, see Aristotle, *Nichomachean Ethics,* trans. with introduction and notes by Martin Ostwald (Indianapolis: Bobbs-Merrill, 1962); John Dewey and James H. Tufts, *Ethics* (New York: Henry Holt, 1908), esp. chs. 18 and 19; and Stanley Hauerwas, *Character and the Christian Life* (Notre Dame: U of Notre Dame P, 1975), esp. ch. 2.

3. See, for example, Richard J. Bernstein, *Beyond Objectivism and Relativism: Science, Hermeneutics, and Praxis* (Philadelphia: U of Pennsylvania P, 1983).

4. Consider Terry Eagleton, *Literary Theory* (Minneapolis: U of Minnesota P, 1983), 194–217; Frank Lentricchia, *Criticism and Social Change* (Chicago: U of Chicago P, 1983), esp. ch. 5; Graff, *Professing Literature;* and Steven Mailloux, *Rhetorical Power* (Ithaca: Cornell U P, 1989).

5. As Struever (15) has put these points, "rhetoric is not so much systematic in the philosophical sense as a mnemotechnical system for making fruitful connections between disparate insights, and the principle which governs its classification and analysis is accessibility. But accessibility here means relevance to particular human performances, not a congruence to a familiar but rigid ontological structure."

6. To give but a sampling of the vast literature on topics, see William M. A. Grimaldi, S.J., "The Aristotelian Topics," *Traditio* 14 (1958): 1–16; Nancy S. Struever, "Topics in History," *History and Theory* 19 (1980): 66–79; Michael C. Leff, "The Topics of Argumentative Invention in Latin Rhetorical Theory from Cicero to Boethius," *Rhetorica* 1 (1983): 23–44; and Richard McKeon, "Creativity and the Commonplace," *Philosophy and Rhetoric* 6 (1973): 199–210.

7. Miller, "Aristotle's 'Special Topics' in Rhetorical Practice and Pedagogy." See also Walter J. Ong, *Ramus, Method, and the Decay of Dialogue* (New York: Octagon, 1979); and Sister Joan Marie Lechner, O.S.U., *Renaissance Concepts of the Commonplaces* (New York: Pageant, 1962).

8. I might indicate at this point that my support of the material, and particularly the special, topics here is not intended to call into question all teaching of formal topics, or of special topics cast at a high level of generality, in courses in composition and speech. For a now somewhat dated overview of some of the literature on "heuristics," see David V. Harrington et al., "A Critical Survey of Resources for Teaching Rhetorical Invention: A Review Essay," *College English* 40 (1979): 641–61.

9. For a recent history of the concept of liberal education and of the "oratorical" tradition in that history, see Bruce A. Kimball, *Orators and Philosophers: A History of the Idea of Liberal Education* (New York: Teachers College, Columbia University, 1986). See also my *Rhetorical Thought in John Henry Newman* (Columbia: U of South Carolina P, 1989), ch. 6, "'A Comprehensive View': The Role of Rhetoric in Liberal Education."

10. Thus it would be correct to say that the term for special topics disappeared in the rhetorics of Cicero and Quintilian, but it would be much mistaken to claim that the *concept* disappeared as well.

11. Thomas De Quincey adverts to this large scope of rhetoric in his essay "Rhetoric" (81): "There was a time when ... it [rhetoric] designated the whole cycle of accomplishments [sic] which prepared a man for public affairs." For the context of debate—arguing *in utramque partem,* on both sides of a ques-

tion—surrounding Ciceronian invention, see Thomas O. Sloane, "Reinventing Inventio," *College English* 51 (1989), 461–73.

12. For two examples, see Victoria Kahn, *Rhetoric, Prudence and Skepticism in the Renaissance* (Ithaca, NY: Cornell UP, 1985); and Eugene Garver, *Machiavelli and the History of Prudence* (Madison: U of Wisconsin P, 1987).

13. For a recent treatment, see George Lakoff and Mark Turner, *More Than Cool Reason: A Field Guide to Poetic Metaphor* (Chicago: U of Chicago P, 1989).

14. As Mark Johnson makes clear (*The Body in the Mind: The Bodily Basis of Meaning, Imagination, and Reason* [Chicago: U of Chicago P, 1987]), this also directly involves *bodily* awareness.

15. See Alasdair MacIntyre, *After Virtue* (Notre Dame: U of Notre Dame P, 1984), and *Whose Justice? Which Rationality?* (Notre Dame: U of Notre Dame P, 1988); Stanley Hauerwas, *The Peaceable Kingdom: A Primer in Christian Ethics* (Notre Dame: U of Notre Dame P, 1983), and *A Community of Character* (Notre Dame: U of Notre Dame P, 1981); Charles Taylor, *Sources of the Self: The Making of the Modern Identity* (Cambridge: Harvard UP, 1989).

16. For an example of rhetorical interconnections across disciplines, see Booth's "Systematic Wonder: The Rhetoric of Secular Religions," *Journal of the American Academy of Religion* 53.4 (1985): 677–702.

17. Thus Michael Leff has observed of "propriety," Cicero's linguistic counterpart to topical inventiveness: "We cannot disentangle propriety from its manifestations, and so it cannot be captured in theoretical abstractions. It can be apprehended only as embodied in a particular discourse. But that does not mean propriety is unteachable, for where one method of instruction fails, another succeeds. . . . *De Oratore* is neither a rhetorical textbook nor a philosophical treatise. It is an oration about the art of oratory, and it instructs by being what it cannot explain" ("Burke's Ciceronianism," 124). See also Leff, "Genre and Paradigm," 313: "The art [of rhetoric] is constituted by its performance, and its application can expand in unlimited and unpredictable ways as oratorical principles are transferred into new domains of practice. . . . Cicero was more concerned about the orator than the art of rhetoric, more interested in concrete practice than abstract precept, and more inclined to view oratory as the central force in civilized life than as one among a number of practical activities open to theoretical investigation."

18. See Quintilian, *The Institutio Oratoria of Quintilian,* trans. H. E. Butler, 4 vols. (Cambridge, MA: Harvard UP, 1920; rpt. 1980), 2: 257–59.

19. See note 8 above.

Bibliography

Bacon, Francis. *The Advancement of Learning.* 1915. London: J. M. Dent & Sons, 1976.

Booth, Wayne C. *Critical Understanding: The Powers and Limits of Pluralism.* Chicago: U of Chicago P, 1979.

———. "The Idea of a *University* as Seen by a Rhetorician." 1987 Ryerson Lecture. Chicago: U of Chicago P, 1987. Rpt. in *The Vocation of a Teacher: Rhetorical Occasions 1967–1988.* Chicago: U of Chicago P, 1989. 309–34.

———. *Modern Dogma and the Rhetoric of Assent.* Notre Dame, IN: U of Notre Dame P; Chicago: U of Chicago P, 1974.

———. "The Revival of Rhetoric." *PMLA* 80.2 (1965): 8–12. Rpt. in *Now Don't Try to Reason with Me: Essays and Ironies for a Credulous Age.* Chicago: U of Chicago P, 1970. 35–46.

———. *A Rhetoric of Irony.* Chicago: U of Chicago P, 1974.

———. *The Vocation of a Teacher: Rhetorical Occasions 1967–1988.* Chicago: U of Chicago P, 1989.

Cicero. *On Oratory and Orators.* Trans. and ed. J. S. Watson, Carbondale, IL: Southern Illinois UP, 1970.

De Quincey, Thomas. "Rhetoric." *The Collected Writings of Thomas De Quincey.* Vol. 10. Ed. David Masson. Edinburgh, n.p., 1889–90. Rpt. New York: AMS Press, 1968. 81–133.

Graff, Gerald. *Professing Literature.* Chicago: U of Chicago P, 1987.

Leff, Michael. "Burke's Ciceronianism." *The Legacy of Kenneth Burke.* Ed. Herbert W. Simons and Trevor Melia. Madison, WI: U of Wisconsin P, 1989. 115–27.

———. "Genre and Paradigm in the Second Book of the *De Oratore.*" *Southern Speech Communication Journal* 51 (1986): 308–25.

———. "Modern Sophistic and the Unity of Rhetoric." *The Rhetoric of Human Sciences.* Ed. John S. Nelson, Allan Megiu, Donald N. McCloskey. Madison: U of Wisconsin P, 1987. 19–37.

Miller, Carolyn R. "Aristotle's 'Special Topics' in Rhetorical Practice and Pedagogy." *Rhetoric Society Quarterly* n.v. (Winter 1987): 61–70.

Newman, John Henry. "University Preaching." *The Idea of a University.* Ed. I. T. Ker. Oxford: Clarendon, 1976. 328–45.

Struever, Nancy S. *The Language of History in the Renaissance.* Princeton: Princeton UP, 1970.

2

Cultural Literacy: Concepts and Information

FRANCIS-NOËL THOMAS

In *Cultural Literacy,* E. D. Hirsch, Jr., addresses a problem that is real enough to be recognized by almost any teacher whose students are more than nine or ten years old. Contemporary Americans from sixth grade to graduate school don't seem to know very much of the information that their teachers take for granted. It isn't unusual today to ask a class of college students about to read *Pride and Prejudice* how many of them have ever heard of Jane Austen and find that fewer than half of them have. College teachers are stunned to realize that their students don't know that the United States and the Soviet Union were allies—or at least fought on the same side—in World War II. If these teachers want to refer to the *Magnificat* or the Annunciation, they quickly find out that they had better explain these terms because they mean no more to an average college humanities class than the binomial theorem means to an average gathering of English professors.

Shocking as it is to stand before a class of college students and discover that most of them have never heard of Jane Austen, haven't any idea of what you are talking about when you say that Bourges was the capital of the duchy of Berry, and don't know if the Battle of Thermopylae is an event that happened before the Vietnam War or is actually an action fought in that war, for most classroom teachers who are also active scholars, it is even more shocking to realize that Hirsch's proposal to right this situation has been taken seriously by so many people.

The people who concern them are not Hirsch's popular audience but his large audience among professionals responsible for making educational policy, running school systems, and buying textbooks. Such people feel a powerful attraction to any reform that promises to show by some "measurable and objective" test that things are improving. Hirsch points to a genuine phenomenon, says it's a problem that must be solved because it is the cause of other, more serious, problems, and has a solution that will bring fast, fast, *fast* relief, as this scientific chart will demonstrate (Hirsch's scientific chart is called the "Chall Curve").

He has been successful enough with this audience to alarm a lot of classroom teachers. People who make educational policy, run school systems, and buy textbooks do not hide their annoyance when teachers tell them that their policies, directions, and textbooks are a menace to teaching and learning. Since the policy makers are unlikely to listen to them, the teachers try to find scholars and thinkers who are not part of the school system to argue their case.

That is how Wayne Booth, a literary scholar, like Hirsch, with a demonstrated interest in educational policy, found himself attempting to argue in a reasonable and almost excessively civil way that the reforms proposed in *Cultural Literacy* will treat symptoms only and end up causing new problems without solving any of the ones we have now ("Cultural Literacy"). Hirsch, invited to respond, dismissed what Booth had to say with all the impatience of a district superintendent and reaffirmed his commitment to "the cultural literacy project." He declined to deal with Booth's argument at all. To do so, he says, would be "easy but tedious" (23).

Wayne Booth's objections to Hirsch's proposals are addressed to teachers and make sense to teachers. Hirsch is a teacher too; that is why, I suppose, Booth wrote in the form of an open letter to him. But Hirsch, it seems to me, has chosen not to address teachers in his response; he is addressing policy makers instead. He tells them that the reason Booth's objections seem so much harder to read than the original proposals is that while he himself is crisp and constructive, Booth, despite his reputation as a thinker, is "rambling and unconstructive" (22). The reason for this contrast, Hirsch claims, is that Booth is not engaged in *thinking*. He is, instead, speaking for a coalition of English teachers—an activity that evidently precludes thinking. Booth, according to Hirsch, is a politician representing notoriously recalcitrant obstructionists.

For Hirsch, Wayne Booth's professional life has a sinister resemblance to the strange case of Dr. Jekyll and Mr. Hyde. There is Booth the thinker, who writes mentally harmonious literary criticism, and Booth the spokesman for a coalition of English teachers, who writes rambling and unconstructive essays full of "cognitive dissonances" (22). Hirsch, in his eagerness to discredit dissent from his own project, argues *ad hominem* and, in doing so, creates a false division. This charge is not merely my pious opinion as Wayne Booth's onetime dissertation student and longtime friend. It will seem to be too evident to require argument for anybody willing to do a little intellectual history of the sort I did myself almost inadvertently.

In the summer of 1965, just after my first year of graduate study at the University of Chicago, I worked as a research assistant for two of my professors, Gwin J. Kolb and Wayne Booth, who were preparing an annotated bibliography of modern scholarship on English literature of the eighteenth century. The job occupied my mornings and left me free afternoons to poke around the half-deserted university. One day I wandered into a class in "Philosophy of Education" taught by Joseph J. Schwab, at that time a legendary Chicago teacher. The members of Schwab's class were, with the exception of one or two very senior classroom teachers, all professional administrators at precollegiate schools from around the country. I was twenty-two years old at the time and had never taught a class anywhere, but somehow talked Schwab into letting me attend on a regular basis. The course proved to be tremendously exciting. By asking a series of strategic questions—and refusing to accept inauthentic answers—Schwab forced us to read *The Republic* not for information but for concepts.

I had read *The Republic* in college but Schwab was getting me to read it in a way I hadn't before. He was also getting me to observe what I was doing as a reader. It brought sharply to mind what Wayne Booth had said one day to his class in "Forms of the Novel" the previous winter: "If you ever find yourself wondering why we are spending all this time examining these novels in such detail, I think we ought to stop and discuss it in class until we have a satisfactory answer, even if we don't get through the list." It is the only thing he said in that course that I still remember. He was the first teacher I had ever heard say such a thing. Where I went to college you read the books because they were on the list. Not getting through the list was regarded as a crime. The punishment was a low mark on the test—almost inevitable, since there were questions on the test about every book on the list. A low mark on the test could keep you out of graduate school and so on down an endless chain of artificial motives creating the conditions for reading as conditioned behavior instead of ethically informed action.

My work as a compiler of lists of modern scholarship on English literature of the eighteenth century slowed to a hot summer's crawl as

I spent more and more of my time in the education library consulting bound volumes of *The Journal of General Education,* to which Schwab had referred me. This journal, new to me that summer, had articles analyzing the same strategies and techniques that Schwab was following in his class. Some of those articles were by Schwab himself, others were by Wayne Booth.[1] They opened what was for me a new way of thinking about both reading and teaching, as a practice, an activity.

To divide Booth, then, as Hirsch does, into two qualitatively unequal parts, literary critic and spokesman for English teachers, defies what the evidence my summer's research and the experience of the subsequent twenty-eight years have established. Booth has always been a spokesman for teachers, even at the outset of his career when he spoke only for himself. It is as wrong to attempt to separate Booth's thought as a literary critic from his thinking about teaching as it would be to attempt to separate Samuel Johnson's thought as a literary critic from his thinking about morality. For Booth, literary criticism is a refinement of a kind of reading that children begin to learn in the first grade; it isn't another world.[2] Literary criticism as Booth has practiced it for all of his professional life is precisely speaking for a coalition of English teachers. The particular coalition he spoke for against Hirsch's proposals taught at every level from primary grades through college, and one of their most pleasant discoveries when they met during the summer of 1987 was that English teachers at all levels can form a professional continuum and become a natural coalition.

This essay, then, is a response to Hirsch's remarks. It is not addressed either to him or to his clients, the school administrators who are too interested in predictions, "findings," "reform," "progress," and "success" to bother much about reason and argument. It is addressed instead to the ultimate policy makers in any society: the community of its citizens, and in the first instance to those members of that community who have the professional knowledge and experience to understand the damage that can be caused by reforms of the sort Hirsch is promoting and who have the public reputations to gain the attention of parents, whose perception of what is good for their children will slowly but ultimately prevail even over the educational bureaucracies.

In responding to Hirsch, it will be helpful to understand why he has made such a positive impression on so many professional administrators in the first place. This too requires a little history, for Hirsch has demonstrated that he is a skillful salesman working in a proven American tradition. In seeking to reform American education, he has adopted the methods of another reformer, a military reformer of the 1950s and 1960s, who commanded the attention of policy makers and became one himself, Maxwell Taylor, "the intellectual general." Taylor's catch phrase was "flexible response." (As a phrase, it bears a structural resemblance to "cultural literacy.") Taylor placed his protégés in charge of the first great test of "flexible response" and assured the president and the secretary of defense that all the other generals who raised objections weren't worth listening to. They were just jealous that Taylor got a war and they didn't. I think Taylor would have admired the phrase "rambling and unconstructive." Taylor and his followers had "projections" and "findings" by the yard. He confidently predicted success and produced statistics that showed continuing progress through years of disaster. The great testing ground of "flexible response" was, of course, Vietnam.[3]

I see considerable reason to fear that Hirsch may succeed in the same way that Taylor did. Like Taylor, he's got hold of an audience that thinks "something must be done to stop this," and, again like Taylor, he is a good salesman, especially when his audience has little direct experience with the situation that something must be done to stop.

Most administrators, like the teachers themselves, are shocked to discover that information they take for granted is simply unknown to the students for whom they are responsible. But unlike most teachers, the administrators feel public pressure directly and seek to cover themselves by adopting programs of reform to remedy the situation. If students have so little information, a program of reform that promises to supply the lack can be seen as just what is wanted. Of course, there is no end to information. Almost all of the English teachers who can't remember when they first heard of Jane Austen know who Michelangelo is, but most of them don't know who Rogier van der Weyden is and practically none of them can identify Philippe de Champaigne. It is impossible to explain why being able to identify Michelangelo in a trivial and superficial way is necessary to being culturally literate for someone who lives in Buffalo, New York, or American Fork, Utah, in the 1990s, but why being entirely ignorant of Rogier and Philippe is no disqualification. There is a tacit system that determines for any community what information can be taken for granted and what is esoterica. College teachers think they belong to what ought to be the cultural community of their students; most of their students disagree.

Hirsch and many others attach a great deal more importance than *that,* of course, to the phenomenon of students who don't know the information their teachers think they should. Hirsch himself thinks that ignorance of the sort teachers see in their students impedes these students' ability to learn. Being able to identify Michelangelo in a trivial and superficial way, taken together with thousands of other similar bits of information, is, Hirsch maintains, a necessary preliminary to literacy and learning. He calls this a "research finding" (23) as if it were something we ought to consider on the same level as, say, the "research finding" that oxygen is necessary to combustion.

Hirsch thinks the best solution to the educational problem he sees is to establish a set of universally required texts, but he concedes that this is unacceptable in the United States for cultural and political reasons. To meet the need without offending American sensibilities, then, he suggests that a list be compiled of all the bits of information people like himself take for granted and that this list be taught to students in the elementary grades.

Hirsch is, I think, disingenuous in his claims for what he proposes. "I predict that [the reforms proposed in *Cultural Literacy*] will result in a greater percentage of high school graduates who are qualified to go to college, and also a greater number of students who are able to do distinguished work after arriving there" (23).

The first part of this prediction will almost certainly prove accurate if we declare that mastery of a list like the one Hirsch composed *is* what will determine who is qualified to go to college. Most of the people who qualify now will, with little effort, be able to master the list and so will many others. It is like saying that many more people would qualify to be licensed as brain surgeons if we accepted as proof of qualification a candidate's ability to name every winner of the Nobel Prize in medicine in chronological order. Anyone who now qualifies to be a brain surgeon might see this requirement as a silly nuisance, but it's a safe bet that any brain surgeon can memorize the list and, of course, so can a lot of people who can't bone a chicken.

The second part of the prediction depends on what we define as distinguished work. Since there is a lot of disagreement right now about what qualifies as distinguished work—some colleges think deconstructive analyses of slasher videos can qualify as distinguished work—who knows what the situation will be after Hirsch's reforms are in place? The elite universities in this country may start giving people Ph.D.'s for dissertations that demonstrate why Aeneas Piccolomini should not be on the list but Howdy Doody should be, or why knowing that Hattie McDaniel won the Academy Award for best performance by an actress in a supporting role in 1939 is a reliable index to a twelve year old's ability to do brain surgery when he's thirty. These might be thought of as research findings some day.

As things stand now, no competent college teacher with any sense stays shocked and immobile, waiting for reforms like Hirsch's to give her students who can identify Jane Austen and don't need to be told that Bourges was the capital of the duchy of Berry, because she knows something from her experience as a classroom teacher that many administrators do not. Once you have done what needs to be done to make one of Jane Austen's novels accessible to a group of students who never read a book that wasn't written in the twentieth century, never read a book that wasn't addressed to people like themselves in background and values, they will know who Jane Austen is. Once you've given people the concepts they need to look intelligently at the Cathedral of Saint-Etienne de Bourges or the *Très riches heures de Jehan, duc de Berry,* they will be able to identify Bourges—and they won't confuse it with Bruges or Burgos, either. To teach concepts effectively is, to be sure, much harder than to teach a list of information, and testing a student's conceptual range requires quite a lot of skill and ingenuity.

It takes a resourceful and knowledgeable person to evaluate learning if she tries to test it by asking, Why were such buildings as Saint-Etienne de Bourges built? Why were they thought to be worth the money and effort? What was their conceptual purpose? Does our own society do anything comparable? It is also time-consuming to evaluate the answers and teach students how to improve them. It is certainly easier to test information, and, of course, a machine can grade the answers.

Machine grading will, in itself, have a certain appeal to the hacks, the incompetents, the indifferent, and the cynical. To teach anybody anything worth knowing requires, in general, actual knowledge about something the teacher believes is valuable, not as an inert lump and not as the coin that will get a student past a test, but valuable in action. The architects of the Vietnam War—both the policy makers in Washington and the commanding generals—knew all sorts of information and are just the kind of people who would have done swimmingly on any test based on Hirsch's list or anyone else's. The insights Wayne Booth fostered about the cognitive process and the ethical value of reading lead me to wish the policy makers and generals had left the directed intelligence reports to gather dust and instead had all read two books with conceptual comprehension: *The Peloponnesian War* and *Pride and Prejudice.* I don't believe that anyone who has read these two books *and learned the concepts required to understand them* won't be equipped to make better decisions in any circumstances than someone who has not. (I am not proposing a sacred canon here; there are books in other cultures that will serve the same purpose; there are others in our own, but the two I have named have a fabulous track record.) I don't believe being able to identify Thucydides as the author of *The Peloponnesian War* with his dates and knowing that the book was written in Greek, or knowing that Jane Austen wrote *Pride and Prejudice* and being able to give her dates and her father's profession and the names of all her brothers and sisters and throwing in Lady Catherine de Bourgh's daughter's governess's name to boot is good for doing anything except taking a test that gives arbitrary value to such information.[4]

Jane Austen, who was neither a snob nor a fool, reminds us how useless such accomplishments are in any situation that actually requires some thinking. In *Mansfield Park,* Sir Thomas Bertrand's daughters are struck at once by their cousin Fanny's cultural illiteracy in precisely Hirsch's sense.

> Fanny could read, work, and write, but she had been taught nothing more; and as her cousins found her ignorant of many things with which they had been long familiar, they thought her prodigiously stupid, and for the first two or three weeks were continually bringing some fresh report of it into the drawing-room. "Dear Mamma, only think, my cousin cannot put the map of Europe together—or my cousin cannot tell the principal rivers in Russia—or she never heard of Asia Minor—or she does not know the difference between water-colours and crayons!— How strange!—Did you ever hear any thing so stupid?"
>
> ... "I am sure I should have been ashamed of myself, if I had not known better long before I was so old as she is. I cannot remember the time when I did not know a great deal that she has not the least notion of yet. How long ago it is, aunt, since we used to repeat the chronological order of the kings of England, with the dates of their accession, and most of the principal events of their reigns!"
>
> "Yes," added the other; "and of the Roman emperors as low as Severus; besides a great deal of the Heathen Mythology, and all the Metals, Semi-Metals, Planets, and distinguished philosophers." (18–19)

People like Julia and Maria Bertrand, who find looking down on their neighbors an important source for preening and find that memorizing Hirsch's list gives them the objective and measurable proof of superiority they crave, easily can be persuaded of the danger of Hirsch's proposals. Implementing his reforms would only spoil their fun. Many others who think some sort of reform is called for could be persuaded in a couple of hours that the reforms Hirsch suggests are useless at best and potentially harmful at worst, since they will promote the docile and the timorous, bore the intelligent to death, and enrage the creative and original.

Although she hadn't the benefit of the Chall Curve, Jane Austen valued reading greatly and was an excellent observer of what is and is not a necessary preliminary to literacy and learning. Being able to recite the list of Roman emperors as low as Severus, as well as all the Semi-Metals, proved of no use to Julia and Maria Bertrand when they were faced with having to make decisions. Neither did it prove to be a necessary preliminary to literacy and learning in Fanny Price's case.

> Kept back as she was by everybody else [Edmund's] single support could not bring her forward, but his attentions were otherwise of the highest importance in assisting the improvement of her mind, and extending its pleasures. He knew her to be clever, to have a quick apprehension as well as good sense, and a fondness for reading, which, properly directed, must be an education in itself. . . . [H]e made reading useful by talking to her of what she read. . . . (22)

I suggest that the evidence of such culturally literate observers as Jane Austen should be taken with as much seriousness as the anonymous "research findings" to the contrary that Hirsch cites so briskly and confidently. Projects such as Hirsch's are the curriculum of the Bertrands, are anything but new, and regularly have been dismissed by the seriously literate. Gustave Flaubert seemed to have devoted his spare time to compiling a massive dictionary of "cultural literacy" of his own to illustrate the mentality of such characters as the progressive pharmacist Homais in *Madame Bovary*. Flaubert called it the "Dictionary of Received Ideas." Some of the entries are almost fit for the *Dictionary of Cultural Literacy*.

> *Archimedes* On hearing his name, say "Eureka!" Or else: "Give me a fulcrum and I will lift the world." There is also Archimedes' screw, but you aren't expected to know what it is.[5]

Flaubert seems to illustrate the results of this sort of education in the conversations and actions of his most foolish characters. At their first meeting Emma and Monsieur Léon repeat all the current clichés about nature, music, and literature. They have learned to parrot things of which they have no experiential knowledge. Emma knows all the sort of information that Fanny Price does not, yet she isn't the reader that Fanny is. Her reading does nothing but lead her into disaster by allowing romantic fantasy to block conceptual maturity. She uses her knowledge of information and clichés to pass a test, a social test that persuades her that she is too good for the conditions in which she lives. That is what mastering detached bits of information leads to, the substitution of conditioned behavior for ethically informed action. It is a point Bernard Shaw takes up in *Pygmalion*.

Professor Higgins's project in *Pygmalion* (perhaps even better known from Alan Jay Lerner's adoption of it in *My Fair Lady*)—passing off a cockney flower girl as a "lady"—fails in its first test, Mrs. Higgins's at home, because the surface of Eliza Doolittle's speech, how it sounds, creates a dissonance with her concept of appropriate action. Hirsch wants to say that we become literate in the way Higgins wanted to make Eliza into a lady: from the outside in. It may be worth remembering here that Higgins's project was simply to pass Eliza off as a lady, not to make her into a *real* one. Higgins despises the social values that create distinctions between flower girls and ladies and thinks they are based on silly and superficial marks. Given a test properly constrained to reveal only certain distinctions in dress and pronunciation, with the help of a cram course and an expense account, anyone endowed with a good ear can pass. Hirsch seems to think the distinction between the culturally literate and the culturally illiterate is a similarly silly one. His project reduces cultural literacy to a mastery of information as a necessary foundation to more complex skills. He can, if he is allowed to control how literacy is tested, pass off almost anyone who can be charmed or threatened into learning a list of information (Higgins's two methods with Eliza) as literate. His project will never be able to make them actually so.

Higgins's project—and Hirsch's too—is at best irrelevant to education for self-directed activity. In both cases, what is learned is directed to a test. Can Eliza succeed in fooling people into thinking she is a lady? Can a sixth grader in Cincinnati, who has never seen a single painting or sculpture by anybody, identify Michelangelo on a test? Why would they want to? Eliza merely wanted to speak proper English so she could get a job in a shop; she didn't want to pass herself off as what she wasn't. That was Higgins's project. The sixth grader will be put into the position of sixteenth-century gentlemen's sons, who were forced to learn Latin without understanding why. The reason was not intellectual, but merely social. Conventionally, gentlemen had to show some knowledge of Latin to separate themselves from lower orders who hadn't the money to hire Latin masters. Almost everyone who was really culturally literate, from Montaigne to Erasmus to John Locke, deplored both the practice and the inevitable means of its achievement.[6]

The archetype of the sort of test Hirsch proposes, analytically if not historically, is the Turing Test, in which, given a certain protocol, a machine when questioned gives answers indistinguishable from those given by a human being and so must be regarded as thinking in the same sense that a human being thinks. For Turing himself, there is no distinction between machines and human beings. If a machine's answers to the questions put to it are indistinguishable from a human being's answers to the same questions, then machines must be regarded as being able to think. It isn't that people are reduced to machines by the Turing Test, since Turing began by thinking that human beings *are* machines who process bits of information; it is just a question of duplicating the ability to process information without all the unnecessary trappings of being human.[7]

The model is a monstrosity and is always rejected by children because children, unlike Turing and Hirsch and sixteenth-century Latin masters, have never accepted the thesis that thinking is processing bits of information. Learning a list of information does not advance a child's ability to read; it is a cheap substitute for the difficult work of satisfying a child's naturally growing desire to read for concepts instead of information. Persuading children that learning is directed exclusively or even primarily toward a test discourages their desire to learn. Early in their education, children hope that the learning they acquire through reading will be directed toward their lives, their choices, their decisions, the way they perceive the world around them. When elementary school reading books present bland characters who never have conflicts or problems, never get frustrated, never raise their voices, never feel like strangling one another, children lose interest because these books teach them that reading has nothing to do with the world they live in; it's just another meaningless school task like long division, which no adult, once out of school, is ever seen doing.[8] When a reader is mature enough to read for concepts, and is about to begin *Pride and Prejudice* or *The Peloponnesian War*, that reader can learn all the necessary information very quickly, even if he is not carrying around dictionary-like bits of information about Austen, Jane (1775–1817) or Culture, Ancient Greek.

I would like to end with a "research finding" of my own. This finding does not require much labor to establish, and the reader can test it by a brief self-examination. It does not require the ability to interpret the Thomas Projection or the Booth Curve (English teachers are easily intimidated by anything that sounds even vaguely like mathematics). It doesn't offer fast relief, just a warning against trying to substitute skillfully promoted fads for the difficult but necessary effort to achieve the most fundamental goal of general education: the ability to read for concepts instead of information.

My finding is the same as Jane Austen's, that knowing lists of information is not a necessary preliminary to literacy and learning. Here is how to test it experimentally. There are fifty-nine items in this essay that might go into a "cultural dictionary." They are

American Fork, Utah
Analysis, Deconstructive
Annunciation
Argument *ad hominem*
At home
Austen, Jane
Award, Academy
Berry, duchy of
Bertrand, Julia
Bertrand, Maria
Bertrand, Sir Thomas
Binomial theorem
Bourges
Bourgh, Lady Catherine de
Bovary, Emma
Bruges
Buffalo, New York
Burgos
Chall Curve
Champaigne, Philippe de
Cincinnati
Doody, Howdy
Doolittle, Eliza
Dr. Jekyll and Mr. Hyde, The Strange Case of
Erasmus
Flaubert, Gustave

Flexible Response, strategic doctrine of
Higgins, Mrs.
Higgins, Professor Henry
Homais
Johnson, Samuel
Léon
Lerner, Alan Jay
Locke, John
Madame Bovary
Magnificat
Mansfield Park
McDaniel, Hattie
Michelangelo Buonarroti
Montaigne, Michel Eyquem, seigneur de
My Fair Lady
Nobel Prize for medicine
Peloponnesian War, The
Piccolomini, Aeneas
Price, Fanny
Pride and Prejudice
Pygmalion
Republic, The
Slasher videos
Soviet Union
Taylor, Maxwell

Thermopylae, Battle of
Thucydides
Très riches heures de Jehan, duc de Berry, Les
Turing, Alan
Turing Test
Vietnam War
Weyden, Rogier van der
World War II

Now ask yourself a few questions. Could you identify all of these items before you started reading my essay? Did the fact that you did not know, let us say, that Bourges was the capital of the old duchy of Berry impede your ability to read this essay or to learn something—perhaps why I think Hirsch's project is silly?

I assume Hirsch would concede that I am culturally literate and so is anybody who has read my essay to this point. It must be clear to my readers that I have a fondness for information of a broadly cultural kind and have collected quite a lot of it from a variety of domains, some of them not usually thought to be at all closely related. Familiar and casual reference to Alan Turing and Hattie McDaniel, Maxwell Taylor and Rogier van der Weyden suggests that I have taken an unusual itinerary across the cultural terrain. Like anyone's range of reference, mine is the by-product of a particular set of activites and interests. I did not sit down and learn to pass a test on what I can now articulate as a list of allusions and references drawn from this essay. Knowing this list did not lead me to write this essay, nor is it a necessary preliminary to such writing. Someone who had learned my fifty-nine-item list as detached bits of information would not, as a result, be able to write an essay like this one. Moreover, I suspect that few of my readers happen to be masters of precisely this list. I don't expect that everyone who reads this essay started off knowing that Bourges was the capital of the old duchy of Berry. Some probably still have no precise idea what or where the duchy of Berry was. For most of my readers, I suppose the binomial theorem could have an entry like Flaubert's on Archimedes' screw: "It exists, but you aren't expected to know what it is." Aeneas Piccolomini makes fine reading, is a fascinating person, and is the only known writer of pornographic romances to have been elected pope, but I don't expect that very many readers of this essay recognized his name or could have identified him. Did this ignorance of detached bits of information—however delicious in themselves—stop you from reading this essay and understanding my ideas?

Hirsch seems to suggest that it should have, and has made a great impression on administrators and an even greater one on bureaucrats. In *The Vocation of a Teacher,* Wayne Booth describes an encounter with one of them, Chester Finn, from the federal Department of Education, speaking to the sixty teachers for whom Booth later spoke in his open letter to Hirsch. Like the good teacher I have always known him to be, Booth is not a talking head offering facile solutions to problems that every generation must solve anew. Booth's analysis of Finn's effect on the teachers shows no more evidence of cognitive dissonance than the best pages of *The Rhetoric of Fiction* or *The Company We Keep*. I end this chapter by quoting Wayne Booth, critic-as-spokesman-for-teachers, doing what the best teachers have always done, framing good questions that lead their readers to activities and practice, not to the possession of dead information.

> When [Chester Finn] told us that we should either buy Hirsch's list of about 5,000 terms, "what every American needs to know" (or as the new jacket has it, "The Thinking American's List") or come up with a list of our own, he set the agenda for the conference in ways he could never have dreamed of. We now know that our task is to combat his way of working; we must try to *think* about how to *educate*. How are we to confront ourselves as we now are—a vast, complex, disorganized group of men and women with a vocation for "English teaching" but without a central, articulated notion of what that vocation requires of us and of our various publics? How can we turn our fellow citizens, who in some sense believe deeply in the importance of "English," into a nation of learners: a learning culture rather than an *information-processing* culture? (267)

Anyone can understand the problems facing "the profession of English" by reading passages such as this one, even if she doesn't know that Wayne Booth was born in American Fork, Utah, and even if she never heard of *The Journal of General Education*. Reading Wayne Booth might also serve some readers as a source for a concept of criticism—one that is sophisticated enough to deepen our understanding of writers as great as Jane Austen and Gustave Flaubert while remaining securely part of the common activity of reading, an activity that extends from the first grade to graduate school. Wayne Booth's practice consistently implies that literary criticism is no more than a nuance added to the immensely more complex cognitive phenomenon of reading, and subsequently that the activity of literary criticism always speaks for a coalition of English teachers. For Wayne Booth, the practice of criticism is the vocation of a teacher, and that is, I suggest, the best and most fundamental reason to celebrate his career.

Notes

1. These articles hold up remarkably well. Schwab's have been reprinted in Joseph J. Schwab, *Science, Curriculum, and Liberal Education*, ed. Ian Westbury and Neil J. Wilkof (Chicago: U of Chicago P, 1978); see especially "Enquiry and the Reading Process," 149–63. Some of Booth's articles have not been reprinted, but see "Reading and Writing on Human Values" (with Ralph M. Sargent), *Journal of General Education* 5 (1950–51): 245–53.

2. When Wayne Booth read this essay in draft, he told me, on coming to this sentence, that he once visited his son's fourth-grade class and discussed with these young readers a story they had recently read. "I used the same principles I wrote about in *The Rhetoric of Fiction*," he said, "Who are the bad guys, and how do you know?" I had never heard this anecdote before, but was glad to have such an authoritative confirmation of my description of Booth as a critic. It stimulated a fantasy: Hillis Miller visits a class of fourth graders. Could he use his normal critical principles in discussing a story with them, *aporia* and the uncanny moment? Miller may be more sophisticated than Booth, but, to my mind, losing touch altogether with fourth graders, when it comes to reading stories, is to achieve the sophistication of the sophists.

3. An account of Maxwell Taylor's career and the success of his strategic doctrine of flexible response can be found in Neil Sheehan, *A Bright Shining Lie: John Paul Vann and America in Vietnam* (New York: Random, 1988), see esp. 59, 116–18, 304–5, 365–67.

4. For a further discussion of this point, see Mark Turner, *Reading Minds: The Study of English in the Age of Cognitive Science* (Princeton: Princeton UP, 1991), ch. 10: "Cultural Literacy and Poetic Thought," 216–38.

5. Flaubert, *Bouvard and Pécuchet* 294. The translation of Flaubert's collection of *idées reçues* is by Robert Baldick and appears on 293–330.

6. See Lawrence Stone, "Radical Wisdom for Elite Boys" rev. of John Locke, *Some Thoughts Concerning Education*, ed. John W. Yolton and Jean S. Yolton, *TLS* (March 2–8, 1990): 229–30.

7. For an account of the Turing Test accessible to nonmathematicians, see Douglas R. Hofstadter and Daniel C. Dennett, *The Mind's I: Fantasies and Reflections on Self and Soul* (New York: Bantam, 1981), 53–95; and Andrew Hodges, *Alan Turing: The Enigma* (New York: Simon, 1983), esp. 415–26.

8. On children learning to read and their desire to connect their reading with their experience, together with an evaluation of reading books used in the primary grades, see Bruno Bettleheim and Karen Zelan, *On Learning to Read: The Child's Fascination with Meaning* (New York: Vintage, 1982), esp. 235–64.

Bibliography

Austen, Jane. *Mansfield Park.* 1814. Ed. R. W. Chapman. London: Oxford UP, 1923.
Booth, Wayne C. "Cultural Literacy and Liberal Learning: An Open Letter to E. D. Hirsch, Jr." *Change: The Magazine of Higher Learning* 20.4 (1988): 10–21.
———. *The Vocation of a Teacher: Rhetorical Occasions 1967–1988.* Chicago: U of Chicago P, 1989.
Flaubert, Gustave. *Bouvard and Pécuchet.* 1881. Trans. A. J. Krailsheimer. Harmondsworth and Baltimore: Penguin, 1976.
Hirsch, E. D., Jr. "A Postscript by E. D. Hirsch, Jr." *Change: The Magazine of Higher Learning* 20.4 (1988): 22–26.

II

Ethics and Fictions

3

Wayne Booth and the Ethics of Fiction

MONICA JOHNSTONE

BEFORE WAYNE BOOTH's article "Kenneth Burke's Way of Knowing" went to print, he had the opportunity to read Burke's reaction. Burke's response compelled Booth to add a "Postscript as Preface": "When I received Kenneth Burke's response to the following piece, I was distressed to find that what was intended as an encomium had given him pain" (1). It is my hope that my similar intention will not give Booth pain. The hazards of working on books that have become friends are many, as are the rewards. Friendship makes objectivity difficult; fortunately for me, Booth's *Rhetoric of Fiction* makes the notion of authorial objectivity suspect (67–88). Therefore, I will proceed as if with impunity to gather together and test what I find to be Booth's most helpful heuristic questions concerning the ethics of fiction. These questions are fully realized in Booth's recent book *The Company We Keep,* but they are also predicted by passages in his earlier works. Not surprisingly, these questions echo concerns implicit in the direction of recent ethical philosophy. Alasdair MacIntyre characterizes the current climate in ethical philosophy this way: "The controversy between emotivism and prescriptivism on the one hand and their critics on the other expresses the fundamental moral situation of our own society" (*Short History of Ethics* 266). The move away from prescriptive ethics and toward descriptive inquiry in ethical philosophy acts as an invitation for literary criticism to reclaim areas it previously explored, this time with new rigor. Booth, as both literary critic and rhetorician, accomplishes this evaluation in a much more helpful way than do others interested in the ethics of rhetoric, such as Richard Weaver and Henry W. Johnstone, Jr. The primary difference lies in the questions each asks.

To test Booth's heuristic questions, I have selected a text that is my personal hobgoblin, Jean Genet's *Querelle*. To illustrate the difficulties that *Querelle* represents, we have only to look at the quotations provided by the critics on the book's jacket. *The New York Times* called this novel, "Genet's purest perverse romance." Michael Levenson writes that *Querelle* "drags us with [Genet] to a confrontation with the basest of angels." And Dotson Rader lauds the work for its "exquisite perversity of imagination." We might ask why this novel inspires such tropes. To put my anxiety about this text into Boothian terms, the most pressing concern may be the lack of distinction I find between the narrator, implied author, and even actual author—if we can trust Genet's self-appraisals.[1] This novel provides us with exactly the kinds of ethical difficulties that can demonstrate the usefulness of Booth's mode of inquiry because this novel undercuts the very norms upon which the ethical systems of other rhetoricians are based. In short, Booth's questions succeed where others' fail. In *The Company We Keep,* as elsewhere, Booth reintegrates literary evaluation:

> The blanket rejection of evaluation, especially in its ethical forms, ignores the variety of *kinds* of judgment that we in practice share. Many an appraisal may indeed be worthless to everyone except the appraiser; but once we make some elementary distinctions, we discover that some appraisals qualify as shared knowledge, no more dubious than many a "factual" claim. (83)

In order to be more specific, I have gathered together ten representative questions that suggest Booth's mode of inquiry.

1. What are the distinctions between the narrator, the implied author, and the actual author?
2. Is the text ironic?
3. Should I believe the narrator?
4. Am I willing to be the kind of person the storyteller is asking me to be?
5. Would I admit this author into the circle of my true friends?
6. What are the text's implicit norms?
7. To what extent do readers take in the values of what they read?
8. Has something been achieved that is *in its own terms* admirable?
9. Has some gift or skill been exhibited here that *those who see and accept its implicit standards* will admire?
10. What is the judgment community in which the text exists?

Though reductive of Boothian inquiry, this list suggests some prime ingredients and preserves Booth's emphasis on *how* we know things about a text and what constitutes assent-worthy reasons for evaluation.

Though the saying goes that the proof is in the pudding, a recipe may be better tested by giving it to an apprentice than to the master chef, whose brilliance might cover the defects of the concoction. We already know that Booth can blend together the delicate flavors of *Emma* in a way that brings us back to the table for delicious discussion. *Querelle* is a tougher cut in less experienced hands. If the outcome of my inquiry is fit for consumption, so much the greater compliment to Booth.

The brand of rhetorical inquiry that leads us to Booth's ethics of fiction is an outgrowth of what Booth has called "ecumenical rhetoric" (*Vocation* 309). Booth's style of inquiry does not so much mend fences as remove entire walls between discourse communities represented by academic departments and critical methods. In his Ryerson Lecture (recounted in *The Vocation of a Teacher*), where he demonstrates how we can and do blend special and common topics with more intuitive judgments of ethos, and in *Critical Understanding,* where he follows competing critical methodologies to their problematic conclusions, we find an undercurrent of rigorous humanism. Loosely speaking, it is Booth's program to give the humanities back to humans by wresting them from departments and dogmas. His attitude of critical *glasnost,* if you will, belies the notion that a rhetorical education is at best elitist and at worst sophistic because he seeks precision while resisting jargon, he demands assent-worthy evidence while scrutinizing unargued assertion, and he renews lines of ethical inquiry while repudiating shortsighted calls for censorship. In short, in Booth's hands the ethics of fiction is a testing ground for a new rhetorical sensitivity that both raises hard questions and suggests rigorous and assent-worthy ways to answer them. This seems a simple enough proposition, but as he so clearly demonstrates in *The Rhetoric of Fiction,* many critics have been asking questions born of prescriptive dogma that obscures difficulties in their reasoning, or have left their evaluations of texts' ethical merits undefended. Both cases split the discourse community into those who agree with the dogma or the evaluation as they stand and those who do not.

In response, Booth asks us to provide reasoned judgments of texts ("Ethical Criticism" 279). His is a call to talk *to* rather than *at* each other. The value judgments we make are not assumed to be made in a vacuum; the discourse community is an integral part of the assessment: ". . . how do I argue for such value judgments about human beings, imagined ones at that? What must I do if someone disputes my evaluation?" (*Irony* 215). In these arguments the ethical appeal of texts is not underrated. He asks us to explore the values implicit in literary works by examining the way these values are transmitted to us: "Should I believe this narrator? Am I willing to be the kind of person that this storyteller is asking me to be? Will I accept the author among the small circle of my true friends?" ("Ethical Criticism" 289–290). The questions Booth asks of imagined human beings, narrators, and authors are all eventually asked of the critical community. "The question in appraising wholes, given their intentions, will always finally be, Has something been achieved here that is *in its own terms* admirable? Has some gift or skill been exhibited here that *those who see and accept its implicit standards* will admire?" (*Company* 111). Booth stresses the idea that we people our lives with the authors we read, calling friendship with books "a neglected critical metaphor" ("George Eliot" 4). If we do, as Booth argues, "underestimate the extent to which we take in the values of what we read," ("George Eliot" 291) then the stakes are high. *The Company We Keep* reminds us that the metaphor of book as friend is central to the questions Booth asks of literature. In practice, often the most deceptively simple questions produce complex answers. We would do well to take seriously a question Booth once posed to fourth graders: "How do you tell the good guys from the bad guys?" (*Rhetoric of Fiction* 457).

These questions seem simple only until we contrast them with other systems intended to help us make reasonable statements about ethical dimensions in rhetorically crafted texts. Booth asks us *how* we tell. Richard Weaver, in *The Ethics of Rhetoric,* suggests a system based on a different sort of questioning. Though Weaver is addressing himself not specifically to fiction but to argumentation, the difference in approach is not determined by genre so much as philosophy. In fact, Booth's approach proves helpful for both fiction and arguments concerning it. In a highly prescriptive fashion, Weaver suggests that a speaker is ethical who demonstrates four qualities:

1. the quality displaying the speaker as seeking mutual agreement with his audience
2. the quality displaying the speaker as recognizing the rational autonomy of the speaker
3. the quality displaying the speaker as recognizing the equality of the listener with himself
4. the quality displaying the speaker as recognizing that the ends of the audience have an intrinsic value for him (102)[2]

The four qualities could be seen as a carefully rendered golden rule for rhetoric or, as the philosopher Henry Johnstone called it, the rule of bilateral argument: "A rhetor may use no device of persuasion that he could not in principle permit others to use on him" (101).[3] It would seem that it should not matter whether the rhetor in question is an actual person or a character in fiction; for certain types of rhetorical situations perhaps it does not.

That these rules have limited power for criticism of discourse like that of Genet's becomes clear when we test them against *Querelle*. In general, we could say that all of Genet's works violate all of these rules in some way. Genet said in an interview that he does not seek our agreement, actively seeks to manipulate the audience, holds himself superior, and places no value on anything outside himself (Fichte 178–90). He receives an "F" on these prescriptive tests. But this failure does little to give us an answer to Sartre's famous defense of Genet:

> I know what can be said: "Let him write, if he wants to, but we don't have to read him. His poems are premeditated crimes, he tries to base his salvation on our destruction and to trick us by means of words. These are excellent reasons for admiring his works from afar and not for buying them."
>
> I admit that Genet treats his readers as means. He uses them all to talk to *himself* about himself, and this peculiarity may alienate readers. When he asks himself: "Should I steal?" Why should he expect the answer to interest *us*? "What I write," says Genet, "is valid only for me." To which the public replies: "What I take the trouble to read should at least be valid for everyone. Let him preach theft! One could at least discuss the matter, could take a stand for or against his views." But he does not say that one should steal. Quite the contrary, he knows that it is wrong to steal and it is in order to be wrong that he steals. But he does not even ask us to be wrong: he asks us nothing at all. If anyone planned to become his disciple, I'm sure he would answer: "How could anyone act like me if he's not me?" This poet "speaks to us as an enemy." (628–29)

Sartre's argument is based on a different perception of authorial intention from that which Weaver and Johnstone imply. We arrive at an impasse. But there *are* ways, following Booth's example, that we might critique Sartre's defense. First, Sartre does not give us assent-worthy reasons to believe that he can be sure of Genet's answer to the questions we might pose; as it turns out, Genet says many things to the contrary in his writings and interviews (Fichte 180–90; Genet, *Journal* passim). Second, we could argue, after examining how Genet's rhetoric functions, that Genet does expect our interest and, beyond that, is asking us to be "wrong" and implies that we already are.

To illustrate these claims, I turn to Genet's *Querelle*. A taste of the novel's beginning reveals that this work was prepared under a system different from the one implied by the prescriptive "rules" of Weaver and Johnstone, or even from the position described by Sartre. Genet, through his narrative technique, actively seeks to break rules such as theirs and to take us with him. *Querelle* begins:

> The notion of murder often brings to mind the notion of sea and sailors. Sea and sailors do not, at first appear as a definite image—it is rather that "murder" starts up a feeling of *waves*. If one considers that seaports are the scene of frequent crimes, the association seems self-explanatory; but there are numerous stories from which we learn that the murderer was a man of the sea—either a real one, or a fake one—and if the latter is the case, the crime will be even more closely connected to the sea. The man who dons a disguise relieves him from the necessity of going through all the rigamarole required in the execution of any preconceived murder. Thus we could say that the outfit does the following things for the criminal: it envelops him in clouds; it gives him the appearance of having come from that far-off line of the horizon where the sea touches the sky; with long, undulating and muscular strides he can walk across the waters, personifying the Great Bear, the Pole Star or the Southern Cross; it (we are still discussing the particular disguise, as used by the criminal) it allows him to assume dark continents where the sun sets and rises, where the moon sanctions murder under roofs of bamboo beside motionless rivers teaming with alligators; it gives him the opportunity to act with the illusion of a mirage, to strike while one of his feet is still resting upon a beach in Oceania and the other propelling him across the water toward Europe; it grants him oblivion in advance, as sailors always "return from far away"; it allows him to consider landlubbers as mere vegetation. It cradles the criminal, it enfolds him—in the tight fit of his sweater, in the amplitude of his bell-bottoms. It casts a sleep-spell on the already fascinated victim. We shall talk about the sailor's mortal flesh. We ourselves have witnessed scenes of seduction. In that very long sentence beginning "it envelops him in clouds . . . ," we did indulge in facile poeticisms, each one of the propositions being merely an argument in favor of the author's personal proclivities. (3–4)[4]

The narrator announces himself to be one and the same with the author, shows us his self-conscious control of his rhetoric, and even demonstrates a tendency to pass aesthetic judgments on his storytelling. Jacques Derrida described Genet's technique as "poisoning the flowers of rhetoric" (13). As readers, we have both witnessed a seduction and been its intended object. We must either enter into the narrator's perspective with its risks or find ourselves described as "mere vegetation" and thus victims. If we look closely at the narrator's initially strange connection between the sea and murder, we find not syllogistic reasoning but the repeated terms of a *gradatio* that mimics logical progression. Our benign willingness to make sense of the narrator's connections and Genet's masterful use of tropes allows this odd passage to track. Propelled by these curious linguistic links, his labyrinthine sentences, and sheer curiosity, the reader becomes enmeshed in the narrator's internal "logic" and becomes the referent, at least by implication, of the narrator's "we." There seems to be no charge on the words "criminal" or "murder" as the narrator uses them. Nor is there any detectable ironic undercutting of the norms the narrator builds into his "argument." In fact, we may strain our internal ear for the entire length of the novel for an implied author who in some way repudiates this narrator's values, but we will hear only silence.

By the end of the novel we find we have been keeping company with a narrator who condones a character who chooses to be a murderer, thief, drug dealer, corrupter, and traitor. The act of continuing to read has made us at least voyeuristic, if not complicit. As accessories, we have allowed ourselves to indulge the narrator's facile poeticisms, to witness scenes of seduction, and to hear arguments for the author's proclivities to the end. Above all, we have entered into a world of violence for at least the time it takes us to read the text. Genet has lived in that world for at least the time it took him to write it.[5] This is as Genet would have it. In his autobiographical *A Thief's Journal,* Genet comments, "Such a definition of violence—through so many contradictory examples—shows you that I shall use words not in order to better describe an event or its hero but in order to provide instruction about myself. To understand me, complicity on the part of the reader is needed" (16). This complicity in his crimes against the community and even the idea of community is a means to secure in our breasts his dark, interior definition of beauty.

We aren't in Kansas anymore. This is the guy our mothers warned us about. Neither Genet nor *Querelle*'s implied author is our friend even in the most tolerant conception of friendship. Genet shows us that there is no honor among thieves even as he invites us to walk along the dock; the seductions in *Querelle* lead to betrayal and murder.

There can be little consolation that this is a relatively isolated literary incident. In his article, "The Reason for Stories: Toward a Moral Fiction," Robert Stone takes on William Gass's "proposition that art and moral aspiration were mutually distant." He sees in Gass's position an "antinomian vision, morality and art are independent and even in opposition" (71).

But does this independence, should it be the case, exclude ethical criticism? We might rightly ask if these texts, given that they do not actually kill us, make us stronger. If truth is beauty, and Genet can make a claim on either, we certainly are presented with some grist for our critical mills. That these questions derive from Nieztsche is telling. MacIntyre locates the modern controversy in ethical philosophy along lines that are on the one hand Nieztschean and that on the other derive from Aristotle. The Nietzschean contention rests on the idea of the individual apart: "It is because this is so that the great man cannot enter into relationships mediated by appeal to shared standards or virtues or goods; he is his own only authority and his relationships to others have to be exercises of that authority" (*After Virtue* 240). This position is clearly anathema to Booth, but is quite like that of Genet. The competing tradition is Aristotelian, and not surprisingly, quite similar to Booth's conception of the questions we ought to explore:

> For if the conception of the good has to be expounded in terms of such actions as those of a practice, of the narrative unity of human life and of a moral tradition, then goods, and with them the only grounds for the authority of laws and virtues, can only be discovered by entering into those relationships which constitute communities whose central bond is a shared vision and understanding of goods. To cut oneself off from shared activity in which one has initially to learn obediently as an apprentice learns, to isolate oneself from the communities which find their point and purpose in such activities, will be to debar oneself to that moral solipsism which constitutes Nietzschean greatness. Hence we have to conclude not only that Nietzsche does not win the argument by default against the Aristotelian tradition, but also, and perhaps more importantly, that it is from the perspective of that tradition that we can best understand the mistakes at the heart of the Nietzschean position. (*After Virtue* 240)

The idea of looking at the narrative unity of life is akin to Booth's questions of implicit norms; it exposes our assumptions as well as some texts' deficiencies. Booth would have us look at the ethos present in the text; in *Querelle* we find the solipsism MacIntyre describes in the Nietzschean position. Here, too, this perspective exposes the mistakes in the heart of the novel's position. Genet preys on our basic trust of the written word, our perhaps naive but customary assumption that authors are trying to do us some good (albeit their own definition of *good*), and our tendency as readers to give the benefit of the doubt to others as an extension of the way we give flexibility to the societal ties that bind us. Genet abuses these virtues of community in the attempt to pull us away from the very norms that allow communities to cohere.

But in an ironic twist not intended by the novel, Genet's antisocial claims are undercut to some extent by the act of his writing and publishing them. Though he writes from a position of alienation, an actual jail cell, his act is communicative even while it is hostile, a kiss of death. Ultimately, he is unsuccessful in conveying the norms he espouses because to convey them he must communicate with us, rendering his position of isolation meaningless.

We are unlikely to allow Genet into the small circle of our close friends unless it is our custom to run with a very tough crowd. What our custom is has some relevance. Turning to Booth's notion of reader's ethics as it applies to me as the reader of *Querelle*, I find that this work reminds me of how very actively values are implied by all works.[6] A dose of Genet makes the camouflaged values in other literary works closer to my own norms stand out in relief. Genet intends me no good, but reading *Querelle* does me some good. My perception of *Querelle* as an inherently inconsistent epistemology is, ironically, its value for me.

When I move from an evaluation of the novel as it affects me as one reader and write about it in this chapter, I open myself and the novel to the coductive process Booth describes in *The Company We Keep*.[7] As my critique enters the larger discussion of the ethics of this novel with Sartre, Levenson, Rader, and others, it becomes an example of Booth's premise that "judgement requires a community" (*Company* 72). My contributions are then judged in terms of the larger discussion. "The validity of our coductions must always be corrected in conversations about the coduction of others whom we trust" (*Company* 73).

Thus Booth can lead us to inquire about the nature of authorial and readers' ethics and the interdependency of criticism itself. We are not limited by proscriptions to what an author *ought* to have done when he or she, in fact, did something quite different. Instead, we are allowed the freedom to inquire beyond the customary boundaries of our predominant methods even into systems that stand in opposition. We are afforded this freedom because Booth's heuristic is relational and invites rhetorical description. By this I mean that by asking us to look at the relationship among authors, readers, and critics, as well as by asking us to examine how these relationships are accomplished and what they imply, Booth avoids the trap of judging one system only by another alien to it. His questions do not constitute some new foundationalism.

MacIntyre would locate this approach in the Aristotelian tradition. Following MacIntyre, I would locate Genet in the Nietzschean. But unlike the positions of Richard Weaver or Henry W. Johnstone, Jr., these locations are not themselves the reason for the judgments made of the text. Belonging to the wrong club is not the reason for censure. That Booth's approach allows us to see this other tradition in relation to the one in which Booth works bodes well for increasing the availability of this sort of discourse to even competing critical communities.

Booth's recipe can be claimed a success because it has rendered Genet's *Querelle* digestible, if not particularly palatable. *Querelle* has a bitter aftertaste but also, for some, a hidden medicinal purpose. Booth's questions concerning how we are invited to partake and what sort of fare we are offered prove to be useful because they ask us to examine ingredients rather than assume them. We make fewer mistakes and reach fewer dead ends because we make fewer faulty assumptions about the norms implicit in texts or the range of values possible in people.

Notes

1. Genet is the first to admit that he sometimes lies in autobiographical writings and interviews. Booth, in *Rhetoric of Fiction*, deals with Celine's *Journey to the End of the Night*. While that text has intricacies that bear some similarity to the difficulties I find in *Querelle*, those in Genet's novel are more pronounced because Genet does not claim to be at any distance from his narrator.

2. Weaver here follows George Yoos's "A Revision of the Concept of Ethical Appeal," *Philosophy & Rhetoric* 12 (Winter 1979): 41–58.

3. In his "Relevance of Rhetoric" Johnstone makes his position clear: "persuasion is responsible when it does not tend to degenerate. One must persuade only in such a way as to maintain the possibility of persuasion" (45). This

Kantian approach relies on the idea that persuasion is of unquestionable value for a community. This communitarianism is foreign to Genet.

4. An earlier "clandestine" version of the original *Querelle de Brest* was circulated in French. Joseph H. McMahon, in his book *The Imagination of Jean Genet* (New Haven: Yale UP, 1963), translates some of this same opening passage from the clandestine version: "We have let ourselves go to a facile verbal poetry in which each proposition is nothing but an argument in favor of the authors *complaisances*. We want to present the drama which unfolds here under the sign of a quite striking inner movement. Furthermore we want to point out that it is addressed to perverts. To the idea of the sea and of murder is added the idea of delight and *naturally* of love—rather of *unnatural* love" (86–87).

5. See *Company* 41–42 for Booth's discussion of ethical dimensions of time spent reading.

6. See "Epilogue: The Ethics of Reading," in *Company* 483–90, for Booth's extended discussion of reader's ethics.

7. Booth defines *coduction* on pp. 72–73.

Bibliography

Booth, Wayne C. *The Company We Keep: An Ethics of Fiction*. Berkeley: U of California P, 1988.

———. *Critical Understanding: The Powers and Limits of Pluralism*. Chicago: U of Chicago P, 1979.

———. "Kenneth Burke's Way of Knowing," *Critical Inquiry* 1 (1974): 1–22. Rev. and rpt. in *Critical Understanding*.

———. *A Rhetoric of Irony*. Chicago: U of Chicago P, 1974.

———. *The Rhetoric of Fiction*. Chicago: U of Chicago P, 1961. 2nd ed., 1983.

———. *The Vocation of a Teacher: Rhetorical Occasions 1967–1988*. Chicago: U of Chicago P, 1989.

———. "'The Way I Loved George Eliot': Friendship with Books a Neglected Critical Metaphor." *Kenyon Review* n.s. 2 (1980): 4–27. Rpt. in *The Company We Keep*. Chs. 6–7.

———. "Why Ethical Criticism Fell on Hard Times." *Ethics* 98 (1988): 278–93. Rpt. in *The Company We Keep*. 25–48.

Derrida, Jacques. *Glas*. Trans. John P. Leavey, Jr., and Richard Rand. Lincoln: U of Nebraska P, 1986.

Fichte, Hubert. "I Allow Myself to Revolt: Interview with Jean Genet." *Genet: A Collection of Critical Essays*. Ed. Peter Brooks and Joseph Halpern. Englewood Cliffs, NJ: Prentice, 1979. 178–90.

Genet, Jean. *A Thief's Journal*. New York: Grove, 1964.

———. *Querelle*. Trans. Anselm Hollo. New York: Grove, 1974.

Johnstone, Henry W. "The Relevance of Rhetoric to Philosophy and Philosophy to Rhetoric." *Quarterly Journal of Speech* (Feb. 1966): 41–46.

MacIntyre, Alasdair. *After Virtue*. Notre Dame: U of Notre Dame P, 1981.

———. *A Short History of Ethics*. New York: Macmillan, 1966.

Sartre, Jean Paul. *Saint Genet*. Trans. B. Fretchman. New York: Mentor, 1963.

Stone, Robert. "The Reason for Stories: Toward a Moral Fiction." *Harper's* June 1988: 71–76.

Weaver, Richard. *The Ethics of Rhetoric*. Chicago: Regnery, 1965.

4

Elie Wiesel and the Ethics of Fiction

SUSAN E. SHAPIRO

ELIE WIESEL'S POST–HOLOCAUST fiction offers a test case for ethical criticism, such as that explicated in Wayne Booth's *The Company We Keep: An Ethics of Fiction*. Wiesel's writings are, among other things, about the grounds of possibility of both discourse and community after the Holocaust. Friendship, both as a theme and as the relation constructed between implied author and implied reader(s), is that which ultimately makes possible for Wiesel the risk of speech, the writing of narrative in particular, and the construction of the possibility for ethical community in confronting the Shoah.[1]

The Holocaust represents, for Wiesel, the radical negation of all ethical and discursive orderings of the world. One of the hermeneutical antinomies facing him, as it does many other post–Holocaust writers, is the act of narrating an event that ruptures such order.[2] For how does one tell in narrative discourse about an event and its effects that have negated or undone the possibility of narrative coherence? By merely constructing a story with a beginning, middle, and end, has one not already teleologically sutured the very rupture that is to be told? Some writers, in response to this antinomy, eschew narrative discourse altogether and write explicitly antinarrativist texts (such as Edmond Jabès) or disrupted poetry (such as Paul Celan and Nelly Sachs).

In thinking through this problem of the testimonial dilemmas and possibilities of, especially, narrative discourse after the Holocaust, I turn here to Booth's ethical criticism.[3] By reading these texts together, as it were "coductively," I intend to read Booth through Wiesel by treating Wiesel as a limit case, testing Booth's arguments about narratological friendship by attempting to apply (at least some of) them to this extreme circumstance of writing, in which narrative is itself questioned as to its ethical viability. By in turn reading Wiesel through Booth I hope to judge whether (and, if so, how) the Holocaust has challenged or further intensified the grounds of possibility of narratological friendship and ethical community.[4]

The problem of fictional discourse "about" the Holocaust is a theme in Wiesel's writings, and is structurally present in the very problem of narration.[5] To project a future is to betray the past, to acknowledge a present (just as surviving itself evoked tremendous guilt for survivors of the Shoah). To write historically, in this case, is to place an event that seems to be isolated and outside of temporality, back into time—past time.

The risk of narration, of telling stories "about," is that of distance and pleasure. Just as speaking at all (in a passionate gesture of communication and community) is a great risk, so also is it problematic to emplot and, thus, impose linear time on the event, giving it a past, present, and future. The event that seemed to eclipse all of history and God's presence in history is surpassed, it seems, in a projection of a future (as possibly different, hence as *future*) in the risk of narrating a story about the event as *past,* with a beginning, middle, and end. The dimensions of the risk of speaking about the Holocaust begin to become clearer. At stake is an intrinsic betrayal, not related to the content of speech or writing but, rather, to the fact that to speak and write at all is necessarily to project a future and, thus, to distance oneself from an event by making it past.

The other side of this risk is the betrayal implicit in forever keeping silent about the event of the Holocaust, not telling, not witnessing, not testifying to its never-ebbing wake of effects. Not to speak about the past is to condemn it to be forgotten to history. It is to repeat too resonantly the awful silencing deaths, themselves become silent if not told.

Speaking and silence, then, this double betrayal, are the opposing and mutually implied poles present within Wiesel's discourse, both as a theme or subject of discourse, and as a structuring principle of Wiesel's narration and, thus, of the discourse itself. I have already treated the first of those manifestations elsewhere.[6] I will here turn to the second and consider the rhetorical grounds of possibility of this narrative structuring.

How does Wiesel dare to take this risk of speech in the face of the double betrayal of speech and silence? Aside from making it an explicit problem in his stories, and of the characters that tell these stories, Wiesel risks this emergence into speech rhetorically; that is, in constituting a peculiar rhetoric of friendship, Wiesel makes the implied reader (as well as his characters) a potential friend: "Gabriel [the protagonist of *The Gates of the Forest*] is my friend and he speaks for me. All my fictional characters exalt friendship; for some it is an obsession. Sometimes I tell myself that I have made them up only because I needed to believe in friendship, because I needed them as friends" ("Celebration" 79). Gabriel asks, "What is a friend? Someone who for the first time makes you aware of your loneliness and his, and helps you to escape so you in turn can help him. Thanks to him you may remain silent without shame and speak freely without risk" ("Celebration" 79). Indeed, it is only in friendship, through the risk of encounter between two "persons" (in this case, two characters and/or the implied author and implied reader), that Wiesel seems to locate the place for the possible reemergence of discourse about God, as well as of speech in general. What is true of the Hasid applies as well to the characters of Wiesel's novels, although perhaps articulated with less optimism.

> A Hasid is never alone nor allowed to be depressed. This is permitted the rabbi, but not the disciple. What, then, is a Hasid to do who is crushed by his memories, shattered by his inability to affirm life while he mourns his dead? How can a Hasid who has lived through the long night of the concentration camps still open himself to joy, to ecstasy? Alone, he would not have the strength. With friends, he can undertake anything, relearn anything; the duty of keeping the faith, of loving, of singing, of sharing with others the salt of his life, and his secret, too, through stories and melodies, through words and silences. The unhappy Hasid will have to choose happiness so as not to be a bad influence on his friends, so as to prevent them from following him into the abyss. ("Celebration" 84–85)

The rhetorical principle of friendship structuring Wiesel's writing and making possible the risk of narration (making past present, projecting a possibly different future, and making past past) is itself a theme, then, of his novels. This rhetorical principle is shown in the way characters relate as they grow toward or away from each other as survivors, that is, as those people who are able to become friends because each has been permeated so thoroughly by silence and death that the usual or ordinary terms of friendship are no longer the determining ones.

The implied reader of Wiesel's novels is constructed and positioned in two ways, as one who either was or was not there, in the Holocaust itself. Nonsurvivor readers are encouraged to imagine that, had fate been otherwise, they could have been there, might even have died there; but this imaginative possibility also ironically heightens the awareness of their distance from the event in recognizing that in fact they were not there. This distance preserves silence even in the risk of speech. Indeed, it is through various strategies of distancing in and through language that silence is inscribed in discourse. For that distance between those who were there and those who were not is, according to Wiesel, unbridgeable. Wiesel writes in "The Holocaust as Literary Inspiration":

> Ask any survivor and he will tell you, and his children will tell you. He or she who did live through the event will never reveal it. Not entirely. Not really. Between our memory and its reflection there stands a wall that cannot be pierced. The past belongs to the dead and the survivor does not recognize himself in the words linking him to them. We speak in code, we survivors, and this code cannot be broken, cannot be deciphered, not by you no matter how much you try.[7]

This distance creates a necessary silence in language. But this distance does not mean that there is not an overall will to, or strategy of, friendship in the narrative structuring of Wiesel's works. Rather, one of the conditions of friendship with the implied author of Wiesel's texts is the recognition of just this necessary silence and distance. The risk required of the implied reader is the risk of understanding the silence inscribed in the text's language: its source, its pervasiveness, its impenetrability. Reading toward the limits of discourse through distance and silence is the implied strategy of Wiesel's narration. This *via negativa* (i.e., knowing that you cannot know) is the ground of possibility of friendship and understanding. It is, in turn, only the desire for and will to friendship that makes possible the risk of speech.

The relation of friendship between the protagonists of Wiesel's novels, especially in *The Gates of the Forest* and *The Town Beyond the Wall,* is of a peculiarly intense sort, friendship in which discourse about death, profound negativity, mad hope, and despair are central.[8] The friends in Wiesel's novels are most often survivors struggling to find themselves, each other, and God in a world that has become abysmal. These friends often are not polite. They hurl angry and, most often, wounded and wounding words at one another, messages sent in an attempt to orient the other to the distinctive, profound, and fundamentally dislocated site in which each struggles. Disconnected from one another, alienated from themselves, apparently abandoned by God, each character whispers and shouts to the other as a way of sharing by recognizing their broken worlds. Struggling toward each other in silence and in fragmented, sometimes "mad," discourse, Wiesel's characters provide the basis for their emergence in the narrative through their risking of speech in the context of friendship.

The relation of friendship between implied author and implied reader is analogously an arduous one. Friendship is the rhetorical ground of possibility for the narrative act of communication. The relations of friendship constituted in Wiesel's narrative discourse between implied reader and implied author may well be understood as analogous to the relations between the characters in his novels. As Booth suggests, there are various kinds of narrative friends.[9]

The kinds of friendship—the quality of companionship during the process of reading—in Wiesel's novels, is, as noted, peculiar. It is constituted through distance and to that extent, ironically, it is shared. Like the disconnected and alienated characters of the novels, the relation between implied author and implied reader(s) is predicated upon distance, separation, and respect. Part of this distancing is, perhaps, maintaining the difference between, and thus memory of, those friends from whom the Holocaust has irretrievably separated the implied author and those who people Wiesel's novels, as well as his implied reader-friends.

> I remember the friends of my childhood as I remember my childhood; I look at them as I look at myself, and a familiar sadness engulfs me. Where are they? Why were we separated? How could I have deserved to outlive them? For most of them are no longer of this world....
>
> Ever since, I have been looking for them. I have never stopped looking for them. Other friends have come to enrich my life, but not one has resembled either of them. When they left they took with them not only a conception of Messianic hope, but also the ideal of friendship.
>
> My new friends and I try to understand what has happened to our people, and sometimes even to act upon its destiny, but my mystical experiences of long ago remain enveloped in memory.
>
> In other words: friendship has not disappeared from my life; it has only changed in nature. Even in a universe of ultimate horror friendship was a haven. ("Celebration" 77, 81–82)

The formidable distance between implied author and implied reader(s) is a rupture for understanding and in discourse that is caused by the Holocaust. It is the silence evoked by this event's uncommunicable, unenunciably horrific dimensions. This rupture in both speech and understanding is itself told in Wiesel's novels through their peculiar modes of negative transgressive discourse and in their impossible, but necessary, mediations of friendship.

Narrating by saying that one cannot fully say is a strategy for talking about the Holocaust without thereby immediately making it simply a subject of, and therefore subject to, discourse.[10] Rather, the event of the Holocaust is understood as being always beyond discourse. It is narrated only to the extent that this unreachability and distance is itself articulated and grasped. As Wiesel remarks, "Only one of my books, *Night,* deals directly with the Holocaust; all the others reveal why one cannot speak about it" (Edelman 18). Thus, the inscription of the failure of discourse is a necessary condition of its testimonial effectiveness.[11] Mediation of the ultimacy of the Holocaust's radical negation of discourse (and of the social and religious coherences that make possible such speech and community) is itself made possible through the confession of this testimonal failure. This narrative confession of the failure of narrative ironically makes possible testimony to the Holocaust as ultimately, but not finally, rupturing discourse and community.

What both the problem of narrating at all about the event of the Holocaust and Wiesel's peculiar use of the rhetoric of friendship that makes possible this narration demonstrate is the difficulty of construing ultimate negation in discourse. The problem is that of narrating a radically disruptive event without either finalizing its negation, thus making impossible its (especially, but not only, narrative) telling, or domesticating its ruptured character and effects in the easy-analogizing and teleological ordering implicit in telling a story to another. Wiesel's peculiar rhetoric of friendship between implied author and implied reader(s), however, makes possible a narrative discourse in which just such a distinction between ultimate and final negation can be made, even as this distinction, as it construes their "proper" narrative distance, makes possible their "proper" narrative friendship.

This peculiar friendship does not in any way erase the rupture the Holocaust poses in discourse and history. It is rather one in which the recognition of the disorienting, silencing event of the Holocaust is itself intensified and shared. As constituting and occupying the place of friend, implied readers who are nonsurvivors understand only to the extent that they also recognize that they cannot fully understand either the event or what surviving fully means.[12] But, as already suggested, implied nonsurvivor readers also know that had fate or historical circumstances been different, they could have been there. This recognition makes the implied readers imaginative or, as it were, potential survivors and both maintains the grounds of distance (one is, as it were, potentially, though not actually, there) and of connectedness (one could have been there had fate and historical circumstance been otherwise).[13]

This is the peculiar friendship Wiesel offers nonsurvivor readers. Friendship is the ground of possibility of narrating what one cannot fully tell. It allows showing how words fail and silence intervenes. This rhetoric of friendship is crucial to the narrative strategies of Wiesel's novels generally.

Just as the recognition of distance, silence, and the negation of the possibility of communicating fully about the Holocaust form the grounds of possible narratological friendship, so is friendship the basis of the risk of speech about and to God. The rhetorical reaching out in communicating negation (of both the radically negative character of the event and of the impossibility of fully communicating this negativity) is present as well in the simultaneous affirmation and denial of Wiesel's peculiar God-language, as in his denial of God's existence in discourse addressed to God (the affirmation coming rhetorically rather than grammatically or logically). It is, likewise, manifest in the metaphorical extension of the term *revelation* as applied to the Holocaust (negative in the similar ultimacy of both Sinai and the Holocaust, and affirming the possibility of difference in the past and future by the metaphorical negation "as if" but not "that" the Holocaust is [i.e., "literally"] a revelation).

The risk of speech, as I have noted, is a testimony of ultimacy, but not of finality. In fact, for Wiesel, if the revelation of the Holocaust had been final, the term would not be metaphorical: indeed, it would not be employed at all. The only response for Wiesel to such finality would be silence.

The rupture within discourse for Wiesel, then, is double (of language in general and of God-language) and also is ultimate, but not final. This rupture, is, therefore, open to further negation, further difference and otherness, as produced in historical events. The site of rupture, then, is within both language and history. The shattering of language by the Holocaust reflects the ultimate and radically negative character of that event and yet, through language's disfiguring, we may both recognize and think about its character. The rupture in language does not take the form of a displacement from history and, as it were, into discourse; rather, it allows discourse to intensify our understanding of the events and eventful character of history, in this case, of the Holocaust.

Events end for the writing of conventional histories on a particular date or a particular moment, effectively sealing them off from other events and times. However, an ultimate event that so radically disrupts our assumptions about humanness and about God, that tears apart even the very social fabric of speech and writing, is inscribed through its rupturing effects in discourse. Discourse thereby becomes testimony to the event in its shattered and ruptured character, in its aporias, its silences, its ellipses, its gaps. And to the extent that the language we "inherit" and learn is so inscribed, our speaking and acting will be affected by this event, whether we are aware of these effects or not. The Holocaust does not, then, simply end, but continues—through its inscription into our language and functioning—to affect us in a wake that we cannot, as linguistic beings, hope to escape.

Our horizons of both understanding and belief have been thus radically altered. Hermeneutical matters are therefore significant in considering this event, for its effects persist in our language, communities, and history/ies. Indeed, as I have suggested, the very temporal ordering of both discourse and history has been radically put into question.

Wiesel notes, "The trouble is that we [survivors] have lived beyond time and therefore find it difficult to distinguish between past and present" ("Why Should People Care?" 17). How can one narrate both the experience of an end of time and the abysmal character of history within the temporal ordering of narration? As stated, the antinomous character of the double betrayal of either writing or remaining silent about the Holocaust is present in the very risk of the temporal ordering of narrative.

To narrate is to construct, in narrative discourse (statement), a temporal account and ordering that is about the story and its temporality.[14] To order temporally is (1) to make the event in some way coherent and, thus, sensible; (2) to construe it as an occurrence in "pseudo" time, that is, to fictionalize it; (3) to structure a temporal mediation of this event that was experienced as out-of-time and end-of-history and, thus, in some way to risk phenomenologically betraying its victims; and (4) to recognize that each of the preceding acts risks domesticating, reducing and, in particular, betraying the radically disruptive and negating force of the event itself. This problem of domestication in discourse applies to, and is exemplified by, the problem of creating a linear narrative of an event that shatters and radically transforms our notions of time and history, as well as our very notions and use of language. How does one avoid domesticating the Holocaust, as a subject of discourse, to speech or writing about the event?[15] About the inadequacy of language to and after the Holocaust, Wiesel writes, "all words seemed inadequate, worn, foolish, lifeless, whereas I wanted them to be searing. Where was I to discover a fresh vocabulary, a primeval language?" ("Why I Write" 201).

Beginning from rupture and silence, how does one emerge into order and speech? According to Wiesel, as a survivor he "enters literature through . . . silence" ("Why I Write" 201). As already noted, Wiesel enters literature through the risk of friendship in the narrative relation of implied author and implied reader(s) through the confession of the testimonial failure of discourse to adequately represent or tell about the Holocaust, a confession, however, given in narrative. This risk of friendship rhetorically makes possible the risk of narrative temporal ordering as well.

The narration of time, constructing the relations between narrative statement time and story time, becomes possible in the context of Wiesel's construal of narrative friendship. Just as Wiesel makes the recognition of distance from the event the basis of friendship, so too does he heighten the distance from historical discourse by writing fiction, increasing the distance between narrative statement time and story time. If readers know that they are not reading history but rather "true fiction" (a true story), then the first-order reference is suspended.[16] The temporality of the story is suspended in favor of the "pseudo-temporality" of the narrative statement. The reference of the temporality of the narrative statement is likewise suspended (i.e., "pseudo"), but for the sake of telling a true story. Truth in this context entails distance from historical narration through a narrative discourse and temporality that is at once "pseudo" and "most true." The "pseudo" characteristic is the necessary condition for narrating a true story that recognizes that writing about the event of the Holocaust is impossible. As Wiesel says,

> I wrote a book called *The Town Beyond the Wall,* which is a novel. . . . And it is written in the third person, which is rare in my books, but if you ask 99 percent of the people who read the book they will tell you it is written in the first person. And for me it was a discovery; it pleased me very much because I was so much there although it was pure fiction. And the same goes for the Holocaust. I never really write about the Holocaust. Yet ask people who read (and there are a few) and they will tell you that I write nothing but about the Holocaust. ("What Is a Jew?" 151–52)

Wiesel has come to consider historical documents of, and personal testimonies to, the Shoah as most veracious and trustworthy.[17] While the split between historical and fictional accounts of the Holocaust is implicit in his hermeneutic practice generally (effacing their shared narrative sources and character), Wiesel's increased concern with the documentary force of historical testimony may be understood not only as a fearful anticipation of the general inattentiveness to the subject and claims of the Holocaust on the part of the public, especially immediately after the war, but as in response to the actual denial that the Holocaust occurred at all. Wiesel's earlier trust in the transformative reception of the truth of his fictional narratives seems somewhat, and perhaps intensely, broken by such denials: "[T]he leader of the SS today in Germany . . . recently told a convention that the Holocaust was a lie, a hoax of the century. . . . I do not know how you react to all this. I can only tell you what one survivor feels. More than sadness, he feels dismay, and more than dismay he feels despair, and even more than despair, he feels disgust" ("The Holocaust as Literary Inspiration" 19). In "Why I Write," Wiesel notes: "And yet the survivor may experience remorse. He has tried to bear witness; it was all in vain. . . . [But] they [the survivors] will continue, for they cannot do otherwise" (205). The essay "The Holocaust as Literary Inspiration" was delivered at Northwestern University, in part in response to the denial, by a professor at that institution, that the Holocaust had in fact occurred. As Irving Abraham notes, "this essay examines the impossibility for fiction to treat the event. Wiesel stresses that a new literary form has grown out of the Holocaust—the literature of testimony—and he offers numerous telling quotations that illustrate this new genre and authenticate the event."[18]

I think, however, that it would be important to consider Wiesel's own writing, his "true fiction," as a part of this genre of testimony, thereby extending (and making more complicated) our notions of narrative truth beyond the radical split between historical and fictive narrative.[19] Despite this hermeneutical fence built around historical narrative in an attempt to protect the veracity of the Shoah from assault, Wiesel's practice opens up the possibility of imagining and thinking about truth in ways not constrained by, or confined to, notions of literal representation. For the peculiar strategies of discourse required for the testimony of ultimacy but not finality, and for telling by saying that one cannot say, are constituted in Wiesel's novels as a kind of "true fiction." The truth of fiction is made possible by heightening the epistemic distance from the event, thus preserving the silence, the character, of the event as beyond discourse, the fictional necessary conditions of the telling of a true story. Writing fiction, then, ironically becomes the literary condition of telling the truth, part of which is the telling of precisely that epistemic distance. Only by first widening this temporal gap in fiction—indeed, by making it unbridgeable—is "true" narrative possible.

The first condition of narration, then, is negative; the inaccessibility of the Holocaust is intensified by the fictional status of the narrative. This negation is again ultimate, but not final. The rhetoric of friendship between implied author and implied reader(s) makes such discourse "about" the Holocaust possible through, among other things, the portrayal of its effects. But this friendship must continue to be distanced. It must not fully bridge the abyss between those who were there and those who were not. The limits of discourse, though rendered not final through the rhetoric of narrative friendship in Wiesel's works, are not eradicated. If recalcitrant "no" is rhetorically transformed into "yes," it still preserves its negativity in the grammar and logic of the text. Grammar and logic are rhetoricized but not sublated in Wiesel's writings in a testifying to the event for the sake of the dead, for those who can no longer tell and on behalf of whose memory Wiesel attempts, however problematically, to speak.

> This is the concentration camp language. It negated all other language and took its place. Rather than link, it became wall. Could it be surmounted? Could the reader be brought to the other side? I knew the answer to be negative, and yet I also knew that "no" had to become "yes." It was the wish, the last will of the dead. One had to break the shell enclosing the dark truth, and give it a name. One had to force man to look. ("Why I Write" 201).

As the rhetorical definalization of the narrative friendship in Wiesel's novels mediates and reorients their negative grammars and logics, and as the relation of friendship is constituted in and by the "quality of the companionship during the time of reading,"[20] so is the odd logic of temporality of Wiesel's "true fiction" that occurs between kinds of temporal ordering governed by the time of reading.[21] The relationship of friendship—through which the temporal aspects of the narrative discourse are construed—is constituted in the terms of the quality of the companionship during the time of reading. Just as story time and the narrative statement time are derived in and from their metonymic displacement in and of reading time,[22] so the relative quality of friendship is derived from and constituted in the quality of the companionship between implied author and implied reader(s) during the time of reading. This displacement into the possibility of saying "yes" to friendship is constitutive, therefore, of the temporal ordering of the narrative as it allows the (ambivalent) projection of a future horizon. This horizon is different from the past, and yet allows its retrieval, as well as a retrieval of those values more fundamental of humanity.

Friendship allows for the emergence of thought of the future as shared destiny rather than as fateful end. The relationship of friendship between implied author and implied reader is thus the ground of possibility for the risk of narrating, however indirectly, the event of the Holocaust. Narrative friendship also reorients the reader(s) (and the implied author) by allowing for a future that recovers the possibility of community. In this way, it makes possible a recovery of just those fundamental relations and assumptions about humanness and the divine that the Holocaust ruptured. As Wiesel retrospectively writes,

> Of course, the technicians of death tried to deprive us of it [the haven of friendship]. Forget your parents, your brothers, your past, or else you will perish. That is what they kept telling us day and night. But what happened was the opposite. Those who lived only for themselves, only to feed themselves, ended up succumbing to the laws of death, while the others, those who knew whom to live for—a parent, a brother, a friend—managed to obey the laws of life. ("Celebration" 83)

Friendship is, thus, a kind of resistance to the relentless attempts by the Nazis to dehumanize, and thus to destroy, the Jews.[23] It is also an affirmation founded in the very risk of friendship.

The move is made in Wiesel's narratives from attempting to bring the Messiah for the sake of the world to the act of one individual character on behalf of another. The saving of one human life is for Wiesel, the saving of a world. And this act is the ground of possibility for redemption more generally, although it is not explicitly performed for the sake of that more general aim. This risk on behalf of another person is the basis for possibly recovering viable God-language. The implied author exhorts his characters (and readers) not to wait for the arrival of the Messiah, not to judge, finally, the effectiveness of God-language in terms of divine intercession. This is not, however, a counsel of indifference.

> "The Messiah may come by accident," said a Hasidic Master, one hundred and fifty years ago. Today he would say: the end of the world may

come by accident. How can it be saved? That's not for the novelist to say. There is a "Savior" for that particular purpose. But the Savior, according to the tradition of my people, is not one person: he is all of us. Which means: we can—we must—help him help us. Which means: we must appeal to our collective memory: only the tale of what was done to my people can save humankind from a similar fate. Which means: we must care—lest we fall victim to our own indifference.

Could this be the answer? No. But—it is the question. ("Why Should People Care?" 18)

But God is not let off easily in Wiesel's works, either. This possibility of saving action *despite* God is achieved through the risk and demand to save another human being, to make a difference in the world through one's own acts. This is very much a retrieval of the praxis character of *Halachah,* but it is not a praxis grounded in a simple, reassuring, covenantal relation between God and the Jewish people or between God and humankind.[24] Historical events appear, rather, to be countercovenantal. This belief in the ultimate value of saving action on behalf of another— and as an act that saves a world—is, in some ways, a postcovenantal religious praxis. It does not necessarily deny the possible truth or validity of the now undisclosed—indeed, seemingly negated—covenantal relation. This postcovenantal religious praxis is grounded, one might say, in the risk of friendship. Saving a world by saving a life is a reaffirmation of the ultimate value of life: this in the face of an event in which the idea of humanness was itself negated, and in which there was an explicit attempt to dehumanize the Jews completely before annihilating them.

Such an affirmation does not proceed through the prior affirmation of God and the guaranteed creation of an ultimately valuable universe. Rather, this affirmation is a risk, and it is a risk of friendship between two "persons" (two characters or the implied author and implied reader) who encounter and struggle with each other as they do with themselves and God.

The affirming of the ultimate value of human life—in a saving act of friendship—mitigates the finality of the Holocaust. This mitigation does not reduce its ultimate negativity. This affirming, this "yes," is the risk of friendship that grounds itself in this very risk. It is not a denial of the ultimate negativity of the event. It is, however, the allowing of a possibly different future: drawing upon what is a fundamental human characteristic and also a ground of possibility for reorientation toward, and retrieval of, a religious tradition for which such humanity is necessay. If the risk of friendship were impossible, then both secular and religious humanistic traditions would be finally irretrievable. This projecting of a potentially different future through the risk of friendship makes possible, but does not guarantee, a retrieval of those traditions. It also grounds the possibility of an ethical criticism, such as Booth's, that draws on and places itself in relation to them.

Reading Wiesel through Booth helps us read Booth through Wiesel. Wiesel's writings "invite" Booth's concern with narratological friendship.[25] If the stakes of an ethical criticism such as Booth's require a limit case for demonstration, surely Wiesel provides such an occasion. For while their works are so very different in style and subject, they share profoundly similar concerns for the continued viability of language and ethical community. Keeping company with Booth and Wiesel thus vividly demonstrates both the breakdown and limits of ethical community and discourse as well as their continued viability and claim upon us.

Notes

1. The terms *Holocaust* and *Shoah* (as is every other such term, e.g., *Churban*) are in different ways problematic. *Holocaust* implies that the event was a (completely consumed) sacrifice to God, and *Shoah* is a term used primarily to refer to natural catastrophes. I use both terms to call attention to the problems and limits of each.

2. See, for example, my "Failing Speech: Post-Holocaust Writing and the Discourse of Postmodernism."

3. Booth, *Company,* especially chapters 5, 6, and 7.

4. The present chapter draws on a chapter on Wiesel (ch. 3) from a larger work of mine, "Recovering the Sacred: Hermeneutics and Theology after the Holocaust" (forthcoming).

5. In this essay, I do not closely read any of Wiesel's novels. Such readings of his *The Gates of the Forest* (New York: Holt, Rinehart & Winston, 1966) and *The Town Beyond the Wall* (New York: Holt, Rinehart & Winston, 1964), two of his novels most concerned with friendship, may be found in "Recovering the Sacred," ch. 3.

6. See my "Hearing the Testimony of Radical Negation" p. 7.

7. Wiesel, "The Holocaust as Literary Inspiration," 7–8. For a brief and thematic discussion of friendship and meaning in the novels of Wiesel, see Michael Berenbaum, *The Vision of the Void: Theological Reflections on the Works of Elie Wiesel* (Middletown, CT: Wesleyan UP, 1979) 37–42.

8. In "Celebration," Wiesel notes that these two works in particular are concerned with friendship.

9. See Booth, "'The Way I Loved George Eliot'" 4–27. These themes are once again developed in *The Company We Keep*, especially chs. 6 and 7, 168–224.

10. See Michel Foucault on the dialectic of subject and subjection, discourse and power, in "The Subject and Power," *Michel Foucault: Beyond Structuralism and Hermeneutics,* eds. Herbert L. Dreyfus and Paul Rabinow (Chicago: U of Chicago P, 1982) 208–25.

11. See my "Failing Speech" 66, 87n. 2.

12. In this chapter, I am treating only the implied nonsurvivor reader. It is this reader, I believe, that forms the primary audience for these novels. The implied survivor-reader represents the degree zero of reading/writing. Like the implied author, the implied survivor-reader(s) is constructed as knowing, but not telling all, both because of the limits of discourse adequately to narrate and, relatedly, because if the survivors did tell, their discourses would be considered excessive and unrealistic and, thus, as unbelievable fabrications of or upon the event. This romantic, absolute horizon of shared knowledge and understanding, however, functions in some ways problematically to efface the constructed and partial character of all knowledge and memory. In construing the nonsurvivor reader(s) as his primary audience, however, Wiesel opens up yet other ways of reading this detour into fiction in order to "truly narrate," as I later demonstrate.

13. Because of its connotation of futuricity, using the term *potential* in this context is somewhat awkward. However, the implied reader's recognition that she or he could have been there is a recognition of fateful potential, the limitations of which are, I believe, that none of us is finally excluded from such fateful negative possibility.

14. See Genette, *Narrative Discourse,* for the narrative terms and their use in this discussion. Although Genette's terms do not necessarily directly correspond to Booth's (see Booth, *Company* 125n), there are some shared insights about the working of stories and narrative discourse that my treatment of Genette highlights.

15. In "Failing Speech" and "Recovering the Sacred," I have shown the risks of this displacement of event by discourse in the grammatical, rhetorical, and logical assumptions and strategies of Edmond Jabès, among others.

16. See Genette 33–35 for a related discussion of this manipulation of narrative distance. The ideas in this paragraph are drawn in part from these pages.

17. See "The Holocaust as Literary Inspiration" 7–8; see also Wiesel, "Myth and History" 20–30.

18. See Rosenfeld and Greenberg, eds., *Confronting the Holocaust* 210.

19. For an insightful criticism of hermeneutically naive understandings of documenting the event, see James E. Young, *Writing and Rewriting the Holocaust* (Bloomington: Indiana UP, 1988).

20. See Booth, "George Eliot" 7.

21. See Genette, 33–85.

22. See Genette, 25–32.

23. In some ways, this risk of friendship might appear to resemble the logic of resistance as explicated by Emil Fackenheim, *To Mend the World: Foundations of Future Jewish Thought* (New York: Schocken, 1982). We must, however, recall that Wiesel's resistance is founded both rhetorically and socially in friendship, not in a quasi-categorical (logical, isolatively founded) imperative as for Fackenheim.

24. *Halachah* means "the way" or "the path" and refers both to the decision-making processes and the determinations of Jewish law, specifically in the Talmud.

25. See Booth's *The Company We Keep*, ch. 4, 90–92, for a discussion of the terms *invite, tolerate,* and *violate,* or *resist* as applied to the relation between texts and particular acts of criticism. See also Wayne Booth, *Modern Dogma and the Rhetoric of Assent* 191–92, for his treatment of Wiesel's *Gates of the Forest*. I have found the resources of his *The Company We Keep* more helpful, however, in reading this (and other) Wiesel works in "Boothian terms" such as those explicated above.

Bibliography

Booth, Wayne C. *The Company We Keep: An Ethics of Fiction*. Berkeley: U of California P, 1988.

———. *Modern Dogma and the Rhetoric of Assent*. Chicago: U of Chicago P, 1974.

———. "'The Way I Loved George Eliot': Friendship with Books a Neglected Critical Metaphor." *Kenyon Review* n.s. 2 (1980): 4–27.

Cargas, Harry James. "What Is a Jew? An Interview with Elie Wiesel." *Responses to Elie Wiesel*. Ed. Harry James Cargas. New York: Persea, 1978. 150–157.

Edelman, Lily. "A Conversation with Elie Wiesel." *Responses to Elie Wiesel*. Ed. Harry James Cargas. New York: Persea, 1978. 9–22.

Genette, Gerard. *Narrative Discourse*. Ithaca, NY: Cornell UP, 1980.

Rosenfeld, Alvin, and Irving Greenberg, eds. *Confronting the Holocaust: The Impact of Elie Wiesel*. Bloomington: Indiana UP, 1978.

Shapiro, Susan E. "Failing Speech: Post-Holocaust Writing and the Discourse of Postmodernism." *Semeia* 40 (1987): 65–91.

———. "Hearing the Testimony of Radical Negation." *Concilium* (1985): 3–10.

———. "Recovering the Sacred: Hermeneutics and Theology after the Holocaust" (forthcoming).

Wiesel, Elie. "A Celebration of Friendship." *From the Kingdom of Memory: Reminiscences by Elie Wiesel*. New York: Summit, 1990. 75–85.

———. "Myth and History." *Symbol, Myth, and Reality*. Ed. Alan M. Olson. South Bend, IN: U of Notre Dame P, 1980. 20–30.

———. "Why I Write." *Confronting the Holocaust: The Impact of Elie Wiesel*. Eds. Alvin Rosenfeld and Irving Greenberg. Bloomington: Indiana UP, 1978. 200–206.

———. "Why Should People Care?" *A Consuming Fire*. Ed. John K. Roth. Atlanta: John Know, 1979. 15–18.

Wiesel, Elie, Lucy Davidowicz, Dorothy Rabinowitz, and Robert McAffee Brown, eds. "The Holocaust as Literary Inspiration." *Dimensions of the Holocaust*. Evanston, IL: Northwestern UP. 4–19.

5

Booth, Bakhtin, and the Culture of Criticism

DON H. BIALOSTOSKY

In an essay in *PMLA*'s centennial number, Geoffrey Hartman portrays the present "culture of criticism" as "within historicism, reacting to the expanded horizon of fact it has brought about, now integrating by an impossible embrace and now violently throwing off the burden of multiplying and fragmenting perspectives" (372). Hartman assumes in the essay the impossible task of integrating the diverse and self-divided culture he imagines, embracing the German, French, British, and American cultures of criticism, and sublimating the violence of the "knowledge explosion" within his own cosmopolitan cultivation of acquaintance with more than one hundred fifty scholars and critics from Aarsleff to Zumthor.

At one point in his argument, Hartman asks whether Bakhtin's dialogics can help criticism cope with its "burden of multiplying and fragmenting perspectives." Hartman thinks that Bakhtin's "dialogic principle" "exposes a constitutive unintelligibility" in both the modern novel and human relations, and he asks whether such a principle can sustain us without our resorting to other powerful structures of thought and discourse: "Can we tolerate such ambiguity, such unresolved diversity," he asks, "without structures of domination or dialectic?" (389). Hartman fears that we cannot, but his commitment to survey the whole present culture of criticism does not permit him to pause and consider the question. I take it up in this chapter as part of a longer inquiry that asks whether a deliberately cultivated dialogic criticism can stabilize and clarify our culture of criticism without giving in to the alternatives Hartman fears.

When Hartman recognizes "domination or dialectic" as alternative practices that threaten to undermine Bakhtin's dialogics, he draws upon powerful Western cultural paradigms. He calls to my mind, for example, the paradigm of political regimes in the eighth book of Plato's *Republic*. There the democratic regime is threatened from below by the temptation to escape from its unresolved diversities into the domination of the tyrant's single voice, the "sinister unifying" Hartman fears (389). But it is also threatened from above by the dialectical philosopher's push to transcend diversities and subordinate them in an ideal scale of forms. In terms more pertinent to my argument here, Hartman's alternatives also recall how easily we can slip from the relatively unfamiliar and unrationalized practices of dialogic thought and discourse back into the familiar cultural tracks worn by the traditional verbal arts of rhetoric and dialectic.

Rhetoric, after all, may be understood as the great storehouse of verbal strategies for imposing "structures of domination." In one of its persistent forms, it teaches its practitioners how to shape their discourse to "win over others," whether the phrase implies persuading them or just plain beating them. Dialectic, I have argued elsewhere, cultivates techniques of manipulating ideas rather than people, teaching its practitioners to organize and overcome ideas without reference to the people who hold them. Because rhetoric resembles dialogics in its concern with the relations among people in a given community and dialectic resembles dialogics in its concern with the relations among ideas, the dialogic figure of the hyphenated person-idea, the ideologist-hero, easily reduces, without a well-known art of dialogics, to a rhetorical person struggling for domination or a dialectical idea contradicting, subsuming, or being subsumed by another idea.[1] Dialogics is always breaking down into the rhetorical and dialectical arts that oppose it and each other.

But the issue is really more complicated than this dialectical formulation allows, because the arts brought forward under the names *rhetoric* and *dialectic* are not all of a piece, and the modes of opposition and cooperation among their advocates and the advocates of dialogics are not uniform. A dialogic survey of some of the many projects for criticism in recent years that have explicitly identified themselves with either rhetoric or dialectic would disclose friends, opponents, and even practitioners of dialogics flying the banners of both the other arts and calling on Bakhtinian dialogics to account for itself in a variety of terms. In this survey, neither domination nor dialectic would maintain a single identity as an alternative to dialogics, but each makes its appearance not only among those who represented rhetoric and dialectic for Bakhtin but also among others who now represent these arts in Anglo-American criticism.

Domination is a significant motif for the writer who most often represents rhetoric in Bakhtin's writings, Victor Vinogradov, a contemporary of Bakhtin's and an influential figure in Soviet stylistics.[2] Vinogradov, who views the novel as a rhetorical genre and analyzes its devices "from the point of view of their effectiveness as rhetoric" (*Dialogic Imagination* 42), helps to shape Bakhtin's zero-sum image of the art. Bakhtin writes in his late notebooks, "In rhetoric there is the unconditionally innocent and the unconditionally guilty; there is the complete victory and the destruction of the opponent. In dialogue the destruction of the opponent also destroys that very dialogic sphere in which the word lives" ("Extracts" 182). Such remarks about rhetoric take on dialogic force in the context of the continuing dialogue Nina Perlina documents between Bakhtin and Vinogradov. She writes,

> Where Bakhtin states that any individual discourse act is internally a nonfinalized, open-ended rejoinder, Vinogradov demonstrates that even a real-life dialogue is built by a set of clear-cut monologic procedures. Where Bakhtin finds dialogic reaccentuation of another person's utterance, the hidden multivoicedness, or the polyphonic "word with the loop[hole]," Vinogradov discovers the speaker's attempt to muffle the voice of the opponent, to discredit his speech-manifestations, and to advance his own monologic pronouncement over the dialogic reply of another person. . . . Within the framework of Bakhtinian poetics, a speech-partner is the protagonist of the idea. Within the framework of Vinogradov's poetic system, a speech partner is the rhetorician whose main intention is to make his oratory the only effective and authoritative speech manifestation. For Bakhtin, the individual utterance is born between the speech partners, in the immediacy of discourse; for Vinogradov, a dialogic rejoinder is generated by and belongs to its absolute owner.

With Vinogradov in the background, Bakhtin associates rhetoric with "style determined by demands for comprehensibility and clarity— that is, precisely those aspects that are deprived of any internal dialogism, that take the listener for a person who passively understands but not for one who actively answers and reacts" (*Dialogic Imagina-*

tion 280). As opposed to the seriocomic genres Bakhtin links with the dialogic, the classical rhetorical genres are one-sided, serious, rational, univocal, and dogmatic (*Problems* 107). Though rhetoric does represent the voices of others, rhetorical double-voicedness does "not extend to the dialogical essence of evolving language itself; it is not structured on authentic heteroglossia but on mere diversity of voices; in most cases the double-voicedness of rhetoric is abstract and thus lends itself to formal, purely logical analysis of the ideas that are parceled out in voices" or to polemically "erecting *potential* discourses for the accused or for the defense (just such free creation of likely, but never actually uttered words, sometimes whole speeches—'as he must have said' or 'as he might have said'—was a device very widespread in ancient rhetoric)" (*Dialogic Imagination* 353–54).

Enter, at last, Wayne Booth, a frequent user of this device, probably the best-known rhetorical critic in the Anglo-American culture of criticism, and in his *Rhetoric of Fiction* the most significant American analog of Vinogradov in the recently renewed critical dialogue with Bakhtin. Just as Vinogradov strengthens Russian formalist poetics by accommodating the novel under the heading of rhetoric, so Booth strengthens Chicago Aristotelian formalist poetics by the same move.[3] In his Aristotelian framework, Booth conceives the rhetoric of fiction as focused on techniques of domination, on "the rhetorical resources available to the writer . . . as he tries to impose his fictional world upon the reader" or on "the author's means of controlling the reader" (*Rhetoric of Fiction* xiii). Booth assumes the end of imposing a unified fictional world of a given kind—such as the tragic, comic, or horrific—and concerns himself with advocating the unrestricted use of all rhetorical means to impose that world upon the reader.

Within Booth's argument for the author's use of all available technical means in imposing a fictional world on the reader, his polemical emphasis is on the uses of the author's voice. He shows the usefulness of direct authorial commentary, and he argues that even when such commentary is lacking and the author resorts to the "hundreds of devices that remain for revealing judgment and molding response," "the author's voice is still dominant in a dialogue that is at the heart of all experiences with fiction" (*Rhetoric of Fiction* 272). Booth's account of the novel at one point as dialogue among the author, narrators, characters, and readers (55) suggests Bakhtin's dialogic model of novelistic discourse, but his repeated insistence on the dominance of the author over narrators, characters, and readers links him more firmly with Vinogradov's monologic rhetorical theories of the novel than with Bakhtin's dialogic account of the Dostoevskyan novel.

Bakhtin's account of the Dostoevskyan novel (*Problems*) gives us an idea of how its ends differ from more familiar tragic or comic or rhetorical ends that Booth prefers. Bakhtin traces Dostoevsky's generic sources along several lines of what he calls the "serio-comic" or *carnivalized* genres. In all these genres, he writes, "there is a strong rhetorical element, but in the atmosphere of *joyful relativity* characteristic of a carnival sense of the world, this element is fundamentally changed: there is a weakening of its one-sided rhetorical seriousness, its rationality, its singular meaning, its dogmatism" (107). The "stylistic unity ... of epic, the tragedy, high rhetoric, [and] the lyric" is replaced by mixed styles in the seriocomic genres (108) as "the epic and tragic wholeness of a person and his fate" is replaced by self-division in which the hero "ceases to mean only one thing" (117). Carnival familiarization suspends the usual hierarchies of social values and destroys "epic and tragic distance" (124). "Deeply ambivalent" responses to fundamental contradictions replace the clarified responses of separate tragic and comic genres; promiscuous participation replaces the conventional "division into performers and spectators" (122).

This highly compressed summary of the seriocomic genre shows how Bakhtin gives *positive* character to a literary effect that Booth reads as a *lack* of the "clarity of distance" provided by the "traditional forms" (*Rhetoric of Fiction* 331). To Booth, who argues for the reader's right to know whether to "approve or disapprove, laugh or cry" (*Rhetoric of Fiction* 331), Bakhtin's "joyful relativity of all structure and order" (*Problems* 124) and his "ambivalent laughter" (166) are a challenge to fundamental distinctions of literary effect. The clarification of response one seeks in Aristotelian tragedy and comedy, and the determinate decision aimed at in some Aristotelian rhetorical genres depend upon the audience's recognition of the hero's standing and the audience's distance from the hero's situation, but the participatory response Bakhtin envisions puts the hero and the audience in a carnivalized proximity to one another that replaces definitive judgment with mutual vulnerability and responsiveness.

In such a fictional world, the author does not design characters to provoke laughter, tears, or admiration but to provoke articulate response. Instead of issuing in a nonverbal recognition or feeling or attitude or decision, the unfinalized interplay of value-charged discourse in the dialogic work continues in the diverse verbal responses it provokes in its readers. Booth's rhetorical emphasis on determinate and generally nonverbal effect leads him to call "the critical disagreement" provoked by stories "a scandal" (*Rhetoric of Fiction* 315). For Bakhtin, that unsettled controversy can be a mark of success in a work designed to dialogic rather than rhetorical specifications.

Although Booth's rhetoric of fiction appears to share a perspective with Vinogradov's that makes their work appropriate to the monologic novel, I shall resist the temptation to set up their monologism in rhetorical or dialectical opposition to Bakhtin's dialogism, because the dialogic perspective finally does not allow for such an opposition in critical theory any more than in novelistic practice. Though Bakhtin himself, despite his dialogic principles, habitually makes use of this heightened opposition, he writes in the essay "Discourse in the Novel" that "even in those places where the author's voice seems at first glance to be unitary and consistent, direct and unmediatedly intentional, beneath that smooth single-languaged surface we can nevertheless uncover prose's three-dimensionality, its profound speech diversity, which enters the project of style and is its determining factor" (315). For Bakhtin, then, neither "monologic" novelists nor critical theorists would "mean only one thing" any more than does the hero of the Dostoevskyan novel, and even rhetorical discourse, Bakhtin concedes, "once [it] is brought into the study [of the novel] with all its living diversity, . . . cannot fail to have a deeply revolutionizing influence [in revealing] the internally dialogic quality of discourse" (*Dialogic Imagination* 269). While monological arguments, then, attempt to reduce their participants to representing single meanings, dialogic criticism recognizes the impossibility of such reduction and remains alert to what remains to be said from the unfolding positions of its concrete participants.

Booth's several recent engagements with Bakhtin's work reveal a more ambivalent dialogue than the reductive opposition between monologic and dialogic would allow. In the afterword to the second edition of *The Rhetoric of Fiction* (401–57), Booth singles out Bakhtin's dialogic poetics of the novel as especially impressive on the topics of language and style, historical and implied authors and readers, objectivity and technique, and ideology and form. Booth's acknowledgment of Bakhtin in his afterword is remarkable for its willingness to see Bakhtin as a challenge on the same issues that *The Rhetoric of Fiction* raises rather than to quarantine him as a theorist of some other critical mode with its own distinctive but unrhetorical questions. In this he shows the effects of the responsive and open-ended pluralism he invents in *Critical Understanding*. But in his introduction to Caryl Emerson's translation of Bakhtin's *Problems of Dostoevsky's Poetics*—an essay he sees as spilling over from the afterword to his own book—Booth combines this stance with the more defensive pluralism of his 1968 essay "The Rhetoric of Fiction and the Poetics of Fictions." He generously acknowledges Bakhtin's challenge to his rhetoric of fiction but also isolates that challenge in a critical mode distinct from his own.

Booth begins his introduction by establishing a common ground between his Chicago school Aristotelianism and Bakhtin's dialogism on the question of ideology and form, claiming that both positions reject the opposition between abstract form and ideological content for an idea of form charged with value or ideology. Booth distinguishes his Chicago Aristotelianism, however, for its focus on the distinction between the effects authors intend in their ideologically charged formal unities and the technical means they use to achieve them. According to the Chicago premises Booth worked under in *The Rhetoric of Fiction,* "Authors," he writes, "were . . . in charge of created unities that consisted of choices exemplified and judged" ("Introduction" xviii).

Booth's introduction presents Bakhtin's position, however, as if it transcended the whole question of fictional techniques and their relation to artistic ends. Bakhtin's challenge, he writes, "has nothing to do with the author's effort to produce a unified effect. Its subject is not the ordering of technical means toward certain effects so much as the quality of the author's imaginative gift—the ability or willingness to allow voices into the work that are not fundamentally under the 'monological' control of the novelist's own ideology" (xx). As Booth recognizes, he has assimilated Bakhtin's position to Longinus—the alternative to Aristotle that the Chicago school has long acknowledged—an alternative concerned to demonstrate the presence of genius or greatness or sublimity in the author rather than to articulate the functioning of parts in the whole in a given work (xx, xxvii). Booth repeatedly emphasizes Bakhtin's transcendence of mere technical concerns for more profound and important issues (xx, xxiv–xxv, xxvii), making his challenge to the rhetoric of fiction seem more like a moral and spiritual challenge to its questions than a technical and artistic challenge to Booth's answers to them.

Booth thus diminishes his direct encounter with Bakhtin by conceding him the high ground and holding onto the low, but, as we have seen, the dialogics and the rhetoric of fiction challenge one another more directly on the common grounds of the author's chosen artistic task and the technical means of realizing it than Booth's account of Bakhtin allows. While Booth repeatedly posits a dialogue in which "the author sees more deeply and judges more profoundly than his presented characters" (*Rhetoric of Fiction* 74), Bakhtin explicitly examines the novel in which not the author's superior consciousness but the hero's self-consciousness is the dominant of representation (*Problems* 49–50). Booth might see such a move as a shift in technical devices that "turns the character whose mind is shown into a narrator" (*Rhetoric of Fiction* 164), but Bakhtin's self-conscious hero is not a "center of consciousness" through whose perspective a story is told but the object of representation itself. The hero's discourse in its response to discourses of the other characters *and* the discourse of the author is, for Bakhtin, the novel's principal object of representation (*Problems* 63–65, 266).

Bakhtin's dialogics of fiction thus reopens the question of what is means and what is end in the novel and suggests that in some cases at least the choices Booth advocates as technically effective would not serve the end Bakhtin imagines. If the hero's self-consciousness is to be the dominant of representation, the author's position must be shifted from the finalizing and judging role Booth defends to an actively dialogic interchange with the hero. "Only in the light of this artistic project," Bakhtin writes, "can one understand the authentic function of such compositional elements as the narrator and his tone . . . and the . . . narration direct from the author" (*Problems* 64). This is not the critical language of someone unconcerned with "unified effect" and the "technical means toward certain effects" (Booth, "Introduction" xx), but that of someone who posits a different kind of effect, one that calls for a radical reconsideration of fictional means and ends. In Bakhtin's seriocomic genre, as we have seen, it is not, as Booth says, that the characters "defy any temptation the author may have to fit them into his superior plans" ("Introduction" xxiii) but rather that, as Bakhtin says, "the freedom of the character is an aspect of the author's design" and "is just as much a created thing as the unfreedom of the objectivized hero" (*Problems* 64–65). Bakhtin has not forfeited an interest in artistic design and the technique that serves it, but has radically enlarged the field of such designs, and so has not only shifted the possible functions of techniques but also shifted the very boundaries between technique and design.

But Booth's linking of Bakhtin to the Longinian tradition may be seen not just as an evasion of this fundamental conflict over the means and ends of fiction but also as part of another agenda. Booth's recent book on the ethics of fiction shows him less interested in Bakhtin's bearings on the technical issues of the rhetoric of fiction than on the evaluative issues that now concern him. Even in *The Rhetoric of Fiction* itself, Booth opens the question of "the moral, not merely the technical, angle of vision from which the story is told" (265), and his identification of Bakhtin's argument with that "more profound" question may serve to acknowledge Bakhtin's challenge where it matters most to him now, rather than to deflect it from the issues of the rhetoric of fiction in which he is no longer engaged.

Booth's and Bakhtin's divergent accounts of the novel are not without implications for the discursive practices of the culture of criticism, but this issue can be joined more directly through examining Booth's *Critical Understanding: The Powers and Limits of Pluralism*, in which he explicitly addresses his version of Hartman's problem of "multiplying and fragmenting perspectives" in criticism. Though Bakhtin's relevant work was not available in translation when Booth wrote *Critical Understanding*, its argument nevertheless bears upon Booth's discussion and complicates the potential relations between Booth's rhetoric and Bakhtin's dialogics. Booth there imagines what he calls the problem of "critical variety and conflict" (3) in characteristically rhetorical terms that produce images of "chaos" (7) and "warfare" (37), but he also gestures repeatedly in the course of his inquiry toward dialogic formulations that would reconstruct his initial rhetorical image of "the immensely confusing world of contemporary literary criticism" (3). Booth's argument shifts from the rhetorical to the dialogic in another sense when he turns from generating potential discourses about poems and pluralism to engaging at length the words and works of three specific pluralist thinkers, all of whom have persuaded him of their diverse views.

Booth's opening formulation of the problem of "critical variety and conflict" envisions a characteristically rhetorical situation of diverse rhetors brought to a given occasion of discourse to mobilize, display, and distinguish their rhetorical resources. Booth imagines a dozen critics given W. H. Auden's "The Surgical Ward" and asked to say what they think is the most important point to be made about it, and he further imagines, in a characteristic hyperbole, that "an infinite number of possible interpretations" of "unlimited variety" would result (1–2). Following something like I. A. Richards's protocols in *Practical Criticism*, Booth's imaginary experiment brings diverse critical rhetoricians to a given occasion and asks them to produce their discourses in isolation from one another without mentioning a context of prior discourse on the poem. In accord with Bakhtin's account of the practices of rhetorical genres, Booth's experiment produces what Bakhtin calls "*potential discourses*" of hypothetical critics instead of using the "actually uttered" words of published critics, and it issues not in what Bakhtin calls "an authentic heteroglossia" but only in "a mere diversity of voices" (*Dialogic Imagination* 353–54). To the "unlimited variety" of that "mere diversity" Booth adds the diverse potential judgments of his critical readers and thus produces his image of "the immensely confusing world of contemporary literary criticism" (3), but this confusing world to which he offers his pluralism as the best response is a function of the monologic rhetorical rules by which he constructs his image in the first place rather than a necessary or adequate portrait of the literary critical world itself.

A dialogic criticism, for its part, would emphasize the artificial isolation of Booth's hypothetical critics and offer the countermodel of the prose writer who

> confronts a multitude of routes, roads, and paths that have been laid down in the object by social consciousness. Along with the contradictions inside the object itself, the prose writer witnesses as well the unfolding of social heteroglossia *surrounding* the object, the Tower-of-Babel mixing of languages that goes on around any object.... For the prose writer, the object is a focal point for heteroglot voices among which his own must also sound; these voices create the background necessary for his own voice, outside of which his artistic prose nuances cannot be perceived, and without which they "do not sound." (*Dialogic Imagination* 278)

Bakhtin's account of this situation may still seem like confusion, but these other voices are many, not infinitely numerous, and they "sound" against the background of each other as the isolated voices of Booth's imaginary experiment do not. Furthermore they belong to a "social heteroglossia" that makes their various utterances reflect the finite, if heterogeneous, possibilities of critical discourse in a given time and place, developing those possibilities, revealing new ones, and making the participants recognizable to one another in their developing concrete diversity. The problem for dialogics is never what to make of the confusing multiplicity of voices and evaluations in general but always what to say in response to the differences among this particular set of actually or potentially interrelated voices.

Booth's initial vision of the production of critical discourse shares a model of the determinants of that discourse with R. S. Crane's response to the questions, "'What *ought* I to say?' or 'What is *important* to say?'": it depends only on "the kind of problem you are interested in and . . . the resources of your 'language'" (43). Bakhtin's image of the prose writer would not only add to these determinants *who* has already spoken and *whom* the critic is addressing but would also reinterpret both the "interests" and the "language" of the individual critic as already derived from and implicated in the social discourses that entail the interests and languages of others. Even critical rhetors called to display their critical resources and interests in response to a given poem speak from a prior conversation and to unnamed mentors and opponents, share or oppose their interests, and revoice their languages.

Booth, however, at another point in his argument, reaches a position very similar to Bakhtin's. He writes,

> No critic makes himself; every one of us discovers his own voice only by listening or mis-listening, to those before us who seem to have spoken best. This much is seldom denied. What seems to be forgotten is that, even after I have begun to speak what I mistakenly call *"my own critical truth,"* my continued vitality as a thinking critic . . . depends on my continuing capacity to take other voices into account. My life, indistinguishable from the life of my critical tribe, requires that my thought be an exchange among "selves" rather than a mere search for ways to impose what I already know. (*Critical Understanding* 223)

Note here Booth's departure from a rhetoric of imposition and domination toward a dialogics of mutual determination through exchange. A different emphasis on these same relations might bring out, in addition, the way in which "my thought" is an "exchange among selves" from the start and "my critical tribe" is already, as Booth elsewhere puts it, "inherently and irreducibly plural" (40). My vitality is not just at stake in my continued engagement with other voices outside my tribe but in its continuing articulations of the conflicts within my tribe and within "myself." And my investment in those conflicts always orients me to the discourse of my tribe and the discourses of other tribes (to which I may in other ways also belong) and shapes my sense of "What I *ought* to say" and "What is *important* to say."

I never encounter a situation, then, in which the critical world is all before me and the choice of critical interests and languages is entirely open, nor do I ever display my critical resources as if no one else had already spoken, or encounter the display of others' resources as if I had never heard of them before. Even utter neophytes in professional critical discussions arrive with investments in critical terms and human relations from familial, religious, political, and other social context that permit preliminary orientation to those discussions, recognition of their participants, and investment in their stakes. At the beginning of my own critical training, a schooling in the texts of American democracy attracted me to Wordsworth's vision of the poet as "a man speaking to men," though feminism had not yet called my attention to how that phrase sounded from a different social location. Similarly, the religious predispositions of some of the New Critics drew them to Coleridge's notion of the Godlike poetic imagination. Both the transcendental mystifications of some schools of criticism and the demystifying gestures of others are continuous with discourses in the precritical culture in which we are schooled, and our interests in the critical sophistications of these discourses are predisposed, though not wholly determined, by our interests in these discourses themselves.

From Crane's dialectical point of view (see Olson), these predispositions may appear as mere "prejudices" that account for any given subject's arbitrary departure from the ideal universal subject, who could disinterestedly entertain all interests and disinterestedly choose the appropriate critical mode of pursuing each interest (*Critical Understanding* 43), but Booth's rhetorical commitments make him aware of both the difficulty of separating critical modes from the individual critics who practice them (28) and of the problem of distinguishing critical modes themselves (94). He approaches a dialogic reinterpretation of Crane's philosophically distinct modes when he identifies the modes we have learned with the "'school' we were trained in" (254) that constitutes our intellectual dispositions, sets our agendas, enables our inquiries, and involves us in a historical conversation, but he concludes with a rhetorical reinterpretation of "critical modes not as positions to be defended but as locations or openings to be explored—in the traditional rhetorical terminology, as *topoi* or *loci*" (339).

As *topoi* or commonplaces, the diverse critical modes lose not only the philosophical discreteness of Crane's dialectical formulation but also the individual, historical recognizability of the dialogic person-idea involved in the cultural discourse of schools of thought. Although Booth characterizes a *topic* as "an inhabited place in which valued activity can occur among those who know how to find their way in" (339), it has lost the historical specificity of a "place" like the Chicago school, inhabited by R. S. Crane and Richard McKeon and engaged with such figures as M. H. Abrams and Kenneth Burke, all of whom constitute the dialogic agenda of Booth's inquiry into pluralism. Both rhetorical *topoi* and dialectical modes have a generality that appears to transcend what Booth calls the "historical accident" (201) of specific affiliations and encounters. Booth wishes he could justify his decision to discuss Crane, Burke, and Abrams as topically or even dialectically representative of "*kinds* of pluralism," but he cannot escape his admission that "my life encountered these lives at such and such moments, and the personal force of these men strengthened the impact of their pluralisms" (201). *The Rhetoric of Fiction,* which distances itself from Chicago Aristotelian poetics by shifting its ground to Aristotle's rhetoric, directs itself against the predominant consensus about fiction in the wider culture of criticism, but *Critical Understanding* is dialogically preoccupied with powerful person-ideas affiliated specifically with the Chicago school. It self-consciously abandons the high ground of philosophical universality maintained in Crane's dialectical pluralism, but its rhetorical pluralism, under the powerful influence of Crane's voice, still ambivalently aspires to transcend the accidents of historically contingent rhetorical community and the violence of aggressively competitive rhetorical domination.

Booth's preoccupation with that violence colors much of *Critical Understanding* with the heightened diction of critics' killing and being killed, annihilating each other, battling, destroying, violating, and living only at the cost of others' death and defeat. Bakhtin's vision of rhetoric's intent "to bring about the destruction of the opponent" is right at home in this rhetorical battlefield. It would be fair to say that Booth strives to formulate a version of what Bakhtin calls "the dialogic sphere in which the word lives" as an alternative to this rhetorical scene of carnage ("Extracts" 182), and it is interesting that Booth makes his closest approach to Bakhtinian dialogics in his sections on the value of vitality. But it would also be fair to observe from our present perspective that the powerful habit of thinking in terms of the opposition between the familiar arts of rhetoric and dialectic limits the alternatives available to him. Booth resists the dialectical reduction of discourse to the "transpersonal" adjudication of "rival propositions" (28–29) just as he wishes for a better world than the bloody rhetorical battle of rival critics, but he is apologetic about using the word "dialogue" (237), deeply invested in the dialectical pluralism of modes he resists, and habituated to turn to rhetoric—in both theory and practice—when all else fails.

The book's most vital and provocative moments for me—its section on the value of vitality (220–23) to which I have already referred and its chapter on "overstanding" (235–56)—reach beyond the familiar alternatives and Booth's avowed affiliations to break new ground. Booth himself recognizes and dramatizes the novelty for him of his thinking in that chapter (236), where he not only defends the imposition of alien terms and questions on a text ("overstanding") against his own powerful commitments to submit to the author's intentions but also recognizes that the repertory, as he puts it, of questions and responses we might bring to any text "will in large part depend on how many other texts we have respected and absorbed in the past" (242–43) and on the " 'school' we were trained in" (254). Booth's closing "image of the reader we seek to propagate" provides also a powerful image of the mode of intelligibility of the dialogic self: such a reader "is one who is so active, so broadly experienced, so thoroughly 'possessed' by texts previously understood that his very individuality, no longer idiosyncrasy, will teach us not only something about himself but something about the text and the world" (256). Such readers individualize in their own texts the possibilities and conflicts of prior texts and thereby realize in themselves possibilities of the social world that are not simply peculiar to them but recognizable to others who are both inside that social world and outside that particular individual location in it. Booth's slightly embarrassed notion of "a kind of conversation or dialogue between a text and a reader" recognizes their participation in a common culture just as his affirmation of overstanding (Todorov translates a related Bakhtinian word as "exotopy") recognizes their inalienable alienation from one another.

The combined effect of these two recognitions would be to rule out the model of isolated critical rhetors from which *Critical Understanding* begins and to open the way to a dialogic model of "critical variety and conflict" that would resist both domination and dialectic for the sake of continuing the lives of historically diverse communities and historically diverse selves. Though a dialectical reading of Booth might expose the *contradictions* between his rhetorical and dialogic premises in order to refute them, and a rhetorical reading might try to exploit the *inconsistencies* between these premises in order to defeat him, a dialogic reading would try, as I have, to identify such divergences as productive sites for further conversation with him and to honor them as vital conflicting identifications within his exemplary life of ideas.

Notes

1. For extended discussion of the ideologist-hero, see Bakhtin's *Problems of Dostoevsky's Poetics* 78–100. For more on the distinction among dialogics, dialectic, and rhetoric, see Bialostosky.
2. Todorov identifies him as "a linguist and marginal Formalist destined to become the official guiding light of Soviet Stylistics" (9), and Shukman calls him "the doyen of the Soviet school of stylistics" (v). See also Busch for an extended discussion of Vinogradov.
3. See Bakhtin's remark that in dealing with the stylistic dilemma posed by the novel, "the re-establishment of rhetoric, with all its rights, greatly strengthens the Formalist position. Formalist rhetoric is a necessary addition to Formalist poetics" (*Dialogic Imagination* 267).

Bibliography

Bakhtin, Mikhail. *The Dialogic Imagination: Four Essays*. Trans. Michael Holquist and Caryl Emerson. Ed. Michael Holquist. Austin: U of Texas P, 1981.

———. "Discourse in the Novel." *The Dialogic Imagination* 259–422.

———. "Extracts from 'Notes' (1970–1971)." *Bakhtin: Essays and Dialogues on His Work*. Ed. Gary Saul Morson. Chicago: U of Chicago P, 1986.

———. *Problems of Dostoevsky's Poetics*. Ed. and trans. Caryl Emerson. Minneapolis: U of Minnesota P, 1984.

Bialostosky, Don. "Dialogics as An Art of Discourse in Literary Criticism." *PMLA* 101 (1986): 788–97.

Booth, Wayne C. *The Company We Keep: An Ethics of Fiction*. Berkeley: U of California P, 1988.

———. *Critical Understanding: The Powers and Limits of Pluralism*. Chicago: U of Chicago P, 1979.

———. Introduction. Bakhtin, *Problems of Dostoevsky's Poetics*.

———. *The Rhetoric of Fiction*. 2nd ed. Chicago: U of Chicago P, 1983.

———. "*The Rhetoric of Fiction* and the Poetics of Fictions." *Novel: A Forum on Fiction* 1 (1968): 105–17. Rpt. in *Towards and Poetics of Fictions*. Ed. Mark Spilka. Bloomington: Indiana UP, 1977. 77–89.

Busch, Robert. "Bakhtin's 'Problemy tvorchestva Dostoevskogo' and V. V. Vinogradov's 'O khudozhestvennoi proze'—A Dialogic Relationship." *Social Discourse* 3 (1990): 311–32.

Hartman, Geoffrey H. "The Culture of Criticism." *PMLA* 99 (1984): 371–97.

Olson, Elder. "The Dialectical Foundations of Pluralism." *"On Value Judgments in the Arts" and Other Essays*. Chicago: U of Chicago P, 1976. 327–59.

Perlina, Nina. "Mikhail Bakhtin in Dialogue with Victor Vinogradov." Unpublished conference paper. University of Cagliari Conference, "Bakhtin: Theorist of Dialogue," June 16–18, 1985. Expanded and revised as "A Dialogue on the Dialogue: The Baxtin-Vinogradov Exchange (1924–65)." *Slavic and East European Journal* 32 (1988): 526–41.

Shukman, Ann, and L. M. O'Toole, eds. *Russian Poetics in Translation*. No. 5 (1978).

Todorov, Tzvetan. *Mikhail Bakhtin: The Dialogical Principle*. Trans. Wlad Godzich. Minneapolis: U of Minnesota P, 1984.

6

From Pluralism to Heteroglossia: Wayne Booth and the Pragmatics of Critical Reviewing

DAVID RICHTER

MOST SCHOLARS WHO have silently suffered from hostile reviews, whether their critics were vapidly incomprehending or actively maleficent, have dreamed vengefully about being granted unlimited space to respond in print. Perhaps it is fortunate that few of us get the chance, because not many would use the occasion for anything better than a return bout with our detractors, whose ignorance or malice tends to be far less permeable than our own thin skins.

Wayne Booth is one of the lucky scholars who have been asked to reply to his own reviewers in a commissioned article for an academic journal; in fact, he has done so not once but twice, in essays spaced nearly ten years apart. True to what one might expect of a critic of his character as well as his stature, Booth eschewed the easy exercise in the countercheck quarrelsome, and used both *"The Rhetoric of Fiction* and the Poetics of Fictions" and "Three Functions of Reviewing at the Present Time" as occasions for discussing the critical scene, the way critics interact with and describe each other's theories and judgments, and the difficulties of critical understanding.

But though one might describe these two essays in similar terms, they are different in tone as well as underlying philosophy: A close examination of the arguments would mark a change in what Booth expects as well as thinks possible in critical discourse, and we can see the results of that change in his subsequent books, both *Critical Understanding* and *The Company We Keep*. The shift is from what Booth himself, in *Critical Understanding,* termed the "pluralism of discrete modes," a position derived from the metatheories of R. S. Crane and the philosophical semantics of Richard McKeon, to a vision of contact through shared *topoi.* This vision in turn anticipates Booth's adoption of a social version of the self as the locus of competing languages and characters, which is reminiscent of the ideas of Mikhail M. Bakhtin.

INSTRUMENTAL PLURALISM

Booth's first stab at his reviewers is, rhetorically, a brilliant example of doublespeak, in that Booth bases a subtle ethical appeal upon his self-restraint in *not* doing several things that he characterizes as futile or self-indulgent (attacking his enemies, rewriting what was unclear about his book), and then does them anyway, but so indirectly that we may not realize what is being done.

The chief victim of Booth's rhetoric is John Killham, whose "The 'Second Self' in Novel Criticism" in the *British Journal of Aesthetics* "attacked me for beliefs I had specifically repudiated, using arguments I myself had used" ("*Rhetoric* and Poetics" 106). Booth is first tempted to ignore Killham as "not worth bothering with," then presents over six hundred words of invective, written at white heat, accusing Killham of distortions so gross and obvious that he has to appeal to malice rather than mere stupidity to explain them—a first draft that Booth allows us to read and savor before he pulls himself up short and repudiates the entire disputational enterprise.

Repudiates it, however, only to continue it by other means: part 2 of Booth's article consists of an analysis of Killham's mode of interpreting literature: the problems he sees as central, the critical terms he uses, and the methodology he employs.

> Mr. Killham's problem is that of reconciling what he calls the "autonomy" of a novel . . . with his knowledge that any novel is, after all, written and read by human beings; he seeks . . . a reconciliation between the autonomous "well-wrought urn" and the world of the author's biography and psychology and intentions. . . . His talk is thus mostly in the expressive rather than the rhetorical mode. . . . [For Killham] true autonomy in a novel comes from our recognition of its independent "sense of life" which is, in fact, what the total creative act of the author, with *his* sense of life, gave it. (109)

As Booth goes on to demonstrate, there is no room within Killham's system—a dialectical method using the central principle of "expression"—for the sort of inquiry Booth is engaged in, or indeed for any inquiry using the problematic method and the principle of rhetoric. For Killham, "rhetoric" is a pejorative term—what inferior novelists are forced into using when they cannot fully develop their "sense of life"; for Booth, of course, it is an inescapable aspect of narrative technique—almost another name for technique. He presents Killham's critical enterprise seriously and sympathetically, and then suavely interposes: "It is easy to see that no author holding Mr. Killham's views uncritically—that is, without thinking through their implications for method—could possibly grasp my way of going about things..." (109).

In eristic terms, Booth understands Killham to death, by reading Killham so much better—and so much more generously—than Killham had bothered to read him. Killham indeed stands convicted, neither of mental incapacity nor of malice, but of something much worse: of holding his views so tightly that he has become incapable of grasping another kind of argument—incapable of learning from anyone who thinks differently than he does.[1]

What Booth demonstrates in his rhetorical victory over Killham (and, implicitly, over all the other detractors who failed to understand the implications of his methodology) is the power of "instrumental pluralism" (Booth's term for the pluralism of his mentor, Ronald Crane): the notion that different critics have worked in discrete critical "languages" or "methods," each capable of its own powers and limitations, each a characteristic mode of insight with its own characteristic forms of blindness. Crane had demonstrated, in *The Languages of Criticism and the Structure of Poetry,* how a question such as, "How many children had Lady Macbeth?" may be meaningless within the formalist New Critical approach of L. C. Knights (in which poetry is seen as a pure symbolic structure), but perfectly apt within the mimetic criticism of A. C. Bradley (in which literary characters are seen as imaginative analogues of real persons).

Both Crane's insight into Knights's meaningless quarrel with Bradley and Booth's insight into Killham's meaningless quarrel with him (Booth) derive directly or indirectly from instrumental pluralisms such as the philosophical semantics of Richard McKeon, who viewed arguments between rival philosophers as derivable from differences in their prior choices of method, principle, organization, and mode of thought. Booth demonstrates the *real* power of this form of pluralism—its power to orient the relationship of one critical enterprise to another—in part 3, where he discusses his choice to write a *rhetoric* of fiction, and how that had dictated major differences in method and vocabulary, not only from those of his mentor Crane, but from other strong modes of criticism: "If [the author] is thought of as *making readers,* then . . . every stroke is in this sense rhetorical, just as in the objective view every stroke is part of the concrete form, or in the expressive view every stroke expresses the artist's psyche, and in the art-is-truth view every stroke reflects a world of values or universals which the book is 'about'" (111–12).

Booth's four terms for critical principles come directly from M. H. Abrams's *The Mirror and the Lamp;* they constitute a critical commonplace that the readers of *Novel* were likely to know. One sees McKeon behind both Abrams and Crane, as the most powerful creator of a meroscopic ("splitting") pluralism in our time.[2] And one sees his direct influence on Booth, certainly in his later work, but even here in his sense that the principle with which he is operating is in potential conflict with another ultimate end he might explore (a "poetics" of fiction), so that Booth speaks of the rhetorical critic as a "stranger in a strange land" when he moves from the question of what authors do to readers to the question of what the literary works they create are by nature.

Booth expresses no dissatisfaction, within *"The Rhetoric of Fiction and the Poetics of Fictions,"* with the pluralism of discrete modes. Indeed, he seems eminently contented with the privileged access to disparate systems of thought, together with the self-critical capacity, that systems such as McKeon's grant their users. Nevertheless, Booth may have a problem with the fact that, as a metaphor, McKeon's system suggests a four-dimensional matrix of 256 pigeonholes, into which any philosophical enterprise may be slotted.[3] Such a metaphor emphasizes both the barriers between systems and the irreconcilability of each system with every other. In the last paragraph of *"The Rhetoric of Fiction and the Poetics of Fictions,"* Booth sees the short-term remedy for misunderstanding as silence—hardly an attractive solution for this lover of discourse—and, in his own metaphor, envisions literary critics as on "a series of climbing expeditions, attempting different peaks or different faces of the same peak" (117). Such a vision of isolated climbers seems clearly preferable to the war of each against all that Booth compares it with ("demolishing each man's shelter to provide materials for our own"), but it does not approach any notion of a scholarly community. For people personally reconciled to the ultimate strangeness of any individual to any other, there may be nothing unpleasant about this, but

Booth is not one of those people, and one suspects that may be why instrumental pluralism was not finally, for him, a sustaining vision.

THREE FUNCTIONS OF REVIEWING AT THE PRESENT TIME

Booth's second essay is a far more intricate (one might almost say "shiftier") piece of rhetoric, not because the values Booth is trying to inculcate are themselves more complex, but because some of the contradictions between the ideology inherent in Crane/McKeon pluralism and Bakhtinian dialogism are beginning to surface in his prose.

Booth opens with a self-deprecating introduction far more extensive than usual, twitting himself for his own bad reading habits: he confesses to misremembering reviews of his work, emphasizing the "careless or inane or hostile strokes," nastier than they were, more given to simple factual inaccuracies. "What I now see are at least three criteria for good reviews, only the first one having much to do with either the reviewers' or the author's ego" ("Three Functions" 3).

Of Booth's three functions of reviewing, only the first, to give the ready-made reader an accurate report and a clear appraisal, establishes a criterion of critical understanding comparable to that posed in "*The Rhetoric of Fiction* and the Poetics of Fictions." The other two, to entice the indifferent and hostile reader into the enterprise, and to advance the inquiry by vexing the author and others into thought, can occur outside the realm of understanding itself.

Booth's examples of the second function are of celebrated theorists who use the occasion of a review to advance their own views. There is a certain degree of covert irony here, particularly in the implication that by virtue of his fame a Kenneth Burke or a William Empson acquires a license to misread denied to lesser mortals. On the one hand, "the author discovers that his own sense of injustice may be less important, *in the long run* and for most journal readers, than the effort to keep a given kind of critical culture alive by making recruits" (6, emphasis added). On the other hand, Booth claims that this job will be most effectively done "by the reviewer who has best understood the book in hand. . . . *In the long run,* making recruits to an enterprise is important only if the enterprise is maintained at the highest possible level, and it seems likely that carefree distortions, however stimulating, will *in the long run* vitiate the enterprise" (6, emphasis added). On both sides of the fence, Booth appeals to the "long run." Perhaps, as with *My Fair Lady* and *A Chorus Line,* there are long runs and longer runs. Critical understanding is in the long run subordinate to vitality, but vitality is in the longer run subordinate to critical understanding.[4]

While in the abstract it seems absurd to argue that A is more important than B, which is more important than A, we frequently find that in the political arena contradictions such as these are more plausible. It happens frequently that a society fighting a war to preserve its freedom may have to suspend, for the duration, some of the very freedoms it fights to preserve. Survival is a precondition of any other good, and we recognize that one is occasionally forced to compromise the good to survive. When the same issue comes up in the case of individual survival, though, as in Plato's *Crito,* the moral issues are less clear. And surely we are likely to disapprove, however well we may understand, a legislator who feels forced to vote in minor matters against his or her best judgment in order to be reelected and fight for more important ideals. What may not be entirely clear are the ultimate consequences of relocating an argument about academic discourse in the political arena, where the collective good always outweighs the individual interest.

Booth's third criterion—advancement of the inquiry—is in some ways the most complex of the lot. One reason is that, unless there is already considerable meeting of minds between reviewer and writer, the former cannot advance the latter's inquiry. Of course, one could always take the position that by saying *Book X is no damn good,* a reviewer is "advancing the inquiry" by forestalling the reader from taking seriously a meretricious argument. But this would be a trivial case; Booth generally presumes criterion (1) as part of criterion (3), which implies that reviews that meet the third criterion will be rare indeed.

Though Booth never discusses how the process of "vexing into thought" works, there may be an analogue to the notion of the carnivalization of language in Bakhtin: "The trick is to vex [the writer] into further thought by allowing the book to goad the reviewer into a genuine encounter with its problems" ("Three Functions" 7). Book goads reviewer; reviewer encounters writer; reviewer vexes writer into thought. We all get dirtied by each other's rhetoric.

How this dialogical approach actually works in practice is not quite so simple, as we shall see. The example Booth chooses to take up is not a casual journalistic assessment but a full-scale *Diacritics* review article devoted to an analysis of his methodology in *A Rhetoric of Irony:* Susan Suleiman's "Interpreting Ironies," published in 1976. The dialogue between Booth and Suleiman extends, in fact, over five works: *The Rhetoric of Irony* itself, Suleiman's "Interpreting Ironies," Booth's commentary on Suleiman in "Three Functions of Reviewing," and a further exchange of views published in 1979 as "Re-Viewing Reviews: Letters by Susan Suleiman and Wayne Booth."

The argument between Suleiman and Booth shifts ground several times over these five texts, but the central area of disagreement is over whether understanding the meaning of a text necessarily includes an emotional participation in its values or only an understanding of its language and the contexts implicit in that language. But it is not entirely clear how Suleiman "advances" Booth's "inquiry," by "vexing the author . . . into thought"; indeed, Booth and Suleiman agree so much more than they disagree that their dialogue might be viewed as a well-choreographed waltz, with Booth deftly leading, rather than the dispute threatened in such verbs as "vex" and "goad."

THE CENTRAL DISAGREEMENT: READING DEGREE ZERO

Suleiman argues that Booth's *Rhetoric of Irony* collapses the valuable distinction between language that we can interpret as irony from an analysis of the meanings of words alone and ironies that require of the reader prior knowledge of the values and intentions of the author.[5] Booth admits to collapsing the distinction, since he does not see how any irony, or indeed any utterance, with the exception of "those texts in which there *was* no intending author," can be interpreted without reference to authorial intent. He admits that it is *possible* for a reader to interpret without regard to this intent, but that, when one chooses to do so, " 'meanings' become infinite" and hence indeterminate ("Three Functions" 9). In insisting upon intention as determining meaning, Booth is opposing the "uncanny" critics—deconstructionists such as J. Hillis Miller—and rhetorically painting Suleiman into that corner.

In her letter of response, Suleiman is prepared to acquit Booth of collapsing the distinction; she concedes, in fact, that the difference between Booth's intentionalism and that of some structuralists and semioticians is that Booth speaks in terms of an *author's* intention, while the others might speak instead of an intentionality inherent in the text. The difference in vocabulary is suggestive, but, for Suleiman as for Booth, it pales beside the more important differences between those "canny" critics who feel that authors or texts can determine meaning through intention and those "uncanny" critics (like Miller) for whom meaning is radically indeterminate. Nevertheless, Suleiman continues to insist that there is a difference between understanding what emotional response a text requires of its implied reader and actually granting that response—citing her own analysis of Drieu La Rochelle's anti-Semitic novel, *Gilles* (Booth and Suleiman 45).

In his reply, Booth refuses to allow Suleiman to acquit him of collapsing a distinction that he indeed intends to explode—the distinction between intrinsic and extrinsic grounds of interpretation. Booth therefore insists upon "the difficulties that underlie your claim that one can somehow *get* a text as a kind of fact without becoming embroiled in its implied author's values" (49). Suleiman appears to be claiming that she performed *less* than a fully sympathetic reading of *Gilles*. Booth disagrees: The repugnance Suleiman registers to the values of *Gilles* suggests that she has performed at least the simulacrum of a sympathetic reading; she must have "in some sense 'gone along' with the intended experience (at least far enough to know how it would *feel* to go all the way)" (49). For Booth, Suleiman has fully understood *Gilles,* but she has also *over*stood it.

By the end of this dialogue, the reader may not be clear whose inquiry has been advanced. Though Booth praised Suleiman's review as one that vexed him into further thought about his problem, it is not clear that he has modified his ideas or conceded any ground, and Suleiman has been driven to qualify or cancel most of the theoretical objections she had raised against his enterprise and its methods. For his part, Booth gives up a skirmish or two—for example, he admits Suleiman's contention that his analysis of irony had skimped on the difficult cases of unlimited global ironies, a point that had been made much less politely by other reviewers—but it is not clear that he has been made to change materially his notion of literary meaning.[6] In effect, her critique has not so much altered or shaken his beliefs as forced him to understand more clearly what his true belief was: namely, that pure linguistic processing, what might be called "reading degree zero," is a chimera, because an ethical assessment of the values inherent in a text is already included within any interpretation of the text's meaning. If this dialogue has genuinely clarified something for Booth that was not clear already, it was the two directions in which his line of thinking was leading him: toward his qualified defense, in *Critical Understanding,* of "overstanding" as a generally valid approach to literature, and toward the pluralistic "ethics of fiction" in *The Company We Keep.*

FROM PLURALISM TO HETEROGLOSSIA

Perhaps the most interesting thing about Booth's approach to Suleiman is that he does not repeat, mutatis mutandis, what he had done to John Killham: that is, he does not explain Suleiman's misunderstanding of insights generated by his method in terms of the blindness inherited from her own. And Booth could have done this very easily: As one can see from her essay on *Gilles,* published in *Neophilogus,* Suleiman is working essentially from a structuralist or semiotic perspective that views meaning as the product of the decipherment of codes; such a logistic method requires some version of the process I have termed "reading degree zero" (pure linguistic processing) as a state from which more sophisticated forms of figural interpretation depart (see, for example, the works by Barthes or Eco, or Suleiman's favorite sources, Genette and Todorov, listed in the bibliography). For Suleiman, understanding language, meanings, and values represent three distinct steps in a hierarchy of semiosis. For Booth, doing a "rhetoric" rather than a semiotics of irony, the reader's grasp of authorial values is already a given, not something to be explained. Their disparate critical languages explain a great deal about the (admittedly minor) ways in which they miss each other's points.

There may have been any number of reasons why Booth did not choose to repeat the lesson in pluralism he had given in the pages of *Novel* ten years before: a preference for novelty over repetition, or courtesy to Suleiman, whose article was generally favorable, who had worked harder than most reviewers had done to understand him, and who was as sophisticated, methodologically, as he was. But as I have already hinted, the most likely explanation, given the terms of his approach and the evidence of *Critical Understanding* (published the following year), is that he had become disenchanted with instrumental pluralism as a metatheoretical principle. Where he had once enjoyed demonstrating its powers, Booth is here at least as much concerned to demonstrate the *limitations* of any pluralism of discrete modes.

The opening chapters of *Critical Understanding* present the limitations of instrumental pluralism in epistemological terms: though any pluralism seems to be better than any nonpluralistic alternative (monism, skepticism, eclecticism, and so forth), Crane's "pluralism of discrete modes" is only one of many methods for organizing the variety of voices into a harmonious (or dissonant) chorus. After examining the rival pluralisms of Kenneth Burke and M. H. Abrams, Booth feels driven to seek a metapluralism (a pluralism of pluralisms), but this quest, even before it begins, is doomed to fail: "Can we imagine a genuine pluralist of pluralisms, one who can accept and use many different . . . metalanguages? . . . How could he avoid an infinite regress of ever more vacuous pluralisms?" (*Critical Understanding* 34). Ultimately, Booth's vision of a pluralism of pluralisms fails, doomed by the "umbrella paradox" from above and from beneath by the humanity of his exemplars (Crane, Burke, Abrams), whose mutual understanding, despite their efforts, was decidedly imperfect. Disappointed of his ultimate "pluralism of pluralisms," Booth settles for a "pragmatic" scheme that will maximize the "inseparable values" of "vitality," "justice," and "understanding."

As James Phelan has shown, this gets Booth out of one difficulty only to get him into another: specifically, Booth becomes incoherent on the degree to which data about literary texts constrain interpretive hypotheses. When he wants to emphasize the respect for and understanding of the exemplary text, "Booth sometimes speaks as if data are fairly fixed and decisive, permitting us to distinguish proper from improper questions and to identify different degrees of violation." At other times, when he seeks a harmonious chorus of pluralistic interpreters, "Booth . . . speaks as if data, though numerous, are not at all decisive" (38–39).[7] Phelan attributes this incoherence primarily to the contradictions inherent in Booth's simultaneous commitments to understanding and metapluralism. This is surely right as far as it goes, but these commitments too derive from prior choices. As Booth says at the end of *Critical Understanding,* "I am not one of those who loves knowledge for its own sake. . . . [M]y goal is practical: how to improve the practice of controversy by increasing the chances of understanding. I have, in fact, made understanding into a supreme goal, running the risk of implying that it is better for two human minds to share erroneous views than for one to have the truth and the other to misunderstand him" (341–42). Without taking Booth as literally committed to communal error as preferable to isolated truth, the social aspect of learning is decidedly important to him. (Booth's mentor Crane, as I have suggested elsewhere [see bibliography], seems to have idealized the positivistic goals and methods of science in ways that have contented few of his students. It would seem that to Crane, the isolated and disinterested pursuit of truth would be satisfying in ways it was not to Booth.)

In the shifting figures of speech Booth has used to describe the critical reading and argumentation, over the twenty years that separate "*The Rhetoric of Fiction* and the Poetics of Fictions" from *The Company We*

Keep, we can observe something about the way in which this social commitment, surely always present to his character, has surfaced in his thought. Where in the *Novel* essay Booth had valorized the image of solitary climbers, by 1979 he views Susan Suleiman and himself as two "who can somehow move together in critical thought . . . because certain settled grounds are shared. As the old rhetoricians might have put it, but never did, certain *topoi,* thank God, remain in *place,* at least long enough for us to talk together" ("Re-Viewing Reviews" 47). Other thinkers, by contrast, "are so unsettled that they simply drift further apart" (47).

While their moving together has been characterized above as a waltz, Booth gently leading, the figure Booth may have had in mind is that of explorers, temporarily sharing tent space on a "settled ground," or possibly the inhabitants of icebergs, which generally drift at random but occasionally settle in one position long enough to allow a community to develop. What he and Suleiman can share is a *topos,* literally a common place, even if their methods and principles do not precisely coincide. It is a metaphor Booth uses even more self-consciously in the conclusion of *Critical Understanding,* where he treats "critical modes not as positions to be defended but as locations . . . to be explored. . . . [The *topos*] is not . . . a pedestal from which one looks out upon a world of error. Rather it is an inhabited place in which a valued activity can occur among all those who know how to find their way in" (339). From here it is not a long way to the center of *The Company We Keep,* where Booth slightly revises Bakhtin's notion that "each of us is constituted in a kind of counterpoint of inherited 'languages,' a multiplicity of voices only the ensemble of which can . . . be called 'my own'" (239) into the vision of the self as a *"character"* within which the various embodied possibilities and roles—social, familial, literary—are all inscribed:

> someone doing my best to enact the various roles "assigned" me. . . . [T]here are no clear boundaries between the others who are somehow both outside and inside me and the "me" that the others are in. . . . I am a kind of focal point in a field of forces, . . . or, as we used to say, a creature made in the image of God and hence essentially *affiliated,* joined to others and more like them than different from them. (239–40)

If we become our metaphors—as Booth insists at length in *The Company We Keep*—it would appear that Booth's own key metaphors for the processes of literary interpretation and argumentation have been undergoing a sea change since the late 1960s, shifting thematically from isolation to affiliation, from the individual climbers each ascending a private mountain to the pioneers who chance to meet and exchange views at a convenient *topos*. The change seems a natural outgrowth of his life and his character, as an individual who sees doing good in the world as one of the principal functions of the intellectual. But if much is gained by this—particularly clarity about Booth's ethical views, so much belabored since the notorious thirteenth chapter of *The Rhetoric of Fiction*—there is also something lost, perhaps, in the waning of the motive behind the earlier metaphor that had also formed a part of Wayne Clayson Booth: those solitary climbers, each making his or her own heroic assault upon a separate mountain peak, symbolic of the pursuit of truth wherever it leads, not for social or personal motives, but for its own sake.

Notes

1. Killham's reply to Booth in the following issue of *Novel* shows that he has learned nothing from the encounter: he keeps attempting to skewer Booth on dilemmas that are pointed within his own frame of reference but not in Booth's (is the narrator of *Tom Jones* a "surrogate for the real Fielding" or "a sort of character in the story"?; is fiction a "category" or an "autonomous form"?) ("Quarrel" 270). A further reply to Killham by Booth, promised for a subsequent issue, never appeared. Either Booth or the editors of *Novel* must have realized that those readers who, like Killham, had not already grasped Booth's methodological point, never would.

2. As Kenneth Burke must be considered the most powerful creator of a holoscopic ("lumping") pluralism.

3. In *The Architectonics of Meaning,* one of McKeon's students, Walter Watson, has further elaborated this system into an eight-dimensional matrix of 65,536 (4^8) slots. But this massive increase in the number of subdivisions does not change the metaphor in the slightest.

4. Booth's incoherence here over whether understanding or a wide-ranging and vital pluralism is more important is also discussed by Phelan in "Data, Danda, and Disagreement," and in his chapter in this volume.

5. One example of irony derived from word meaning alone might be the opening of Anatole France's *Penguin Island:* "The penguins had the mightiest army in the world. So had the porpoises."

6. As with *"The Rhetoric of Fiction* and the Poetics of Fictions," Booth's careful reading of Suleiman has guaranteed a debating victory over her.

7. Phelan goes on to imply that Booth's pluralism of pluralisms is a chimera, since the real remedy for the problems inherent in holding to a single form of pluralism is to be a better pluralist in one's own chosen mode.

Bibliography

Barthes, Roland. *Writing Degree Zero*. 1967. London: Cape, 1984.
Booth, Wayne C. *The Company We Keep: An Ethics of Fiction*. Berkeley: U of California P, 1988.
———. *Critical Understanding: The Powers and Limits of Pluralism*. Chicago: U of Chicago P, 1979.
———. *The Rhetoric of Fiction*. Chicago: U of Chicago P, 1961.
———. "*The Rhetoric of Fiction* and the Poetics of Fictions." *Novel: A Forum on Fiction* 1 (1968): 105–17.
———. *A Rhetoric of Irony*. Chicago: U of Chicago P, 1971.
———. "Three Functions of Reviewing at the Present Time." *Bulletin of the Midwest Modern Language Association* 11 (1978): 2–12.
Booth, Wayne C., and Susan Suleiman. "Re-Viewing Reviews: Letters by Susan Suleiman and Wayne Booth." *Bulletin of the Midwest Modern Language Association* 12 (1979): 43–52.
Crane, R. S. *The Languages of Criticism and the Structure of Poetry*. Toronto: U of Toronto P, 1953.
Eco, Umberto. *The Role of the Reader*. Bloomington: Indiana UP, 1978.
Genette, Gérard. *Figures II*. Paris: Seuil, 1969.
Killham, John. "The 'Second Self' in Novel Criticism." *British Journal of Aesthetics* 6 (1966): 272–90.
———. "My Quarrel with Booth." *Novel: A Forum on Fiction* 1 (1968): 267–72.
Phelan, James. "Data, Danda, and Disagreement." *Diacritics* 13 (1983): 39–50.
Richter, David. "The Second Flight of the Phoenix: Neo-Aristotelianism Since Crane." *The Eighteenth Century: Theory and Interpretation* 23. 1 (1982): 27–48.
———. "Ronald S. Crane." *Dictionary of Literary Biography* 63 (1988): 87–98.
Suleiman, Susan. "Ideological Dissent from Works of Fiction: Toward a Rhetoric of the *Roman à thèse*." *Neophilologus* 60 (1976): 162–77.
———. "Interpreting Ironies." *Diacritics* 6.2 (1976): 15–21.
Todorov, Tzvetan. *Théories du symbole*. Paris: Seuil, 1977.
Watson, Walter. *The Architectonics of Meaning*. Albany: SUNY P, 1986.

III

Rhetoric and Politics

7

Pluralism, Politics, and the Evaluation of Criticism

JAMES PHELAN

There can be no such thing as keeping out of politics.
GEORGE ORWELL

Become a pluralist.... Become a pluralist.... Become a pluralist....
WAYNE C. BOOTH

FIFTEEN YEARS AFTER its publication, Wayne Booth's *Critical Understanding* remains a major statement on pluralism in literary criticism.[1] In these fifteen years, however, criticism in general has paid less attention to the powers and limits of pluralism than to the pervasiveness of politics—in interpretation, in theory, in the intersection between one's identity and one's critical beliefs and values, especially where matters of race, gender, and class are involved. Furthermore, as theorists have come to regard Orwell's dictum above as a universal truth, they have typically become more dismissive of pluralism.[2] From the perspective of Orwell's epigram, a pluralism such as Booth's is suspect because it pretends to be above politics while its efforts to reduce conflict by advocating the validity of multiple perspectives actually performs the political function of preserving the status quo. In this chapter, I would like to counter such objections by arguing that it is desirable for critics to attend to both Orwell's dictum and Booth's injunction; that, in other words, politically committed critics and pluralists have much to teach each other. For any politically committed criticism to do more than preach to the converted, it must move beyond implicit assertions of the "more-left-than-thou" variety, and pluralism provides some useful lessons in how to do that. Pluralism, for its part, needs to be more cognizant than it has typically been to the political dimensions of both the general program and any practical application of it. In a sense, then, I am seeking to build on some of the principles of *Critical Understanding* in order to address an issue Booth never takes up explicitly: the relation between politics and pluralism. I will be working not so much to defend the details of Booth's pluralist program as to realize a potentiality in its spirit.

Because one of the charges frequently leveled at pluralists is that they are unable to discriminate strong positions from weak ones, I will develop my argument by focusing on the questions that surround the act of evaluating criticism. On what grounds do pluralists evaluate other critics? Are those grounds ultimately political, that is, explainable as the imposition of a privileged set of interests on the other's discourse? Or are those grounds not entirely explainable in political terms? In other words, what force and emphasis ought pluralists give to Orwell's dictum as they reflect on their own procedures of evaluation? More generally, what are the politics of pluralism? To give an added twist to the inquiry, I will focus on a specific example of political criticism, Sandra Gilbert and Susan Gubar's *The Madwoman in the Attic,* considering, first, Toril Moi's evaluation of it from the vantage point of her feminist stance, and then an evaluation conducted from the vantage point of pluralism.[3]

Because dismissals of pluralism often proceed from an inadequate understanding of it, and because I am less interested in the detailed argument of *Critical Understanding* than its general project, I would like to begin by clarifying my version of pluralism. My work is indebted to Booth's, and before him to R. S. Crane's, though I part company with Booth in his conclusion that there is no philosophical foundation for pluralism and part company with both Booth and Crane with their privileging of understanding over other purposes of criticism.[4] Pluralism is the stance I arrive at through the following chain of reasoning: (1) to engage in critical discourse is to implicate oneself, whether consciously or not, in some theoretical positions. If I utter the apparently unstartling statement that "In *Pride and Prejudice* Jane Austen created one of the most lovable characters in English fiction," I imply a theoretical commitment to many ideas that will be seen as startlingly erroneous from the perspective of some other theoretical commitments: authors create the meanings of texts; characters are representations of possible people; readers share responses to texts; fiction is a category distinct from nonfiction. Thus, (2) to speak critically is to speak with principles and assumptions that both enable and give meaning to the speech; to speak critically is to speak within a *mode* or a *framework*. These terms denote an implicit or explicit critical system (which may or may not be internally consistent, well formed, efficient, or effective). A mode includes (a) a characteristic set of questions; (b) some methods for answering those questions; (c) a set of principles and assumptions about such things as the nature of the text, the importance of the author (or authorial function) in the creation of meaning, the role of the reader in interpretation, the significance of history to the creation or interpretation of a work, and the relation between the text and the world outside the text; (d) some general purpose toward which the questions, methods, principles, and assumptions are directed. Answers to critical questions about a given text can be seen as a result of the interaction of these four parts of a mode with the particulars of the text.

(3) Some modes are fundamentally discrete: the questions they ask, the methods they adopt, the principles and assumptions on which they are built, and the purposes they serve are so different that even though they may share some terms (e.g., the "meaning" of the text), they are not offering competing kinds of critical knowledge. A Marxist who asks how a text reveals its relation to the conditions of production within its culture and a psychoanalytic critic who asks how a text reveals the psyche of its author may focus on the exact same textual data but because they interpret that data in light of their discrete frameworks, they offer interpretations that do not compete.

(4) More than one mode is capable of yielding results that are fully adequate to the data it seeks to explain. There are two related points here: first, the different kinds of knowledge offered by different modes can't always be ranked; one kind isn't necessarily better or worse than others, it can sometimes just be different. Second, the different kinds of knowledge are not partial in the usual sense of the term. The Marxist may be able to use her framework to explain the whole text with admirable precision—and so may the psychoanalytic critic. Each explanation is itself total, but each explanation occurs within a framework that is one of several possibilities.

(5) Some modes, and especially some executions of a mode, are deficient: there are many ways to be wrong. If a mode's first principles lead its practitioner to reductive views of data, then the mode will be flawed. If a mode's characteristic methods lead to distortion of the data or to a kind of reasoning that is severely limited, then the mode will be

inferior to others that are more methodologically sound. Furthermore, if a given practitioner violates principles of the mode or employs the method in a sloppy fashion, then the execution of the mode will yield dubious results.

At first glance the consequences of pluralism for critical practice may seem minor: because pluralism is a metacritical stance, a position on positions, the pluralist must still operate within a single mode when doing practical criticism.[5] The consequences can, however, be very significant, because the pluralist's understanding of what it means to operate within a mode is radically different from the nonpluralist's. On the one hand, the pluralist develops a keener sense of the limits of her interpretation: she abandons the belief that her interpretation is *the* truth about the text and adopts the belief that it is one of multiple truths. On the other hand, the pluralist, believing that there are many ways one can go wrong, becomes much more attentive to the methodology of the mode in which she is working—and to her execution of that methodology. Furthermore, the pluralist will both eagerly welcome and carefully scrutinize the work of other critics. Believing in the validity of more than one mode, the pluralist operating on a particular occasion as, say, a Freudian, will not reject out of hand the interpretation of a Marxist, but will consider such things as whether the Marxist addresses elements of the work that she might have unwittingly neglected within her psychoanalytic approach. At the same time, given the belief that there are many ways to go wrong, the pluralist will pay special attention to the Marxist critic's execution of the mode, probing for both weak and strong features of the argument. In short, as a practical critic, the pluralist will be at once more modest and more rigorous than the nonpluralist.

Notice that once I talk about rigor and about being wrong, the questions about the relation between pluralism and politics in the task of evaluation immediately and unavoidably emerge. If methodologies vary from one framework to the next, whose conception of rigor do we use? Are there transmethodological tests of methodologies and their execution? If there is no such thing as keeping out of politics, then we also need to ask about the political dimensions of the tests we use—and the political consequences of the results we obtain. I will keep these questions in mind as I turn to Gilbert and Gubar and to Toril Moi.

Gilbert and Gubar's central question is, "How did women writers of the nineteenth century establish a distinct female literary tradition within a patriarchal literary culture that wanted to deny them the authority of authorship?" Gilbert and Gubar's chief methodological steps are to analyze the patriarchal literary culture and the woman writer's place within it, and to read women's texts for signs of their resistance to or subversion of the patriarchy and for signs of their awareness of female precursors. More specifically, they conduct their analyses of patriarchal culture by reading the gender politics involved in metaphors about writing employed by male writers as well as the gender politics implied by male writers' typical representations of women as either monsters or angels. Gilbert and Gubar read women's texts in three main ways: First, they seek to uncover the textual details that reveal resistance to or subversion of patriarchy, typically finding recurring images of enclosure and escape, disease and health, and fragmentation and wholeness, as well as characters who play off the angel–monster dichotomy; they then use these details to construct their feminist readings of women's texts.

> Women from Jane Austen and Mary Shelley to Emily Brontë and Emily Dickinson produced literary works that are in some sense palimpsestic, works whose surface designs conceal or obscure deeper, less accessible (and less socially acceptable) levels of meaning. Thus these authors managed the difficult task of achieving true female literary authority by simultaneously conforming to and subverting patriarchal literary standards. (73)

Second, Gilbert and Gubar analyze the structure of a narrative text according to what the structure reveals about the nature of men and women's relations under patriarchy. Third, they employ analogical reasoning to establish connections between women's texts and their precursors (indeed, sometimes ancestors as well) in both the male and female traditions. For example, they argue that because both texts are crucially involved with the concepts of heaven, hell, and a fall, *Wuthering Heights* is a response to *Paradise Lost*.

Gilbert and Gubar's main assumptions, some of which I have already touched on, are the following: They view the text as the site of a revelation of male–female relationships within the culture in which it was produced. They regard the author as the source of the text's meaning. They posit an implied reader who can understand the covert story of women's texts. They assume that history restricts authors but not readers: authors inevitably respond to their cultural moments but readers can move across cultures—Gilbert and Gubar imply that the meanings available to them in the twentieth century were also available to readers in the nineteenth. Thus, they claim that the women writers themselves were aware of the tradition they describe in the book; Gilbert and Gubar see themselves as uncovering rather than constructing that tradition. They assume further that texts relate to the world by representing and adopting stances toward cultural attitudes, situations, and ideologies.

The purpose of Gilbert and Gubar's criticism is political. They want to refocus attention on the gender politics of the texts they read, and they want to establish the power of the female literary tradition they uncover. Indeed, by emphasizing the adverse cultural conditions under which women wrote, their history of the female tradition is in part a celebration of women writers' power of resistance, insight, and creation. By accomplishing these tasks of reading politically and establishing the power of the tradition, Gilbert and Gubar also want to achieve the political purpose of making feminist criticism more important in their own cultural moment of the late 1970s. Their book is not only an analysis of the power of the woman writer in the nineteenth century but also a demonstration of the power of the feminist critic in the twentieth.

In *Sexual/Textual Politics,* Toril Moi praises Gilbert and Gubar's "often inventive and truly original readings," but she objects strongly to their assumption that the woman writer is the source of the meaning of her text: Gilbert and Gubar's insistence, writes Moi,

> on the female author as the instance that provides the only true meaning of the text . . . actually undermines [their] anti-patriarchal stance. Having quoted Edward Said's *Beginnings* with its "miniature meditation on the word *authority*" as a description of "both the author and the authority of any literary text," they quote Said's claim that "the unity or integrity of the text is maintained by a series of genealogical connections: author-text, beginning-middle-end, text-meaning, reader-interpretation, and so on. *Underneath all these is the imagery of succession, of paternity, of hierarchy.*" But it seems inconsistent . . . to accept with Said that the traditional view of the relationship between author and text is hierarchical and authoritarian, only to proceed to write a book of over 700 pages that never once questions the authority of the *female* author. For if we are truly to reject the model of author as God the Father of the text, it is surely not enough to reject the patriarchal ideology implied in the paternal metaphor. It is equally necessary to reject the *critical practice* it

leads to, a critical practice that relies on the author as the transcendental signified of his or her text. For the patriarchal critic, the author is the source, origin, and meaning of the text. If we are to undo this patriarchal practice of *authority,* we must take one further step and proclaim with Roland Barthes the death of the author. (62–63)

From my perspective, the most important feature of Moi's argument is its political nature, and especially its assumption about the relation between critical positions and political ones. This assumption becomes clearer once we break the argument down into the twin syllogisms at its crux:

1. Any critical position that perpetuates patriarchal beliefs is politically objectionable.
The belief that authors are the source of meaning is patriarchal.
The belief that authors are the source of meaning is politically objectionable.

2. The work of critics who subscribe to a politically objectionable position should be repudiated.
Gilbert and Gubar subscribe to the politically objectionable position that authors are the source of meaning.
Gilbert and Gubar's work should be repudiated.

Note, first, that the argument as a whole turns round on itself and convicts Moi of the same political crime she finds Gilbert and Gubar guilty of: her discussion treats them as the source of meaning for their book. Thus, either her argument participates in the perpetuation of the patriarchy and should be repudiated or her premises need to be questioned. I will question one of those premises as I relate it to the assumption Moi makes about the relation between critical positions and political ones.

Perhaps the most notable feature of Moi's reasoning is that the linchpin of the whole argument, the minor premise of the first syllogism (the belief that authors are the source of meaning is patriarchal) is not demonstrated but simply asserted. This point has greater force when we go back to Gilbert and Gubar and recognize that the apparent support Moi gives for the belief—their use of Said's analysis of the traditional image of an author—functions very differently in *Madwoman* from the way Moi claims.

Gilbert and Gubar turn to Said not to *accept* "the traditional view that the relationship between author and text is hierarchical and authoritarian" but to show that patriarchal culture has adopted the metaphor of author as "father" and "authority" of the text and thereby has given women an anxiety of authorship. At no point do Gilbert and Gubar agree that the patriarchal view accurately describes authorship; not only are they objecting to it from the very first sentence of their book ("Is the pen a metaphorical penis?"), but they are also offering their account of the success of women writers as a refutation of that view. Moi seems implicitly to acknowledge that Gilbert and Gubar want "to reject the model of author as God the Father of the text" and its attendant patriarchal ideology, but she in effect denies the possibility of separating a belief in authors as the source of meaning from a perpetuation of patriarchy. "It is surely not enough to reject the patriarchal ideology implied in the paternal metaphor. It is equally necessary to reject the *critical practice* it leads to, a critical practice that relies on the author as the transcendental signified of his or her text. For the patriarchal critic, the author is the source, origin, and meaning of the text." In short, *Moi assumes that a given critical position—in this case, a belief in authorial meaning—has a single politics—in this case, perpetuation of the patriarchy.* This assumption is so deeply embedded in her work that she never questions it and thus never questions—or feels the need to substantiate—the minor premise of the first syllogism.

The assumption is doubly troubling here: not only does Moi fail to offer a warrant for it, but Gilbert and Gubar also implicitly reject it and posit a different relation between critical and political positions. They do not see any necessary connection between a belief in authors as the source of meaning and any specific political belief; for them, the politics derives not from the critical position but from how it is appropriated. In other words, for Gilbert and Gubar the politics of criticism do not inhere in specific critical first principles but in how those principles are used. The nineteenth-century patriarchal culture used the belief in authors as the source of meaning to reinforce patriarchal ideology. Gilbert and Gubar's book works in conjunction with the texts of the women writers they analyze to subvert that ideology. For Moi's case to have force, she would have to take on the task of *showing* that the belief in authors is *not* politically neutral. Because she does not do that, she does not genuinely engage with Gilbert and Gubar's book, and thus her commentary tells more about her critical position than about theirs.

Let me engage her position on authorial meaning more fully by examining its specific logic. Moi's view equates authors with authority, authority with the authoritarian, and the authoritarian with patriarchy. The problem arises in the equation of authority and the authoritarian. Proclaiming the death of the author does not *eliminate* authority but merely *transfers* it—to the reader or to history or to culture or to the play of signification or perhaps to some synthesis of these forces. If authority is to be equated with the authoritarian, then these other positions are also authoritarian (note, too, that the proclamation of the author's death exercises a strong authority *against* one kind of reading), and thus, within Moi's logic, equally patriarchal. Gilbert and Gubar's position is no more—and no less—patriarchal than Barthes's. The larger point is that once we recognize that authority will always be located somewhere and thus will always privilege something, we must give up making arguments about the necessary connection between authors, authority, and patriarchy. Whatever is privileged can always be analogized to the male and whatever is marginalized can always be analogized to the female. If, for example, authority is located in the reader, then readers can be seen as in the male position of appropriating and claiming dominance over the work of authors who are in the female position of laboring in the service of the dominant sex. And so on for the other locations. This kind of analysis, of course, is just playing games with terms, games that are themselves authorized by the erroneous assumption that there is a direct link between one's critical and one's political position.[6]

This analysis of Moi's evaluation leads to a larger question: Is her failure to engage meaningfully with Gilbert and Gubar just a local problem, a failure of execution on her part, or something that is more revealing of what happens when we read other critics in terms of our own politics? It is, I think, revealing of what typically, though not invariably, happens. Furthermore, it is typical not so much because it is political but because it is dogmatic. As I have implied above, Moi's failure to engage derives from her deep, unquestioning commitment to her assumption about the relation between critical and political positions. In that respect, she is no different from a critic who is not at all overtly concerned with political positions but who has some deeply entrenched assumption about the nature of texts. For both of them, some direct—or, more frequently, indirect—appeal to that assumption will be sufficient to carry the argument (note Moi's "it is surely not enough" just before she invokes the consequences of her assumption).

The trouble here is the trouble with all such arguments from monism: assertion replaces argument, declaring one's superiority replaces engaging the other's position.

At the same time, despite all my complaints about Moi's analysis, I must recognize that she has brought into focus a significant dimension of Gilbert and Gubar's text that was absent from the account based on my pluralism. While that account acknowledged the overarching political purpose of Gilbert and Gubar's project, it did not address the political dimension of their position on authorship. Moi's attention to the political *in combination* with the strategies of pluralist reading allow for the recognition that the politics of the principle must, as we have seen, be understood not in the abstract but in the uses to which it is put.

How then would a pluralist evaluate Gilbert and Gubar's book more generally? One way of conducting that evaluation is to go to their answer and assess the case they make for it. Here is the central passage in their argument that the covert story of *Jane Eyre* is one that makes Bertha Jane's double, the argument that gives them one of their chief warrants for titling their book as they do:

> ... Bertha has functioned as Jane's dark double *throughout* the governess's stay at Thornfield. Specifically, every one of Bertha's appearances—or, more acurately, her manifestations—has been associated with an experience (or repression) of anger on Jane's part. Jane's feelings of "hunger, rebellion, and rage" on the battlements, for instance, were accompanied by Bertha's "low, slow, ha! ha!" and "eccentric murmurs." Jane's apparently secure response to Rochester's apparently egalitarian sexual confidences was followed by Bertha's attempt to incinerate the master in his bed. Jane's unexpressed resentment at Rochester's gypsy-masquerade found expression in Bertha's terrible shriek and her even more terrible attack on Richard Mason. Jane's anxieties about her marriage, and in particular her fears of her own alien "robed and veiled" bridal image, were objectified by the image of Bertha in a "white and straight" dress, "whether gown, sheet, or shroud, I cannot tell." Jane's profound desire to destroy Thornfield, the symbol of Rochester's mastery and of her own servitude, will be acted out by Bertha, who burns down the house and destroys herself in the process as if she were an agent of Jane's desire as well as her own. And finally, Jane's disguised hostility to Rochester, summarized in her terrifying prediction to herself that "you shall, yourself, pluck out your right eye; yourself cut off your right hand" (chap. 27)

come strangely true through the intervention of Bertha, whose melodramatic death causes Rochester to lose both eye and hand. (360)

The case is both detailed and concrete; if it holds up to a closer look, it will be very persuasive. That closer look, however, undermines its persuasiveness. The first serious problem arises in the second association they find—Jane's apparently secure response to Rochester's sexual confidences being followed by Bertha's attempted arson. If Jane gives no sign that she is angry (and she says "I had a keen delight in receiving the new ideas he offered, in imagining the new pictures he portrayed, and following him in thought through the new regions he disclosed, never startled or troubled by one noxious allusion"), then how do we know that Bertha's action ought to be associated with Jane's anger? Gilbert and Gubar solve the problem by reversing the direction of their argument: they go backwards from Bertha's action to Jane's response to Rochester. Because Bertha acts Jane must be angry; if she doesn't express the anger it is because she is repressing it. But those inferences will be valid only if Gilbert and Gubar have already established the association they're trying to prove. Their argument at this point is circular and unconvincing. It is failing the test of coherence.

The third association, between Rochester's gypsy masquerade and Bertha's shriek and attack on Richard Mason, again acknowledges that Jane's resentment is unexpressed, and so runs into similar problems. Furthermore, the reasoning here faces the additional problem of dealing precisely with the data: if Bertha is to be seen as acting out Jane's anger toward Rochester, why is Mason the object of the attack? Rochester, after all, would be glad to have Mason out of the way.

With the fourth association, between Jane's anxieties about marrying Rochester and Bertha's appearance, Gilbert and Gubar are on firmer ground, though of course alternative explanations for Bertha's appearance, including foreshadowing, are also possible. With the fifth association, the problems recur and multiply: first, Gilbert and Gubar assert that Jane has a profound desire to destroy Thornfield but they give no evidence that she does. Second, they say that Bertha will act out this desire. But the case they have been making is that Bertha's manifestations are associated with an experience or repression of Jane's anger. Bertha's burning of Thornfield is associated with no such experience— it occurs while Jane is beyond her anger at Rochester, if indeed, that anger ever exists—while she is living with the Rivers and thinking of becoming a missionary. The association also overlooks the fact that after setting fire to hangings in the room next to her own, Bertha went and set fire to the governess's bed. When placed within Gilbert and Gubar's hypothesis, this detail must be seen as a sign of Jane's self-hatred—again, something we have no evidence for. The reasoning fails the tests of both coherence and correspondence.

Finally, they claim that Jane's disguised hostility toward Rochester is carried out through the intervention of Bertha whose death causes Rochester's maiming. The main problem here is the gap between cause and effect. Bertha provides the occasion for Rochester's maiming but she is not its cause; she does not set fire to him but to the house; it is made clear that he could have easily escaped injury, even after his unsuccessful and unselfish attempt to save Bertha. Instead, he wants to make sure that everyone else is out of the house before him and so gets burned when the beam falls on him. Again, the argument suffers from a lack of precision.

Of course, to conclude that the reasoning in this single, albeit very important, paragraph from a 700-page book is flawed is not to establish that the argument of the whole is flawed. Indeed, although I do think that the analysis I have just scrutinized is far from an isolated example of their reasoning, I also find that in many places their readings become more convincing under such scrutiny.[7] So it might seem that what I should do here is conclude that their work is flawed but not fatally so and then reflect on the politics of this pluralist evaluation. But I am not ready for that step just yet, because the pluralist position asks me to take one more step toward understanding.

Can my reconstruction of their framework tell me something about the sources of the flaws in the argument? Why should readers who are as skillful and sophisticated as Gilbert and Gubar sometimes produce readings that seem as questionable as the one we have analyzed? One powerful feature of their framework is their definition of the text as a site of the female writer's responses—and especially resistance—to patriarchy. Part of the significance of their book is its demonstration of how such a view of the text opens up some understandings of Austen, the Brontës, Eliot, Dickinson, and others, that were not available before. This conception of the text joins with their goal of showing that the women writers themselves created the tradition to lead Gilbert and Gubar into the position of having to offer comprehensive readings of the texts as resistances to patriarchy. Once in that position, however, they are virtually committed in advance to reaching certain conclusions about their texts. In other words, by implicitly defining the text not just as a political document capable of revealing its author's attitudes about male–female relations under patriarchy but also as a document that will be more powerful the more it reveals about the woman writer's *resistance* to patriarchy, they become powerfully predisposed to finding that resistance. And that predisposition leads to some strained readings. If they gave up the predisposition, then they would be less likely to offer such readings. They would, however, also have to give up the conclusion that the tradition they are describing is one that they are *uncovering* from the women writers' texts because those texts cannot be *comprehensively* read as resistances to patriarchy. Nevertheless, the convincing readings of parts of texts could be recombined into a different kind of narrative, one in which Gilbert and Gubar could take more responsibility for constructing a pattern of resistance in the female literary tradition.

On this view, the flaws in the reasoning have important consequences for our evaluation of the whole project: the flaws detract from the persuasiveness of Gilbert and Gubar's large claim about the female tradition. At the same time, these flaws do not touch Gilbert and Gubar's powerful demonstration of how to do literary history when the text is conceived not as a formal object but as a political document. Furthermore, when we step outside their framework and historicize it in the larger context of literary critical politics, the flaws become even less important. By demonstrating in 1979 on a grand scale what a literary history built on the notion of text as political document would be like, Gilbert and Gubar helped to consolidate the growing power and influence of feminist criticism in the academy. Their voices loudly joined those of many other feminist critics to produce a compelling case for the necessity of rereading familiar texts with new principles in order to attain a different kind of knowledge about those texts. Even if one wants to argue with specific readings, their larger case for the importance of reading politically remains intact. As a result, the book has contributed in an important way to the emphasis on political interpretation in the last decade.

What then are the politics of the pluralist evaluations of Moi and Gilbert and Gubar I have conducted in this chapter? This question, I think, needs to be broken down into three separate questions, because politics operates here on three different levels. First, there is the "internal" politics involved in the analysis of the critics' arguments.

Because I have attempted to conduct those analyses according not to transmethodological standards but to the ones Moi and Gilbert and Gubar implicitly set for themselves, and because those standards involve some conception of the relation between evidence and conclusion in argument, then the politics here are the politics of rational argument. Privilege accrues to those who generate the best reasons according to the standards agreed upon in advance. In Moi's case, the test is whether the inferences she draws are adequately based upon the data that she is working with. In Gilbert and Gubar's case, the test is whether their account of the data is sufficiently precise and coherent to support their inferences about the relation between Jane's anger and Bertha's actions. And for my analysis, in turn, the question is whether I have met them on their own terms and whether my conclusions follow from my evidence. For other critics with different standards, the politics of such "internal" pluralist evaluation would shift and become the politics implied in those standards. Orwell is right that there is no getting outside of politics, but for the pluralist doing internal evaluations of others' arguments, the politics themselves are plural.

The second level on which politics operates here is in my evaluation of Gilbert and Gubar from outside their framework. My case about the significance of their book is based at least in part on an assumption about the importance of their feminist ideology. And that assumption itself is supported by two political positions. One derives from the politics of pluralism, a politics that valorizes the multiplication of critical perspectives for the different kinds of knowledge that they can offer. The second derives from my personal belief in the validity and importance of the feminist ideology itself. That belief arises out of more deeply embedded assumptions about such matters as justice and equality but those, too, of course have a political dimension. It is crucial to recognize, then, that in the final evaluation conducted in the last section both my commitment to pluralism, which prompted the question—why should these kinds of problems develop in this project—and my political commitments to feminist ideology converged.

The third, and most complex, level on which politics operates here is in my choosing feminist criticism as the illustrative case. First, the choice itself reinforces the power of feminist criticism because it assumes that one way to get a hearing for my case about pluralism is to pose the problem of evaluation in this way. At the same time, the structure of the whole chapter privileges pluralism over these feminist positions—they are being evaluated from the perspective of pluralism—and in that respect the politics of pluralism *in this chapter* are the politics of any discourse that is trying to establish its own power. But to reduce the politics of this chapter, let alone the politics of pluralism in general, to that stance is to deny the other levels on which politics are operating here. Thus, though there is no getting outside of politics, there is also no good reason to treat discourse *only* as political. To evaluate our conversations only in light of Orwell's dictum is to impoverish our sense of the work they do; to think of those conversations pluralistically is to enrich our understanding of them. At the same time, to think of pluralism as escaping the realm of politics is to fool oneself; to pay attention to the political dimensions of pluralistic anlayses will heighten our self-understandings. And it is these last assertions that form the ultimate message—political and philosophical—of my discourse.

Notes

1. Other important works on pluralism in criticism in this period include Walter Davis, *The Act of Interpretation* (1978), Paul Armstrong, *Conflicting Readings* (1990), and James Battersby, *Paradigms Regained* (1991). For a more general philosophical treatment of pluralism, see Watson.

2. Note, for example, that the special issue of *Critical Inquiry* (Spring 1986) devoted to pluralism is entitled not "Pluralism and Its Powers" but "Pluralism and Its Discontents" and that the great majority of the contributors (Booth, Richard McKeon, and Kenneth Burke are the exceptions) focus on perceived discontents.

3. I will comment later on the politics involved in the choice of this example.

4. For Crane, see *Languages of Criticism*. For my detailed assessments of *Critical Understanding,* see "Data, Danda, and Disagreement," and "Pluralism and Its Powers." Booth himself talks about Crane's tendency to privilege his neo-Aristotelian mode of understanding as the one best way to do interpretation.

5. The mode a pluralist chooses will depend upon the kind of knowledge that he wants to acquire, and thus, the purpose he sets for his act of criticism.

6. Moi has other objections to the book, and some of these strike me as more cogent precisely because she is more successfully engaging with it. When she questions Gilbert and Gubar's practice of identifying female characters with their authors, she can appeal at least implicitly to the common ground of the authors' lives and their texts.

7. To take just one example, it seems to me that their analysis of how

Edgar Linton in *Wuthering Heights*, though lacking the physical attributes of the strong male, nevertheless acquires power from his social position as patriarch of Thrushcross Grange, offers a new and powerful insight into the dynamics of the relationships among Edgar, Catherine, and Heathcliff after Catherine gets married.

Bibliography

Armstrong, Paul. *Conflicting Readings*. Chapel Hill: U of North Carolina P, 1990.

Battersby, James L. *Paradigms Regained: Pluralism and the Practice of Criticism*. Philadelphia: U of Pennsylvania P, 1991.

Booth, Wayne C. *Critical Understanding: The Powers and Limits of Pluralism*. Chicago: U of Chicago P, 1979.

Crane, R. S. *The Languages of Criticism and the Structure of Poetry*. Toronto: U of Toronto P, 1953.

Critical Inquiry 13. 3 (1986). Special issue, "Pluralism and Its Discontents."

Davis, Walter. *The Act of Interpretation*. Chicago: U of Chicago P, 1978.

Eagleton, Terry. *Literary Theory: An Introduction*. Minneapolis: U of Minnesota P, 1983.

Gilbert, Sandra, and Susan Gubar. *The Madwoman in the Attic: The Woman Writer in the Nineteenth-Century*. New Haven: Yale UP, 1979.

Moi, Toril. *Sexual/Textual Politics*. London: Methuen, 1985.

Phelan, James. "Data, Danda, and Disagreement." *Diacritics* 13 (1983): 39–50.

———. "Pluralism and Its Powers; Metapluralism and Its Problems." *College English* 46 (1984): 63–73.

Watson, Walter. *The Architectonics of Meaning*. Albany: SUNY P, 1984.

8

Wayne Booth and the Politics of Ethics

BARBARA FOLEY

ETHICAL CONCERNS HAVE always been at the heart of Wayne Booth's critical enterprise. The early *The Rhetoric of Fiction* (1961) as well as the subsequent *A Rhetoric of Irony* (1974) proposed pioneering critical methodologies for locating authorial point of view—a point of view that was, Booth always insisted, while mediated through structure, style, and voice, necessarily ethical in its implications. *Modern Dogma and the Rhetoric of Assent* (1974) and *Critical Understanding: The Powers and Limits of Pluralism* (1979) offered rigorous commentaries on the logical grounds upon which readers, critics, and authors might achieve a common terrain for critical dispute—and, in so doing, articulate their common or divergent ethical concerns. It is, however, in *The Company We Keep* (1988), subtitled "An Ethics of Fiction," that Booth shrugs off the formalistic aspects of his Chicago school heritage and undertakes his fullest encounter with the ethical questions that are involved in the activities of writing, reading, and commenting upon literary texts. In this discussion of the relation of politics to ethics in Booth's work, I shall therefore focus upon this book, which, in its encounter with questions of interpretation and value that have been urgently raised by recent critical theory, combines an abiding passion for the literary classics with a lively concern for social justice and a strong intellectual commitment to discovering the connections between the two.

There are certain crucial respects in which Booth's attempt to propose an ethics of reading is made problematic by the very question he is asking: Can the "ethics" embedded in literary texts be meaningfully discussed apart from an analysis of the social and political assumptions and practices that endow any given ethical system with its aura of legitimacy? However fully it may wish to historicize the values invoked in a text, can any project taking "ethics" as its ground succeed in relating these values to the competing ethical systems generated by actual social groups in conflict? Does the very invocation of the term *ethics*—even if qualified by the modest singular article "an"—fetishize questions of textual morality, setting them apart from—and prior to—the messy and embattled terrain of political practice? Before I plunge into a consideration of the relation of ethics to politics in Booth's study, however, I must acknowledge the massive dimensions of Booth's achievement in *The Company We Keep*. For, in this landmark study, Booth builds upon the most valuable insights of Chicago school theory, which was by no means as unremittingly formalistic as is often supposed, to construct a compelling model for describing the ways in which a text's "power of form" implicates readers in its author's values.

Arguing that ethical considerations are intimately bound up with any encounter between an author and a reader, Booth declares that it is incumbent upon critics to engage in "ethical criticism," which he defines as the "attemp[t] [to] describe the encounters of a story-teller's ethos with that of the reader or listener" (*Company* 8). As he develops what he means by the theory and practice of "ethical criticism" in *The Company We Keep,* it becomes clear that Booth has relinquished much of the ahistoricism and abstraction at times accompanying the Chicago school's formulations about the relation of form to ideology and reception. In stipulating that an author's "patterning of desire" articulates historically grounded social beliefs at the same time that it shapes these intentionally into a certain type of artistic whole, for example, Booth supersedes the rigid and artificial distinctions between "extratextual" and "literary" causalities proposed by earlier Chicago school critics such as R. S. Crane and Elder Olson (see Olson, "Outline"; Crane, *Principles* 52; Crane, "Introduction" 20). Thus in his remarks on e. e. cummings's "ygUDuh," ostensibly a satire upon white American workers' crudely racist attitudes toward the Japanese in the World War II era, Booth points out that the "formal" cause of cummings's clever play with linguistic opacity is inseparable from its "final" cause, namely, the poet's desire to expose the ways in which patriotism can mask—but also enable—a fascistic characterization of the "other." Booth also notes, however, that a recognition of cummings's simultaneously aesthetic and social intention should prompt the critic to scrutinize closely the particular ways in which the poet positions his reader:

> Looked at more closely . . . the poem may come to seem tainted by another form of bigotry; in capitalizing on one rejected act of stereotyping on the basis of race, it relies on another, on the basis of class, as it suggests that people who speak substandard English embrace substandard moral notions. . . . The elite position of the poet attacking bigotry, reinforced by the elite assumptions of readers who take pride in performing an intricate act of linguistic deciphering, is vulnerable to the reader's question: "as you mock these slobs for their blindness to the Japanese as 'other,' where do you stand toward them as *your* 'other'?" (218)

Booth's ethical criticism of the "patterning of desire" in cummings's poem entails not only an examination of the satisfactions afforded by the (educated) reader's decoding of cummings's play with "typical" working-class language but also an inquiry into and judgment upon the elitist social assumptions encoded within the generalizations about the working class that the poem encourages. After a point, Booth demonstrates, historical and aesthetic causalities are indistinguishable from one another.

In *The Company We Keep,* Booth continually points out how generic convention and *dynamis* mobilize social values: the text is, for Booth, by nature ethical to the core. In setting forth his ethics of reading, Booth demonsrates the various axes along which a neo-Aristotelian concern with such matters as instabilities and resolutions in plot is not merely compatible with, but actually requires, analysis of the specifically literary ways in which fictional texts work upon readers. In a subtle and highly dialectical commentary upon Jane Austen's *Emma,* he shows how the text's adherence to romantic plot conventions would appear to entrap the reader into endorsing the notion that marriage is the necessary context of female self-realization: by being urged to desire Emma's consignment to the custodianship of the gallant but sober Knightley, readers are entrapped within sexist social values by their own vicarious "literary" desires. Yet Booth also analyzes the narrator's persistently ironic deflation of the expectations routinely accompanying romantic closure, which, he argues, functions to undercut the notion that Emma's selfhood, hard won through her own experience, can really consist in nuptial bliss. The text's manner of representation interacts with, and alters, its mode of representation. Booth salvages Austen for feminism by demonstrating that the text's meaning cannot be equated with any single narrative element but must be inferred from a description of the specific narrative experience afforded by the text. A Chicago school examination of the text's "power" as an instance of narrative comedy thus provides privileged access to its embodiment of ideology.[1]

But the ethical criticism of narrative form does not always yield ideological recuperation of the classics for contemporary readers. After a close consideration of the alternative interpretive possibilities embodied within Rabelais's dialogic treatment of the status of women in *Gargantua* and *Pantagruel,* Booth concludes that these texts' refusal to include the voices of their many female characters leaves the reader with the indelible impression that women are simply material for "masculine laughter" (394). Similarly, after undertaking a careful reading of *Adventures of Huckleberry Finn* that focuses not only on the novel's vexing ending but also on the shifting attitudes and judgments orchestrated throughout the narrative, Booth feels compelled to conclude that the representation of Jim implies very damaging generalizations about the responses of slaves to their conditions of servitude. Although he continues to insist that *Adventures of Huckleberry Finn* is a "wonderful" book, he also concedes, "I cannot, by sheer act of will, restore Twain's former glow" (477). The application of ethical poetics to an examination of the *dynamis* informing various classic works of literature is thus as likely to produce a lowering of the critic's estimate of a text as it is to yield "proof" of the text's untarnished and enduring value.

At the heart of Booth's ethical enterprise, then, is a conception of the rights—and responsibilities—of the reader that substantially alters the notions of textual reception originally postulated by the Chicago school critics, who generally stipulated an undifferentiated "we" receptive to an apolitical "pleasure" and "beauty" (Olson 566). While Booth, as an unreconstructed intentionalist, rejects the subjectivism he sees implied in many versions of reader-response criticism, he also grants that different readers will bring different ethical values to texts and come away with different assessments. A key "character" introduced at the outset of *The Company We Keep* is one Paul Moses, a black member of the University of Chicago professorial staff, who in the early 1960s refused to teach *Huck Finn* because of its "many distorted views of race" (3). Moses's principled stand—which, Booth freely admits, he failed to grant sufficient legitimacy at the time—haunts Booth throughout his study, functioning as a social conscience continually challenging the formalist abstractions of a "pure" (that is, nonethical) criticism. Booth continues to insist, as he did in *The Rhetoric of Fiction,* that literary texts work upon their readers by "creating" them as "peers" (*Rhetoric of Fiction* 397). But he now insists with equal force that it is the task of criticism to query "the offer of disinterested friendship" held out by the implied author—who may "prove to be a wolf in sheep's clothing" (177). The "we" who, for Olson or Crane, served as the author's perfect mirror is now dissolved into multiple social and historical selves, each claiming the right to engage in reading and criticism along the lines dictated by distinctive ethical imperatives. "Pleasure" is no longer a form of potential energy stored within the text, awaiting transformation into kinesis by an ideal reader, but a material measure of the extent to which the text's implied values have been made moving and acceptable to an actual reader experiencing an actual evaluative response.

What Booth urges in *The Company We Keep*, in other words, is a view of the reading process, and of the critical acts elucidating that process, that enlists the best features of the Chicago school's concern with texts as instances of persuasive *praxis*. Booth's rehabilitation of neo-Aristotelian poetic and rhetorical theory for socially committed criticism thus prompts us to consider exactly *how* poetic and fictional texts do their ideological work. While much valuable semiotic inquiry has recently been undertaken by critics arguing that all texts need to be scrutinized *as* texts, without exempting the so-called "nonfictional" genres, Booth's study usefully illuminates the rhetorical strategies peculiar to the "specifically literary" genres. In short, *The Company We Keep* enriches our understanding of the ethical powers of literature, helping us to see both *how* literary works perform their rhetorical tasks and *why* we should take seriously their function as purveyors of social values. It brings us to the threshold of a rhetoric of politics.

If Booth's study brings us to this threshold, however, it does not take us over the lintel. It fails in this enterprise, in my view, largely because it never directly confronts the relation between the ethical and the political, but instead continually slips from the former to the latter without clarifying their points of tangency or difference. Booth evinces an awareness of this problem at the outset, declaring that

> [w]e might ... broaden the term "ethical" even further, making it carry the weight of all political criticism as a rough synonym for what many people would call ideological criticism. I must often use it in that broad sense, but although I raise political issues throughout, I cannot pretend to offer the full encounter with them that the enterprise inherently demands. (12)

At subsequent points in *The Company We Keep*, Booth expressly points to the embeddedness of political considerations within ethical judgments, as, for example, when he refers to the "political questions that naturally spring from any serious thinking about the ethical powers of fictions" (137), or when he notes that the capacity to acknowlege one's beliefs requires "a fully developed art of ethical (and, by implication, political) criticism" (290). Booth's careful wording in these passages suggests that he does not see the political and the ethical as precisely equivalent to one another, though they may be closely related. His abstention from defining this relation, however, leaves the reader with the impression that what "comes first"—and really "matters"—is ethics: politics may in some sense flow from ethics, but ethical decisions and judgments are prior in both temporal sequence and importance.

Booth's reluctance to confront the relation of ethics to politics results in two major omissions in *The Company We Keep*. The first of these consists in his almost exclusive concentration upon acknowleged "classics" and his refusal to engage in sustained critical dialogue with any work that is not squarely situated within the established canon. To make this charge is not to claim that Booth makes no mention of noncanonical texts; *The Company We Keep* is in fact replete with passing references to soap operas, detective stories, popular romances, and sensationalistic potboilers such as *Jaws*. He offers laudatory assessments of several texts—for example, Alice Walker's *The Color Purple,* Toni Morrison's *Beloved,* Tillie Olsen's *Tell Me a Riddle*—that have in fact become canonical, or near canonical since the publication of this book six years ago. But Booth refrains from discussing the particular sorts of ethical criticism that can be prompted by the works of serious writers who, for reasons having to do with race, gender, class, or simply historical contemporaneity, have not (or not yet) emerged as creators of cultural monuments. His most fully fleshed out examples are drawn from Yeats, Pound, Joyce, Austen, Lawrence, Rabelais, and Twain—all white, all but one male, and all—with the exception of Rabelais, for whom such a label would be anachronistic—bourgeois.[2]

No doubt Booth could justify his choice of textual examples by arguing that his principal point is that even—indeed, especially—the classics need to be scrutinized for ethical shortcomings: Rabelais, Austen, Lawrence, Twain, and others warrant close investigation precisely because they are commonly held to propound incontrovertible wisdoms and articulating universal values. The fact remains, however, that the reader of *The Company We Keep* is left with the distinct impression that the most significant (if flawed) company one should choose to keep is the "classic" writer, who offers a "richer, fuller life" than any of his or her lesser counterparts. Thus, by a curious turn of the wheel, the classic writers whom Booth chastises for their questionable ethics emerge as, if not "morally" rehabilitated, at least rehabilitated as the principal objects of critical inquiry. As Booth notes,

> [R]ather than finding reasons to ban narratives, we are now more interested in protecting them—and thus ourselves—from premature, unacknowledged, and irresponsible judgments. The classics need not fear us if we look them in the eye; most of them—we cannot know which ones in advance of fresh reading—can more than hold their own in any fair encounter. Perhaps the supreme value of ethical criticism is that once we have practiced it vigorously in the presence of a classic, that classic becomes more fully alive in our culture than it was before. (423)

Indeed, Booth's repeated use of the word "classic," as well as his continual deployment of honorific adjectives such as "wonderful" and "beautiful" to describe even works he finds ethically lacking, has the effect of protecting his cherished texts in advance from even the most searing criticism. The current debate about canon busting is thus largely defused by Booth's emphasis upon the classics, which, he assures us, contains sufficient meat—delicious meat—for the most voracious political critic.

Booth is of course entitled to his love of the classics. But the absence in *The Company We Keep* of any detailed analysis of texts by working-class writers or writers of color substantially limits the range of his description of the powers and functions of ethical criticism. My point here is not simply that Booth has violated some pluralistic notion of "equal time" for all comers on the literary scene; although, given his evident enthusiasm for other sorts of pluralism, this point could also be made. My complaint is that he has sloughed over one very important type of ethical effect that a text can produce—namely, that of immersing readers in a represented world that calls into question their sense of moral purity or that simply teaches them something new about social reality. If ethical criticism consists simply of describing and judging the ways in which classic texts encode social values that may, upon closer examination, appear morally repugnant, the critic is assumed to inhabit a superior ethical stance: possessed of egalitarian values the author does not hold (or at least not fully enough), the critic confronts her or his own agonized contradiction between aesthetic pleasure and social belief. But if ethical criticism is to address the real political problems that many of us encounter, not only in our own reading experiences but also in those of our students, it must additionally theorize the dynamics of situations where writers challenge readers to assume *more* egalitarian attitudes (antiracist, antisexist, antielitist) than they might already espouse. Ethical criticism must take into account that the writer may be the principal "ethical critic," and the would-be emancipated reader his or her pupil—chastened, bemused, guilt-ridden, indignant, even resentful.

Booth by no means ignores the transformative power that books can have: indeed, at one point in *The Company We Keep* he offers a fascinating catalogue of instances in which numerous friends and acquaintances have attested to the liberating influence certain books have had upon their attitudes and lives (278–79). But, in a study that is generally quite remarkable for its candor and self-critical openness, Booth himself offers no detailed ethical criticism of his *own* encounter with any of the noncanonical texts he finds compelling, even though doing so might significantly buttress his ethical criticism of classic texts. His incisive commentary upon the racism embedded in *Huck Finn,* for example, would be immeasurably enriched by a juxtaposition of his reading of this novel with an account of an "ethical" response—his own or someone else's—to the representation of the lives of slaves in *Beloved* or Frederick Douglass's *Narrative of the Life of an American Slave.* To be sure, as Booth himself points out, a critical discussion of any text is no substitute for the actual narrative encounter itself. One very important type of ethical criticism is accomplished when a reader "corrects" the version of reality tendered in one text by counterposing it with the lived experience of another "rival" world with which it is "in dialogue" (344). Nonetheless, by refraining from describing how attitudes or knowledge gained from an encounter with an "emancipated" text intersect with those gained from an encounter with a "retrograde" text, Booth leaves the reader with the impression that the ethical critic's presumably enlightened judgmental stance derives from principle alone, rather than from the experience that shapes and alters principle. No doubt one's lived experience—such as many of us have had in recent decades with social movements against racism and sexism—is the best teacher of such principles. But we cannot underestimate the role played by exposure to texts that embody and articulate the ethical values at the heart of such movements, providing political experiences of a valuable if different kind.

To ask the question, then, How might Frederick Douglass tell the "story" of Jim? is not to substitute literature for life, but to ask how the representation of social practices in Twain's novel might be subjected to scrutiny through the lens of a narrative particularly empowered to tell us things about those practices that Twain himself could never have known. Posing this question entails a risk, however. For it exposes Twain's novel to an ethical criticism perhaps more searching than any criticism derivable from an examination of implied social beliefs embedded within the "text itself." The juxtaposition of Douglass with Twain might require not only a careful consideration of what *is* represented in the text, as Booth does so ably, but also a consideration of what is *excluded*—namely, a depiction of the institution of slavery (including the whippings, the daily humiliations, the back-breaking labor, the emotional pain, the psychological alienation) that would render plausible Jim's decision to cut all his social ties and take off down the river. The risk entailed here, in short, is that, after his ethical scrutiny "by" Douglass, Twain might in fact never fully recover from the shock: the terms "classic" and "wonderful" that Booth lovingly (if ambivalently) bestows upon *Huck Finn* might indeed get stuck in the mouth. The impact of considering at length the "ethical criticism" offered by a text that is both noncanonical and oppositional, in short, might be to demonstrate that the "rival" worlds offered in the two books are not simply in dialogue, but in conflict—*political* conflict. It might be impossible to continue to cherish the former if one takes seriously the ethical burden of the latter.³

For Booth to have included more extended discussions of the ethical criticism embedded in texts by ethnic minority and working-class writers would not simply have called into question his abiding veneration of the classics; it would also have put in a new light the aesthetic criteria for adjudicating literary value that justify this veneration. Booth notes at one point that "[w]hat we all admire (though the details of our admiration vary tremendously) are works that are either consistent with themselves, and thus in some sense unified, or works that acknowledge their own inconsistencies and thus reflect a genuine encounter with recalcitrant materials" (193–94). Jane Austen undertakes an exemplary feat of ethical criticism in *Emma,* he claims, because she ably deploys the conventions of sentimental romance in constructing an emotionally and aesthetically satisfying plot at the same time that she subtly undermines these conventions by refusing to narrate scenes of romantic fulfillment, substituting instead ironic summaries and laconic judgments. Rather than attacking completeness and closure, in other words, Austen indicates her dissatisfaction with the ideologies embedded in conventions.

In positing that "we" all "admire" works that are either consistent and unified or at least self-conscious in their inconsistency and disunity, Booth is arguing in a polemical context. His antagonist is the currently fashionable notion that rupture or inconsistency or disunity is in itself a sign that a text has made a "genuine" ethical encounter with social reality. I readily grant his point, as well as his judgment of the particular feminist strengths of *Emma*. But I question whether ethical criticism should place as high a premium upon unity (or upon self-consciousness regarding disunity) as Booth suggests. For what is the ethical critic to make of a writer such as Harriet Wilson, who, in *Our Nig*, attempted to construct a bildungsroman around her agonized and profoundly restricted life as "free black" in a "white house, North"? Or, to expand the analysis to another black woman writer not so visibly hampered by the particularities of her own experience, what should the ethical critic make of such an accomplished and sophisticated writer as Jessie Redmon Fauset, who, in *Plum Bun*, also attempted to enlist the conventions of the bildungsroman to recount the ironically self-defeating life of a light-skinned woman trying to "pass" in the New York of the 1920s? Did not the very requirements of the genre within which they were working—the notion that character is fate, for example, or that selfhood entails the attainment of autonomy—run counter to the social experience these writers wished to describe? Does the "ill fit" between subject matter and form simply reflect upon Wilson's or Fauset's lack of skill with plot or characterization? Or might it point to the ideological premises of the presumably "formal" qualities in a successful bildungsroman—namely, the notion that we are largely free to choose the selves we become? And, if this is true, might not it be appropriate to view genre itself as implicitly political—and problematic—for large numbers of writers possessing little if any access to such assumptions? And, if *this* is true, should not the literary standards that presuppose unity and wholeness as an "aesthetic" value be themselves subjected to ethical scrutiny? Is adequate recognition of the difficulties posed by conventional forms to marginalized or oppositional writers granted by Booth's stipulation that these writers' conflictual relation to these forms should be articulated as a matter of conscious concern and control? To raise such questions is not, I repeat, to enshrine "incoherence, incongruity, or uncontrolled dissonance" (108n). It is, however, to suggest another way in which noncanonical writers can provide ethical instruction. Such writers may not only reveal submerged aspects of social reality but also query the political presuppositions undergirding the literary conventions through which that reality is ordinarily represented.

In short, Booth's abstention from any serious or extended encounter with the problems raised by the recent movement to open up the canon has the effect of isolating ethical criticism from politics. Booth's passion for the classics, his conviction that they deserve the most serious ethical commentary, enables him to tease out many of their points of political vulnerability. Yet this very loyalty prevents him from turning his attention to whole sets of texts that provide a fascinating plurality of ethical standpoints from which to criticize not only the implied ethical contents of classic works but also the ideological premises of classic forms. The narrowing of the domain of relevant literary texts entails the narrowing of the domain of relevant ethical issues. Ethics is collapsed into politics only at the cost of obscuring the various types of morality or immorality that can accompany the act of reading.

The Company We Keep would benefit not only from a broader sense of literary tradition but also from a consideration of more, and different, ethical standards that might be brought to bear in ethical judgments of classic texts. My second major complaint about Booth's depoliticizing of ethics is that he does not adequately introduce considerations of social class into his discussion of the ethical critic's strategic practice. For, with the exception of the brief—though powerful—analysis of class bigotry in cummings that I mentioned above, Booth refrains from raising questions about the representation of classes and class hierarchy throughout the book. Of course, Booth's defenders, seeing where I am heading (ah! here comes the Marxist!), might interrupt me here, arguing that, in faulting Booth for his failure to address these issues, I am simply disappointed that he does not happen to share *my* particular ethics. A writer's failure to exhibit sensitivity to inequalities stemming from social class, they might declare, may simply not be Booth's particular concern. This absence does not imperil the integrity of Booth's argument, these critics might continue, for he explicitly states that his own ethics may not coincide with those of other ethical critics and that he is simply attempting to delineate the parameters within which *any* act of ethical criticism can be performed, regardless of its specific social content. Booth's preponderant emphasis upon a feminist critical approach, they would conclude, is not to be taken as prescriptive, but simply as exemplary: the strategies of feminist criticism should be taken as "representative" of those of ethical criticism generally, rather than as constituting an exhaustive repertory of specific social values.

I acknowledge that different critics may wish to emphasize different ethical concerns as they consider literary texts. But I question whether the strategies of feminist ethical criticism can be taken as "representative" of all ethical criticism, especially a criticism based on considerations of class. Feminist and Marxist analyses share, of course, certain important concerns: both stipulate that the classics contain egregious instances of ethical blindness and, moreover, that this blindness *matters* in interpretation and evaluation. Nonetheless, feminist and Marxist criticism do not always adopt similar critical maneuvers. To be sure, gender issues are elided in whole genres or authorial oeuvres addressed to male readerships or focusing on male experience (I think here of Westerns, various types of adventure narratives, and the sea novels of Joseph Conrad). More often than not, however, women are at least a marginal presence in even the most sexist of the classics. Sexist representation usually takes the form of denigration or distortion, not of wholesale omission. Feminist criticism thus generally addresses itself to the ideological implications of something that *is* represented. An examination of personal interactions among characters, narratorial intervention, and other textual features will ordinarily yield up sufficient material for the feminist critic to formulate an ethical commentary.

Feminist criticism has developed useful strategies for examining such concerns, and in what I am about to say I in no way intend to detract from its achievement. But certain types of feminist criticism end up reinforcing the notion that the ethics of a text are projected through its representation of personalities; understanding the portrayal of the personal is the key to grappling with the political. Criticism emphasizing issues of class, by contrast, is more frequently confronted with absence; in any number of classics, the vast numbers of peasant and proletarian producers who enable the very existence of the narrative's interacting elite characters—male *and* female—are simply invisible. To be sure, this is not always the case: Joyce and Lawrence give us enough of working-class experience to whet our appetites, while Dickens treats problems of class hierarchy by boldly juxtaposing characters from diverse social levels. But generally the working class figures in literary texts in the bourgeois "great tradition" as an invisible presence. In Edith Wharton's *House of Mirth,* the fastidious Selden may intuit that "a great many dull and ugly people must, in some mysterious way, have been sacrificed to produce [Lily Bart]" (7). But this recognition does not seem to compel Wharton herself to grant more than the most passing recognition to such sacrifices or to explore the mystery of their cause. In *The House of Mirth,* as in a great number of classic novels, the reader is left with the distinct impression that, however fully a character's personality and values may be grounded in his or her social environment (and Wharton is, it should be granted, better than many on this point), that environment itself is an autonomous world. This world may be juxtaposed in interesting ways with the world of the laboring and the poor, but is in no significant way dependent upon it. One result of this fetishization of wealth and leisure, I would argue, is a fetishization of morality. Questions of alienation, oppression, and injustice—questions that are political to the core—take shape as "moral" issues, embodied in the "good" and "bad" polarities signaled by the elite characters who ordinarily constitute the text's ethical spectrum.

If it is true that class is often obscured in classic texts in ways that gender is not, then the ethical project of the critic concerned with issues of class is in certain crucial ways very different from that of the feminist critic. The Marxist critic treats as political both textual presences and textual absences. The final ethical judgments the Marxist critic arrives at may thus diverge significantly from those reached by the feminist critic; the "correct" ethical judgment of a text is not a preexistent given, waiting to be discovered by the enlightened critic, but a contested terrain, where different political premises require different critical maneuvers and produce potentially divergent ethical conclusions. As Booth ably demonstrates, the various textual presences in *Emma*—both explicit and implicit—allow the feminist critic to conclude that Austen offers an emancipatory ironic commentary that recuperates her for contemporary feminism. But what are we to say of Austen's (or, Austen's narrator's) blithe remark that Emma had the "good fortune" to be possessed of great wealth? There are no represented elements in the novel that invite us to interpret this statement ironically. Austen's attitude toward the plot of romantic fulfillment can be inferred from the subtle interplay of action with tone; but the author's silence on the question of the sources, and legitimacy, of "fortunes" suggests that the conditions of their being got and spent are irrelevant to her ethical universe. For the reader who is concerned with ethical criteria encompassing considerations of both gender and class, then, assessing *Emma* is deeply problematic. If this reader's discontent with Austen's blindness to the implications of early nineteenth-century class hierarchy is then fueled by encounters with texts that describe what class hierarchy meant in the lives of real people—Marx's searing account of the consequences of the enclosure movement in *Capital,* volume 1, for example, or Mayhew's description of the urban poor—it may become still more difficult for the ethical critic to respond with pleasure to Austen's account of self-discovery and love among the leisure classes. Like *Huck Finn* after its encounter with Frederick Douglass, *Emma* after its meeting with Marx or Mayhew may never be so "wonderful" again.[4]

No doubt the argument could be made that any ethical critic who relies so heavily upon a judgment of what is *not* represented in a text is a spoilsport in the groves of academe, anachronistically condemning great cultural monuments and, moreover, raising considerations that are fundamentally irrelevant to the sort of criticism Booth is describing. It is one thing to criticize a writer for failing to grant full humanity to characters who actually appear in the pages of a text: at least then the "ethics" of the text can be seen as consisting in its failure to grapple fully with its own *donnée*. It is quite another thing, however, to insist that authors talk about something that did not even occur to them. Indeed, the argument might be—and here a frown might be cast toward Booth as well as the Marxist—that the above comments on Austen, Marx, and Mayhew demonstrate why the whole enterprise of ethical criticism is of questionable value to begin with. Once the door is opened to the proposition that critics have the right—indeed, the responsibility—to inject social values into literary evaluation, can it ever be closed again? Is there no domain of aesthetic evaluation exempt from political judgment?

I would respond that the Marxist arguments I have raised are entirely compatible with Booth's inquiry into the ethics of reading and criticism; to an extent I expect that Booth would back me up. Certainly he would grant little validity to the argument that complaints about earlier writers' failure to be aware of the realities of exploitation are irrelevant or ahistorical. As he notes with regard to the potential accusation that he is imposing a 1980s-based ethics of gender relations upon Rabelais, "The only 'Rabelais' I can be fully responsible to confronts me here and now. I do not possess Rabelais's works *then;* I possess them, or they attempt to possess me, *now*. I read him as I read anyone: *in my own time*. Whatever he does to me will be done within my frame of values, not his" (412). Where Booth and I would part company, however (and I would regret to see him go, for he is such splendid company to keep) would probably be around a disagreement regarding my claim that the forms of ethical criticism are inextricably bound up with their substance. He would assert, I suspect, that the particular ethics guiding a given critic's act of ethical criticism are logically separable from the adopted strategy of critique. I, by contrast, would insist that different social values necessitate different sorts of inquiries and that certain specific ethical contents—central among these being a full recognition of the ideological workings of assumptions regarding gender, race, *and* class—are indispensable to a "full" ethical engagement with a text, one that accounts not only for what the text represents but also for what it sloughs over and obscures. The critic who ignores such considerations, I would argue, runs the risk of dissolving ethics into a matter of personal sensitivity, obscuring the important political questions at stake when we encounter texts and traditions that purport to represent a culture to itself.

Much of *The Company We Keep* is given over to a discussion of the logical grounds upon which ethical criticism makes its claim to legitimacy. Near the beginning of the book, Booth asks, "Can we hope to find a criticism that can respect variety and yet offer *knowledge* about why some fictions are worth more than others?" (36). The argument that follows offers an eloquent refutation of the notion that ethical criticism can be nothing more than the imposition of subjective value judgments upon literary texts and traditions. There is, Booth emphatically argues, no valid basis for distinguishing between fact and value, interpretation and judgment, nor should we look for one. Even though Booth's own writing is largely directed toward a rehabilitation of the classic tradition as the object of ethical inquiry, his book serves to legitimate and support the activity of a broad range of canon-busting critics who have been engaging in their own brands of "ethical criticism" for some years now. In many ways Paul Moses is generously vindicated by Booth's committed response to the issues his colleague posed twenty-five years ago. In this sense, *The Company We Keep*, coming as it does from a critic widely esteemed for his adherence to "traditionalist" values, offers aid and sustenance to the insurgent modes of cultural criticism at a crucial moment in their development. For we should not be overly complacent about the foothold that the proponents of feminist and ethnic studies have gained in literature departments. While presently enjoying considerable prestige, these scholars are coming under increasing attack by cultural conservatives dedicated to expunging the barbarians in our midst and to lampooning "political correctness" as a new McCarthyism. Booth, for all his abiding dedication to the study of the classics, will clearly not allow himself to be enlisted in the conservatives' ranks. He may not be branded a barbarian or neo-McCarthyite himself, but as time goes by, he may well be seen as a renegade who, by theorizing the inseparability of the ethical from the aesthetic, gives succor and comfort to the mob at the gates.

I hope I have not been looking a gift horse too much in the mouth, then, when I direct attention to what I think are significant limitations in Booth's ethical program, limitations that are simultaneously ethical and political. For Booth can set forth his version of *critique engagée* with such aplomb—and can argue that its validation is primarily a logical matter—partly because his book does not raise particularly incendiary political questions. His success in urging the logical integrity of his thesis is a function not so much of his avoidance of politics as it is of his endorsement of a distinctively nonthreatening politics. The antiracism informing Booth's critique of Twain, while powerful within its limits, confines ethical judgment to the domain of stereotyping; it bypasses the more fundmental issues about economic and institutional power that would be raised by such texts as *House Made of Dawn* or *Native Son*. The antisexism informing his discussions of Austen and Rabelais, while perspicacious in its analysis of the limitations on female potentiality projected in classic conventions and texts, speaks to constructions of feminism currently enjoying widespread acceptance (at least at the level of lip service) among middle-class academics. Considerations of class that would emphasize issues of exploitation or the legitimation of class hierarchy are virtually absent from the range of standpoints Booth presents as possible premises for ethical criticism. Booth can collapse politics into ethics because he invokes a version of the political that is inseparable from the moral stance of contemporary liberal humanism. A Marxist version of the political, I hope to have shown, does not simply generate a different series of examples to make the same points. Instead, it places the ethical in tension with the political, requiring that "ethics" themselves—a plural, not a singular noun, we should note—be situated in the conflicted zone of social practice before they be invoked in the process of literary evaluation. Booth sets forth with passion and clarity the assumptions and strategies of an ethical criticism practiced from the vantage point of liberal humanism. Critics further to the left, taking up Booth's cue, need to theorize with equal rigor how ethics are embedded in their own strategic practices of reading, criticism, and evaluation.

Notes

1. The fullest application of Chicago school principles to the study of narrative fiction is Sheldon Sacks, *Fiction and the Shape of Belief*. Kenneth Burke's various works undertake an imaginative politicization of Aristotelian poetics that explores potentialities only partially realized by Sacks's work and

the earlier work of Booth. See, for example, *The Philosophy of Literary Form* and *Counter-Statement*.

2. The use of the term *bourgeois* here refers not specifically to class origins but to a writer's general placement within a philosophical/political tradition that can be loosely described in this way. Clearly the term has somewhat more problematic application to a D. H. Lawrence than to a Jane Austen, but it remains useful in characterizing an overall ideological orientation.

3. My own interpretation of *Adventures of Huckleberry Finn* does not necessitate such drastic conclusions regarding Twain's racism. While I concede that the portraiture of Jim is sterotyped and involves serious omissions regarding the institution of slavery, I subscribe to the more "ironic" reading of the novel that Booth dismisses as overly ingenious (470–73). This reading—which is, I believe, amply buttressed by the text, and not simply imposed by 1990s wish fulfillment—does a good deal to salvage Twain for contemporary antiracist discourse. For antiracist readings of *Huck Finn,* see Wilding, "The False Freedoms of Huckleberry Finn," in *Political Fictions* 21–47; and David L. Smith, "Huck, Jim, and American Racial Discourse," in Leonard, Tenney, and Davis 103–20.

4. I have not directly confronted here the relation of class to race: clearly the remarks I have made about the ways that criticism focusing on questions of class requires special attention to gaps and omissions are also true of criticism focusing on questions of race. Indeed, as my remarks on *Huck Finn* suggest, a writer's inattention to the position of blacks within the socioeconomic structure is closely related to the invocation of racial sterotypes. In terms of representational presences and absences, class is a good deal more closely aligned with race than it is with gender. Yet the treatment of racism differs from that of class, and shares certain similarities with that of gender, insofar as an ethics of the "personal" can more frequently emerge as central to a text's ideological stance.

Bibliography

Booth, Wayne. *The Company We Keep: An Ethics of Fiction*. Berkeley: U of California P, 1988.

———. *The Rhetoric of Fiction*. Chicago: U of Chicago P, 1961.

Burke, Kenneth. *Counter-Statement*. New York: Harcourt, 1931.

———. *The Philosophy of Literary Form*. Baton Rouge: Louisiana State UP, 1941.

Crane, R. S. *Critical and Historical Principles of Literary History*. Chicago: U of Chicago P, 1967.

———. "Introduction." *Critics and Criticism: Ancient and Modern*. Chicago: U of Chicago P, 1952.

Leonard, James S., Thomas A. Tenney, and Thadious M. Davis. *Satire or Evasion? Black Perspectives on Huckleberry Finn.* Durham: Duke UP, 1992.
Olson, Elder. "An Outline of Poetic Theory." In Crane, *Critics and Criticism.*
Sacks, Sheldon. *Fiction and the Shape of Belief: A Study of Henry Fielding, with Glances at Swift, Johnson and Richardson.* Berkeley: U of California P, 1967.
Wharton, Edith. *The House of Mirth.* 1905. New York: NAL, 1980.
Wilding, Michael. *Political Fictions.* London: Routledge, 1980.

9

Learning to Read Martin Luther King's "Pilgrimage to Nonviolence": Wayne Booth, Character, and the Ethical Criticism of Public Address

FREDERICK J. ANTCZAK

To imagine a language is also to imagine a way of life.
                                                              WITTGENSTEIN

MOST OF US KNOW something of Wayne Booth's contributions in bringing ethical concerns to the study of literary narrative, of his persistent efforts and signal accomplishments at a moment in critical history when such activity had run counter to the intellectual fashion. Surely Booth is right in thinking narrative an important subject, one "of universal concern," for "in the beginning, and from then on, there was story, and it was largely in story that human beings were created and now continue to recreate themselves" ("Ethical Criticism" 289, 290). But it is not only, and not always most importantly, in literary narrative that human beings constitute and progressively reconstitute their characters and communities; the study of narrative has recently been extending itself into the study of the narratives that structure our practical discourse, including those of public address.[1] Booth remains a largely untapped resource for this line of inquiry; but he is a resource worth tapping, for his recent work can contribute to this study both theoretical insights and methodological approaches, both ideas and methods.

In this chapter, I first explore three of Wayne Booth's theoretical insights that challenge contemporary critical and ethical dogmas, and which for our purposes happen to stand in particularly productive interrelation. Then I suggest how they generate ways of examining the narrative dimensions of our practical discourse for their ethical nature. Finally, following Booth's consistent good example, I apply these lessons to a particular text that has a special importance and interest, to which such a mode of criticism has productive access. I hope to show how Booth enables us to describe and evaluate texts in terms of the capacities of character they realize.

THREE BOOTHIAN CONCEPTS

In *Modern Dogma and the Rhetoric of Assent,* Booth unpacked his notion of what it means to be human and to communicate to others who share our substance, describing the human self as "a field of selves," whose "primary mental act . . . is to assent to truth rather than to detect error, 'to take in' and even 'to be taken in'" (126, xvi). This view of human nature and agency mandated a new emphasis in rhetorical inquiry, a focus on character in the context of practical discursive communities: "what is thus demanded by the principle of systematic assent is more rigorous thought than is customary about who 'we' are, the axiological experts whose shared experience confirms what we know together" (108).

This rhetorical redefinition of the self, departing from modernist dogmas of both scientism and irrationalism, led to a consequent shift in the object of ethical criticism. "Most modern critics who have attempted any kind of ethical criticism," Booth acknowledges, "have sought ways of judging the effects of literary works on the lives of their readers—what modern jargon would call after-effects" ("George Eliot" 4); granting such empirical studies their place but noting their extraordinary difficulties, Booth offers an alternative:

> to shift our attention from consequences to qualities of experience sought or achieved by authors and readers *during the time* of reading or listening. Instead of asking whether this book or poem or play will make me a better person after I put it down, we might ask whether we can describe with any precision what sort of relation I have with it *before* I put it down. ("George Eliot" 5–6)

Booth's concern is with the quality of life lived in the company we keep with a work's implied author,[2] an ethically relevant concern because, "insofar as the fiction has *worked* for us, we have lived with its values for the duration: we have been *that kind of person* for at least as long as we remained in the presence of the work."[3]

One of the novelties of Booth's approach is that by this nonconsequentialist focus, he resists the modernist separation of description from evaluation practiced both by the scientismist (who emphasizes description and dismisses evaluation, at least as a form of knowledge) and by the irrationalist (who privileges the latter and disdains the former, at least as morally relevant). Such divisions and dismissals make little sense for a mode of analysis that is "practiced by *characters* who have been to some degree formed by the sort of thing they are judging, using a range of mental powers that will have been already affected by the narrative being judged" ("Ethical Criticism" 291); that is, for an ethical study that is in some part inescapably *reflexive*. But such a study must just as inescapably take into account the implied audience, its values, and their evolution over the reading of the piece. Booth is not utterly dismissing effects. He is, rather, reshaping our concepts of what counts as an effect in the ongoing rhetorical reconstitution of our own characters, and redirecting our notions about which of these effects are relevant for our study so as to include "not only the effects on listeners . . . but also the effects on tellers themselves." Because narrative ethics are inescapably *reciprocal,* as "any story told with genuine engagement will affect its teller fully as much as it affects listeners," we must expand our range of critical vision to consider both parties in every narrative exchange—both implied audience and implied author. "When we do that we discover a surprising range of responsibilities that might be explored" ("Ethical Criticism" 292).

Those responsibilities emerge in the *ethos of rhetoric* constituted and enacted between implied author and implied audience. I use *ethos* here not in the technical Aristotelian sense familiar to rhetorical critics, to refer to the character of the speaker as projected in the speech; rather, I refer to the underlying and distinctive character of a practical community, its constitutive and ongoing way of life—more precisely in this case, its distinctive and characterizing *way of life in language*. These Boothian concepts—the self as a field of selves, the nonconsequentialist focus, and the vision of narrative ethics as a reflexive, reciprocal activity—can generate at least an approach, if not a full-blown critical methodology, for how such a range might be explored.

ETHICAL CRITICISM

So what does an ethical criticism based on Boothian insights into narrative do, exactly? First, we know we are to explore how character is shaped in the field of selves shared by author and audience; it might be slightly more precise here to say "*implied* author" and "*implied* audience," but remember that it is Booth's premise that insofar as the rhetoric works for us, we live with and enact those values, and thus we become that kind of person for at least as long as we are engaged with the text. In such an ethical criticism, further, we are to focus not primarily on the measuring of effects, but on describing with intersubjectively testable precision the way of life constituted and enacted, the quality of life lived while we are the kind of people, communicators, and moral agents whom the text invites and teaches us to be—the kind of people who take its starting point as our own, who move as we must move and who stop our interpretive deconstructions and reconstructions where we must stop if the text is to have its full intended effect. And finally, in such an ethical criticism we must take into account narrative's reciprocal and reflexive nature; we must take into account how the stories, as embedded in and constitutive of a way of life, affect both their teller and their listeners. Tellers and listeners are human characters, to some degree inescapably shaped by the sort of thing which they are both judging and participating in; indeed, reshaped continuously by their processes of participation and judgment, depending on a range of intellectual and moral powers inescapably touched and triggered by experiencing the narrative that also is their object.

Ethical criticism based on these principles—and this is one of the features that makes it distinctive in both contemporary ethical and rhetorical thought—unites the descriptive with the evaluative. If we follow Booth, we would begin by doing the best—by which he means the most intersubjectively verifiable—job possible in describing the text as an action. That is to say, in saying how the text acts, we must locate the means the text uses to constitute and enact its rhetorical relation with the intended audience. Then we must go on to describe the possibilities and limits of such a relation—but not, of course, exclusively in terms the critic imposes from outside the text, rather as ethical terms held in common with the audience of the criticism and affected by the experience of the text. We must describe the world of perception, choice, and action encountered in the text, seeing and evaluating as the text permits and enables us to do. For it must be our aim as ethical critics of this kind to articulate the moral possibilities and limits of this particular ethos of rhetoric; to describe (and inevitably, by our very choice of descriptive terms, to begin to evaluate) what it is like to live, move, and grow in this way of life in language, in the practice of seeing and saying things this way.

There is another way of putting this: Booth's contribution to the ethical criticism of American public discourse is to prompt us to clarify and criticize the *ken* of the discourse—the moral vision in terms of which the world may be seen and characterized for purposes of decision and action. As ethical critics, we must analyze the text's characteristic terms of description and evaluation, and explain how they work with one another to create the text's constitutive lines of argument, and to rank-order the possibilities for appeal and intersection of motive. This requires us to examine the language in which specific rhetorical situations are to be recognized; the values, assumptions, kinds of attention, and notions of authority with which that language is freighted; the thinkable alternatives for attitude and action therein to be characterized and made determinate for conscious and freely willed choice. It is our task to note how these terms clarify some possibilities (and obscure others) for sustaining or denying, extending or transforming the immediate community of discourse and the wider world of experience in which that discourse is given to operate. By pursuing such concerns, the ethical critic aims to determine what one can and cannot say, can and cannot do, or even aspire to do, through discourse constituted and enacted in the text's characterizing way—to determine who we have to become, in our interactive relations with the author and with the text in its habits of language and dispositions of persuasion, in order to belong and to move appropriately and effectively in the world the text establishes. In short, Booth gives us an ethical criticism uniquely concerned with character as it is realized in author and audience "dancing together the dance" of the text.

What is distinctive about this sort of ethical criticism is that in its own practice it remains persistently rhetorical—uniting value and fact, uniting critical evaluation to sharable, testable, improvable description of the text and of its ethos of rhetoric. For that ethos has a kind of recoverable public existence, an existence that may be the object not only of personal response, but also (and in a prior way) of sharable description and reasoned critical debate—intersubjective testing that itself becomes a matter of character, an influence on how we may hear and tell stories, and how we may draw from them practical public conclusions.

The proof of any criticism, especially rhetorical criticism of public address, lies in what it can reveal about texts. In the hard case of Martin Luther King, Jr.'s "Pilgrimage to Nonviolence," ethical criticism becomes less a mode of passing judgment—the kind of verdict that usually reveals more about the critic than the object criticized—than a mode of noticing and explicating issues of character in understanding and evaluating the text.[4]

MAKING KING'S PILGRIMAGE

Ethical criticism based on the principles that Booth has made available would seem a particularly appropriate and promising approach to studying the rhetoric of the civil rights movement, since the movement drew so much of its remarkable (one might even call it transformatory and reconstitutive) persuasive force from moral appeals—not only in how it "talked its talk," but in how it "walked its walk" true to its principles. This also seems true of Dr. King in a variety of ways; for example, King's willingness to accept arrest was itself symbolic and persuasive, an expression of respect for democracy in general and American public opinion in particular, a kind of living appeal to conscience while being an unflinching enactment of its call to nonviolence. Surely Dr. King had vivid stories to tell, of confrontations, jailings, beatings, narrow escapes, radiant triumphs. But were one to select a King discourse particularly likely to demonstrate the insights of ethical criticism, "Pilgrimage to Nonviolence" would not be an obvious choice. However, employing ethical criticism enables us to see how "Pilgrimage" tells a character-shaping story, a story after which neither King nor the movement—nor, perhaps, the reader and critic of the movement—can ever be quite the same.

While "Pilgrimage to Nonviolence" does tell a story of sorts, it does not directly concern King's colorful public life; rather, by the way it asks its audiences to read in order to understand and appreciate it, it breaks down whatever distinctions between the *vita activa* and the *vita contemplativa* its intended audiences might bring to the reading. This essay is an account of his intellectual journey toward an idea that at least one critic has described as the most important contribution to American intellectual history since Dewey, at a minimum: the idea of nonviolent action.[5] Originally appearing in 1958 as a chapter in his *Stride Toward Freedom: The Montgomery Story*, it might have seemed a curiosity:

an uncharacteristically scholarly and unblushingly abstruse disquisition about the relative merits of such esoteric thinkers as Niebuhr, Jaspers, Kierkegaard, Nietzsche, Heidegger, Sartre, and Rauschenbusch, appearing anomalously in the middle of a rousing story of one of the most interesting episodes in King's life. Revised for publication in 1960 in the journal of theology and social ethics *Christian Century,* it might have seemed a little like preaching quite literally to the choir. Both kinds of audiences needed to learn how to read such a peculiar narrative; an ethical criticism of "Pilgrimage to Nonviolence" reveals how King taught such readers by moving them through a narrative that in several ways embodied and enacted its own message.

The story begins with King himself at a formative learning stage, in theological seminary. There he is torn, not only intellectually but morally, between the "rather strict fundamentalist tradition" ("Pilgrimage" 35) in which he was raised, and the liberal theology in which he was being trained. Each tradition was "inadequate both for the church and for personal life"; each proved inadequate in the crucible of moral experience—much as, perhaps, King's readers may have found themselves torn between hopeful philosophy and unbending reality. Fundamentalism "fell into a mood of antirationalism ... stressing a narrow, uncritical biblicism"; it was "too pessimistic" in defining man "only in terms of his existential nature, his capacity for evil." Liberalism was "all too sentimental concerning human nature and ... leaned toward a false idealism" in coming to terms with "the complexity of human motives and the reality of sin on every level of man's existence"; in displaying a "superficial optimism concerning human nature," liberalism "failed to see that reason by itself is little more than an instrument to justify ... distortions and rationalizations." In short, "an adequate understanding of man is found neither in the thesis of liberalism nor in the antithesis of neo-orthodoxy, but in a synthesis which reconciles the truths of both" (36). And it is just here in the text that King enacts the importance of this intellectual quest, this characteristic quest for synthesis.

Fundamentalism seemed to King to accept the unacceptable, to tolerate the intolerable ravages of bigotry in this life, overemphasizing the "better world" beyond. "Any religion that professes to be concerned about the souls of men and is not concerned about the slums that damn them, the economic conditions that strangle them and the social conditions that cripple them is a spiritually moribund religion awaiting burial." But liberalism's optimism about the prospects of change underestimated not only the tactical problems of politics, but the deeper problem of intractable evil in human hearts, which drove King to suspect that "the 'turn the other cheek' philosophy and the 'love your enemies' philosophy," the very Gospel itself, had only a limited practical application, that "when racial groups and nations are in conflict a more realistic approach is necessary" (38).

King's audiences came at this narrative from different directions, each with their own blind spots; King was asking of each a new ken, a new kind of reading activity, calling on new sorts of personal resources from each. The scholars were used to dealing with and assessing ideas as such; indeed, it must have seemed to them circuitous to confront ideas in an explicit narrative rather than in what would have seemed to them the more straightforward form of a treatise. King asked them now to examine those ideas as they would be embodied in human events, and to care about their outcomes. The members of the popular audience on the other hand were no doubt ready to read about events in the story of civil rights; King asked them now to inquire about how those events could be perceived and interpreted with greater moral insight if put in the context of deeper philosophical questions. In other words, to catch the full meaning and force of King's story of synthesis, these different audiences had to perform a synthesis themselves: each had to animate their concerns with the concerns of the other, each had to exercise new personal resources of empathy in order to read on.

At that point King explains how he himself had performed his synthesis, how he had been taught to perform it by his intellectual and practical engagement with Gandhi's philosophy of *satyagraha* (quite literally a synthesis: "truth-force or love-force"). King came to terms with it first intellectually; however committed the members of the civil rights movement might be to their activity, to appreciate its origins and its hold on their leader they had to learn to see their cause as informed with a truthful philosophy that needed to be struggled with and thought about. But at first King "had a merely intellectual understanding" (38). However scholarly the theologians might be about their philosophy, to appreciate the force of that "merely" they had to become interested in King's forceful enactment of his ideas, at Montgomery and beyond.

King goes on to discuss practical applications of Gandhi's philosophy about which Gandhi had not directly spoken: the implications of nonviolence on international relations in a nuclear age, and the reality of a personal God. The story of King's learning to read Gandhi only reaches a conclusion that is to be regarded as satisfying when it becomes a story of how he extended those ideas to new intellectual problems and new fields of human endeavor and experience. Our story of learning to read the pilgrimage to nonviolence—King's journey, and our own—cannot find a satisfactory ending in merely changing others' hearts: "it first does something to the hearts and souls of those committed to it. It gives them new self-respect; it calls up resources of strength and courage that they did not know they had"; and ultimately, it reaches out to the other so that synthesis may occur, and "reconciliation becomes a reality" (39).

"Pilgrimage to Nonviolence" is a pivotal text for the character of the civil rights movement and of King's work in particular, and ethical criticism can help us see how. Afterward, the movement could never be the same, for it was now made accountable, not only for its pragmatic effectiveness but its intellectual content and moral character. But at a time when "discerning the subject" has become more complicated—and the very notion of *agency*, that seems essential to the history of rhetoric and potentially important in some form to retrieve, is a region of theoretical controversy—Booth's ethical criticism brings even more within our ken: it opens a path for critical inquiry and discourse that can recover some sense of subjectivity, can as it were relocate it in the ethical field of texts and readers, from which self is continuously constituted and reconstituted.

By examining the author's self as a field of selves, we find that King, by becoming the storyteller of the pilgrimage, could never be the same either, henceforward being bound to practice a kind of leadership that synthesized expediential concerns with philosophical ones. By approaching the ethos of rhetoric practiced in this text nonconsequentially, we can appreciate the kind of engagement it offers and the qualities that mark and characterize it.

But in practicing narrative ethics as a reflexive, reciprocal activity, the readers of "Pilgrimage"—at least the readers who have moved with the text, and done all they had to do to understand and appreciate its suasive effects fully in the way they were intended—are also changed. Having performed these syntheses, having called on new resources of strength and courage and empathy, they are readied to extend those powers to new areas of their experience. Learning to read "Pilgrimage to Nonviolence" enacts, at least for the time of engagement with the text, a way of life in language that prepares its readers to make similar pilgrimages in their own lives. We can describe and appreciate the importance of this text because Booth has equipped us with an ethical criticism focused on the capacities of character realized in the author and audience dancing together the dance of the text.

Notes

1. Perhaps the most important recent move in this direction has been Walter Fisher's articulation of "the narrative paradigm," along with the critical responses it has stimulated. See Walter R. Fisher, *Human Communication as Narration: Toward a Philosophy of Reason, Value and Action* (Columbia: U of South Carolina P, 1987). See also Barbara Warnick, "The Narrative Paradigm: Another Story," *Quarterly Journal of Speech* 73 (1987): 172–82, and Robert C. Rowland, "Narrative: Mode of Discourse or Paradigm?" *Communication Monographs* 54 (1987): 264–75.

2. See especially *The Rhetoric of Fiction,* part 2, "The Author's Voice in Fiction."

3. Booth, "Ethical Criticism," 291–92. In this way he has much in common with James Boyd White's concern with "textual community," but I take it to be one of Booth's distinctive and more richly implicative contributions for the study of narrative ethics to characterize them as reflexive and reciprocal. See James Boyd White, *When Words Lose Their Meaning: Constitutions and Reconstitutions of Language, Character and Community* (Chicago: U of Chicago P, 1984), especially 14–20. It would be fair to characterize my critical enterprise as an attempt to elaborate what seems to public address scholars still somehow implicit (and what has been in any case still largely unexamined) in the important work of Booth and White, and to make their contributions more clearly relevant and readily usable in the analysis of public address. To the extent that I would claim an original contribution, it would be in adapting the focus of ethical criticism from individual texts to larger bodies of materials of various kinds over time and changing circumstance.

4. The rhetorical critic Edwin Black, in "The Second Persona," has described an essential difficulty with current forms of ethical criticism: "the moral judgment of a text is a portentious act in the process of criticism, and ... the terminal character of such a judgment works to close critical discussion rather than open or encourage it" (109). I discuss this difficulty and the possibilities that Booth and James Boyd White provide for circumventing it in "Discursive Community and the Problem of Perspective in Ethical Criticism," in *Conversations on Communication Ethics,* ed. Karen Joy Greenberg (Northwood, IL: Ablex, 1991).

5. The critic in question was myself, at the Speech Communication Association's January 1988 Conference on the Oratory of Dr. Martin Luther

King, Jr., in a presentation entitled "When 'Silence is Betrayal' ": An Ethical Criticism of the Revolution of Values in Martin Luther King's Speech at the Riverside Church"; and in "Remembering Martin Luther King, Jr.," in the *Iowa City Press-Citizen* 20 Jan. 1988: 3A.

Bibliography

Black, Edwin. "The Second Persona." *Quarterly Journal of Speech* 56 (1970): 109–19.

Booth, Wayne C. *Modern Dogma and the Rhetoric of Assent*. Notre Dame, IN: U of Notre Dame P, 1974; Chicago: U of Chicago P, 1974.

———. *The Rhetoric of Fiction*. Chicago: U of Chicago P, 1961; 2nd ed., 1983.

———. " 'The Way I Loved George Eliot': Friendship with Books a Neglected Critical Metaphor." *Kenyon Review* n.s. 2 (1980): 4–27.

———. 'Why Ethical Criticism Fell on Hard Times." *Ethics* 98 (1988): 278–93. Rpt. in *The Company We Keep: An Ethics of Fiction*. Berkeley: U of California P, 1988, 25–48.

King, Martin Luther, Jr. "Pilgrimage to Nonviolence." *A Testament of Hope: The Essential Writings of Martin Luther King, Jr.* Ed. James M. Washington. New York: Harper, 1986.

IV

Booth across Disciplines

10

"Three Times out of Five Something Happens": James M. Cain and the Ethics of Music

PETER J. RABINOWITZ

IN JAMES M. CAIN's 1937 novel *Serenade,* the down-and-out narrator John Howard Sharp arrives in Acapulco with his mistress, a prostitute named Juana Montes, to help her open a brothel. But even before a fit of sexual jealousy encourages him to punch out one of the town's leading politicos (at which point he finds himself a wanted man), he decides he wants to get away; and at a local hotel, he comes across a feisty ship captain who might be able to smuggle him across the border. To get his help, of course, Sharp needs to *prove* himself; and in a traditional and highly coded macho confrontation, parallel to the one between Robin Hood and Little John, his worthiness is put to the test. But despite the reference to "feinting and jabbing" (62), it is a verbal rather than a physical sparring. More significant, the subject is neither sports, nor politics, nor sex, although the style used is appropriate for such topics. Rather, the struggle climaxes in a dispute over the relative merits of Mozart and Beethoven—and Sharp wins the argument (and hence saves his life) by tossing off the serenade from *Don Giovanni* ("Deh vieni alla finestra"), accompanying himself on a guitar that he borrows from a *mariachi.*

Cain, author of the notoriously successful *Postman Always Rings Twice* (1934), is of course remembered as one of the toughest of those tough writers that Edmund Wilson called "the boys in the back room."

The *New York Times* review by Harold Strauss that helped launch *Postman* claimed that "Cain can get down to the primary impulses of greed and sex in fewer words than any writer we know of"; and David Madden, besting that *Times* reviewer's characterization of Cain as a six-minute egg, dubbed him the "twenty-minute egg of the hard-boiled school" (*James M. Cain* 23). Indeed, he's so tough that even Raymond Chandler dismissed him as "the offal of literature": "Everything he touches smells like a billygoat" (qtd. in Madden, *Cain's Craft* 6). Given this reputation for toughness, given the plot situation, and given the language, "Deh vieni alla finestra" is sufficiently incongruous that one might at first suspect irony. But while the hard-boiled label helped market Cain, over the years he found it an increasing hindrance. In a letter to Alfred Knopf, he protested that "Being tough or hard-boiled is the last thing in the world that I think about. . . . I am shooting for something quite different" (qtd. in Hoopes 256). And in the preface to *The Butterfly* he warned his readers, "I belong to no school, hard-boiled or otherwise, and I believe these so-called schools exist mainly in the imagination of critics, and have little correspondence in reality anywhere else" (352).

Indeed, Chandler may have been closer to the truth than he thought when he knocked Cain as "a Proust in greasy overalls" (qtd. in Madden, *Cain's Craft* 6). For like Proust, Cain was not only obsessed with sexuality, but also with music. Indeed, Cain considered his writing career a "consolation prize" failing as an opera singer (qtd. in Hoopes xii), and singing figures as the central subject in three of his best novels, and as a subsidiary concern in many of the others. Even the mobster Sol Caspar, in *Love's Lovely Counterfeit* (Cain's icy equivalent of Hammett's *The Glass Key*), takes time out from running the rackets in Lake City to assess a new recording of *Il Trovatore*. And what I would like to argue here is that, if treated seriously, Cain's novels can offer valuable insights into the relationship between music and ethics.

That vexed relationship, of course, has been explored by a wide variety of theorists from Plato onward. But as Wayne Booth points out, no one has yet come close to a "full *ethical* criticism" of music (*Company* 19, italics in original). What might that entail? Ethical analysis is always an analysis of actions, not of objects. As Booth's rhetorical analyses since *The Rhetoric of Fiction* have continually made clear, there is thus no way to talk seriously about literary ethics simply by looking at the doctrines espoused in a text, without taking into account the *transaction* between author and reader. Similarly, while it might be possible to produce an ethics of composition or an ethics of performance, such study would inevitably be subsidiary to an ethics of listening—in particular, a study of the way musical meaning is tied, not simply to abstract shapes, but to the rhetorical dynamics through which works of art "change" us (*Modern Dogma* 165). Booth himself, in his occasional forays into music, invariably takes this position. Thus, for instance, one of his discussions of "what art teaches" starts with a "mental experiment" that attempts to unpack the experiences of listening carefully to Beethoven's A Minor Quartet (*Modern Dogma* 168–80).

But although Booth, in his stress on reception, points clearly in the right direction, he has never explored the dynamics of listening with anything like the scrutiny he has applied to the dynamics of reading—especially the increasingly contextualized notion of reading that has come to ground some of his later work.[1] What follows, then, is not so much an analysis of Booth, nor even a debate with him, but rather an expansion beyond his work, asking what kind of insights we might gain if we treated the process of listening with the same kind of detailed attention, say, that Booth gives the process of reading irony in *A Rhetoric of Irony*.

It is perhaps not surprising that Booth has not taken this next step, for until recently *most* theorists of music—whether they have praised music for its ethical benefits, blamed it for its corruptive influence, sorted it out into various ethical categories, or steadfastly refused to admit its ethical dimensions at all—have started with questionable postulates that have deflected our attention from the complexities of listening. In particular, they have tended to assume that, as W. J. Henderson put it in a once-popular guide, the best music "exercises her sway upon us wholly by means of her own unaided powers" (87).[2] Of course, not everyone is so flowery; but for all the differences in vocabulary and style, Henderson, in this regard, is not far distant from Leonard Meyer or Milton Babbitt.[3] That is, all of these theorists skim over, or at least fail to develop, that process of mediation through which the composer's acts are transformed by the listener. In this context, it is perhaps not surprising that Booth too, even though he is not unaware of this intermediate process, is apt, like Henderson and Meyer, to treat it as outside the realm of his analysis, as if, like the best digital–analog processing, it were for all practical purposes a self-canceling coding-decoding procedure.

Thus, it is not, as it might at first appear, a hubristic claim when he tells us that "listening well [to Bach], totally engrossed in the musical moment, Bach and I—the implied Bach and the postulated listener—

become indistinguishable" (*Critical Understanding* 238).⁴ Rather, this vision of unity is but the logical consequence of bracketing the complexity and variety of the mediation between listener and music—of assuming, as he puts it, that "music does not offer me as many invitations [as literature does] to create epicycles of meaning on my very own" (*Critical Understanding* 238) and of assuming, as well, that "whether all such meanings [of detailed musical structural relationships] are conventional and learned, or (as I believe) some are innate and universal, the repertoire of such 'reasons of art' possessed by everyone in a given culture, in advance of any one experience, is immense" (*Modern Dogma* 169).

In going beyond Booth, I would like to complicate this model by asking what the process of listening would look like if we don't assume that those "invitations to create epicycles of meaning" are negligible and if we look, not at the shared repertoire of interpretive procedures, but at the points where cultural agreement breaks down. In other words, I would like to propose that listening, no less than performing (or reading), is an *interpretive* act, and that like any other interpretive act, it is always grounded in mediating principles that are both ideologically charged and contextually variable. I will be using Cain's novels in my case study to illustrate the process of listening; but before turning to them, I need to respond to the traditional assumptions of theorists of music with some countertheorizing, specifically by setting out a musical distinction that Jay Reise and I have developed in detail elsewhere.⁵

As Reise and I conceptualize it, the act of listening involves the braiding together of three separate strands. The first is what we call the *technical,* and it consists of only those elements that are specifically represented in the notation—or, in the case of un-notated music, those elements that would be captured by a transcriber. Statements about the technical level would include, for instance, "The first note of Scott Joplin's *Maple Leaf Rag* is an eighth-note octave E-flat on the second half of the second beat of a measure." To a large extent, traditional analysis has assumed that the technical component is the totality of the music. It is this assumption, for instance, that supports Alan Walker's claims not only that meaning is inherent in the notes, but that quality is inherent as well ("You need not prove that the *Eroica* symphony is a masterpiece before you can be certain that it is a masterpiece . . . : its mastery is self-evident") (xii).

In fact, though, the technical is only the raw material of the music. In and of itself, for instance, it has no hierarchy of importance, no shape, no content, no symbolic force. To put it more sharply, on its own the technical is meaningless—which is why we are generally disoriented when we hear pieces from radically different cultures. Despite the long tradition of theorizing to the contrary, listeners can only make sense (and I would like to stress the act of "making" here) of the technical in combination with what Reise and I call the *attributive,* a second component of the listening process that assigns (or proposes) meanings (in the broadest sense), a component that is inevitably extracompositional (usually even what traditionalists would call "extramusical"), a component that is always at least provisionally in place before the act of listening begins.

Many types of information coexist on the attributive level, but they can be loosely divided into two categories, what Reise and I call codes and mythologies. *Codes* consist of "regulations" of conventional behavior, and are often arrived at through statistical analysis. Harmonic practice, at least during Western classical music's common practice period, is especially subject to codification.[6] But for my purposes here, the second type of attributive information, the mythological, is more relevant. The *mythological* consists of the verbal discourse and the other cultural apparatus that surrounds and in a sense grounds the experience of the music in question. It includes, for instance, the stories about Beethoven raging against his deafness, stories that help determine, before we start to listen, what kind of stance we will take toward the music. Many music-appreciation analyses of "sonata form" (especially those couched in narrative terms, which often assign gender roles to various themes) are, despite their apparent stress on technical matters, mythological in spirit. Performance practice, too, is a part of the mythological—as are the systems, such as Schenker's, that provide the philosophical underpinnings for the claims made for particular analyses or analytic techniques.[7]

Especially in its more overt forms, the mythological makes many contemporary musicians uneasy. Ernst Krenek went so far as to try to exorcise it completely, calling on composers "to avoid the dictations of such ghosts" as "recollection, tradition, training, and experience" (90). Milton Babbitt is an even more fiery ghostbuster. He takes as his example the sentence (unattributed, but taken from a work by Paul Henry Lang) "There can be no question that in many of Mendelssohn's works there is missing that real depth that opens wide perspectives, the mysticism of the unutterable." Such a "verbal act," Babbitt insists, should not "be allowed"—indeed "a book containing a sentence such as this [should not be saved] from the flames" (11).[8]

But Babbitt's incendiary arguments light up serious misconceptions about the nature of what we are calling mythological discourse. He sets himself up in opposition to any utterances in which there is "virtually nothing to be communicated." In theory, of course, it is hard to take issue with such a wholesome (albeit Quixotic) position. But in practice, his argument depends on the assumption that "responsible normative discourse" is synonymous with "cognitive communication"—which is in turn equated with empirically verifiable statements (11). That is, he depends on the assumption that the only valid form of communication is through the kind of speech act that J. L. Austin called *constatives*, "'statement[s]' [that] 'describe' some state of affairs, or . . . 'state some fact,' which [they] must do either truly or falsely" (1). In fact, however, the statement about Mendelssohn is more properly viewed as what Austin calls a *performative* (an utterance that performs an act rather than describes a situation), specifically as an *advisory*.[9] That is, instead of describing a state of affairs, Lang's sentence offers a framework within which to make sense of and evaluate Mendelssohn's art.

Babbitt's complaint that such statements are nonfalsifiable, while undeniable, thus has no bearing on the issue. For to judge the legitimacy of the sentence, we need to assess not its "truth" but its utility: its ability to provide a grid that can help guide and support listeners as they attribute meaning (or, in this case, a lack of a certain kind of meaning) to the music at hand. The same holds true, as I have suggested, even for many supposedly formalist statements that appear on the surface to be descriptions of what is "objectively there" on the technical level: they too, more often than not, turn out to be not descriptions at all, but advisories in formal attire. Whatever his claims to the contrary, Alan Walker's complex thematic analyses do not in fact reveal a preexisting unity within the "masterpieces" he discusses. Rather, they *attribute* unity to them, to persuade us to hear them in the same way he does.

Although listeners can switch or merge attributions (even during listening), attributive screens are only available if they precede the particular act of listening. Likewise, the technical is always in place before the act of listening begins; even in improvised music, the performer decides what sounds to play before the audience hears them. Where is the activity of the listener in all of this? Listening is an active process: although it requires both the technical and the attributive, their mere presence only make the music potentially available. It is up to the listener to *apply* (whether self-consciously or not) attributive screens to the technical material at hand in order to transform it into a particular listening experience. Reise and I call this the *synthetic* level.[10]

The difference between the levels can be seen as follows: "The next-to-last chord of Joplin's *Crush Collision March* (reduced to closed position) is FACE♭" is a statement about the technical level; "*Crush Collision* is a turn-of-the-century parlor piece ending in B♭ major, and in that context, such a dominant seventh chord is most likely to be followed by a tonic" is an attributive statement; "On hearing that dominant seventh, I expect a B♭ major chord to follow" is a synthetic conclusion drawn from the application of attributive information to technical facts. The lines between technical, attributive, and synthetic, of course, are imprecise: one listener's synthetic activities, for instance, can become part of the attributive information for another listener, or even for that same listener at a different time. Despite the smudged boundaries, however, these distinctions, as we will see, are of considerable analytic use.

What does all this have to do with ethics? If our analysis is correct, then, *even when talking about music without texts,* "the music itself" (especially the music *as listened to*) is not to be found in the sounds on their own, but in a complex interaction between sounds and the discursive practices that surround them and open up their potential for meaning. And whatever the ethical dimension of that raw sonic material, those *discursive practices* are inevitably ethical in Booth's broad sense of the term, which refers not simply to morals or to "the approved side of choices," but rather to "the entire range of effects on the 'character' or 'person' or 'self' " (*Company* 8). In other words, the ethical dimension of music should be sought not in the technical, but rather in the attributive and the synthetic. For regardless of what, if anything, the music teaches us that we could not otherwise know (*Modern Dogma* 169), and regardless of whether we are, in the long run, "better" because we have been exposed to Bach, the attributive and synthetic levels, by their very nature, require us to engage in one or another kind of ethically implicated practice before and while we listen. And Cain's novels, because they provide such highly charged examples of how attributive screens and synthetic strategies operate, give us a sharpened vision of the way listening is intertwined with ethics.

Cain might seem an unlikely source of insight into the ethical grounding of so-called absolute (that is, non-texted) music, for his musical interest is directed primarily to opera—and this preference would seem to sneak the problem of texts back into our discussion. In fact, though, while Cain writes extensively about operas, he hardly ever touches on their texts. Indeed, he seems to hold opera plots in contempt: when Columbia Pictures asked him for a film script to star Rita Hayworth in *Carmen,* one of his favorite operas, his response was blunt: "It is a skimpy, dated little tale, and considerable work would have to be done to it to explain why Columbia Pictures Corporation saw fit to bring up the subject in connection with Rita Hayworth in this year 1945" (qtd. in Hoopes 377).[11]

Why was Cain so consumed with music? In part, I suspect, it was the result of nostalgia for his lost career, or for his opera-singer mother. But he also had an aim that makes his work especially valuable for my project. Like most of us, he wanted to offer (and perhaps justify) what he loved to those he respected; and opera, he felt, was the property of the wrong crowd.[12] As John Dillon notes in *The Moth,* "There's something about a guy who uses steel that goes for football more than he does opera" (215). Conversely, in Cain's eyes opera audiences were dominated by the decadent: by the "gray-haired women with straight haircuts and men's dinner jackets, young girls looking each other straight in the eye and not caring what you thought, boys following men around" that we see attending Winston Hawes's concerts in *Serenade* (131); by the woman "that goes to concerts because they give her the right vibrations, or make her feel better, or have some other effect on her nitwit insides" (*Serenade* 128); by the Social Register types who were "so cultured that even their eyeballs were lavender" (*Career* 4). In other words, opera audiences are effete in ways that link to both class and sexuality.

Cain's perceptions do not come out of nowhere; they replay familiar myths about opera, class, and sexuality. They may have their origins, in part, in the ambiguities of gender introduced by the castrati of early Italian opera. Certainly, in the Anglo-American tradition, these myths go back to the early eighteenth century, and the works of Defoe, Swift, and especially Pope, who was particularly concerned with opera's breakdown of clear sexual difference.[13] It is found, as well, in the portrayal of Maggie and Jiggs's responses to opera in George McManus's long-running comic strip *Bringing Up Father,* a portrayal that neatly illustrates Herbert Gans's claim that while "high culture condemns popular culture as vulgar and pathological," popular culture can counterattack by insisting that high culture is "overly intellectual, snobbish, and effeminate" (43). Things haven't changed much in the past sixty or seventy years: the same image of opera as effete, pretentious, and unfit for men showed up a few years back [March 4, 1990] on *The Simpsons.* Indeed, even Catherine Clément, who should know better, falls into gay-bashing when her anger at opera audiences is aroused.[14]

The issue, of course, is not whether Cain's sociological analysis of the interconnections of culture, class, and sexuality is correct. The point, rather, is that Cain tries to remedy the perceived problem by proposing *an alternative way of listening,* one that is straight, masculine, and working class. Or, to put it more accurately, he tries to come up with a set of attributive strategies that is consistent with what he believes to be the worldview of the working-class guy who uses steel and goes for football. And the resulting strategies provide an especially vivid illustration of the ways in which ethics and listening intersect.

Cain's musical aesthetics snuggle up against the "art for art's sake" tradition (he criticizes producers who haven't yet understood that singing might be "good for its own sake") (*Serenade* 99), but the object under scrutiny is almost always a *performance.* That is, for Cain, you don't listen to music in the abstract, but rather to a particular act of music making. When he describes an operatic event, he's directing our attention neither toward the relationships among the characters, nor toward what traditional music analysis would call the music's eternal formal properties. Instead, he proposes a set of interpretive strategies through which a performance can be redefined and made comprehensible.

As I have argued in *Before Reading,* literary interpretive strategies fall into four basic categories: what I've called rules of notice (which tell us where to focus our attention), rules of signification (which allow us to draw the meaning from particular elements), rules of configuration (which allow us to predict the future course of events), and rules of coherence (which allow us to ascribe generalized meaning to the completed experience of the work). Such procedures are not exclusively "literary"; they have analogs in other arts, as well. In particular, the scheme is useful for charting out the synthetic activities of listening, and I would therefore like to use it to clarify what synthetic activities Cain is proposing. And since the core of Cain's attributive screen is found in his recommendations for acts of signification, I will start there. Cain offers two major strategies of signification: he equates meaning and technique, and he equates voice and body.

The first strategy advises us to judge musical events less in terms of so-called musical expression than in terms of virtuosity. Not for Cain's stars is the slow, painful process of spiritual self-discovery undergone by Thea Kronborg in Willa Cather's *Song of the Lark;* the quality of your musicality has little to do with the quality of your soul.[15] It is consistent with this virtuosic vision that Cain's best singers are immediately recognizable, and that they learn quickly. Once coloratura Veda Pierce is discovered by her teacher Treviso—who can measure her singing talent simply by hearing her hum a few bars of Schubert on her way home after a concert (*Mildred* 212–13)—she emerges as a great singer in just a few months.

Because Cain is concerned with the meaning of an event, not an object, the virtuosity involves the ability to handle not only the demands of the written music, but also whatever unanticipated difficulties arise out of external circumstances. A good singer, Sharp points out, "can spot trouble a mile away" (*Serenade* 90)—and can improvise his or her way around it. When the scheduled Escamillo backs out of a Hollywood Bowl *Carmen,* Sharp can jump into the role without preparation—even though he has to sing some music added to the opera in order to accommodate a local ballet school. Since the interpolated music comes from *L'Arlésienne*—and was not even originally scored for voice—he has never sung it before; he consequently sails past a repeat. "The dancers were all frozen on one foot, ready to do the routine again, and there was I, camped on an E that didn't even belong there." But he shows his musicianship in the way he handles the crisis: the conductor "looked up, and I caught his eye, and hung on to it, and marched all around with it, while he spoke to his men and wigwagged to his ballerina. Then he looked up again, and I cut, and yelled 'Ha, ha, ha.' He brought his stick down, and the show was together again" (*Serenade* 93–94).

But besides valuing virtuosity, Cain also believes deeply in the sensuality of the human voice, and he proposes a second set of synthetic strategies to enable his readers to interpret that sensuality in a way that he thinks will appeal to them, equating voice and body, often through fairly direct analogy. "What makes a great voice," notes Sharp, "is beauty, not size, and beauty will get you, I don't care if it's in a man's throat or a woman's leg" (*Serenade* 77). Consequently, in Cain's novels voice often becomes the locus of the erotic. Indeed, *Mildred Pierce* ends as clumsily as it does because of Cain's fixation on the voice he had created. The "keystone" of the novel is "the implication of having a big coloratura soprano in the family" (qtd. in Hoopes 348) and the story pivots around Veda, a singer whose musical talent is equalled only by her moral bankruptcy. At the climax, Veda's mother Mildred learns that her husband has been seduced by her daughter; finding them in bed together, she turns against that crucial throat, strangling the young woman for whose musical advancement she has sacrificed so much, and "destroying," as Cain himself put it, "the one thing she loved most on this earth, Veda's beautiful voice." But Cain could not follow through.

Instead, he engineered an improbable denouement where Veda only pretends to lose her voice to get out of an onerous contract. As he later admitted, "It got the curtain down, but that's about all I can say about it. Believe it or not, I had by that time fallen in love with Veda's totally imaginary voice, and I couldn't bear to think it was permanently gone" (qtd. in Hoopes 309).

Cain's infatuation with so monstrous a character as Veda, a passion so strong that he forfeited the integrity of his novel to preserve her voice, makes it clear that he listens in a way that elevates voice over character, at least over moral character. But if, according to Cain's attributive screen, voice is divorced from moral character, his attempt to counteract High Cultural effeteness leads him to marry it all the more tightly to sexual character. Specifically, Cain gives his own twist to some traditional mythology about the voice. There's a long history, of course, connecting sexuality, variously defined, and vocal quality. Catherine Clément, for instance, summarizes *Phantom of the Opera* as follows: "Voices bring down lights; they do things, they kill. But their power depends on a pitiless chastity" (27). Thus, the soprano will lose her voice (or stop singing) when she becomes married. *Song of the Lark* presents a variation of that theme. So, more distantly, does the legend of Echo, whose reduction to pure voice derives from erotic failure.

None of these stories, of course, would appeal to Cain's intended audience, so he proposes a countermythology, one that explicitly reverses the Echo story (simultaneously conflating it with a distorted reference to the corollary story of Narcissus): in *Serenade,* Sharp is enraptured by the echo of his own voice which—following his crackup—is *restored* precisely through sexual activity. Cain's tough style may cloak his argument in a crudeness that seems laughable in an academic essay. But in fact, his strategic equation of voice and body (especially his emphasis on the throat) bears a striking kinship to the academically respectable strategies in Roland Barthes's "The Grain of the Voice." Barthes privileges the throat over the lung (the lung "swells but gets no erection" [183]), equates "the grain" with "the body in the voice as it sings," and proposes an orgasmics of listening that overlaps considerably with Cain's. "I am determined," notes Barthes, "to listen to my relation with the body of the man or woman singing or playing and that relation is erotic" (188).

Of course, for Cain's intended audience, proper erotic activity is strictly bounded. Indeed, it is precisely the assumed association with homosexuality that helps make opera distasteful. So it is no surprise that Cain and Barthes part company when it comes to the *nature* of the sexual component of listening. Cain insists that you can determine the affectional preference of a singer, at least a male singer, by his voice, and that good singing is congruent with straight sex. As Juana puts it in *Serenade,* men who love other men " 'have no *toro* in high voice, no *grrr* that frighten little *muchacha,* make heart beat fast. Sound like old woman, like cow, like priest' " (*Serenade* 142). Or as Cain puts it himself, a good singer sings "with his balls," and there is a "peculiar color of a homo's voice" (qtd. in Hoopes 266). *Serenade* represents a scandalous version of this myth, for the tale centers around the deterioration of Sharp's voice whenever his homosexual side (the "five per cent" he claims that every man has in him [*Serenade* 144]) is brought out. From the perspective of the 1990s, the novel may seem distastefully homophobic, but (especially considering its historical context) its ambiguities are many. After its publication, Cain found himself attracting numerous gay men who thought he was, as he put it, a "brother" (qtd. in Hoopes 287). More interestingly, Leonard Bernstein (whose sexuality was more complex than Cain thought his own to be) met with Cain in 1948 with the hopes of turning *Serenade* into an opera. The project never materialized, but a few years later Bernstein wrote another work of the same name—a violin concerto based on *The Symposium* and celebrating Platonic love.[16]

Given this traditional masculine approach to signification, Cain's proposed rules of notice, if unconventional, follow readily. Standard guides to music offer varying suggestions about what to listen for, where to direct our primary attention, but more often than not it is something formal, something divorced from the particular performance—melodic contour, or harmonic motion, or contrapuntal structure. Booth, for instance, starts his analysis of the act of listening with the "innumerable detailed structural relationships that must be perceived before even the simplest fragment [of the slow movement of the Beethoven A Minor Quartet] can be experienced" (*Modern Dogma* 169). Cain, in contrast, urges us to give priority to something quite different. First, in terms of the body/voice equation, you listen for the color, for the balls. Second, in terms of the meaning/technique equation, you pay attention to virtuosic difficulties. Thus, in *Career in C Major,* Leonard Borland describes the quartet from *Rigoletto:* "Well, you've heard the Rigoletto quartet a thousand times, but don't let anybody tell you it's a pushover. The first part goes a mile a minute, the second part slower than hell, and if there's one thing harder to sing than a fast allegro it's a slow andante, and three times out of five something happens" (*Career* 108–9). Likewise, we are warned, in *Serenade,* that the interpolated high F-sharp at the end of the *Don Giovanni* serenade is treacherous, because it "catches a baritone all wrong, and makes him sound coarse and ropy" (*Serenade* 119). Thus, as we imagine listening to a particular performance he describes, the traps that await the singers are highlighted.

From this, Cain's proposed rules of configuration also follow readily. When Borland tells us that "three times out of five something happens," the something that happens has little to do with the kinds of events (motivic repetitions, thematic variations, modulations, and returns) that traditional guides to music teach us to anticipate, nor even with what Irving Kolodin calls the quartet's *"dramatic effect"* (170, italics in original). Rather, the something that happens is performative disaster. From this perspective, the repetition of the Duke's opening phrase is anticipated not because of its contribution to formal balance, but because it provides a potential trap for the person singing Maddalena, who might thoughtlessly come in at the wrong time. For Cain, music is less an organic structure than, say, a roller coaster, and anticipation is primarily directed toward the virtuoso challenges that remain. Thus, a Proppian analysis of Cain's narratives might see the operatic performances as functionally equivalent to such activities as driving a train (in *Past All Dishonor*) or drilling for petroleum (*The Moth*): as we look ahead, we steel ourselves for the possibility of a collision or a blowout. It is thus appropriate that Borland's disaster with the *Rigoletto* quartet is described in terms similar to those Cain uses to describe the catastrophic explosion of the oil well John Dillon is managing in *The Moth*. And, as we have seen, how a skilled musician handles those challenges is more a matter of quick thinking and practical know-how than it is of traditional "musicality."

Technical expertise, quick thinking, sexual glamor, stamina, ingenuity, successful negotiation of difficult challenges: these are among Cain's key points of orientation, and they provide the attributions by which he urges us to map the raw sounds into coherent experiences. And this map is consistent with his larger cultural project of making classical music accessible to a broad audience, for the coherence he proposes is both familiar and highly valued. A rite of passage that tests the character of the performers, it is more like a battle or athletic contest than an abstract form of expression or communication.[17] Indeed, the contest exists not only between the performer and the composer, but between the performer and the audience as well. As Cecil Taylor warns Borland, the audience is "'always a pack of hyenas, just waiting to tear in and pull out your vitals, and the only way you can keep them back is to lick them. It's a battle, and you've got to win'" (*Career* 37). Opera is often loosely referred to as a sport.[18] But rarely is that metaphor treated as seriously as it is in Cain. No wonder Sharp compares John McCormack to Ty Cobb (*Serenade* 75)—and no wonder Borland compares himself, after his failure at the Hippodrome, to Georges Carpentier after his defeat at the hands of Jack Dempsey in 1921 (*Career* 112–13).

That strategy of coherence makes good rhetorical sense: since Cain's aim is to open up opera to the guy who uses steel and goes for football, what better way than by showing him (and the masculine term is crucial) that opera and football can be viewed and evaluated according to the same principles? But it is worth looking at some of the ideological baggage this recasting involves. Cain once praised opera singers as "a separate breed" because "opera is ten times as tough as any other challenge to a singer" (qtd. in Hoopes 508). *Toughness* is a loaded term, and it signifies roughly the same thing here that it does in his novels. That is, opera becomes just one more arena in which traditional male American virtues can be demonstrated: the ability to think quickly, to meet challenges, to improvise, to "troupe" (that is, to operate as part of a team).[19] Thus, Sharp is a musical hero because he consistently shows his mettle by doing what has to be done with whatever he's got on hand—for instance, by knocking off the prelude to the last act of *Carmen* on a guitar: "You may think that's impossible," he tells the reader, "but if you play that woodwind stuff up near the bridge, and the rest over the hole, the guitar will give you almost as much of what the music is trying to say as the whole orchestra will" (*Serenade* 15). Likewise, he manages to save a mediocre movie by composing an elaborate five-part overdubbed version of "Git Along Little Dogies" that allows the filmmakers to incorporate some visually spectacular footage of a snowstorm that otherwise wouldn't fit in. It's no wonder that one of Sharp's idols is a man named Harry Luckstone, who insisted that you didn't have to know a song to sing it (93); no wonder, either, that in Hollywood, he is most appreciated by the tech people who, unlike the producers, know what they are doing.

Given his project of opening opera up to guys who like football, it is obvious why Cain found it useful to cast music in such terms—terms with provocative ties to the aesthetics of such American musicians as

Gottschalk and, especially, Ives, and terms with serious implications for both the sexual politics and the class politics that surround high art in America today. But for my purposes here, it is important to see not only the content of Cain's implied ethics, but also its locus: for Cain's novels seriously challenge traditional musical thinking in two ways. First, like any significant analysis of music, Cain's turns out to be not a description but a proposal for a way of listening, and that way of listening is profoundly contaminated by a preexisting ethical (especially sexual) hierarchy, a contamination that inevitably colors whatever he hears. You can, of course, reject the masculinist assumptions of his proposals; but you cannot do so without falling back on some equally ideological alternative. Thus, for instance, while she is not responding specifically to Cain, Clément is clearly trying to escape from masculine habits when she remarks, "One day, I became aware that opera did not come to me from my head. . . . Opera comes to me from somewhere else; it comes to me from the womb" (176). Listening for the balls and listening with the womb are obviously different strategies; but together they suggest that the very act of listening is bound up with the ideological categories with which we live; and using them as a background, we can see that Booth's image of listening as if we could become "indistinguishable" from Bach is not a description of the ethical consequences of immersing oneself Bach's notes, but an ethically charged piece of advice that encourages us both to listen in a certain kind of way and to attribute a certain kind of ethical value to that act.

Second, this analysis suggests that if we want seriously to understand the ethical implications of music, we have to learn to attend less to what used to be called "the music itself" and more to the processes by which listeners make sense of it: for as surely as Cain's novels represent the ideology behind the act of listening, they remind us that the act of listening is in fact an *act* that alters the object listened to. In *Opera and Ideas,* for instance, Paul Robinson distinguishes the politics of Mozart and Rossini. Specifically, he points out the "striking emotional difference" between their Beaumarchais operas (*Figaro* and *The Barber of Seville*), and argues that this difference "reflects . . . the changes in the European climate of opinion over the thirty-year span separating the two works" (11). The post-Enlightenment reaction, the "modulated cynicism" (16) of Rossini is marked particularly by the fact that, for instance, in "Largo al factotum," what we listen for is "the demonstration of vocal technique, not the revelation of character" (29). What is significant here is not simply that *Serenade* takes on the relative merits of Rossini and Mozart, too, but even more that Cain presents Mozart in the same terms that Robinson reserves for Rossini alone. Robinson, in other words, clings to the formalist notion that the attitudes he finds in Rossini are "forced on us by the composer himself" (29). Cain demonstrates, in contrast, that the differences are as much brought *to* the music by the procedures through which we choose to interpret it.

In the end, then, my interest lies less in the particular cultural reformation Cain has in mind than in the means he chooses for putting it into effect, and the implications those means have for ethical study. Booth's work, from *The Rhetoric of Fiction* on, has always reminded us that rhetoric and ethics are inextricably linked. And if Booth's own work on music has been limited by its tendency to privilege the technical level, Cain's fiction suggests a direction in which his insights can be profitably expanded. For if music exists, as his novels seem to confirm, not simply in the notes, but in the verbal discourse around them and the synthetic acts that this discourse encourages listeners to engage in, then rhetoric *about* the notes may be more significant than the rhetoric we used to think was *in* the notes. If we want to think seriously about the ethics of music in the ways that Booth has thought seriously about the ethics of fiction, therefore, we have to turn away from the technical level and concentrate instead on the attributive and the synthetic: on those stories we tell about music, whether as novelists or critics or theorists, and the ethical dimensions they inevitably bring with them.

Notes

1. See, in particular, his discussion of Rabelais in *Company*, ch. 12.

2. Other critics, of course, have analyzed the ethical implications of the words set to music. But although words, as we shall see, are important in any music criticism, analysis of the texts *that are set* hardly leads to an ethics of music.

3. In the past few years an increasing number of musicologists—in particular, feminist musicologists—have come to question the traditional assumptions of the field; and I see my work here as a complement to that of such colleagues as Lawrence Kramer (for instance, in *Music as Cultural Practice*), Susan McClary (in *Feminine Endings*), and Ruth Solie (in "Whose Life?"). There has also been an increasing interest in the semiotics of music; see, for instance, Nattiez. For the most part, however, the study of music remains wedded to formalist principles. For a fuller discussion of this point, see my "Chord and Discourse" and "Whiting the Wrongs of History."

4. A similar model is found in *Modern Dogma:* "I take the work in, or, as phenomenologists say, it enables me to dwell in it. I live the work; it lives its life in me. Its creator and I become, in a part of our lives, indistinguishable as we live in the work together" (169).

5. Indeed, this analysis of listening is so much a product of our collaboration that claims to authorship of this essay are hardly unencumbered. For further discussion of this issue—the subject of a forthcoming, jointly authored book—see also my "Chord and Discourse" and our "The Phonograph Behind the Door." I appreciate Jay's willingness to allow me to use these ideas here.

6. While traditional analysis, of course, often deals with such codes, it usually treats them as if they were part of the technical level, rather than a cultural apparatus for processing the technical. Such analysis thus ignores the degree to which the choice of what code to apply when listening to a given piece is an *interpretive* decision, subject to debate. For a fuller discussion, see our "Phonograph."

7. For a fuller discussion of sonata form from this perspective, see my "Chord and Discourse."

8. The citation comes from Paul Henry Lang, *Music in Western Civilization* (New York: Norton, 1941) 811. Thanks to Fred Maus for helping me find the original source. Babbitt's burn-the-books rhetoric is an allusion to the final paragraph of Hume's *Enquiry Concerning Human Understanding*.

9. Of course, by the end of *How to Do Things with Words,* Austin has dismantled the constative/performative distinction; it is, nonetheless, useful for our purposes here. What I call *advisories* would fall under Austin's general class of "exercitives"; see Austin 155–57.

10. In the "mental experiment" described above, Booth begins with "a highly intelligent, sensitive adult who had never heard any music but who had ... a complete capacity to 'take in'" the Beethoven A Minor Quartet (*Modern Dogma* 168). Booth recognizes this as an "impossibility"; but although he never explains where the impossibility comes from, it seems to be a kind of sociological impossibility: in our culture (indeed, in any culture I know of), no intelligent, sensitive adult capable of hearing at all could grow up without experiencing music. I would agree that his experiment hinges on an impossibility, but would argue instead that it is a cognitive impossibility: such a listener would not know how to perform synthetic activities at all, and would thus be listening to sounds, but not to music.

11. Sharp talks enthusiastically about this opera—indeed, he calls the Prelude to the last act "one of the greatest pieces of music ever written" (*Serenade* 15). There's good reason to believe that he is echoing Cain's sentiments at this point, too, since Cain elsewhere called Bizet one of his "favorites" (qtd. in Hoopes 552).

12. See Bloom's claim that in the 1950s, "emotive experience" with classical music "was probably the only regularly recognizable class distinction between

educated and uneducated in America" (69). Cain would agree, in the 1930s, with the fact; he would, of course, disagree with its significance or its possible remedy.

13. See Robert Ness; see also Michael Bronski on Defoe's *The True Born Englishman* (1701) (Bronski 137). Thanks to John O'Neill for advice on this issue.

14. In her discussion of the men who posthumously adulated Callas, she remarks: "She died a banal death. But her ashes were stolen from the Père-Lachaise cemetery; a pyre of books was built for her; hastily pressed records were sold in abundance. Come on, men, shut up. You are living off her. Leave this woman alone, whose job it was to wear gracefully your repressed homosexual fantasies" (Clément 28).

15. Bronski, in contrast, argues that stress of form over content is one of the features that ties opera to gay sensibility (136).

16. Although the violin piece sits right next to Cain's novel in the index, Joan Peyser—surprisingly—makes no connection between them, although it would fit neatly into her lurid Bernstein biography.

17. Richard Ohmann insists this applies to television news broadcasts as well (173–74).

18. Arthur Groos, for instance, refers to "the blood sport of opera" (2).

19. See also Ann Douglas's praise of "toughness" as an antidote to sentimentality (11).

Bibliography

Austin, J. L. *How to Do Things with Words*. 2nd ed. Cambridge, MA: Harvard UP, 1975.

Babbitt, Milton. "The Structure and Function of Musical Theory." *Perspectives on Contemporary Music Theory*. Ed. Benjamin Boretz and Edward T. Cone. New York: Norton, 1972. 10–21.

Barthes, Roland. "The Grain of the Voice." *Image—Music—Text*. Trans. Stephen Heath. New York: Hill, 1977. 179–89.

Bloom, Allan. *The Closing of the American Mind*. New York: Simon (Touchstone), 1987.

Booth, Wayne C. *The Company We Keep: An Ethics of Fiction*. Berkeley: U of California P, 1988.

———. *Critical Understanding: The Powers and Limits of Pluralism*. Chicago: U of Chicago P, 1979.

———. *Modern Dogma and the Rhetoric of Assent*. Notre Dame: U of Notre Dame P, 1974.

Bronski, Michael. *Culture Clash: The Making of Gay Sensibility*. Boston: South End P, 1984.

Cain, James M. *The Butterfly*. 1947. In *Three by Cain*. New York: Vintage, 1989.
———. *Career in C Major*. 1938. In *Three of a Kind*. Philadelphia: Blakiston, 1944.
———. *Mildred Pierce*. 1941. New York: Vintage, 1978.
———. *The Moth*. New York: Knopf, 1948.
———. *Serenade*. 1937. In *Three by Cain*. New York: Vintage, 1989.
Clément, Catherine. *Opera, or the Undoing of Women*. Trans. Betsy Wing. Foreword by Susan McClary. Minneapolis: U of Minnesota P, 1988.
Douglas, Ann. *The Feminization of American Culture*. New York: Avon (Discus), 1978.
Gans, Herbert J. *Popular Culture and High Culture: An Analysis and Evaluation of Taste*. New York: Basic, 1974.
Groos, Arthur. "Introduction." *Reading Opera*. Ed. Arthur Groos and Roger Parker. Princeton: Princeton UP, 1988. 1–11.
Henderson, W. J. *What Is Good Music? Suggestions to Persons Desiring to Cultivate a Taste in Musical Art*. 3rd ed. New York: Scribner's, 1899.
Hoopes, Roy. *Cain*. New York: Holt, 1982.
Kolodin, Irving. *The Opera Omnibus: Four Centuries of Critical Give and Take*. New York: Dutton, 1976.
Kramer, Lawrence. *Music as Cultural Practice 1800–1900*. Berkeley: U of California P, 1990.
Krenek, Ernst. "Extents and Limits of Serial Techniques." *Problems of Modern Music*. Ed. Paul Henry Lang. New York: Norton, 1962. 72–94.
Madden, David. *Cain's Craft*. Metuchan, NJ: Scarecrow, 1985.
———. *James M. Cain*. New York: Twayne, 1970.
McClary, Susan. *Feminine Endings: Music, Gender, and Sexuality*. Minneapolis: U of Minnesota P, 1991.
Nattiez, Jean-Jacques. *Music and Discourse: Toward a Semiology of Music*. Trans. Carolyn Abbate. Princeton: Princeton UP, 1990.
Ness, Robert. "*The Dunciad* and Italian Opera in England." *Eighteenth-Century Studies* 20. 2 (1987): 173–94.
Ohmann, Richard. *Politics of Letters*. Middletown, CT: Wesleyan UP, 1987.
Peyser, Joan. *Bernstein: A Biography*. New York: Beech Tree, 1987.
Rabinowitz, Peter J. *Before Reading: Narrative Conventions and the Politics of Interpretation*. Ithaca, NY: Cornell UP, 1987.
———. "Chord and Discourse: Listening through the Written Word." *Music and Text: Critical Inquiry*. Ed. Steven Scher. Cambridge: Cambridge UP, 1992. 38–56.
———. "Whiting the Wrongs of History: The Resurrection of Scott Joplin." *Black Music Research Journal* 11. 2 (1991): 157–76.
Reise, Jay, and Peter J. Rabinowitz. "The Phonograph behind the Door: Some Thoughts on Musical Literacy." *Reading World Literature*. Ed. Sarah Lawall. Austin: U of Texas P, forthcoming.

Robinson, Paul A. *Opera and Ideas: From Mozart to Strauss.* Ithaca, NY: Cornell UP, 1985.

Solie, Ruth. "Whose Life? The Gendered Self in Schumann's *Frauenliebe* Songs." *Music and Text: Critical Inquiries.* Ed. Steven Paul Scher. Cambridge: Cambridge UP, 1992. 219–40.

Strauss, Harold. "A Six-Minute Egg." *New York Times Book Review,* 18 Feb. 1934: 8.

Walker, Alan. *An Anatomy of Musical Criticism.* London: Barrie, 1966.

Wilson, Edmund. "The Boys in the Back Room: James Cain and John O'Hara." *New Republic* 11 Nov. 1940: 65–66. A longer version appeared in *Classics and Commercials: A Literary Chronicle of the Forties* (New York: Farrar, 1950), 19–56.

11

Keeping the Company of Sophisters, Economists, and Calculators

DONALD N. MCCLOSKEY

> *It is now sixteen or seventeen years since I saw the Queen of France, then the Dauphiness, at Versailles.... Little did I dream that I should have lived to see disasters fallen upon her in a nation of gallant men.... I thought ten thousand swords must have leaped from their scabbards to avenge even a look that threatened her with insult. But the age of chivalry is gone. That of sophisters, economists, and calculators, has succeeded; and the glory of Europe is extinguished for ever.*
>
> EDMUND BURKE, *REFLECTIONS ON THE REVOLUTION IN FRANCE*

ADAM SMITH WAS a professor of moral philosophy. John Stuart Mill was a moral and political philosopher. Since then the worldly philosophers have withdrawn from morality.

Kurt Heinzelman places this "divorcing philosophy from economics" in the emblematic year of 1871, when Mill issued the last edition of *Principles of Political Economy, with some of their Applications to Social Philosophy* and William Stanley Jevons, the new scientist of British economics, published *The Theory of Political Economy* (Heinzelman 85–87). The Truce of Modernism took place unheralded sometime in the late nineteenth century, the truce that placed science from 8 to 5 in business hours, art for an evening's entertainment, and morality on Sunday. By 1894 an article by F. C. Montague in the *Dictionary of Political Economy* could formulate the business of economics in a way that few economists would now dispute, under the article "Morality":

> The relation of morals to economics is often misunderstood. Political economy is, properly speaking, a science rather than an art. It aims in the first instance at the explanation of a certain class of facts. . . . The special knowledge of economic facts possessed by the economist may enable him to give valuable advice on economic questions, but this, strictly speaking, is not his business. His business is to explain, not to exhort. It is therefore beside the mark to speak of economists, as such, preaching a low morality or rejecting morality altogether.

The economist was to be seen as a man of business, not a preacher. He sold Gradgrind facts, not the mere preaching of morality. In 1900 the word *preach* already sneered, as teenagers now sneer at their parents' "preaching" (or, worse, "lecturing"). The *Dictionary* claims that economic facts are Science rather than Art.

By 1900 the specialization of *science* in English to mean "lab-coated and quantitative" had already been accomplished. No other language did it. In French, Italian, Spanish, German, Dutch, Norwegian, Swedish, Icelandic, Polish, Hindi, Hungarian, Finnish, Turkish, Korean, Hebrew, Tamil, and all the other languages where the question arises the *science* word to this day means "disciplined inquiry" (*Wissenschaft*), as it did in English until the last quarter of the nineteenth century. The first occurrence of sense 5b in the *Oxford English Dictionary* is from the *Dublin Review* of 1867: "We shall . . . use the word 'science' in the sense which Englishmen so commonly give to it; as expressing physical and experimental science, to the exclusion of theological and metaphysical." The pre-nineteenth-century (and non-English) sense is found for instance in Johnson: "Of Fort George I shall not attempt to give any account. I cannot delineate it *scientifically,* and a *loose and popular description* is of use only when the imagination is to be amused" (Johnson 50, emphasis added). John Stuart Mill, writing in 1836 on the "science of political economy," refers to "moral or mental sciences," of which political economy is a part, and in the next paragraph uses "reasoners" and "inquirers" as though synonymous with "scientists" (a word he does not use, because it is a later coinage; Mill 55). Mill later in the same passage distinguishes "art" from science; but by "art" he means applications of the abstractions of science, not the fine arts, the Truce of Modernism being still fifty years away. And John Ruskin in *The Stones of Venice* (1851–1853) warns that "the principal danger is with the sciences of words and methods; and it was exactly into those sciences that the whole energy of men during the Renaissance period was thrown" (3.ii.32, 58, emphasis added).

By 1882 Matthew Arnold is struggling against the new specialization of the word, and against the biologist Thomas Huxley: "all learning is scientific," asserts Arnold, "which is systematically laid out and followed up to its original sources, and . . . a genuine humanism is scientific" (411). He applies the word here to the study of classical antiquity (in German, *Altertumswissenschaft*), as he had applied it in 1867 to chairs of Celtic literature at Oxford and Cambridge. Some time after Arnold's tug of war with Huxley over the word the English economist Alfred Marshall, in his style of writing an old-fashioned man, declares that to say that supply or demand dominates a particular market, as against the scissors of both, "is to be excused only so long as it claims to be merely a popular and not a strictly scientific account of what happened" (Marshall 348 [5.iii, 7]). The physicist Lord Kelvin would have nothing of the broader and now old-fashioned usage, sneering as early as 1883 at the nonmeasureable, excluded by 5b: "When you cannot measure it, when you cannot express it in numbers, your knowledge is of a meagre and unsatisfactory kind. It may be the beginning of knowledge, but you have scarcely in your thoughts advanced to the state of *science*" (1). The statistician Karl Pearson's *The Grammar of Science*, the bible of neopositivism, claimed that to use the word "in no narrow sense" (24), but in opposing his Science to "philology and philosophy" (10) showed that he meant to convert "anthropology, folklore, sociology, and psychology into true science" (16) by the standard of "geology, or biology, or geometry, or mechanics" (11). (And yet [37], "To draw a distinction between the scientific and philosophical fields is obscurantism.") Huxley, Kelvin, and their allies won the quarrel over the word. The peculiarly English definition—by 1933 the Supplement to the *OED* notes that sense 5b is of course "the dominant sense in ordinary use"—made it easy for Jevons and other English-speaking economists over the past hundred years to suppose that a science would have nothing to do with morality.

It would be a strange economics, of course, that did not treat at least the pursuit of happiness, and therefore the morality of doing well. Economics has a branch called "welfare economics" into which moral questions have been diverted since Jevons and the coming of scientism. The graduate schools teach that economists need merely the distinction of positive from normative, "is" against "ought," the way things are against how they should be. Though philosophically mistaken (Searle, see "Deriving 'Ought' from 'Is'" in *Speech Acts*), as a theory of ethics it has the merit of brevity. The sole moral judgment an economist is supposed to make is the least controversial one: if every single person is made better off by some change, the change should take place. Such a change is said to be "Pareto optimal," in honor of the economist who first made the point, in 1906. Even philosophers like John Rawls have adopted the notion of Pareto optimality, trying in the economist's manner to pull a decently detailed moral theory out of an empty hat. Welfare economics has shown recently some stirrings of more complex moral life, as in the works of the economist and philosopher Amartya Sen and a few others. But welfare economics is for the most part late-Victorian neoutilitarianism stuffed and mounted and fitted with marble eyes.

The demise of moral reasoning among economists in the late nineteenth and early twentieth century, of course, would not come as news to Wayne Booth. He sees it happening in literature, too, noting how thoroughly since modernism (in both his sense and mine) the moral questions have been segregated, the better to sidestep them. "There is no such thing as a moral or an immoral book," proclaimed Oscar Wilde. "Books are well written or badly written. That is all." As was his talent, Wilde spoke only a little ahead of his time. Biologists, historians, economists, even theologians subscribed in the end to the modernist amorality. There is no such thing as a moral or an immoral economy, says the economist. Economies are efficient or inefficient. That is all. In this life, we want nothing but Facts, sir, nothing but Facts!

Booth's book gives a reply, and suggests to an economist that the "ethical criticism" it propounds can reach beyond literature. Booth himself takes it as far as the Ajax Kitchen Cleanser jingle. It can be taken all the way to economics, and particularly to the use in economics of ethics-laden stories. Tzvetan Todorov put the matter so: "literature ... is a discourse oriented towards—let us not be intimidated by the ponderous words—truth and morality. . . . If we have managed to lose sight of that essential dimension of literature, it is because we began by reducing truth to verification and morality to moralism" (164). For "literature" here read "economics." The subject of economics is ethical in any case, which makes worrisome a claim by the economist to sidestep ethics. We do not worry overmuch if an astrophysicist refuses to think ethically about her stories. We should be more worried if an economist does.

Economists are not willing to elaborate their ethical opinions (cf. Booth, *Critical Understanding* 27). No ethical talk, please—we're economists. One day at lunch in the late 1970s the Chicago economists (of whom I am one) were talking over lunch about the economics of capital punishment. Gary Becker, the embodiment of economic thinking (for which he received in 1992 a well-deserved Nobel Prize), was explaining the finding of his colleague and student Isaac Ehrlich that one execution appeared to deter seven murders. I objected, not to the statistics or to the economics, with which I agreed, but to the ethical notion that an execution was the same as a murder. An execution elevates the Government to life-and-death power; whereas a murder is an individual's act. The two are not ethically comparable, said I, and so their ratio is no knock-down argument in favor of capital punishment. Becker was irked, because he was unprepared to argue on ethical grounds. No economist is prepared to argue on ethical grounds, at least since the demise of moral reasoning in the West. The facts were there, said he, seven to one. In this life, we want nothing but Facts, sir. What's this maundering about ethics? Becker truncated the conversation (a habit among modernists, incidentally), collected his dishes on the cafeteria tray, and strode off towards the door muttering, "Seven to one! Seven to one!"

In one way the story is unfair to Becker and to economics. Welfare economics contains ethical arguments, conclusive in their sphere, which can be used indifferently to attack or support, say, private property. Economists, including Gary Becker, speak wonderfully explicitly about certain ethical matters. (Becker preaches against welfare economics, but his practice of course is different.) No other social science can approach economics in the thoroughness of its ethical reflection, when it reflects. Political philosophers and literary folk accustomed to sneering at the ethical naïveté of economists are mostly pikers when it comes to the details of ethical theorizing, and are left gaping at the economists' astounding equations concerning Mr. A's happiness and Ms. B's chances in the lottery. Still, a reasonable complaint about the economist's style of ethical thinking is its razoring away of certain issues (the image of "razoring away" comes from the article on "Morality" in Eatwell et al., eds., *The New Palgrave* [1987], the modern successor to Palgrave's *Dictionary of Political Economy* [1894]). Economists think ethically, if within a narrow sphere.

The easiest point to make in reproach is that economists have ethics, perforce. Booth remarks that "even those [economists] who work hard to purge themselves of all but the most abstract formal interests turn out to have an ethical program in mind" (*Company* 7). Ideology motivates economists, despite their protestations of ideological innocence. Admittedly, the economists have a wider ethical purpose in mind, which it is true they do not acknowledge. To use the magic word, the economists are in the grip of Ideology. Some of them love capitalism; others hate it. But both sides find it hard to articulate their reasons, or to know that they have them.

Nowadays students of literature are quick to make the Ideological

Point. Score one for the Department of English. Yet one can ask, So what? Lacking a fuller sociological analysis—an analysis more commonly demanded than supplied—there is not much more to say. After one has pinned the tag of "ideological" on a scientific analysis, what then? An ideological purpose is unveiled: "Aha, Professor Becker! Caught favoring capitalism again, I see!" Well, so what?

To suppose that the mere unveiling of motive suffices to annihilate Becker and his economistic tribe is what Booth has called elsewhere "motivism" (*Modern Dogma* 24f; and the case of Russell, *Modern Dogma* 71–72). *Motivism* is the notion that an argument is wrong if it can be shown to arise from a hidden motive. Santayana describes Bertrand Russell's motivism during the First World War: His "information, though accurate, was necessarily partial, and brought forward in a partisan argument; he couldn't know, he refused to know everything; so that his judgments, nominally based on that partial information, were really inspired by passionate prejudice and were always unfair and sometimes mad. He would say, for instance, that the bishops supported the war because they had money invested in munition works" (441).

It is understandable that professors of economics would favor motivism. The argument fits with their model of humankind. The late George Stigler, for example, America's leading vulgar Marxist (though a Chicago economist), routinely reduced politics to the pocketbook. But it is less easy to see why professors of literature sneer at the force of political words, and yearn to reduce ethical questions at once to amateur sociology. When the professors hear the word *ethics* they reach for their ideology. Compared to the average social scientist, the best professors of literature are ill armed for the task. As Gerald Graff put it, "[m]aking political judgments and classifications of theories requires an adequate analysis of social practices. Is there any reason to think current literary critics possess such an analysis?" (604–5). The literary people would perhaps do better to pause with Booth on the literary matters, about which they can claim plausibly to speak. When Wallace Stevens regretted in the 1940s "that we have not experimented a little more extensively in public ownership of utilities," he had the sense to add it was "rather a ridiculous thing for me to be talking about" (qtd. in Longenbach 145). One wishes such diffidence were more widely shared by literary folk, most of whom are ignorant of economics and content to remain so. (Most literary folk since about 1880 have not read any economics, imagining that a smattering of Marx and *The New York Review of Books* will suffice.)

The big point is not ideology and its inability to see itself; we know that already, and not much follows from it. The big point is a literary one, from which things do follow, namely, that economists are storytellers, like Twain or Austen or Lawrence, and that their stories, as Booth argues in detail for novelists, have an ethical burden. "We all live a great proportion of our lives in a surrender to stories.... [E]ven the statisticians and accountants must *in fact* conduct their daily business largely in stories: the reports they give to superiors; the accounts they deliver to tax lawyers; the anecdotes and parables they hear...." (*Company* 14). "[A]ll of us spontaneously make narratives out of just about every bit of information that comes our way" (162). "[I]t is impossible to shut our eyes and retreat to a story-free world" (236). If we enter into it we "embrace the patterns of desire of any narrative" (285). As Peter Brooks put it, "Our lives are ceaselessly intertwined with narrative, with the stories that we tell, ... all of which are reworked in that story of our own lives that we narrate to ourselves.... We are immersed in narrative." (3). Or as the historian J. H. Hexter put it: story-telling is "a sort of knowledge we cannot live without" (8).

Economics has not lived without fictional stories, not ever. That economics purports to be a *true* fiction does not of course exempt it from the rules of fiction. Economics (at any rate my sort) is true. But that does not keep it from being fiction all the way down. Economic scientists, like everyone else, use a rhetorical tetrad—fact and logic, to be sure, but also metaphor and story, their explicit models and their tacit narratives. The stories of the first three minutes of the universe or the last three months of the recession are shaped by the conventions of human storytelling, even if constrained by considered human opinion about the nonhuman and the human facts.

The philosophically inclined need not at this point commence kicking stones and pounding tables, showing thereby that facts are facts, nothing but facts, and therefore all we need. Thinking of science as also involving stories and metaphors does not entail skepticism about the facts. The facts are there, killing the story or giving it life. The story is made by people, the facts are made by God. We of course need both to make sense. It's like fishing in the sea. Humans make the nets to catch the fish, but the fish are there by God's command, "really" there. We can believe trustingly that the fish are there even when our backs are turned, yet still admit that the design of the nets is a human job. Or we can believe skeptically that the fish are after all themselves fish by human construction (is a guppy a fish?), yet admit that the world's best net trailed through a sea without something we call fish in it would be hauled in empty. "We receive in short the block of marble," wrote William James, "but we carve the statue ourselves.... Altho the stubborn fact remains that there *is* a sensible flux, what is *true of it* seems from first to last to be largely a matter of our own creation" (247, 255). As Richard Rorty puts it, "The world is out there, but descriptions of the world are not" (5). Any professor of English knows: She was the single artificer of the world / In which she sang.

But any professor of economics knows that a narrative criticism of the field needs to come at least in part from economists themselves. People other than economists can read the texts, making a text of their own, and then can think usefully about it all (see, for example, Heinzelman or Woodmansee on copyright and the Romantic idea of the author). But by definition the economists themselves have most thoroughly internalized the writings of economists. The rhetorical study of the sciences and social sciences had better involve the artificers of the worlds in which they sing, who best understand (see Klamer; Gergen and Gergen; Geertz; Billig; and Carlston, Davis and Hersh, Landau, Megill and McCloskey, and Rosaldo in Nelson, Megill, and McCloskey).

Booth makes the point repeatedly. It is the second item in his "Hippocratic Oath for the Pluralist": "I will *try* to publish nothing about any book or article until I have *understood* it, which is to say, until I have reason to think that I can give an account of it that the author himself will recognize as just. Any attempt at overstanding will follow this initial act of attempted respect" (*Critical Understanding* 351). Economists are better placed to understand and respect what they write than are literary critics.

Therefore, most attacks on economics by law professors and sociologists or even professors of literature do not bite (I can think of a few exceptions, such as the strictures on economics raised by the political theorist Brian Barry, which make even an economist uncomfortable; but they are rare). In this respect, by the way, many economists themselves are incompetent to judge the ethical effect of so-called neoclassical economics, the mainstream of economics and an oppressor of minorities to the left and right, because they do not and cannot read it with comprehension.

Yet Booth notes the danger of being too good a reader of a text: "To understand a book well enough to repudiate it, I must make it a part of me, . . . and to that degree I will have already experienced an ethical change, for better or worse" (*Company* 239). There is no alternative to giving the best readers a good deal of attention—Fish on Milton, Bloom on Stevens, Booth on Austen. But the expert readers become, for better or worse, Miltonic, Stevensish, Austenian. Likewise, if there is going to be a serious ethical criticism of economic writing, the part accomplished by economists is going to exhibit whatever corrupting influence the arguments may have (such as McCloskey, *Rhetoric of Economics; If You're So Smart; Knowledge and Persuasion*).

Start the ethical criticism of economics, then, with Booth's central question about the corrupting influence of literature (*Company* 11): "What kind of company are we keeping as we read or listen?" As our mothers told us, keeping good or bad company is good for us, or bad. Though Booth can hardly be faulted for not reflecting elsewhere on scholarship more generally, he does not in *The Company We Keep* examine the reading and listening to the stories of scholarship itself (as against literature), and the company therefore that scholars keep.

The levels at which we are asked to be a kind of person by economic scholarship can be distinguished.

First, the scientific paper in economics has an implied reader it shares with other self-consciously scientific productions of the culture. The implied reader has some unattractive features: he is cold-blooded, desiccated, uninvolved. Isaac Newton, in many other ways an unattractive man, invented some of the attractive rhetoric of the scientific paper (Bazerman ch. 4; contrast the dialogues of Galileo and the personal confessions of Pascal). It is an ethical stance claiming to avoid an ethical stance.

For example, in the typical scientific paper in economics, as much as in physics or biology, certain high-minded precepts about the ethics in science are accompanied by low-minded notions that other ethical questions are "just matters of opinion." The scientific paper in economics treats the matter of how income should be distributed, for example, as an unarguable matter of opinion, sheer opinion, like one's preference for chocolate ice cream. If you say "I like chocolate ice cream" you are not inviting a discussion. Either you like it or you don't. No argument could move you. The economist's conveniently brief $3'' \times 5''$ card for ethical reasoning, dividing positive from normative, leads to a chocolate ice cream theory of ethics. Heh, either you like murder or you don't.

The eminent economist Mark Blaug, for example, believes "there are long established, well-tried methods for reconciling different methodological judgements. There are no such methods for reconciling different normative value judgements—other than political elections and shooting it out at the barricades" (Blaug 132–33). The economists think that either you like chocolate ice cream or you don't; you shoot it out or you shut up. As Blaug's master, Joseph Schumpeter, put it, "We may, indeed, prefer the world of modern dictatorial socialism to the world of Adam Smith, or vice versa, but any such preference comes within the same category of subjective evaluation as does, to plagiarize Sombart, a man's preference for blondes over brunettes" (Schumpeter 330). The theory is *emotivism,* "the doctrine that all evaluative judgments and more specifically all moral judgments are *nothing but* expressions of preference" (MacIntyre 11; emotivism is of course self-contradictory, since the sneer at evaluation applies to the evaluation of evaluation).

Undergraduates and many of their professors become uneasy and start giggling when a moral question arises. The agreement to disagree that ended the wars of religion in Europe can be traced in their unease, and in their stock remarks expressing it: "That's just a matter of opinion"; "Religion should not be mentioned in polite conversation"; "In questions of morality, it is thy blood or mine"; "The only methods for reconciling different normative value judgments are political elections or shooting it out at the barricades"; "It is within the same category of subjective evaluation as a man's preference for blondes over brunettes." The highbrow, philosophical doubt of the Vienna Circle that moral statements were even meaningful has this lowbrow, chocolate ice cream trace. According to modernist theory, therefore, to be caught making moral statements is to be caught in meaningless burbling.

The chocolate ice cream theory pervades academic life and explains why academics are so unwilling to discuss—as against assert or impose—their judgments. The question remains, of course, "How do we think about our judgments, once we decide that our goal is to *think* about them and not simply to assert them?" (*Company* 59; and Booth any year, *passim*). The values asserted by the scientific paper in economics and elsewhere are certainly not all bad. We should not burn people at the stake on account of their opinions on transubstantiation and we should not lie about our data on the IQs of identical twins. But it is worth remarking sharply that the values narrated in the scientific paper are not all good, either, even though Scientific.

The second point about the people we are asked to be in the reading of economic texts is more particularly economic. The economist asks the reader to take on certain ethical positions for the sake of the economistic argument. Most of us do not like the implied reader of economic stories: "Am I willing to be the kind of person that this story-teller is asking me to be?" (*Company* 33). About the coldly calculating *Homo economicus,* no, say we, for the fellow has a levelling, rancorous, rational sort of mind / That never looked out of the eye of a saint / Or out of a drunkard's eye. And yet (I will be making this point repeatedly— and yet) the cold calculation had better be done, by someone, or else we will again ban Japanese autos at a cost to American auto buyers of $200,000 annually for each job saved in Detroit or we will again bomb German civilians indiscriminately at night without affecting the outcome of the war or we will again regulate airlines for the benefit of the present holders of landing rights at O'Hare. The person you are asked to be in a modern economic argument is not entirely attractive, but is not a character that society can do without. The economic persona is usefully realistic about constraints, and thinks hard about certain of the ethical choices we must face, albeit ignoring certain others.

On utilitarian grounds, in other words, the economist is necessary; on wider grounds she is sometimes ethical. In policy questions, the ethical position that economics recommends is that of the social engineer, who provides her masters the plans indifferently for full employment or extermination camps. The social engineer will protest that she would have had nothing to do with extermination camps. She must ask where she draws the line, or where German engineers in 1942 in fact drew the line, an ethical deliberation that economists are reluctant to undertake. They will argue, remarkably, that they are not specialists in ethics and should stick to their comparative advantage.

Third, as Booth says, "artists often imitate the roles they create. The writer is moved, in reality, toward the virtues or vices imagined for the sake of the work itself" (*Company* 108). The same is true of scholars; perhaps more so. Historians of the medieval papacy or students of comparative politics adopt their subjects' methods, at least in spirit. It is not irrelevant that Henry Kissinger's first book was on Metternich. Anthropologists have begun to wonder recently about how their people affect them. It's about time.

For economics, the analysis of the ethical effects of the roles they create is simple, and partly true. Some economists imitate the role of that *Homo economicus* they have created. Anyone who has administered economists will report that a third or so of them behave in frankly selfish ways, and will justify their behavior when challenged by smirking reference to the economic model of humanity. "If I serve on the search committee I want a more than an average raise next year." "Jim, you're kidding: I can't hitch salary to service in such a mechanical way. We're in this together." "Ha! Don't talk to me about togetherness. You believe in economics, don't you?" What he means is, Don't you believe that people are unsocialized SOBs, disciplined only by the invisible hand of the marketplace, and therefore that professors of economics should act the same way? Historians and, I suppose, professors of literature have their own occupational diseases, but cheeky selfishness is not one of them. It's not done in their circles; in economics, believe me, it is. It would be impossible to get a group of modern economists to vote each a strictly equal raise in salary, so deeply do the economists believe in the ethics of competition. The egalitarian solution regularly occurs in history departments, by vote.

And yet (there it is again) the ethical effect of paying close attention to economic behavior, I repeat, is not entirely bad. Economists suggest sometimes that the splendid rationality they study is worthy of imitation. Economics provides the rudiments of ethical thinking for a bourgeois age: accumulate; think ahead; be methodical if it suits the task; be as honest as is the local custom; above all, do not feel socially inferior to an impulsive aristocracy—their day is done. The ethical thinking of the bourgeosie is not worthless (reflexively, an economist would make the joke that after all it has sold well). The intellectuals who sneer at it are the beneficiaries of its virtues, which, "during its rule of scarce one hundred [now near 250] years, has created more massive and more colossal productive forces than have all preceding generations together." And since Marx and Engels penned these lines, the real income per head of Americans has increased by a factor of ten and of latecomers to capitalism, such as Korea or Mexico, by more. Viewed socially, the economic man is no pest.

Even viewed from a strictly individual point of view the merchant's virtues, though not those of Achilles or Jesus, are not ethical nullities. In his wretched play at the dawn of bourgeois power (1731), George Lillo makes his priggish ideal of the London merchant, Thorowgood, assert that "as the name of merchant never degrades the gentleman, so by no means does it exclude him" (294). Lillo lays it on thick. Thorowgood in his exit instructs his assistant to "look carefully over the files to see whether there are any tradesmen's bills unpaid." Hah. One can smile from an aristocratic height at the goody-goody tendencies of bourgeois virtue, and scorn the earnest lists of virtues in how-to-succeed-in-business books from Ben Franklin's autobiography down to the latest best-seller. But after all is it not a matter of ethics to pay one's tailor?

What kind of person accepts the wares of tradesmen and then refuses to give something in return? No merchant he.

And one cannot leave the matter at "a strictly individual point of view." That is the main point of the eighteenth-century philosophers, that there are wider, unintended consequences of this or that individual act, such as publishing a book or paying a bill. In 1830 Macaulay noted the elementary instance: "A man who owes large bills to tradesmen, and fails to pay them, almost always produces distress through a very wide circle of people with whom he never dealt" (152).

The honesty of a society of merchants in fact goes beyond what would be strictly self-interested in a society of rats, as one can see in that much-maligned model of the mercantile society, the small midwestern city. A reputation for fair dealing is necessary for a roofer whose trade is limited to a community of 50,000. One bad roof and he's finished. A colleague once refused to tell me at a cocktail party the name of a roofer in Iowa City who had at first done a bad job (he redid the job free, at his own instigation), because she knew he would be finished in town if his name got out. But her behavior itself shows that ethical habits of selfish origin can grow into ethical convictions, the way a child grows from fear of punishment to servicing an internal master. An unsocialized SOB, or DOB, would have told me the name of the roofer, to improve the story. After all, the DOB's own reputation in business was not at stake.

The economist who relishes the telling of a story of greed could be seen as its advocate, whatever she may say about the distinction between "is" and "ought." Since the beginnings of modern economics the economist has urged us to look on the good side of greed. Again I say: The morality of the almighty dollar is not the worst of moralities. Dr. Johnson said, "There are few ways in which a man can be more innocently employed than in getting money." "The more one thinks of this [said Strahan], the juster it will appear" (Boswell 532; 27 March 1775). Economists have been arguing since the eighteenth century that the ancient and aristocratic distaste for acquisitiveness is naïve ethically. It is naïve because it fails to see that greed prospers in a market economy only by satisfying the ultimate consumers. A capitalist prospers by supplying what consumers demand (the power of advertising is grossly exaggerated: were it as powerful as it is portrayed any business could be profitable merely by advertising). The state or the church, free of greed, are no better as employers and are worse as suppliers than the market.

Donald Trump offends. But for all the jealous criticism he has provoked, he is not a thief. He did not get his billions from aristocratic cattle raids, acclaimed in bardic glory. He made, as he put it, deals, all of them voluntary. He did not use a .38 or a broadsword to persuade people, but honeyed words. Both sides at the outcome of persuasion, as in any free exchange, are better off than they were when they began, in contrast to the violence or hectoring favored by most intellectuals.

The businessperson is a rhetor, as David Lodge notes in *Nice Work*. Robyn Penrose, the professor of literature, watches the businessman persuading:

> [I]t did strike [her] that Vic Wilcox stood to his subordinates in the relation of teacher to pupils. . . . [S]he could see that he was trying to *teach* the other men, to coax and persuade them to look at the factory's operations in a new way. He would have been surprised to be told it, but he used the Socratic method: he prompted the other directors and middle managers and even the foremen to identify the problems themselves and to reach by their own reasoning the solutions he had himself already determined upon. It was so deftly done that she had sometimes to temper her admiration by reminding herself that it was all directed by the profit-motive. (219)

Donald Trump persuaded bankers to finance his buying of the Commodore Hotel. He then sold it for a profit, persuading people to come there. Penn Central, Hyatt Hotels, and the New York City Board of Estimate—and behind them the voters and hotel guests—put the old place at a low value and the new place, trumped up, at a high value. Trump earned a suitably fat profit for seeing that a hotel in a low-value use could be moved into a high-value use. An omniscient central planner would have ordered the same move. Market capitalism can be seen as the most altruistic of systems, each capitalist working to help someone else, for pay. Trump does well by doing good.

And yet there is an ethical problem in the theory and practice of economics. The problem lies deeper than the mere distaste for greed and calculation. Booth argues persuasively that a good author is a good friend, the good friend being "a kind of company that is not only pleasant or profitable, in some immediate way, but also good for me, good for its own sake. . . . Hours spent with this best kind of friend are seen as the way life should be lived. . . . [M]y true friend is one who [quoting Aristotle] 'has the same relations with me that he has with himself'" (*Company* 146–47).

The model of economics conserves on this sort of friendship, trying to get along on as little of it as possible. Economics has been described as the science of conserving love. The notion is that love is scarce, and that consequently we had better try to get along without it, organizing our affairs to take advantage of the abundant selfishness instead. The argument is economic to the core. As Adam Smith said famously, "It is not from the benevolence of the butcher, the brewer, or the baker, that we expect our dinner, but from their regard to their own interest" (1. 1. 2, 16).

Smith did not overlook love—on the contrary, he wrote what he himself thought was his best book on "the theory of moral sentiments." Yet he did not connect his theory of love with his theory of selfishness. The problem is that conserving on love, treating it as terrifically scarce, and not expecting it, may be a bad way to encourage its growth. That is the modern social democratic position against market capitalism: that market capitalism discourages love (the social democrats believe that bureaucracies located in London or Washington, on the contrary, encourage it).

The novelists in the eighteenth and early nineteenth centuries did better in thinking about love and selfishness. I do not think I am saying anything new in observing that not economists but novelists first gave prominence to commercial greed and calculation. Novelists, poets, and playwrights, not primarily social theorists, first portrayed a society of the bourgeoisie. I just described Smith's *The Wealth of Nations* as a "theory of selfishness." That is the reading that a modern economist gives the book, projecting back onto the father the sins of the children. In truth, the book itself does not support such a reading very well. Smith never describes a project of rational selfishness without noting the emotional and ethical obstacles to achieving it. Foreign trade free of tariffs, for example, is recommended by more than "police" (that is to say, policy, expediency, the achieving of high incomes). Most fundamentally, Smith asserts, free trade accords with the natural right of a person to use her own labor as she wishes.

The idea of *Homo economicus* itself arrives late in economics, toward the end of the nineteenth century, by way of an analogy with physical molecules. (It arrives at the same time that morality drops out.) Yet it comes early to the English novel, full blown in Defoe circa 1719, and prominent later in, say, Austen's comedies of calculation circa 1800 or Dickens's satires of greed circa 1840.

Homo economicus is a facer of choices, a considered spurner of the option foregone, known in economics as "opportunity costs." The notion of opportunity cost does not become clear to economists until the so-called Austrian economists explain it in the 1870s. Yet it has been a commonplace of poets since the beginning, two roads diverging in a yellow wood, and I, being one traveler, able to take only one, and facing therefore the opportunity cost. Achilles spurns fighting in preference to sulking in his tent; Satan spurns Heav'n to reign in Hell.

Robinson Crusoe selects what to load on the first raft trip from the wreck:

> It was in vain to sit still and wish for what was not to be had, and this Extremity rouz'd my Application. . . . [H]ope of furnishing my self with Necessaries, encourag'd me to go beyond what I should have been able to have done upon another Occasion. My raft was now strong enough to bear any reasonable Weight; my next Care was what to load it with. . . . [H]aving considered well what I most wanted, I first got three of the Seamen's Chests . . . and lowered them down. . . . [T]he first of these I filled with Provision, *viz*. Bread, Rice, three Dutch Cheeses. . . . [T]his put me upon rummaging for Clothes, . . . but [I] took no more than I wanted for present use, for I had other things which my Eye was more upon, as first Tools to work with on Shore, and it was after long searching that I found out the Carpenter's Chest, . . . much more valuable than a Ship Loading of Gold. . . . My next Care was for some Ammunition and Arms. . . . (41–42)

The raft is not of infinite size; at any moment the weather may turn and sink the wreck; this may be the only trip. Crusoe cannot have everything, and so must make choices. He takes only the clothing "wanted for present use," because there were "other things which my eye was more upon." That is, he chose to have fewer clothes and more carpenter's tools. He could not in the circumstances have both. He faced a road of many clothes or a diverging one of many tools and had to choose between them, spurning one. He later "resolv'd to set all other Things apart [so incurring the opportunity cost of projects elsewhere], 'till I got every Thing out of the Ship that I could get" (44).

Each time Crusoe, or any *Homo economicus,* faces a choice he draws up a balance sheet in his head. Crusoe speaks in the passage just cited of calling "a Council, that is to say, in my Thoughts, whether I should take back the Raft," but more commonly he uses commercial metaphors, especially those of accounting (most particularly on 53–54). It is the rational way to proceed—understanding the word *rational* to mean merely the sensible adjustment of what you can do to what you want; calculation, but of course humanly imperfect. Crusoe is the first calculator, projector, undertaker, entrepreneur. The rational person is a calculator making rough and ready choices about what next to put on the raft. After the second storm destroys the wreck, "I . . . recover'd my self with this satisfactory Reflection, *viz.* That I had lost no time, nor abated no Diligence to get everything out of her that could be useful to me" (47).

Opportunity cost says that Crusoe cannot have every scarce thing. He is a commercial man making choices under conditions of "scarcity" (another notion articulated late in economics, well after the novelists had shown it working in a bourgeois society). In the book the details of the style throughout contribute to the force of scarcity—a contrast to the stories of shipwrecks in the *Odyssey* or the *Aeneid,* over which hover intervening gods willing to perform miracles of abundance. The miracles in Crusoe's world are naturalistic, reflecting always Adam's Curse. Defoe's story is filled with realistic disappointment, signaled often by an ominous "but": "[T]here had been some Barly and Wheat together" on the wreck, "*but,* to my great Disappointment, I found afterwards that the Rats had eaten or spoil'd it all" (41). The wreck had "a great Roll of Sheet Lead: *But* this last was so heavy, I could not hoise [*sic*] it up to get it over the Ship's Side" (45). He takes a kid from a she-goat, and "hopes to have bred it up tame, *but* it would not eat, so I was forc'd to kill it and eat it myself" (50). He endeavored to breed some young wild pigeons, "*but* when they grew older they flew all away" (62). "May 4. I went a fishing, *but* caught not one Fish that I durst eat of" (68). "I searched for a *Cassava* root, . . . *but* I could find none" (79). He spent three days bringing grapes to his cave, "*But,* before I got thither, the Grapes were spoil'd" (80). The "but" (all emphases added above) is unsentimental, aware of life's scarcity. It is the economist's master conjunction.

Homo economicus may or may not be bad company for us, but literary artists, not worldly philosophers, are responsible for getting us acquainted.

And finally, the doctrines of economics themselves have ethical consequences. Booth argues in the manner of Aristotle that there are many kinds of goodness, which depend for their effect on the character the reader brings to the text. Narratives are to be thought of as "a botanical garden full of many beautiful species, each species implicitly bearing standards of excellence within its kind" (*Company* 47). Booth, like MacIntyre and other modern Aristotelians after virtue, does not want to reduce The Good to one all-purpose juice.

Economics has both its Platonists and its Aristotelians, ethical plungers and ethical hedgers. The labor theory of value, reducing all value to an ideal juice, is Platonist. The utilitarians were also Platonists: "the principle of utility," wrote Jeremy Bentham on the first page of *Introduction to the Principles of Morals and Legislation* (1789) "approves or disapproves of every action whatsoever, according to the tendency which it appears to have to augment or diminish the happiness of the party whose interest is in question."

The so-called marginalists of the 1870s and after them the modern economists are Aristotelians masquerading as unreconstructed Platonists. Their "marginal utility" of water and diamonds was dressed up as utilitarian and Platonist, but in fact admitted that the value of different goods could *not* be reduced to one number. Value could not be reduced to embodied labor, say, or God's own valuation of water or of diamonds. The science turned gradually away from the question of what the single juice might be that constituted value; and turned toward the answerable question of what *relative* value consumers put on one good as against another—in the vernacular, the "tradeoff," or in the economist's jargon, the opportunity cost. It was like the seventeenth-century turning away from the question of what gravity *was* to the answerable question of the rate at which two things fell toward each other. Water and diamonds in such a story are not merely sources of utility to be added up into one number. They are different, un-add-up-able goods. Their values depend on individual tastes and circumstances, not on something measureable independently of human choice. The human choice reveals a relative value.

Modern economics would do well to recognize its Aristotelian *ethos*. ("Austrian" economists make the point frequently, though not quite in these terms.) The economist can do a cost-benefit analysis as measuring one juice, in which case the economic wizard in her tower will be left to make the determination of what is to be done. Clearly, if society's valuation of the distinct goods of a clean environment and of cheap auto travel can be reduced to a single dollar measure then the economist should recommend arrangements that maximize the dollar measure. To hell with democracy. The best use of Prince William Sound might well be as a fluid medium for oil tankers, if that is how the calculation of cost and benefit comes out, in which case the otters and water birds be damned.

Aristotle would properly object that cost-benefit analyses should not be brought down to a universal juice. The analyses should be stopped before the juicing stage, and should present alternatives. In a democracy it should be the people who choose between otters and gasoline, not an economist king. The rhetoric of advising real kings makes it difficult to resist, but the economic expert should avoid forcing moral conclusions on his clients. Some economists would agree, though they keep on saying that good counselorship consists in *not* thinking about ethical matters.

If economists tell stories and exercise an ethical sense when telling them, then they had better have as many stories as possible. "Powerful narrative," writes Booth, "provides our best criticism of other powerful narratives" (*Company* 237). This is an economic justification of pluralism, an argument for not keeping all one's eggs in a single narrative basket. The application to economics is straightforward: we need pluralism in our economic narratives. Marxist narrative provides a criticism of the bourgeois "neoclassical" narrative, and vice versa. "The serious ethical disasters produced by narratives occur when people sink themselves into an unrelieved hot bath of one kind of narrative" (*Company* 237).

If you are accustomed to thinking in Platonic terms, within which knowledge consists mainly of propositions like the irrationality of the square root of two, provable now and forever, then monism looks attractive. There's One Truth out there, isn't there? If you are by contrast accustomed to thinking in Aristotelian terms, within which knowledge consists of judgments like the desirability of democracy, uncertain even when agreed to after much discussion by people of good will, then monism looks foolish. Dogmatic Marxists, dogmatic neoclassicals, dogmatic Austrian economists, dogmatic institutionalists, who have put the other's writings on an index of forbidden books, are foolish and ethically dangerous, all of them. They are true believers, or, rather, believers in Truth: The best lack all conviction, while the worst / Are full of passionate intensity.

The Boothian pluralism of stories, then, speaks to economics. Albert Jonsen and Stephen Toulmin have recently noted the failures of "principled dogmatism," the one-story world, as an approach to morality —"legalism without equity, and moralism without charity" (342). Economics is an encouragement to such dogmatism, attempting to reduce ethical questions to a system of axioms. The stories of economists could better be used casuistically, as Jonsen and Toulmin would put it. The case-by-case method is quite opposed to modernism, and was attacked on modernist grounds by Pascal in his *Provincial Letters* of 1656–1657 (Jonsen and Toulmin, ch. 12). It does not seek universal principles to be applied by social engineers. It seeks an ethical conversation in which principles of less-than-universal applicability are discovered.

The best economists do exactly this. Ronald Coase, for example, is a British-educated economist for a long time on the faculty of the Law School of the University of Chicago (in 1991 he received the Nobel Prize). His approach to economics is casuistic, looking for the stories and metaphors and facts and logics that fit the case at hand, and avoiding the unreasonable obsession with one of them alone. His most famous article, "The Problem of Social Cost" (1959), is exactly casuistic. It has therefore been misunderstood by modernist economists, who see in it a "theorem" for their social engineering. The theorem they have in mind, as it happens, is due to Adam Smith, some years in advance of Coase (namely, that exchange free of trammels works well to decide about air pollution and property rights; Coase's actual point was the opposite, that in a world of trammels the particular trammels need to be examined one by one). A style of ethical storytelling that insists that cases matter as much as principles is foreign to most of modern economics.

The Boothian pluralism of stories, then, has something to teach economics. The application of an ethics of fiction to economics, though, can hardly fail as well to teach in the other direction. It would violate Booth's maxims of critical pluralism if it were not so. Students of literature can learn a thing or two about ethics from economists, and not only the ethical point that we must be grownups and face scarcity when after all it exists.

The main lesson in ethics that literary people can learn from economics—economics of any sort, or indeed social science of any sort—is that action is social. Booth takes ethical matters to be one-on-one affairs. He uses Wallace Stevens's "The House Was Quiet and the World Was Calm" as a motto for *Company:*

> The house was quiet and the world was calm.
> The reader became the book....
> ... the reader leaned above the page,
> Wanted to lean, wanted much most to be
> The scholar to whom his book is true....

Literary people will naturally take the reader and the poet-novelist-scholar as the relevant pair. But this is a mistake, an economist (and critics like Northrop Frye) would note. Reader-response criticism is one thing, and very nice. But a full rhetorical criticism would be an audience-response criticism, fully social, noting the linguistic and, yes, ideological consequences unintended in the dyad of writer and lone reader. You cannot fully understand forests by examining trees one by one. You cannot take a fish out of its school and expect to learn much about schooling. An economist listening to the stories told by Adam Smith, David Ricardo, Knut Wicksell, John Maynard Keynes, or Paul Samuelson resists narrowing the ethical question down to me and thee. She has a lively appreciation of the we.

A book with economic implications—Ayn Rand's *Atlas Shrugged,* for example, or Keynes's *The General Theory of Employment, Interest and Money*—can have the consequences in wholly unintended ways on the individual reader (which Booth emphasizes) and in social ways, too (which he does not, that being the point here). *Atlas Shrugged,* for instance, can sustain a country-club Republicanism far removed from the romance of the novel. *The General Theory* can sustain a perpetual class of welfare recipients and perpetual employment for college graduates enriched by service to the welfare recipients. The economist looks for moral consequences beyond the dyad of author and reader. A book can have obviously "good" ethical effects on individuals, encouraging them to save (to take the standard Keynesian example), yet the saving can have disastrous effects in the society at large. We recognize the pursuit of profit as in some ways an ethical failing in an individual, yet it can lead to great good.

The classic definition of economics was given by Alfred Marshall in 1890 on the first page of his *Principles of Economics*—"a study of mankind in the ordinary business of life." To this Northrop Frye would have added: "The fundamental job of the imagination in ordinary life ... is to produce, out of the society we have to live in, a vision of the society we want to live in" (140). Economists preach ethics unaware, but have limited their imagination in the telling of ethical stories.

Economics seems to be ready to get back to ethical thinking. Many economists have realized that the utilitarian and Platonist hat does not have a rabbit inside it. We cannot do economics without ethical thinking in detail, and we cannot do ethical thinking in detail without varied and Aristotelian stories. An economist comes to recognize that he is a teller of tales and therefore, as Booth notes, a giver of judgments. When he does, he writes better economic stories, truer and with sager morals at the end. He trusts less in models on a blackboard and more in an ethics of fiction read from people's lives. And he makes better, much better, company to keep.

Bibliography

Arnold, Matthew. "Literature and Science." 1885. *The Portable Matthew Arnold.* Ed. L. Trilling. New York: Viking, 1949. 405–29.

Barry, Brian. *Sociologists, Economists and Democracy.* Chicago: U of Chicago P, 1970; 1978.

Bazerman, Charles. *Shaping Written Knowledge: The Genre and the Activity of the Experimental Article in Science.* The Rhetoric of the Human Sciences. Madison: U of Wisconsin P, 1988.

Billig, Michael. "Psychology, Rhetoric, and Cognition." *History of the Human Sciences* 2 (1989): 289–307.

Blaug, Mark. *The Methodology of Economics: Or, How Economists Explain.* Cambridge: Cambridge UP, 1980.

Booth, Wayne C. *The Company We Keep: An Ethics of Fiction.* Berkeley: U of California P, 1988.

———. *Critical Understanding: The Powers and Limits of Pluralism.* Chicago: U of Chicago P, 1979.

———. *Modern Dogma and the Rhetoric of Assent.* Chicago: U of Chicago P, 1974.

Boswell, James. *The Life of Samuel Johnson, LL. D.* 1791. Vol. 1. Everyman edition, 2 vols. London: Dent, 1949.

Brooks, Peter. *Reading for the Plot: Design and Intention in Narrative.* New York: Vintage, 1985.

Carlston, Donal E. "Turning Psychology on Itself: The Rhetoric of Psychology and the Psychology of Rhetoric." Nelson et al. 145–62.

Davis, Philip J., and Reuben Hersh. "Rhetoric and Mathematics." Nelson et al. 53–68.

Defoe, Daniel. *Robinson Crusoe.* 1719. Ed. Michael Shinagel. Norton Critical Edition. New York: Norton, 1975.

Eatwell, John, Murray Milgate, and Peter Newman, eds. *The New Palgrave: A Dictionary of Economics.* London: Macmillan, 1987.

Frye, Northrop. *The Educated Imagination.* Bloomington: Indiana UP, 1964.

Geertz, Clifford. *Works and Lives: The Anthropologist as Author.* Stanford: Stanford UP, 1988.

Gergen, Kenneth J., and Mary M. Gergen. 1986. "Narrative Form and the

Construction of Psychological Science." *Narrative Psychology: The Storied Nature of Human Conduct.* Ed. T. R. Sarbin. New York: Praeger, 1986. 22–44.

Graff, Gerald. "The Pseudo-Politics of Interpretation." *Critical Inquiry* 9 (1983): 597–610.

Heinzelman, Kurt. *The Economics of the Imagination.* Amherst: U of Massachusetts P, 1980.

Hexter, J. H. "The Problem of Historical Knowledge." Unpublished manuscript. Washington University, St. Louis, 1986.

James, William. *Pragmatism: A New Name for Some Old Ways of Thinking, together with four essays from The Meaning of Truth.* 1907, 1909. Rpt. (with pagination of the 1907 edition). New York: Longmans, 1949.

Johnson, Samuel. *A Journey to the Western Islands of Scotland.* 1775. Harmondsworth: Penguin, 1984.

Jonsen, Albert R., and Stephen Toulmin. *The Abuse of Casuistry: A History of Moral Reasoning.* Berkeley: U of California P, 1988.

Kelvin, William Thompson, Lord. "Electrical Units of Measurement." 1883. *Popular Lectures and Addresses.* Vol. 1. London, 1888–89.

Klamer, Arjo. *Conversations with Economists: New Classical Economists and Opponents Speak Out on the Current Controversy in Macroeconomics.* Totawa, NJ: Rowman, 1983.

Landau, Misia. "Paradise Lost: The Theme of Terrestiality in Human Evolution." Nelson et al. 111–24.

Lillo, George. "The London Merchant." 1731. *Eighteenth-Century Plays.* Ed. Ricardo Quintana. New York: Modern Library, 1952.

Lodge, David. *Nice Work.* Harmondsworth: Penguin, 1988.

Longenbach, James. *Wallace Stevens: The Plain Sense of Things.* New York: Oxford UP, 1991.

Macaulay, Thomas Babington. "Southey's Colloquies." *Edinburgh Review.* 1830. Reprinted with revisions in *Macaulay's Essays.* 1860. Riverside Edition. Boston, 1881. 1. 2: 132–87.

MacIntyre, Alasdair. *After Virtue: A Study in Moral Theory.* Notre Dame: U of Notre Dame P, 1981.

Marshall, Alfred. *Principles of Economics.* 1895. London: Macmillan, 1 1961.

Marx, Karl, and Friedrich Engels. *Manifesto of the Communist Party.* 1848. *Basic Writings on Politics and Philosophy: Marx and Engels.* Ed. L. S. Feuer. New York: Anchor, 1959.

McCloskey, Donald N. *If You're So Smart: The Narrative of Economic Expertise.* Chicago: U of Chicago P, 1990.

———. *Knowledge and Persuasion in Economics.* Cambridge: Cambridge UP, 1993.

———. *The Rhetoric of Economics.* The Rhetoric of the Human Sciences. Madison: U of Wisconsin P, 1985.

Megill, Allan, and Donald N. McCloskey. "The Rhetoric of History." Nelson et al. 221–38.
Mill, John Stuart. "On the Definition of Political Economy and the Method of Investigation Proper to It." 1836 (1844, 1877). *The Philosophy of Economics.* Ed. Daniel Hausman. New York: Columbia UP, 1984. 52–69.
Montague, F. C. "Morality." 1894. *Dictionary of Political Economy.* Ed. R. H. Palgrave. London: Macmillan, 1901.
Nelson, John, Allan Megill, and Donald N. McCloskey, eds. *The Rhetoric of the Human Sciences: Language and Argument in Scholarship and Public Affairs.* The Rhetoric of the Human Sciences. Madison: U of Wisconsin P.
Pearson, Karl. *The Grammar of Science.* 1892. 2nd ed. London: Black, 1900.
Rorty, Richard. *Contingency, Irony, and Solidarity.* Cambridge: Cambridge UP, 1989.
Rosaldo, Renato. "Where Objectivity Lies: The Rhetoric of Anthropology." Nelson et al. 87–110.
Ruskin, John. *The Stones of Venice.* 1851–53. 3 vols. New York: Peter Fenelon Collier, 1890.
Santayana, George. *Persons and Places.* 1943–53. Vol. 1 of *The Works of George Santayana.* Cambridge, MA: MIT P, 1986.
Schumpeter, Joseph A. *History of Economic Analysis.* New York: Oxford UP, 1954.
Searle, John R. *Speech Acts: An Essay in the Philosophy of Language.* Cambridge: Cambridge UP, 1969.
Smith, Adam. *An Inquiry into the Nature and Causes of the Wealth of Nations.* 1776. Ed. E. Cannan. Chicago: U of Chicago P, 1976.
Todorov, Tzvetan. *Literature and Its Theorists: A Personal View of Twentieth-Century Criticism.* Trans. C. Porter. Ithaca, NY: Cornell UP, 1984; 1987.
Woodmansee, Martha. "The Genius and the Copyright." *Eighteenth-Century Studies* 17 (1984): 425–48.

12

Saying What Goes without Saying: The Rhetoric of Bacon's *Essays*

EUGENE GARVER

FROM *The Rhetoric of Fiction* through *The Company We Keep: An Ethics of Fiction,* Wayne Booth has devoted himself to showing how literature can make us into better, or worse, people. His work is rhetorical not only in that he is concerned with the effects of literature on an audience, but because his terms of analysis are rhetorical, viewing literature as a transaction between writers and readers. Like Sidney's *Apology,* his defenses of literature and his exposition of its powers translate traditional defenses and expositions of the powers of persuasion into a new realm. But Booth's work also departs from traditional rhetoric by directing attention to literature, and novels above all, which achieve practical effects through an independence from the institutional setting and practical purpose that were essential to classical rhetoric.

While he expands the range of materials to which rhetorical criticism applies to include literature, he also narrows the scope of the literary, and of his criticism, by excluding didactic writing. The preface to the first edition of the *Rhetoric of Fiction* begins by excluding "didactic fiction" to look at "the rhetorical resources available to the writer of epic, novel, or short story as he tries, consciously or unconsciously, to impose his fictional world upon the reader." He defends this restriction by

Don Bialostosky, Wayne Booth, and Victoria Kahn were useful readers of an earlier version of this piece. Participants in the faculty workshop entitled "Machiavelli and the Renaissance" at Lebanon Valley College patiently raised helpful objections to some less temperate expositions of my thesis. Jim Phelan helped make the "Wayne Booth" who appears in this essay somewhat closer to the person of that name.

claiming that the "problems raised by rhetoric in the sense [mentioned above] . . . are seen more clearly in non-didactic works" (xiii).

Someone not educated and chastened by Booth might call the situation ironic. Booth's shift of rhetorical attention from the didactic to the literary was revolutionary and productive. But that change of focus was meant to expand the field of rhetoric to include the fictional, not to shift it from the didactic to fiction. This chapter is designed to see some significance in the above quotation from Booth. If "problems raised by rhetoric . . . are seen more clearly in non-didactic works," then it is time to see how much light can be reflected back on rhetoric's more traditional home among the didactic.

I want to ask Boothian questions about a kind of discourse or literature that he does not consider, a kind that is didactic by design, and ask how reading Francis Bacon's *Essays* can make us better (or worse) people. The noninstitutional character of literary rhetoric becomes especially interesting in looking at works whose purpose is to teach. The *Essays* are not a random choice for a test case, because they occupy middle ground between traditional instances of oratory and genres like the novel, which have freed their purposes from institutional settings. Without entering into the extensive debates concerning the ideology of the novel, I think it fair to say that the *Essays* are worth exploring because, while not tied to institutions or particular practical decisions, neither author nor reader is fully abstracted from specific ethical and political context. The individualism that is often a part of the presuppositions and outcome of the ethics of the novel, and which I think is presupposed by Booth, will itself be called into question by an ethics of the essay that is simultaneously self-asserting and self-effacing.

Bacon explains what the *Essays* are for and how they work in the *Advancement of Learning*. He says that it is strange that wisdom concerning the "husbandry" as opposed to the "fruit" of life, has not been presented: "This part therefore, because of the excellency thereof, I cannot but find exceedingly strange that it is not reduced to written inquiry: the rather, because it consisteth of much matter, wherein both speech and action is often conversant; and such wherein the common talk of men, (which is rare, but yet cometh sometimes to pass), is wiser than their books" (*Advancement* 2.22.3, 167–68).[1] He supplies the beginning for an explanation for the puzzling fact that this wisdom has not yet been collected: "This part of knowledge we do report also as deficient: not but that it is practised too much, but it hath not been reduced to writing" (2.23.13, 188). But why has something so useful not been reduced to writing? It has not been "reduced to writing" because to do so transforms the nature of such knowledge. Unlike the secrets of nature, which are given up only when she is tortured, truths that are unknown because we so far lack the right method of investigation, this kind of learning is deficient for a different reason. Secrecy is connected not to obscurity and difficulty but to darkness and shame. Bacon notices that there are things that are best left unsaid because they are not decent to talk about: "some things are secret because they are hard to know, and some because they are not fit to utter" (2.23.47, 205). Consequently, and here is the central point to the rhetoric and ethics of the *Essays,* if reducing this knowledge to writing transforms it, performing these sorts of actions from learning transforms the nature of the acts. If negotiation is an object of knowledge, then successful negotiating can be taught, can become a commodity, potentially accessible to everyone, and potentially matter for specialization and profit. When something becomes a craft, then it can be used for ends outside itself. It can be displayed as well as used. It is ungentlemanly to try too hard to succeed; much better to be upright and let success follow as God and luck allow.

What is most interesting and troubling in the *Essays* is what happens to What Everybody Knows when it becomes publicly stated and collected into an art, how What Everybody Knows becomes transformed into something quite different simply by being known, and, more specifically, by being collected, by being presented in writing. The novelty of the *Essays* and their moral force is in their existence, not just in what they say. If these things have until now been tacit, there is good reason why. The transformations involved in making common knowledge explicit are enormous, and make more complicated the claim that Booth makes in the afterword to the second edition to *The Rhetoric of Fiction:* "The reader whom the implied author *writes to* can be found as much in the text's silences as in its overt appeals. What the author felt no need to mention tells us who he thinks we'll be—or hopes we'll be. . . . The same holds for our beliefs about values: what the author feels no need to mention, of the values the story depends on, tells us who he thinks we are before we start to read" (423). Those silences may be signs of tacit agreements, but some of them, including those that bear most directly on moral teaching, will be signs of *agreements to hold certain things tacit.* An author may "feel no need to mention" things that everyone knows, because to mention such things proves that either author or audience is not part of that community in which they go without saying. The things that go without saying might go without saying because they are too obvious, or because they are hidden too deep to be seen—some foundations don't work when they're above ground—or because they are unsightly.[2] Writers and readers are parts of communities, communities of silence as well as of speech. *The Rhetoric of Fiction* considers "authorial silences," but Bacon brings to our attention communal silences.[3]

The *Essays* present what everybody knows, and by the act of presentation change the nature of such knowledge. Everybody knows that necessity and fortune create gaps between what is and what ought to be and between what should be and what can be. To be ignorant of that fact is the ethical immaturity called youthful idealism. But to announce that necessity creates such discrepancies is in bad taste, and to acknowledge that one realizes that such gaps exist is to accuse oneself of bad character and loose living.[4] It is part of sociability and individual goodness to present a face to others that insists that goodness is rewarded, that we are all equally submissive to the demands of what should be. There is, for example, an affront to decency in Bacon's declaration in "Of Ambition": "Since we have said it were good not to use men of ambitious natures, except it be upon necessity, it is fit we speak in what cases they are of necessity" (*Essays* 113). Such declarations are in questionable taste, and are signs of bad character, because it is an easy road from admitting that circumstances sometimes create exemptions to moral laws to declaring that the *speaker* is exempt from those laws. We want presidents who say that they will not negotiate with hostage-takers, and we want them to negotiate. When someone points out a gap between what should be done and the demands of necessity, there is at least the danger that that gap increases by being mentioned.

We all know that sometimes necessity dictates that we not act as we would like, that we not do what is right, but the more we admit necessity as an excuse, the easier it becomes to appeal to necessity as an excuse, and the more often we act against reason and goodness. Excuses become justifications; we start out doing wrong because it is necessary, and end up thinking that because it's necessary, it's not wrong after all. Among the excuses that become justification, the notion that Everybody Does It must be high on the list, and so stating what everybody knows, through the act of exposure, widens the discrepancy between what is and what ought to be. Once *ought* no longer implies *can,* obligations seem less compelling. Maybe it's better not to mention such things.

Bacon himself sees the connection between saying what goes without saying and turning to necessity and fortune. When he claims in the

Advancement of Learning that the novelty of his approach is to note the existence of wisdom that exists but which has not yet been collected in writing, he simultaneously proposes to offer practical advice concerning fortune as well as goodness: "Fortune layeth as heavy impositions as virtue; and it is as hard and severe a thing to be a true politique, as to be truly moral" (2.23.13, 188). But he does not tie the project of "collecting" to its subject matter, fortune and necessity. Expanding the realm of the practical to fortune seems innocent and optimistic, but it turns out that acting in the *face* of necessity can often become acting in the *guise* of necessity.[5] Consequently Bacon's moral teaching—both his didactic practice and the practice he preaches—inverts Aristotle's advice to the rhetorician: "Do not seem to speak from thought [*dianoias*] as men now do, but from choice [*prohaireseos*]. Say, for example, 'I wished this. Indeed, I *chose* this. But if I gained nothing, still this is better.' For the one way of speaking is the mark of a practically wise man [*phronimou*], the other way is the mark of a good man [*agathou*]. The practically wise man is involved in pursuing the advantageous, but the good man in pursuing the noble" (*Rhetoric* 3.16.1417a24–28). Instead of that advice of Aristotle's, Bacon shows that recognizing the force of necessity provides an all-purpose excuse and denial of responsibility, one that applies to the *Essays* themselves. And so Bacon says in "Of Cunning," "In things that a man would not be seen in himself, it is a point of cunning to borrow the name of the world; as to say, *The world says,* or, *There is a speech abroad,*" (*Essays* 69). The inversion of Aristotle's point goes beyond persuasiveness: if knowledge of things outside our control, rather than our attitude towards things we can do something about, determines success, then such knowledge is now to be valued over goodness. By stating what everybody knows, Bacon offers a kind of knowledge that is a substitute for character. Hence the inversion of Aristotle's precept.

Bacon's writing is more than just another case of the moral act of saying what goes without saying; it makes discursively accessible the entire realm that must go without saying, the realm of necessity, the fortuitous, those things that lie outside human control. There are many rhetorical genres that say what everybody knows, debunkings and exposés among them. But *fortuna* is the realm of events for which people, especially powerful people, cannot be held accountable. Making necessity and fortune amenable to advice and teaching threatens the excuses that prevent misfortunes from being read as injustices. When Bacon presents an art for dealing with necessity, necessity becomes at the same time both more available and more suspect as an excuse and rationale. The realm of the practical is things within our power as opposed to things we cannot do anything about. The realm of the ethical is reliably located in our characters as opposed to the vicissitudes of the fortuitous external world. The realm of the moral, finally, is those things for which praise and blame are accorded regardless of outcome, as opposed to an amoral realm in which success is the measure of goodness. Making husbandry, negotiation, and fortune subjects for teaching and for practice threatens conventional equations between the practical, the moral, and the ethical.

Stating what everybody knows also widens the reference of *everybody* as stating rules for action makes successful action accessible to new, upstart, actors. The moral thing to do is right regardless of consequences, but only people who possess sufficient wealth and power can afford to act without regard for consequences; the rest of us have to worry about success, and when Bacon's *Essays* present an art of husbanding one's fortune, he legitimizes the unseemly concerns of us outsiders.

In making negotiation and dealings with fortune subject to teaching, Bacon upsets the division of labor between the moral realm in which consequences do not count and the nonmoral domain in which consequences are everything, a division of labor that seems conveniently equivalent to a division of classes in society between those who act gracefully and those who must be industrious. His work can be read as domesticating the fortuitous, making chance subject to policy, and so leading the moral into new territory, civilizing something still in a state of nature. It can also be read as a process of infection and corruption running in the opposite direction, with vulgar considerations of worldly success tainting the moral and the ethical.[6]

Although it is easy to think that Bacon's project is one of undermining conservatism and replacing it with selfish opportunism, the opposite case can be made equally well: he expands the realm of the moral to match the broadened domain of the practical. Saying what goes without saying is alternatively conservative and upsetting, preserving and overthrowing traditional moral rules and the social roles that are aligned in a privileged way with the practical, the moral, and the ethical.[7] While it is easy to see a concern for successfully making it in the world as a leveling one, Horkheimer, for example, insightfully argues instead that success is an essentially conservative concept: "The pragmatic concept of truth in its exclusive form ... corresponds to limitless trust in the existing world. If the goodness of every idea is given time and opportunity to come to light, if the success of the truth—even after struggle and resistance—is in the long run certain, if the idea of a dangerous, explosive truth cannot come into the field of vision, then the present social structure is consecrated.... In pragmatism there lies embedded the belief in the existence and advantages of free competition."[8] The reason that Bacon's rules for making it in the world can seem alternatively conservative and destabilizing, can appear either to extend or to contract the territory of the moral, is that in different circumstances, the same teaching can either serve to expose hypocrisy in others or it can itself become instruction in manipulation. Those circumstances are not themselves contained within the *Essays*.[9] Therefore, the ethics of the *Essays* is a rhetorical problem in that its ethical value and effect depend on circumstances and purposes outside itself, unlike a purely aesthetic object, if such a thing exists, which carries its principles of application within itself, and unlike a traditional rhetorical appeal, which is tied to its circumstances of production and reception.[10] Because those circumstances of application cannot be given within the *Essays* themselves, reducing this wisdom into writing opens up possibilities for manipulation that did not exist before.[11] Bacon has made a way of acting into a rule-guided technique, and by that transformation his wisdom becomes something that can be used for any purpose, good or bad. When Aristotle noted that that character is to be preferred to knowledge, his evaluation relies on just that morally indeterminate feature of knowledge: character is oriented towards ends, knowledge looks back to its justifying principles. There were good reasons why these things went without saying, at least good reasons for the people who knew them but didn't say them.[12] Saying them makes them into matters of technique by loosening the bonds between action and circumstance. The very act of announcing how people act brings into question the appropriateness of actions.

The distinctions Booth develops in *The Company We Keep* permit a more sophisticated statement of the problem of character and knowledge as he distinguishes the moral effects of reading from the moral work *in* the act of reading itself. It is true that the moral effects of reading depend on circumstances of reception outside the text. But the moral values of the activity *of* reading are something within the control of the author. Every method for confronting fortune and for success in business and negotiation can be used for good or bad external purposes. In addition, corresponding to Booth's idea of the morality *in* reading, each method for confronting fortune articulates a set of principles that define a person; the rhetoric of fiction and, more generally, of noninstitutional discourse, develops a conception of character that is relatively independent of circumstances. Consequently, such character can be understood as a set of principles used by a person, and so it becomes a kind of knowledge that substitutes for character. Every precept and example can be read and then can be imitated as a kind of faking or as a kind of incorporation. They are all, that is, subject to use in what *The Company We Keep* calls upward and downward hypocrisy.[13]

For this inner, ethical side, which Booth expresses as the moral experience in the act of reading, therefore, Bacon not only has to teach his readers how to act—that is the easy idea of reading literature as causing moral effects—but also has to teach them how to read, to read his directions on how to act—the more sophisticated idea of reading literature as itself an ethical activity. To that extent Stanley Fish is right to direct the attention of the critic to the experience of reading the *Essays,* although it does not follow at all, as Fish claims, that that experience of reading is therefore the "subject" of the *Essays*.[14] That latter inference is not only a danger for the literary critic, but for the moral agent as well.

The practical equivalent to thinking that the experience of reading is the subject of the *Essays* is the thought that what one learns from the *Essays* is a certain ability to use language, not to refer to what language is about but to use language to refer to and thereby define oneself as a certain kind of person, a person who speaks the right way. The danger of the *Essays* is not Booth's general conception of the downward hypocrisy of the sophist who uses a better mask to cover a worse cause, but a quite specific kind of hypocrisy, subject to frequent attention in the Renaissance, that uses a mask to substitute for any face at all, the kind of chameleonlike concealing that occurs when knowledge replaces character. In terms to which I will return, *mention* becomes a substitute for *use,* as aesthetic style becomes a substitute for practical action. As Johnson puts it in a sentence (*Idler* 84) that perfectly fits the difficulties with Bacon, "The examples and events of history press, indeed, upon the mind with the weight of truth; but when they are reposited in the memory, they are oftener employed for shew than use, and rather diversity conversation than regulate life."

Without thinking about how to read Bacon's precepts and examples, the critic will be forced to make the elisions from "ambiguity" to "secrecy" to "unintelligibility" that Hexter makes in talking about More's *Utopia:* "While ambiguity may enhance the value of certain special kinds of poetry, it does not enhance the value of social comment.

We should think rather poorly of any present-day social thinker whose intention was inscrutable or mysterious, and unintelligibility is no more a virtue in a criticism of society written four hundred years ago than it is in current social criticism" (11).[15] Hexter's thesis makes sense only if Bacon, or any social thinker, need not teach the readers how to read, only if reading consists in drawing out some informative content. If part of Bacon's project must be to teach his readers to read, then ambiguity can have more intelligible functions. This further dimension is essential to Bacon's enterprise, since without reading the *Essays* prudently, the reader will either make them, and himself, into aesthetic objects, or make them into amoral techniques and instruments distinct from any particular uses.

Bacon's practice in the *Essays* has the dual function that imitations have of both providing a model and providing an authority, offering both resources for action and resources for argument in support of actions one wants to undertake anyway, including the future resource of citing Bacon's arguments. That provision of authority offers the dimension in which his arguments can be mentioned as well as used, the sense in which mention becomes an unusually efficient and productive form of use.[16] Mentioning becomes a form of use, since to cite Bacon, and to cite Bacon's citations, is a way of authorizing one's behavior. In negotiation and in confronting fortune, everybody knows what to do, namely to win; Bacon's teachings offer a way of respectably clothing one's actions. His teachings are then used for ownership and display. Analogous to the use/mention distinction applied to language is the distinction between use value and exchange value applied to commodities.[17] While it might seem obvious, and while it is true on a grammatical as opposed to a rhetorical understanding of language, that use is prior to mention, Bacon shows ways in which mentioning a rule, moral principle, authority, or example is prior to or constitutive of using it, ways in which displaying a line of argument is its use. In the same way, an understanding of economics that grounds economic value in demand and need will naturally make use value prior to exchange value, but the range of economic activity obviously explained by a connection to demand seems so small that instead needs become products of economic activity, not its genesis, and exchange value determines use value. We can learn what is good for us by what sounds good.

So the essay "Of Usury" begins by distinguishing between the many, who have made "witty invectives" against usury and Bacon himself, who will speak "of usury usefully," constructing a new kind of didactic rhetoric that realigns the practical, the moral, and the ethical. Speaking usefully means, it turns out, first pointing to the "discommodities of usury" (*Essays,* all 123), then its advantages, and finally of the "reformation and reiglement of usury; how the discommodities of it may be best avoided, and the commodities retained" (125). What begins as a necessary evil turns out to be necessary, and therefore not evil after all. (Rhetorically, there is an important innovation here: Aristotle says that deliberative rhetoric concerning the useful and epideictic rhetoric about the good are convertible by a change of phrase [*Rhetoric* 1.9.1367b37–1368a10]. The differences between witty invectives and useful maxims are greater than that.) The essay ends with a formula that captures Bacon's intent of saying what goes without saying: "If it be objected that this doth, in a sort, *authorize* usury, which before was in some places but *permissive;* the answer is, that it is better to mitigate usury by *declaration,* than to suffer it to rage by *connivance*" (126, emphasis added). According to that ending, saying what goes without saying and speaking usefully *reduce* rather than expand the gap between *is* and *ought.*[18] But, I have been claiming, such reduction and consequent realignment of the practical, the moral, and the ethical is possible only if Bacon teaches a method of reading as well as a method of acting and imitating what one reads, which is in turn possible only if he grounds the ethical in the activity of prudent reading itself. Only then will speaking usefully have the added dimension of doing more than providing seemly clothing for what one wanted to do anyway; only then can we learn what is good for us by what sounds good.

In the *Advancement of Learning,* Bacon makes the activity of the learner turn on the method of presentation drawn through a series of "diversities of method." I want to show how some of them permit a characterization of prudent reading, and then add a couple of diversities of method of my own that seem to me to capture the work of the *Essays* more specifically. First, the method of probation is opposed to the magistral method, which is founded on a "kind of contract of error between the deliverer and the receiver: for he that delivereth knowledge, desireth to deliver it in such form as may be best believed, and not as may be best examined; and he that receiveth knowledge, desireth rather present satisfaction, than expectant inquiry; and so rather not to doubt, than not to err: glory making the author not to lay open his weakness, and sloth making the disciple not to know his strength" (2.17.3, 141 [4, 449; cf. *De Augmentis* 10, 123]). The *Essays* will have an internal ethical side, as well as external practical effects, if the author instead employs the method of probation, and if the reader recognizes that this is what the author is doing. "Knowledge that is delivered as a thread to be spun on, ought to be delivered and intimated, if it were possible, in the same method wherein it was invented: and so is it possible of knowledge induced" (*ibid.*). The reader acquires a character, and not just knowledge, by imitating Bacon's process of invention, including his processes of observation, qualification, quotation, and appropriation.[19]

Next, Bacon contrasts "the delivery of knowledge in aphorisms" as opposed to delivery in method: aphoristic writing is, among other things, a better test of whether the writer has something to say. Moreover, "methods are more fit [than aphorisms] to win consent or belief, but less fit to point to action"; finally, "Aphorisms, representing a knowledge broken, do invite men to inquire farther; whereas methods, carrying the show of a total, do secure men, as if they were at farthest" (2.17.7, 142).[20] For the subject of the *Essays*, though, inquiring further would not be directed towards the growth of knowledge, but towards further husbanding of fortune. The civil or ethical project is not of a piece with scientific investigation. Bacon's method for scientific investigation, as spelled out in the *New Organon,* is based on a *grammatical* analogy between language and nature, in which elements and rules of combination are fundamental to both. His method for articulating and teaching conduct is based on a *rhetorical* analogy between language and action, stressing competence and performance.[21] Neglect of this difference leads Fish fallaciously to suppose that because the essays are scientific and descriptive, they cannot be practical or prescriptive. Similarly, Box thinks that the *Essays* are not scientific or even Baconian because they do not contribute to a kind of progress that would be inappropriate to business and negotiation.[22]

Bacon's series of contrasts of methods—there are more—concerns the quite general problem of how writing makes its readers active, and so I think the *Advancement of Learning* is a fundamental theoretical contribution to the general problems of the ethics of teaching to which Booth has forced attention. More specifically, these distinctions bear on the perennial problem of moral education, how to make readers active rather than passive, how to make readers regard one's teaching as engaging character rather than a narrower kind of knowledge. Although these first diversities of methods are quite general, later in the *Advancement of Learning* he offers a further contrast specifically designed to show how discourse about negotiation, husbandry, and fortune can be organized to issue in activity rather than passivity on the part of its readers. The first dichotomy is worth quoting at length:

> The form of writing which of all others is fittest for this variable argument of negotiation and occasions is that which Machiavel chose wisely and aptly for government; namely, discourse upon histories or examples. For knowledge drawn freshly, and in our view, out of particulars, knoweth the way best to particulars again; and it hath much greater life for practice when the discourse attendeth upon the example, than when the example attendeth upon the discourse. For this is no point of order, as it seemeth at first, but of substance: for when the example is the ground, being set down in history at large, it is set down with all circumstances, which may sometimes control the discourse thereupon made, and sometimes supply it as a very pattern for action; whereas the examples alleged for the discourse's sake are cited succinctly, and without particularity, and carry a servile aspect towards the discourse which they are brought in to make good. (2.23.8, 186 [5, 56])

The realm of fortune is the realm of particulars resistant to generalization in rules, and so examples rather than precepts are the best teachers. Fortune is unpredictable, and the behavior appropriate to managing and husbanding fortune is similarly resistant to statement in rules. Consequently, the reader who successfully learns Bacon's lessons will know how to follow a rule loosely and conveniently.[23] In classical rhetoric, the best art is the art that looks natural and hides its artful quality, and the rules Bacon teaches must be followed in a similarly disguised and ingenuous-looking way. No one is supposed to be fooled into thinking that one is acting naturally; it's just that here is something new that goes without saying. In a realm in which examples rather than precepts are authoritative, the place of rules must be loose and tacit. The aristocratic lack of concern for consequences is universalized into a nonchalance, *sprezzatura,* towards rules of good behavior.[24] His description in "Of Ceremonies and Respects" applies to his method of teaching throughout the *Essays:*

> To attain [good forms] it almost sufficeth not to despise them; for so shall a man observe them in others; and let him trust himself with the rest. For if he labour too much to express them, he shall lose their grace: which is to be natural and unaffected. Some men's behaviour is like a

verse, wherein every syllable is measured; how can a man comprehend great matters, that breaketh his mind too much to small observations? Not to use ceremonies at all, is to teach others not to use them again; and so diminisheth respect to himself; especially if they be not omitted to strangers and formal natures; but the dwelling upon them, and exalting them above the moon, is not only tedious, but doth diminish the faith and credit of him that speaks. And certainly there is a kind of conveying of effectual and imprinting passages amongst compliments, which is of singular use, if a man can hit upon it. (6, 500–501)

I want to suggest two further "diversities of method" not mentioned in the *Advancement of Learning* that also characterize the ethics of the *Essays,* and characterize Bacon's contribution to the ethics of moral education. First, there is a diversity of method between transparent writing that puts the reader's attention on what is said, and more opaque prose that directs attention to itself.[25] The structure and tactics of the *Essays* are apparent on the surface as Bacon uses techniques in a way that makes his audience aware of those techniques: His style constantly directs attention to itself not, though, as an object for delight, but instead to increase a certain kind of reflection and suspicion. In the description of the "rhetoric" best suited for negotiation quoted above, he recommends "knowledge drawn freshly, and in our view," and the *Essays* work by constantly keeping the acts of fresh drawing in view. The prudence needed to read the *Essays* is less an increased facility at a method of reasoning than an increased facility at speaking a new language, and Bacon's teaching resembles that required for teaching a second, nonnative language, allowing foreigners, or social upstarts, to pass for natives. This facility at a second language is rhetorical rather than grammatical, centering on rules of application and performing appropriately rather than competence at correctness and well-formedness.

Although the things that go without saying are not difficult to know, they have been left unsaid. There is a further reason, beyond the fact that it is not only a sign of ill-breeding and social climbing to admit that one is acting from knowledge rather than nature. These things seem unknowable because of their particularity or, as Bacon also puts, it, their immersion in matter.[26] This immersion in matter is characteristic of practical problems of confronting fortune, as opposed to ethics and practical problems of directing one's own intentions, and so the neglect of knowledge of fortune comes from the particularity of the accidental. Bacon will have to change the meaning of counsel accordingly. Things which from one point of view are shameful to talk about are also too indeterminate to say anything dignified about. As they are made more discursively accessible, the nature of counsel must transform the manifold that counsel is about, the realm of fortune, and change the relation between the useful and the noble, and consequently the relation between the useful and the shameful.

Given the "immersion in matter" and ascendency of examples that characterize negotiations with fortune, it would be just the sort of passivity Bacon wants to avoid to make his teachings into rules. By making explicit What Everybody Knows, mentioning as well as using principles of action, he transforms such knowledge, transforms what it means to follow, or violate, a rule.[27] Following a rule loosely, or prudently, or opportunistically—in a word, rhetorically—is different from the grammatical conception of following a rule that authorizes its instances. What it means to follow a rule is made problematic when following naturally is distinct from following the rule artfully and loosely, thus changing the nature of advice and the rhetoric of the *Essays*. Following a rule prudently cannot be an excuse for bad behavior, the way obeying a law removes one's accountability for bad consequences: "Don't blame me; I was obeying the law when I arrested the shoplifter; if she subsequently killed herself that's none of my business." Following a rule does not remove the need for thought and responsibility.

Making his own persuasive tactics explicit, while it has one advantage, seems in another respect to backfire. In order to make his readers active, and thereby increase their chances for success in the world, Bacon shows them how he is working, exhibits the lack of fit between rule and example, between goodness and utility, between what we say and what we do. But the more we understand Bacon's method, the less we should in fact follow it. The rules he offers work only if actors do not look as though they are following rules.[28] In other words, they work only when they go without saying. Bacon the teacher must lay bare his own techniques and therefore act tactlessly so that his audience can become decorous.

I think that it is to address that problem and those possibilities for rule following, rule citing, and exploitation that we need a final "diversity of method" to characterize Bacon's moral teaching in the *Essays*. These *Essays*, especially in comparison with their model in Montaigne, are astonishingly impersonal, especially in contrast to the self-assertion they enjoin, but that too is a part of their teaching. Knowledge once again becomes valued over character; in this final paradox and final diversity of method morality becomes separated from self-knowledge. Once there are rules for success, Bacon's method will suppress the role of individual talent or nature in ethics as much as in science.[29] Common knowledge is common, available to all, and so exploitations are different from deviations based on individual insight. It is hard to see how character, and ethics, can survive such publicity and impersonality, but of course the history of ethics is full of transformations of the relations of knowledge and character that suppress individuality.

The innovation of the *Essays* is to teach successful negotiation with fortune, and such success takes knowledge, not character. "It is not possible to join the wisdom of the serpent with the innocence of the dove, except men be perfectly acquainted with the nature of evil itself; for without this, virtue is open and unfenced; nay, a virtuous and honest man can do no good upon those that are wicked, to correct and reclaim them, without first exploring all the depths and recesses of their malice" (*De Augmentis*, 5, 17).[30] In the end, then, the moral geography of the world is revised. In Bacon's world (both the world in which he writes and the world constructed and implied in his writing) the task of discriminating prudence from opportunism, moderation from perfidiousness, accommodation as a form of making one's values real and accommodation as a form of deviating from one's values, is a permanent job.[31] There are no sure signs that make the discrimination for the reader; it simply takes prudence. (Or opportunism.) It is no easier or safer to tell whether one is oneself being accommodating in the one way or the other than it is to make that decision about others. The lack of reflection on one's inner life and conscience in the *Essays* directs the reader's attention to acts, circumstances, and consequences, rather than intentions, but it is only a judgment of intention—a judgment one no longer has available—that can make a distinction between prudence and opportunism. Perhaps this is a world that one gains only by losing one's own soul.

In such a world, one learns not to avoid evil but to use it. Evil thereby becomes neutralized in being used. As part of that process, its dangers are deflated, and so he says in "On Cunning," "There be that can pack the cards, and yet cannot play well." Facility at rule exploiting is unseemly, but not very dangerous, since the contraction of attention becomes self-defeating. Moreover, by a kind of parody of the economy of nature, the more someone practices deception and relies on the gullibility of others, the more he himself turns out to be credible. Just as the principal purpose of intelligence agencies is to counter other intelligence agencies, and the main use of advertising seems to be to negate competing advertising campaigns, so Bacon pictures the cunning use of rules and the cunning display of rule following to be an activity mainly directed at others engaged in similar practices: "If we observe, we shall find two differing kinds of sufficiency in managing of business; some can make use of occasions aptly and dexterously, but plot little; some can urge and pursue their own plots well, but cannot accommodate or take in; either of which is very imperfect without the other" (*Advancement* 2.23.35, 198). The more loosely we follow the rules of business, Bacon implies, the less harm will be done by cunning. Cunning is the false form of prudence (in Booth's terms it is hypocrisy downwards rather than upwards), but it works by promoting a misunderstanding of what it means to follow a rule concerning what everybody knows. Therefore Bacon associates the "delight in deceiving, and aptness to be deceived":

> This vice [which concerneth deceit or untruth] therefore brancheth itself into two sorts; delight in deceiving, and aptness to be deceived; imposture and credulity; which, although they appear to be of a diverse nature, the one seeming to proceed of cunning and the other of simplicity, yet certainly they do for the most part concur: for as the verse noteth, *Percontatorem fugito, name garruluae idem est* an inquisitive man is a prattler; so, upon the like reason a credulous man is a deceiver: as we see it in fame, that he will easily believe rumours, will as easily augment rumours, and add somewhat to them of his own; which Tacitus wisely noteth, when he saith, *Fingunt simul creduntque:* so great an affinity hath fiction and belief. (*Advancement* 1.6.8, 28)[32]

But this neutralizing of the vices cannot supply too happy an ending. The virtues too become neutralized in being used, and so Bacon will describe the good and bad uses of the virtues: "Virtue in ambition is violent, in authority settled and calm" ("Of Great Place," *Essays* 33). The goodness of virtues then consist in their use and their appearance: it is good to have friends because they can praise you when it would not be decent to praise yourself. Once they can be used, and once exchange, display, and mention become prominent forms of as well as use—they are not good and evil in any stable sense any longer: *Misanthropi* "are the very errors of human nature; and yet they are the fittest timber to make great politics of; like to knee-timber, that is good for ships that are ordained to be tossed, but not for building houses that shall stand firm" ("Of Goodness, and Goodness of Nature," *Essays* 38). If the instability of the distinction between prudence and opportunism is permanent, then "there is no better way to moderate suspicions, than to account upon such suspicions as true, and yet to bridle them as false" ("Of Suspicion," *Essays* 100). Ultimately, we have no place left from which to judge the morality of the *Essays*. Instead of making such judgments, we learn to "speak usefully."

What can Bacon, and the *Essays,* show about the rhetoric and ethics of reading? Bacon's attention to the social uses of saying, and not saying what goes without saying, opens an expanded set of connections between writer, reader, and the material talked about. If one conceives the rhetoric of fiction to be a transaction between authors and readers completely defined by the written object, saying what goes without saying might be bad manners, but nothing more.[33] Bacon constructs a momentous work out of what might otherwise be simply a breach of etiquette. Social silence has problems of its own that reach beyond those of authorial silence narrowly considered. Bacon shows that there are ways of being didactic that increase ethical activity by the reader. I would hope—although it cannot here be more than a hope—that this display of how Bacon works might force a reconsideration of the explicitly didactic purposes of novels, dramas, and poems, purposes that we are currently too inclined to discount. Regardless of that hope, Bacon's *Essays* add to the dimensions of how literature can make us better, and worse, people. Bacon's exhibition of a readjustment of the practical, the moral, and the ethical makes the rhetoric of fiction and the ethics of reading all the more central to how we ought to live.

Notes

1. References are to the standard edition of the *Works,* ed. Spedding et al., 1857–61. In addition, I give page numbers to the Everyman edition of *The Advancement of Learning* and the *Essays,* both ed. Kitchin.

2. Gadamer, *Truth and Method* 16–17: "By 'tact' we understand a particular sensitivity and sensitiveness to situations, and how to behave in them, for which we cannot find any knowledge from general principles. Hence an essential part of tact is inexplicitness and inexpressibility. One can say something tactfully; but that will always mean that one passes over something tactfully and leaves it unsaid, and it is tactless to mean to avert the gaze from something, but to watch it in such a way rather than knock against it, one slips by it. Thus tact helps one to preserve distance, it avoids the offensive, the intrusive, the violation of the intimate sphere of the person."

3. Contrast White, "Thinking About Our Language" 1975: "Part of maintaining a community is maintaining the agreement not to speak or ask about the ways in which its language means differently for different members," with Bernard Williams, *Ethics and the Limits of Philosophy* 102: "It is one aspiration, that social and ethical relations should not essentially rest on ignorance and misunderstanding of what they are, and quite another that all the beliefs and principles involved in them should be explicitly stated. That these are two different things is obvious with personal relations, where to hope that they do not rest on deceit and error is merely decent, but to think that their basis can be made totally explicit is idiocy."

4. That the *Essays'* intent is one of removing gaps between *is* and *ought* is noted by Levy. "Bacon shifted his emphasis from man's ability to train and control himself to resist the onslaughts of fortune to man's ability to control fortune herself, to be the architect of fortune. That shift was heralded by replacing the effort of *cultum animi* by an examination of the arts of rising at court, that is, by replacing how to 'be' with how to 'seem'" (113). See also, more generally, MacIntyre, "Epistemological Crises."

5. Plato notes the connection between claims of necessity and rationalization for what one wanted to do anyway at *Rep.* 6.493b–c: The sophists know "nothing in reality about which of these opinions and desires [sc. those of the many] is honorable or base, good or evil, just or unjust, but should apply all these terms to the judgments of the great beast, calling the things that pleased it good, and the things that vexed it bad, having no other account to render of them, but should call what is necessary just and honorable, never having observed how great is the real difference between the necessary and the good."

6. Whigham, *Ambition and Privilege* 170: "To the established aristocrat these [new competitive forms of political advancement] were, in Bacon's term, not virtues but 'activity.' Political accomplishments based on new kinds of ability were now read as subversive of the old order. But the members of that order had long recognized the role of ability (those raised as humanists could do no less); the powers manifested by the promotions therefore had to be denied *qua* virtues. Political success was redefined as failure, that is, as moral ugliness; political failure was redefined as a moral purity in one who chooses to turn aside from public life rather than to occupy its roles at the expense of integrity. . . . This attitude has long been familiar as a way of mystifying the direct engagement of a leisure class in political dominance by denying its engagement in the most obvious manifestations of power."

7. So Levy 120: "The man of judgment, the friend of the great, could offer two sorts of advice: how best to wear a mask, and how to discover the reality behind the masks of others."

8. "On the Problem of Truth" 423. See also Lovibond, esp. 99–101.

9. Whigham x–xi: "The received sense of personal identity, seen as founded on God-given attributes such as birth, was slowly giving way to the more modern notion that the individual creates himself by his own actions.

This new view was enticing to those on the rise, but it threatened those who resisted sharing their positions or who feared they would be displaced. The latter proposed the distinction found in courtesy theory in order to maintain their preeminence; the former read the courtesy books, hoping to avoid being too distinguished. The effect of this practical intellectual struggle was to articulate a sophisticated rhetoric, indeed an epistemology, of personal social identity—a new understanding of *how people tell who they are.*"

10. White, *Heracles' Bow* 65: "One way to identify what is misleading about the form of a legal rule might be to say that it appears to be a language of description, which works by a simple process of comparison, but in cases of any difficulty it is actually a language of judgment, which works in ways that find no expression in the rule itself. In such cases the meaning of its terms is not obvious, as the rule seems to assume, but must be determined by a process of interpretation and judgment to which the rule gives no guidance whatever. The discourse by which it works is in this sense invisible."

11. Levinson 112–13: "There is a fundamental way in which a full account of the communicative power of language can never be reduced to a set of conventions for the use of language. The reason is that wherever some convention or expectation about the use of language arises, there will also therewith arise the possibility of the non-conventional *exploitation* of that convention or expectation. It follows that a purely conventional or rule-based account of natural language usage can never be complete, and that what can be communicated always exceeds the communicative power provided by the conventions of the language and its use." Dewey 26: "Just because circumstances are really novel and not covered by old rules, it is a gamble which old rule will be declared regulative of a particular case, so that shrewd and enterprising men are encouraged to sail close to the wind and trust to ingenious lawyers to find some rule under which they can get off scot free."

12. Whigham 41: "Obscurantism is the code of the religious and courtly ruling elites; disruptive literalism is that of the unruly oppressed, ambitious for social and religious mobility."

13. For a suggestive remark that indicates just why texts like Bacon's *Essays* should be central to an ethics of literature, see *Company* 253n23: "Along with the strange history of the word 'hypocrisy,' we should add the ambiguous history of the word 'practice.' The earliest recorded sense of the word is 'the action of scheming or planning; artifice; a trick or plot.' Yet the word quickly developed more favorable senses, since—as we say—practice makes perfect." For details, see Orsini, "'Policy' or the Language of Elizabethan Machiavellianism." Booth's discussion of hypocrisy, a crucial but not deeply examined factor in his account of the ethics of fiction, would be enriched by consideration of the complexities of Renaissance debates about imitation, both literary and practical. While the literature is enormous, for some of the interesting details, see Greene, *The Light in Troy.*

14. See Fish, *Self-Consuming Artifacts.* I was glad to be confirmed in my as-

sessment of Fish's readings of Bacon by Richard Strier's unpublished consideration of the image of the reader and the reader's experience in *Self-Consuming Artifacts.* See also Whitney, *Francis Bacon and Modernity.*

15. For an application to the *Essays,* see Fish 80–81: "The characterization of the *Essays* as objective, dispassionate, and concisely analytic is hardly borne out by the collective response of those who so characterize them. An impersonal report does not leave its readers wondering about the inner life of the author; nor does it encourage speculation as to whether its own focus is 'traditional,' 'utilitarian,' 'moral,' or blurred."

16. For some purposes it is useful to distinguish several species of mention, all opposed to use. Equally, though, it is important to see how *in use* these different practices of mention run together. The Searle-Derrida debate turns in part on whether, as Searle claims in the name of common sense and logic, use is primary and mention parasitic, or whether, as Derrida more perversely claims, mention is primary and use derivative. For some complications, see Farrell, esp. 56: "I do not see that Derrida distinguishes clearly among four sorts of things: the mentioning of an expression in our talking about it; the quoting of a speaker's earlier speech; the sort of citing we do when, in using an expression rather than mentioning it, we deliberately make a reference to an earlier use of the expression (as when I use the phrase 'Parting is such sweet sorrow' not in order to quote it but to make an assertion to a friend); and the use of language in a play or poem when I am not making assertions about the world." That the idea of *use* includes a diverse set of phenomena, including what goes without saying, is noticed in Cohen 174: "Wittgenstein remarked that under normal conditions it would be odd to say, when I have a pain, *I* KNOW *I am in pain.* But perhaps this oddity tells us nothing of interest about the meaning of *know,* since it may be due just to the oddity of saying things that are too obvious to be worth saying. The 'use' terminology tends to confuse problems about the conditions under which a concept is applicable to problems about the conditions under which it is appropriate to make utterances involving the concept." See also Sperber and Wilson, "Irony and the Use-Mention Distinction."

17. Whigham 29–30: "All these texts function as commodities, in two ways. First, each offers a specimen of its author's worth, epideictically; many criteria are at work here besides interior intellectual ones. Second, each offers itemized concepts that may be traded anew by its consumer. . . . The Renaissance conversation in which such coin was spent was often organized by the canons of the *querrelle,* wherein the conduct of argument was *primarily* epideictic and formal, rather than substantive. In such a case ideas as quotable segments of texts may be analyzed in terms of exchange value rather than use value."

18. *Pace* Fish 118: "Bacon is not rejecting the *ideal* of goodness, but pointing out how far from it are the practices of men. It is this that distinguishes him from Machiavelli, or at least from the Machiavelli of popular reputation, a cynic who counsels self-interest at the expense of morality. Bacon is neither

immoral or amoral, but *pre*moral. He accepts the moral ideal as a point of departure, and measures everything against it. The conclusions that follow, then, are conclusions to matters of fact, not directives for future action. When Bacon has finished, the ideal remains; what does not remain is any illusion we may have had about the ease of living up to it. And without illusions, Bacon would argue, our chances of doing just that are much better." On the more general question of what happens when rules become explicit, see Schneewind 535: "Explicit articulations make sense where unspoken consensus seems to have reached its limits. An appeal to principle is a way of seeing whether that consensus can be projected into a novel area of controversy. Statements of rules and principles thus have a social function in this sort of context, one quite different from that envisaged by moral philosophers but important nonetheless."

19. Fish 92: "The *Essays* are to be read not as a series of encapsulations or expressions, but as a refining process that is being enacted by the reader; and to some extent, the question, in any one essay, of exactly what abstraction is being refined, is secondary." I have already argued against Fish's tacit and qualified inference to the conclusion that "to some extent" the emphasis on teaching the audience to read prudently somehow makes the content of that teaching irrelevant. See also Box 42: "Most of the essays of 1625 present an initial declaratory statement followed by qualifications and exceptions that undermine our confidence in the initial claim. The effect of this is unsettling but far from provocative in the Baconian scientific sense."

20. Booth, *Rhetoric of Fiction* 424: "The fictive experience, in contrast to the experience of most narrative in history and journalism, is thus made out of a special kind of double role-playing: as the actual listener or viewer, capable of joining an unlimited number of authorial audiences, I am 'made' to join the ones that are postulated by this particular story—to join them, as we might say, *really* and not just in pretense; but as a member of the narrative audience, I pretend to go much further and may even weep tears that I know to be 'false' even though they are physically real.

"The resulting tension between belief systems (a tension ordinarily *not* brought into consciousness) is the essential mark of the domains of fiction and it is the source of many distinctive effects, including our freedom to dwell in worlds expanded beyond what we could permit ourselves to dwell in 'really.' And it is utterly missing from all historical narratives except those that deliberately and openly contradict what the auctorial audience believes about historical fact—in short, those that become fictional."

21. Rossi 15. "Bacon analysed substances to determine their primal natures or irreducible qualities, so that gold becomes a combination of yellowness, specific weight, a degree of pliancy, malleability and so forth. This process is akin to that of reducing a word to its component letters, and so these primal natures are 'nature's alphabet' and constitute the ultimate elements to which the whole of nature can be reduced."

22. Fish 94. "Such a morality, [Bacon] implies, may well be immoral (use-

less), for it leaves a man ignorant of and defenseless against the real complexity of the situations that will confront him.... The essays advocate nothing (except perhaps a certain openness and alertness of mind); they are descriptive, and a description is ethically neutral, although, if it is accurate, it may contribute to the development of a true, that is, responsible, ethics." Box, after refuting some of Fish's stranger mischaracterizations of Bacon's aphoristic method, questions whether Bacon's description of the method in fact applies to the *Essays*. "It would seem a simple matter to decide whether the *Essays* are aphoristic and therefore scientific in Bacon's sense. Unfortunately, this is not the case because . . . the Baconian aphorism is defined by use and effect rather than by length, pithiness, or any other structural quality. . . . Accordingly, in passing judgment on the scientific style of Bacon's writing it is necessary to pay more attention to the effects of the content on the reader than to the actual form of the work in question. The question is whether the *Essays*, by presenting fragmentary but suggestive data, exert a 'pressure in the direction of "further enquiry"' [quoting Fish quoting Bacon]. . . . The later essays are not aphoristic in the 'Baconian' sense. Rather, the systematic presentation of assertions followed by qualifications is intended to impart to the reader a sense of the uncertainty and contingency of social life" (34).

See also Whitney 183: "Like the *Novum Organum*, the *Essays* reveal the modern paradox of the aphorism, that the literary effort to present the naked truth with all the force of its flashing moment of discovery occludes, veils, or all but dissolves naked truth."

23. "There is no greater impediment to action than an over-curious observance of decency, and the guide of decency, which is time and season" (2.23.3, 180). "Behavior seemeth to me as a garment of the mind and to have the conditions of a garment. For it ought to be made in fashion; it ought not to be too curious; it ought to be shaped so as to set forth any good making of the mind, and hide any deformity; and above all, it ought not to be too strait, or restrained for exercise or motion" (2.23.3, 181).

24. Kant, *Critique of Judgment*, sec. 29. 136/275: "*Simplicity* (artless purposiveness) is, as it were, nature's style in the sublime. Hence it is also the style of morality, which is a second (namely, a supersensible) nature, of which we know only the laws, without being able to reach, by means of intuition, the supersensible ability within ourselves that contains the basis of this legislation."

25. For an elementary treatment of this distinction, see Lanham, *Style: An Anti-Textbook*.

26. 2.17.13, 145: ". . . rule unto what degree of particularity a knowledge should descend. . . . For certainly there must be somewhat left to practice; but how much is worthy the inquiry. We see remote and superficial generalities do but offer knowledge to scorn of practical men; and are no more aiding to practice than an Ortelius' universal map is to direct the way between London and York. The better sort of rules have been not unfitly compared to glasses

of steel unpolished, where you may see the images of things, but first they must be filed: so the rules will help, if they be laboured and polished by practice." Compare the following: "Of Seditions and Troubles" (*Essays* 45): "For the remedies [of seditions]; there may be some general preservatives, whereof we shall speak; as for the just cure, it must answer to the particular disease, and so be left to counsel rather than rule." "Of Counsel" (*Essays* 65): "Neither is it enough to consult concerning persons *secundum genera*, as in an idea or mathematical description, what the kind and character of the person should be; for the greatest errors are committed, and the most judgment is shewn, in the choice of individuals." 2.23.1, 179 (5, 32): "Civil knowledge is conversant about a subject which of all others is most immersed in matter, and hardliest reduced to axiom. Nevertheless, as Cato the Censor said, *That the Romans were like sheep, for that a man might better drive a flock of them, than one of them; for in a flock, if you could but get some few to go right, the rest would follow:* so in that respect moral philosophy is more difficult than policy." (Cf. 2.23.15, 189: "Although the knowledge itself falleth not under precept, because it is of individuals, yet the instructions for the obtaining of it may.") 2.25.11, 214: "As to brevity, we see, in all summary methods, while men purpose to abridge, they give cause to dilate. For the sum or abridgement by contraction becometh obscure; the obscurity requireth exposition, and the exposition is diduced into large commentaries, or into common places and titles, which grow to be more vast than the original writings, whence the sum was at first extracted."

27. For what it means simultaneously to follow a rule and to be active, see Vining 45: "How does one imagine oneself going about *following* a decision? What are called 'the rules laid down by a decision' are verbal formulations of the reasons relied upon by a decision maker in making the decision. Those reasons are values, importances; any decision maker acting in a particular role necessarily gives relative weights to them in making a particular decision. One *follows* the decision by focusing upon the values appropriate for that role and discovering the weights used by the decision maker."

28. Cf. Cavell 307: "No rule or principle could function in a moral context the way regulatory or defining rules function in games. It is as essential to the form of life called morality that rules so conceived be absent as it is essential to the form of life we call a game that they be present."

29. Rossi 33. "What debars magic and alchemy from the status of science ... is precisely the burden they entrust to individual judgment and skill."

30. *Advancement of Learning*, 2.21.9, 165–66: "Men of corrupted minds presuppose that honesty groweth out of simplicity of manners, and believing of preachers, schoolmasters, and men's exterior language: so as, except you can make them perceive that you know the utmost reaches of their own corrupt opinions, they despise all morality; *Non recipit stultus verba prudentiae, nisi ea dixeris quae versantur in corde ejus*." This view is expressed in the *Republic* by Adiamantus: "Except that a man by inborn divinity of his nature disdains

injustice, or, having won to knowledge, refrains from it, no one else is willingly just, but that it is from lack of manly spirit or from old age or some other weakness that men dispraise injustice, lacking the power to practice it" (2.366d).

31. Consider, for example, the first essay, "Of Truth." We are told both that a pure truth is less and more desirable than one mixed with falsehood: "Truth may perhaps come to the price of a pearl, that sheweth best by day; but it will not rise to the price of a diamond or carbuncle, that sheweth best in varied lights. A mixture of a lie doth ever add pleasure" (*Essays* 3). On the other hand: "It will be acknowledged even by those that practise it not, that clear and round dealing is the honour of man's nature; and that mixture of falsehood is like allay in coin of gold and silver; which may make the metal work the better, but it embaseth it" (*Essays* 4). For a similar sentiment in the *Advancement of Learning,* see 2.23.33, 197: "These grave solemn wits, which must be like themselves, and cannot make departures, have more dignity than felicity."

32. See also 2.23.35, 198, quoted previously, and 2.14.6, 131: "This part concerning *elenches* is excellently handled by Aristotle in precept, but more excellently by Plato in example; not only in the persons of the Sophists, but even in Socrates himself; who, professing to affirm nothing, but to inform that which was affirmed by another, hath exactly expressed all the forms of objection, fallacy, and regardution. And although we have said that the use of this doctrine is for regardution, yet it is manifest the degenerate and corrupt use is for caption and contradiction, which passeth for a great faculty, and no doubt is of very great advantage: though the difference be good which was made between orators and sophisters, that the one is as the greyhound which hath his advantage in the race, and the other as the hare which hath her advantage in the turn, as it is the advantage of the weaker creature." See also *Advancement* 6, 268–69, discussing "lesser forms" or "those parts of a speech which answer to the vestibules, back doors, antechambers, withdrawing-chambers, passages, &c., of a house; and may serve indiscriminately for all subjects. Such are prefaces, conclusions, digressions, transitions, intimations of what is coming, excusations, and a number of the kind. For as in buildings it is a great matter both for pleasure and use that the fronts, doors, windows, approaches, passages, and the like be conveniently arranged, so also in a speech these accessory and interstitial passages (if they be handsomely and skilfully fashioned and placed) add a great deal both of ornament and effect to the entire structure."

33. In addition to *The Company We Keep,* the final section of *Critical Understanding* is an important reflection on connections between "flesh and blood" authors and readers and implied and constructed authors and readers.

Bibliography

Bacon, Francis. *The Advancement of Learning*. Ed. G. W. Kitchin. Everyman Edition. London: Dent, 1973.

———. *Essays*. Ed. G. W. Kitchin. Everyman Edition. London: Dent, 1972.

———. *Works*. Ed. J. Spedding, R. L. Ellis, and D. D. Heath, 7 vols. London, 1857–1861.

Booth, Wayne C. *The Company We Keep: An Ethics of Fiction*. Berkeley: U of California P, 1988.

———. *Critical Understanding: The Powers and Limits of Pluralism*. Chicago: U of Chicago P, 1979.

———. *The Rhetoric of Fiction*. Chicago: U of Chicago P, 1961; 2nd ed., 1983.

Box, Ian. "Bacon's *Essays*: From Political Science to Political Prudence." *History of Political Thought* 3 (1982): 31–49.

Cavell, Stanley. *The Claim of Reason*. New York: Oxford UP, 1979.

Cohen, L. Jonathan. "Speech Acts." *Current Trends in Linguistics* 12 (1990): 173–208.

Dewey, John. "Logical Method and Law." *Cornell Law Quarterly* 10 (1924): 17–27.

Farrell, Frank B. "Iterability and Meaning: The Searle-Derrida Debate." *Metaphilosophy* 19 (1988): 53–64.

Fish, Stanley. *Self-Consuming Artifacts: The Experience of Seventeenth-Century Literature*. Berkeley: U of California P, 1972.

Gadamer, H. G. *Truth and Method*. New York: Seabury, 1975.

Geertz, Clifford. *Local Knowledge: Further Essays in Interpretive Anthropology*. New York: Basic, 1983.

Greene, Thomas. *The Light in Troy: Imitation and Discovery in Renaissance Poetry*. New Haven, CT: Yale UP, 1982.

Hexter, J. H. *More's Utopia: The Biography of an Idea*. Princeton, NJ: Princeton UP, 1952.

Horkheimer, Max. "On the Problem of Truth." *The Essential Frankfurt School Reader*. Ed. Andrew Arato and Eike Gebhardt. New York: 1982. 423.

Lanham, Richard. *Style: An Anti-Textbook*. New Haven, CT: Yale UP, 1974.

Levinson, Stephen. *Pragmatics*. Cambridge: Cambridge UP, 1983.

Levy, F. J. "Francis Bacon and the Style of Politics." *English Literary Renaissance* 16 (1988): 101–22.

Lovibond, Sabina. *Realism and Imagination in Ethics*. Minneapolis: U of Minnesota P, 1983.

MacIntyre, Alasdair. "Epistemological Crises, Dramatic Narrative and the Philosophy of Science." *Monist* 60 (1977): 453–72.

Orsini, Napoleone. "'Policy' or the Language of Elizabethan Machiavellianism." *Journal of the Warburg and Courtauld Institutes* 9 (1946): 122–34.

Plato. *Republic*. Trans. Paul Shorey. 2 vols. Loeb Classical Library. Cambridge, MA: Harvard UP, 1930–35.

Rossi, Paolo. *Francis Bacon: From Magic to Science*. Trans. S. Rabinovitch. Chicago: U of Chicago P, 1978.

Schneewind, Jerome B. "Moral Crisis and the History of Ethics." *Midwest Studies in Philosophy* 8 (1983): 525–42.

Sperber, Dan, and Deirde Wilson. "Irony and the Use-Mention Distinction." *Radical Pragmatics*. Ed. Peter Cole. New York: Academic, 1981. 295–318.

Vining, Joseph. *The Authoritative and the Authoritarian*. Chicago: U of Chicago P, 1986.

Whigham, Frank. *Ambition and Privilege: The Social Tropes of Elizabethan Courtesy Theory*. Berkeley: U of California P, 1984.

White, James B. *Heracles' Bow*. Madison: U of Wisconsin P, 1987.

———. "Thinking about Our Language." *Yale Law Journal* 96 (1987): 1960–83.

Whitney, Charles. *Francis Bacon and Modernity*. New Haven, CT: Yale UP, 1986.

Williams, Bernard. *Ethics and the Limits of Philosophy*. Cambridge, MA: Harvard UP, 1985.

V

Booth, Assent, and Argument

13

Wayne Booth and the Ethics of Argument

PATSY CALLAGHAN AND ANN DOBYNS

ARGUING AS AN ETHICAL ACT

WAYNE BOOTH'S WORK has been dominated by ethical concerns, from his early *The Rhetoric of Fiction* with its overtly ethical conclusion, in essays proclaiming the need for reasoned discourse collected in *Now Don't Try to Reason with Me*, to his defense of shared literary experiences in *A Rhetoric of Irony*, in his faith that some truth is to be found in the mutual exchange of differing opinions in *Critical Understanding*, and recently by his advocacy of friendship as the metaphor for the interaction of author and reader in *The Company We Keep*. While all of these works are predicated on the assumption that as human beings discourse they make meaning together, they also present a philosophy of argument as primary in the testing and embracing of values. Argument is then the theoretical heart of the ethical pursuit. In 1974 Booth explicitly defined his philosophy of argument in a book written in part as a response to the protests of the 1960s and the "failure of communication" between warring factions (*Modern Dogma* ix). Originally a lecture series at the University of Notre Dame in 1971, the essays presented in *Modern Dogma and the Rhetoric of Assent* constitute what is perhaps Booth's most direct explanation of his rhetorical position. Rhetoric, he explains in his introduction, is "the art of discovering warrantable beliefs and improving those beliefs in shared discourse" (*Modern Dogma* xiii).

Why argue anyway? To pursue an answer, we must set two lines of reasoning that render the question pointless. First, if it were possible to address the question through objective observation of available facts, people would have no need to discuss it, for the answer would be self-evident. Second, if the question is not one of "hard fact" but instead one of "soft faith," then whatever answer is proposed would necessarily be an assertion of "value" or belief, and thus mere personal preference. To go on talking about the question in either case would be to join a "world of futile babblers" (*Modern Dogma* xi). As Booth sees it, these ways of addressing the question assume a passive, almost unconscious acceptance of the "dogmas of modernism," dogmas which have created a rhetorical crisis that is also an ethical one: "We have lost faith in the very possibility of finding a rational path through any thicket that includes what we call value judgments" (*Modern Dogma* 7). And yet, Booth holds out hope for such a rational path. As users and sharers of symbols, and as imperfect beings in an imperfect world, humans act ethically when they reason together toward probable and contingent truths. In the process of discovering assent, humans seek a point of agreement from which to begin a dialogue. The dialogue itself builds the self, so we discover who we are and become who we are through communicating with each other. Through this process the world and truth are both found and made, and the act of finding meaning together supercedes the importance of any particular product. The sense of this stance seems as practical as the humor in the old story about the three blind philosophers and the elephant: The first feels the trunk and declares he's found a snake; the second feels the tail and pronounces it a rope; the third feels a side and knows he faces a wall. Wayne Booth asks us to consider the possibility of discovering the whole elephant: reasoning together, accepting that which we have every reason to believe and no good reason to doubt, we argue in order to agree.

Assent Instead of Skepticism

As Booth represents them, the two "sects" of modernism present man as an atomic, physical mechanism, the universe as impersonal and value free, and knowledge as the provable. The first sect of modernism Booth identifies, scientism, posits a neutral universe, inherently impersonal, in which truth exists apart from the individual as a set of facts to be discovered through the systematic doubt of empiricism. The individual in this universe is isolated, the mind a material organ that operates mechanically by chemical and physical laws. Our human responsibility consists, then, of seeking certainty through the examination of facts, of discovering knowledge and truth while avoiding the self-delusion of opinion, belief, and value by doubting all pending proof. The second sect, irrationalism, recognizes the limit of scientism to be that it fails to cope in other than empirical terms with multiple, simultaneous, even contradictory truths. Since little, as we know, is invulnerable to the probings of empiricism, scientism must eventually disprove all external truths; thus certainty would be found only in self-knowledge. Isolated in a self-constructed reality, the individual seeks truth through the subjective examination of internal feelings, since each person's truth is uniquely valuable for that person alone. Seeming opposites, the two schools of modernism share the methodological assumptions of science, the mechanical metaphors of technology, the isolation of the individual, and the goal of certainty. Though in one case facing human responsibility means finding the world through objective observation and in the other case creating the world out of our own perceptions and feelings, in both cases individuals seek certain truth through retreat to skepticism—into the corner they find by doubting all pending proof, or into a "self" of preconceived notions and biases.

Given these assumptions, argument—all discourse about values—will be necessarily divisive, mechanistic, competitive, and isolationist. The only answers to the question "why argue" would either be "to win" or "to assert the self," and the only way to go about arguing would be to pronounce assertions at each other. Booth regards such a situation a failure of rhetoric resulting from a "radically mistaken conception of the nature and possibilities of argument" (*Modern Dogma* 11), and posits instead a habit of mind that radically alters the epistemological groundings of our process of communicating: a rhetoric of assent. Rather than rejecting hypotheses or approaching them with skepticism, people ought rather tentatively to accept any premise (1) that they have no particular reason to doubt, (2) that they have good reasons to believe, and (3) that others who are educated about the problem also believe (*Modern Dogma* 40). "It is reasonable," Booth insists, "to grant (one *ought* to grant) some degree of credence to whatever qualified men and women agree on, *unless* one has specific and stronger reasons to disbelieve" (*Modern Dogma* 101).

Rhetorical Communities

Countering what he has called "dogmas," Booth asserts that the "primary act of man is to assent to truth rather than to detect error" (*Modern Dogma* xvi). Rather than seeing humans as isolated, material beings operating by mechanical laws, he presents the self as existing in a community of individuals who build each other through symbolic exchange. Instead of existing in a universe that is value free, found through objective examination of facts or through subjective examination of feelings, Booth's individual operates as a field of selves, both discovering and changing the world through dialectic. The answer to "why argue" becomes then a matter not of asserting positions or winning ground, but of discovering "together, in discourse, new levels of truth (or at least agreement) that neither side suspected before" (*Modern Dogma* 11). Individuals do this, Booth argues, to exercise responsible judgment, to achieve cooperation, to solve problems, and finally, to survive. "If," Booth asks, "language is not a means of communication but the source of our being, and if the purpose of rhetoric is not to persuade but to meet other minds in the best possible symbolic exchange . . . everything we value, including the achievements of science and mathematics, depends on this fact which is a value: men ought to attend to whatever good reasons are offered them by other men" (*Modern Dogma* 142). Thus the responsibility placed upon us is clear: "we must build new rhetorical communities, we must find a common faith in modes of argument, or every institution we care about will die" (*Modern Dogma* 150).

Seen this way, the process of argument is essentially ethical: we ought to attend to whatever good reasons are offered to us by others, and we ought to seek the conditions under which a meeting of minds is likely to occur. As participants in the dialogue, we should react with common sense, accepting only premises that in some way are true to our experiences. We should begin not with doubt, as many theorists of critical thinking would have us do, but with assent, giving credence to a valid, shared position as a starting point in a line of reasoning. We should test our ideas through discourse, listening with understanding to the arguments of others. And we should be willing to change our minds. Thus the process of rhetorical inquiry becomes more important than any possible conclusions, as individuals discover and test not just what they believe, but what they find they *should* believe, creating a rhetorical community based on shared values.

Community and Good Reasons

Rhetoric is the "art of discovering good reasons," and individuals pursue that art because good reasons provide the only basis for rational behavior. "Good rhetoric" is not what is successful or effective in the face of "pig-headed" audiences, but what "any reasonable person ought to be persuaded by" (*Modern Dogma* xiv). Conversely, "bad rhetoric lacks genuine power to move reasonable auditors" (*Modern Dogma* xv). To argue well, individuals should argue honestly, genuinely, attending to their own assumptions and making sure they have good reasons for believing that to which they would encourage others to assent. Furthermore, individuals should argue critically, listening to the arguments of others with understanding. As Booth explains, "To be genuinely critical—to judge on the basis of thought—is to have no easily predictable relationship with belief or doubt, with yes or no, with joining or splitting. The critical mind does not know in advance which side it will come out on" (*Now Don't Try to Reason* 66).

Essential to this process of arguing is the grounding of the rhetorical community in common sense, or those principles agreed upon by "any thoroughly informed and rational—any thoroughly qualified—human being" (*Modern Dogma* 110). As humans, individuals have more common than different experiences. And because of our common experiences, we share many beliefs or values. In other words, we choose to hold many postulates first because they ring true to our patterns of experience, and further, because they stand up when tested against others' patterns of experience. Rather than an argument for universal principles, Booth's position suggests that humans make meaning together and do so through dialogue about shared experiences. Further, the strength of the testing of such agreements rests on the rationality and experience of the testers. Our rhetorical communities then comprise ourselves and those whose empirical testing qualifies them as experts on the question at issue. Such a concept seems to come dangerously close to that of the bandwagon, and Booth acknowledges the comparison. What makes Booth's explanation of assenting to values in rhetorical communities different is his faith in the credibility of the educated examination of experience. Fanatical groups exist whose beliefs seem based on common experience, but it does not follow that reasonable humans will assent to such beliefs, precisely because the beliefs would contradict their own experiences and those of other reasonable humans.

Such a definition of systematic assent allows Booth to find a starting place for discussion when individuals disagree, thus identifying a rhetorical community in which real dialogue is possible. It is only in real dialogue, Booth argues, that humans create themselves as they propose good reasons for the positions they hold and seriously entertain the good reasons offered by those with whom they disagree. Such a mutual exchange, on issues important to all participants and discussed on common ground with respect for opposing arguments, promises what Booth calls "improving beliefs in shared discourse" (*Modern Dogma* xiii). Attending to a multiplicity of voices is for Booth inherent in ethical argument. Individuals may choose to ignore what Booth elsewhere calls the "dialogic imagination" (see "Freedom of Interpretation: Bakhtin and the Challenge of Feminist Criticism"). But by doing so they miss opportunities to see the world in new ways, to grow and change consciously as they participate in the exciting social interaction of "being persons together" (*Modern Dogma* 134).

The Rhetoric of Assent and the Study of Literature

In many ways, *Modern Dogma and the Rhetoric of Assent* shows the coherence of Booth's writings. Though clearly a work about reasoning, Booth's *Modern Dogma* presents a philosophy of good reasons that has less to do with logic than with ethics. The self, Booth argues, is "*essentially* rhetorical, symbol exchanging, a social product in process of changing through interaction, sharing values with other selves" (*Modern Dogma* 126). In the dialogue with other selves, whether face to face or with the implied author of an artistic work, humans are making and remaking themselves. This process is an ethical one, first because human actions form human character, or ethos, and further because the dialogue Booth describes involves judging good reasons offered by other selves. Booth's philosophy of good reasons rather than being an inquiry into certain truth concerns the formation of character.

Throughout his discussions of argument, Booth explores the way humans change through their interactions with others, whether people or ideas or art, music, or literature. Having concluded *The Rhetoric of Fiction* with a consideration of the ethical dimensions of literary works, Booth comes back repeatedly to the discussion. In *Modern Dogma,* he claims that art "is of fundamental importance in making and changing our minds (or souls or selves or identities)" (168). The study of literature for Booth is less a matter of the attempt to find the meaning of a text than to engage in dialogue with a writer about values. Literary works, he suggests, present positions on questions of value and, further, give good reasons for those positions. Readers engage in dialogue by considering the strength of the reasons and by judging them against their own experiences and the experiences of other careful readers. In *Modern Dogma,* Booth describes this process as one in which the writer presents a position on a question of value by performing a narrative act and in that performance affirming an attitude toward a question of value. Stories are the reasons writers give for their position—the experience of the story expresses a worldview. Readers participate in the constructed experience and judge the validity of the attitude expressed through that experience. When readers participate in the experience, they are in some way changed, and because art has the power to change us, Booth argues, we ought to read critically and examine the reasons writers give for the positions they espouse.

In *The Company We Keep: An Ethics of Fiction,* Booth takes on the task of presenting a definition of ethical criticism and giving good reasons for engaging in such an activity. In this book, he explicitly shifts the issue from the determinacy of meaning to the value of the narrative experience and the ways in which that experience is sharable. Booth acknowledges that "the question of whether value is in the poem or in the reader is radically and permanently ambiguous," but to admit the inherent ambiguity is not to suggest that all judgment is subjective. Booth explains, "Of course the value is not there, *actually* until it is actualized, by the reader. But of course it could not be actualized if it were not there, *in potential,* in the poem" (*Company* 89). The process of actualizing the potential value system of a literary work initiates a dialogue between author and readers that develops into a larger critical conversation about the values at issue. While readers may not evaluate the experience in precisely the same ways, they can discuss their judgments and their reasons for such judgments. The ethical inquiry is one conducted in a critical community. For Booth "the most important of all critical tasks is to participate in—and thus to reinforce—a critical culture, a vigorous conversation, that will nourish in return those who feed us with their narratives" (*Company* 136).

TEACHING ETHICAL ARGUMENT

If it is ethical to argue, to seek shared understandings regarding values, then it is also good to promote rhetorical inquiry. We should ask "what 'rhetorical communities' can be discovered that may in fact unite seemingly warring factions, and what are the real conflicts that separate rhetorical communities based on conflicting assumptions?" (*Modern Dogma* xiv). We study rhetoric to learn to argue "ethically," to increase the possibility that we can reach shared understandings with others. As teachers, we are in a position to create communities of inquirers in our own classrooms, and yet we often have to work against the traditional authority of writing texts based on the dogmas of scientism, which have taught "that the goal of all thought and argument is to emulate the purity and objectivity and rigor of science, in order to protect oneself from the errors that passion and desire and metaphor and authority and all those logical fallacies lead us into" (*Modern Dogma* 88). We also have to work against the traditional authority structure of the classroom, which inhibits notions of community and sharing.

Two textbooks by Booth and Marshall W. Gregory, the Harper and Row *Rhetoric* and the Harper and Row *Reader,* help teachers and students consider the value of thinking about ideas together. The *Rhetoric,* subtitled *Writing as Thinking, Thinking as Writing,* introduces the choices writers must make in the symbolic exchange as they attempt to change the minds of others, while the *Reader* approaches the symbolic exchange from the recipient's perspective and thus examines the ways other writers share their intentions, values, and meanings. The distinctions are, of course, not so neat as the contrast might make them appear. One way the authors of the *Rhetoric* discuss the various choices student writers might consider is by analyzing the strategies that were employed in completed essays. Likewise, in the *Reader,* Booth and Gregory ask students to participate in the dialogue invited by the essays they read, not merely to analyze the strategies of argument. Throughout both texts, the dialogic nature of the processes of reading and writing, as well as the importance of those arts, is reinforced. Writing is treated as a 'conversation' with potential readers" (*Rhetoric* xiv), a conversation that will involve students in a process of inquiry through which they will repeatedly be making themselves—finding, testing, evaluating, and frequently changing their beliefs, and thus it is clear that the composition course is not a service course but potentially the most significant college experience.

As in *Modern Dogma,* the emphasis is on the importance of finding common ground. The process of becoming educated, the authors say, is "in part, learning to take in the contrasting perspectives of other lives" (*Rhetoric* 157), and writing itself "is one of our most effective ways of learning, for it not only forces us to attend to other people's arguments and opinions, but also forces us to *think through* our own views" (*Reader* 12). Unlike in other introductory writing texts that include the inevitable warning of the danger of discussing controversial and apparently irresolvable issues (for example, Maxine Hairston's *Contemporary*

Rhetoric, in which she argues in chapter 4, "Where Rhetoric Starts and Stops," that communication is impossible when *a priori* premises conflict), Booth and Gregory demonstrate ways to discuss and even sometimes resolve apparently irresolvable issues. In analyses of pieces of completed writing, Booth and Gregory put the reader in the mind of the writer, most importantly by making them consider the rhetorical context that compelled the writer to write.

An early example from the *Rhetoric* illustrates their approach. The authors reprint a letter written to the editor of the *New York Times* in which the writer recounts the martyrdom of Sir Thomas More, an act of conscience claimed inspirational by many politicians, such as New York's Governor Cuomo. In his narration of the events leading to More's martyrdom, the writer emphasizes the consistency of More's private principles and his public actions. Today, the writer concludes, public officials claim private disapproval of abortion while publicly defending laws that allow its practice. Such officials, he suggests, have not learned the lesson the martyr's death ought to teach. The analysis that follows the letter demonstrates the kind of critical understanding Booth and Gregory advocate. Why did the writer compose his letter, they ask; what was the situation that compelled him to write, and to whom was the letter addressed? Given his particular rhetorical situation, what strategies did he employ—strategies of argument, design, cohesiveness, character, and style? Throughout the discussion, Booth and Gregory withhold judgment as to the correctness of the writer's position, taking on the task as if it were their own. If you were to tackle this situation, they seem to say, how might you choose to proceed? By taking the reader through the writer's hypothetical thinking process, they encourage the reader to consider the writer's concerns, beliefs, ways of approaching the task—to examine the issue from his perspective and thus enter into real dialogue with him.

Writers also are obliged to do all they might to seek understanding of others' positions as they attempt to discover the best possible reasons in support of their own arguments. As the letter to the *Times* illustrates, purposes consist of both writers' motives and the changes writers hope to make in their readers. While considering strategies, the authors argue, writers must explore issues in light of the positions their readers might hold—they must, in other words, "bring in the voice of the opposition" (*Rhetoric* 82). The processes of discovering arguments then involves critically questioning one's own principles and thus, potentially, changing one's mind. But while there are no infallible rules for judging good reasons, Booth and Gregory establish some principles to help writers consider their options. To argue well, writers should know the variety and kinds of reasons available to them because the modes of argument, shared as they are by humans, provide the most obvious common ground (or *commonplaces,* in Aristotelian terms) from which to argue. Further, writers should spend time thinking about their audience's beliefs and needs, should strive to meet their readers' standards as well as their own, and should adjust the strength of their own claims to the strength of their reasons. Keeping these principles in mind could make it less likely that writers would fall into the dishonest practice of trying to "get readers to follow without *thinking* about the cost, the direction, or alternative paths" (*Rhetoric* 241). To do so is, according to the principles espoused in *Modern Dogma,* dishonest to both writer and reader because such a practice misses the point of argument. "The supreme purpose of persuasion in this view could not be to talk someone else into a preconceived view; rather it must be to engage in mutual inquiry or exploration. In such a world, our rhetorical purpose must always be to perform as well as possible in the same primal symbolic dance which makes us able to dance at all. If it is good for men to attend to each other's reasons—and we all know that it is, because without such attending none of us could come to be and questions about value could not even be asked—it is also good to work for whatever conditions make such mutual inquiry possible. Whatever imposes belief without personal engagement becomes inferior to whatever makes mutual exchange more likely. The purpose of mental change is thus to fulfill one's nature as a creature capable of responding to symbolic offerings" (*Modern Dogma* 137).

These texts, then, explicitly endorse Booth's vision of argument as coming face to face with human responsibilities. Booth and Gregory offer students reasons for writing that appeal not to their desire for better grades or better wages, but to their personal, social, and cultural identities, reasons that reinforce the notion of argument as the basis of human existence. Writers write to gain greater control over their own lives, and "to help create the kind of world—presumably a 'better' one—that [they] want to live in" (*Rhetoric* 11). Writers discover that "[l]earning to think critically about the way powerful language is used in our culture is really the same as learning to think about the culture itself: about freedom and community" (*Rhetoric* 244). And they find that language, rather than being something they inherit like property, is "more like the air we breathe, the medium that sustains our very life" (*Rhetoric* 28); it is, Booth and Gregory point out in their introductory comments in the *Reader*, the form of behavior that characterizes humans.

Thus the textbooks, in admitting, even insisting on, the discussibility of values, clearly include an agenda of ethical beliefs. In addition, the authors provide the best model of their teachings, refusing to allow readers to adopt that agenda uncritically. The dialogic process is reinforced both in the manner and the matter of the approach. As the authors observe in the *Rhetoric*, "Instead of leading you like sheep, we keep inviting you to think critically about our claims and our arguments" (241). In fact, at the end of the first chapter, they list some of the claims about writers and writing they have made so far—claims that assert the uncertainty of "truth," the social and dialogic nature of the self and language, and the value of seeking assent—and ask that students "argue" the claims, finding good reasons to support their truth or falsehood.

Teachers, following the model of the authors of the *Rhetoric* and the *Reader*, thus have a dual role: they act both as participants in the rhetorical community, exhibiting their own "high excitement about learning steadily toward higher standards for their answers" (*Rhetoric* 22). To establish the dialogic nature of the classroom, teachers are advised to start modeling "active learning" on the first day, getting students to talk, read, and write together; to hold personal conferences early; to use editorial teams and workshop sessions; and to practice discussion, a difficult art in an environment plagued by naive relativism and a constant devaluing of "opinion" in favor of "fact." They are asked directly to follow in their teaching the same rhetorical ethics they would encourage in their students, exhibiting openness, tolerance, and liberality of mind and heart. As Booth and Gregory put it, "we address each other, and try to change one another's minds, because we all know that nobody *is* perfect, either in knowledge or behavior. In learning to write better— without hope of perfection—we join the age-old, never-ending human project of trying to make life better for us all" (*Rhetoric* 467).

ETHICAL ARGUMENT BEYOND THE WRITING CLASSROOM

If the limited "vision" of the three blind philosophers is obvious enough to be the basis of the old story's humor, then why is it that a similar absence of common ground so often seems to muddle public discourse about issues? Booth's own observations of the complicated entanglements characterizing campus rhetoric in the 1960s prompted his concern with the ethics of arguing, but our own experiences offer little evidence that, twenty years later, a discussion about values is less likely to result in an impasse. On the national front recently, a row of senators with furrowed brows contemplated the testimony of Clarence Thomas and Anita Hill at hearings concerning Thomas's nomination for Supreme Court Justice. The senators' puzzlement was painfully obvious. They sought diligently and hopefully for the fact, the single witness, the piece of news that would take the situation out of the realm of probability and into the empirical science of certainty. Without that missing fact, they seemed to lack even an awareness of how to go about regarding the information they had. It was obvious from both the questions and answers that the senators had not articulated, much less agreed upon, assumptions about the nature and seriousness of sexual harassment, the qualifications of the candidate, or the relevance of the charges to their understanding of the qualifications for the job. Because they had not undertaken the chore of articulating their positions, of defining their common ground, of establishing the nature and limitations of their task, they were left with the impossibility of determining who was telling "the" truth. Given this example of public discourse, it is obvious why students have difficulty accepting that it is even possible, much less desirable, to make decisions in a situation where the facts aren't enough.

In the 1992 presidential elections, media personalities made much of the difference in the candidates' "styles." George Bush, it seemed, was more "decisive." Clinton, the continuing story asserted, was "indecisive." Time and time again what the examples illustrated was that Clinton, unlike Bush, not only changed his mind when confronted with new knowledge or good reasons, but was willing to admit such changes publicly. Far from considering the possible ethics of the strategy, many regarded this openness as a lack of character: a suspicious weakness. Given this assumption, it is no wonder that students presume in their courses that their task is to assert their preconceived ideas—that they have a right to say only what they can assert with certainty, or what they can assert with pretended authority. We think of one student who came to class in tears on the day a paper was due. "I'm sorry," she said. "I have to write about something else. While I was reading about my other topic, I changed my mind."

In our public involvements beyond the writing classroom, we also witness the frequency with which discussions of values result in an impasse. With the help of an administration practiced in the art of collaborative dialogue, a local school district recently extricated itself from what could have been a devastating crisis. It began when a parent objected to some of the contemporary stories included in a recently adopted anthology of short fiction. Some teachers joined in the call for review of the decision; others were appalled at the possibility of self-censorship among their ranks. Suddenly and without warning, tempers flared. Anger divided long-term colleagues. Assumptions about knowledge, training, learners, aesthetics, responsibility, and public trust were articulated as if permanent, paramount, and uncomplicated by situation and particulars. Though the issue seemed hopelessly polarized, an administrator asked the faculty to name and invite a panel of parents and university faculty to participate in a dialogue on the decision. He required that the meeting continue until the participants reached some agreement, and agreed to support that decision to the school board. The panel was instructed to establish, first, a list of criteria for selecting literary texts, and then to evaluate the anthology in light of those criteria.

In the end, no one, it seemed, questioned the quality of the literature included in the anthology. Second, everyone accepted the principle that the appropriateness of the material depended on how a good teacher might handle it. Third, and this was an essential discovery, many of the teachers, already overworked, admitted that their stance was influenced by their fear of having to prepare to teach literature they had not "mastered" in their university training. Having identified this common ground, the panel proposed a resolution acceptable to all parties: Because no one should have to teach a text with which they are unfamiliar, and because no one should be prevented categorically from using a text they can justify professionally, the story anthology should remain available as an optional text for teachers to use depending on the needs and backgrounds of their students and the specific teaching goals.

The warrant is simple. It recognizes and acknowledges matters of value, even though it may not resolve them permanently. It recognizes that solutions to problems are contextual, and yet that people can agree on the ethical grounds of the answers. But possibly more important than the particular wording of the resolution were its other effects: a release in the tension surrounding the issue that allowed more honest inquiry, a greater understanding of purpose and goals among the language arts professionals, and the survival of dialogue in an essential teaching community far in time and space from Booth's Chicago campus, but identical in its need for ways to arrive at shared understandings through the art of discovering warrantable beliefs.

If we argue to agree we must also agree to argue. Understanding, justice, even our existence as a human community depend upon our ability to keep critical interchange vital: "The Babel of critical voices is transformed at the moment when each critic decides that his survival depends not on shouting down all the others but on granting them a hearing" (*Critical Understanding* 232). Thus Booth enjoins us all to employ the ethics of argument, to create community through rhetoric, to discover warrantable beliefs, and to improve those habits in shared discourse.

Bibliography

Booth, Wayne C. *The Company We Keep: An Ethics of Fiction*. Berkeley: U of California P, 1988.

———. *Critical Understanding: The Powers and Limits of Pluralism*. Chicago: U of Chicago P, 1979.

———. "Freedom of Interpretation: Bakhtin and the Challenge of Feminist Criticism." *Critical Inquiry* 9.1 (1982): 45–76.

———. *Modern Dogma and the Rhetoric of Assent*. Chicago: U of Chicago P, 1974.

———. *Now Don't Try to Reason with Me: Essays and Ironies for a Credulous Age*. Chicago: U of Chicago P, 1970.

———. *A Rhetoric of Irony*. Chicago: U of Chicago P, 1974.

Booth, Wayne C., and Marshall W. Gregory. *The Harper and Row Reader: Liberal Education Through Reading and Writing*. New York: Harper, 1984; 2nd ed., 1988.

———. *The Harper and Row Rhetoric: Writing as Thinking, Thinking as Writing*. New York: Harper, 1987; 2nd ed., 1991.

Hairston, Maxine. *Contemporary Rhetoric*. 3rd ed. Boston: Houghton, 1985.

14

The Logic and Rhetoric of Systematic Assent

ALAN BRINTON

Modern Dogma and the Rhetoric of Assent is a provocative book, both in its attacks on "modern dogma" and in its own affirmative rhetoric. As I read *Modern Dogma,* the attack on what Booth takes to be governing presuppositions of modern thought is meant to clear the decks for a rhetoric of assent and to lay the groundwork for a series of affirmations. Among modern dogmas, "a kind of unproved and unprovable conviction that *thought doubts;* that that's its job" (57) is of central importance in the overall plan of *Modern Dogma.* Booth especially identifies this dogma with Bertrand Russell, among twentieth-century philosophers, but sees Russell's views about doubt and certainty as arising from "a tradition willed to him by centuries of western skepticism" and "brought to a head" by Descartes in his method of systematic doubt (55).[1] The Cartesian method of systematic doubt is apparently regarded by Booth as constituting the dominant methodological dogma of modern philosophy. As an alternative to it, he proposes a diametrically opposed method of systematic *assent.* And in opposition to a "habit of negative rhetoric" (as manifested in the negative political rhetoric of the 1960s, but also in more "metaphysical" modern nay-saying about the meaning of human life), he means to affirm rhetorical and epistemological policies of communal yea-saying, as well as to engage in some significant yea-saying of his own.

So *Modern Dogma* attempts a clearing away of "dogmas of doubt," to make way for an assentive rhetoric, but also in preparation for Booth's own experiment in assenting—assenting to propositions that give rise to the conception of man as "essentially" rhetorical, as "a rhetorical animal," created and defined symbolically in interaction with other persons. The rhetoric recommended in *Modern Dogma* purports to be a rhetoric of good reasons; and the introduction of his method of assent is meant to provide justification for an outbreak of assenting in chapter 4.

Some aspects of the early stages of *Modern Dogma* are worthy of hearty approval, such as the treatment of the dogma of "motivism." And some of the details of the constructive program of the later parts seem to me also to be important and able to stand on their own, independent of what goes on in earlier chapters. In particular, much of what is said in chapter 4 about ethical and emotional proof seems important and essentially correct. But the critique of the method (and attitude) of Cartesian doubt and the attempt to replace it with a method of systematic assent strike me as highly problematic. In any case, it is the conception of a *method of systematic assent,* along with the suggestion that there can and ought to be one, which I find to be a most provocative aspect of *Modern Dogma,* and which I would like (as a self-confessed "analytic" philosopher, I must add) to examine in this chapter.

THE METHOD OF SYSTEMATIC DOUBT

A Cartesian method of systematic doubt, Booth claims, underlies and gives the impetus in modern thought to both "scientism" and irrationalism, in both cases by engendering a kind of skepticism about values and about discussion of questions of value. But just what *is* this method of doubt, and what really are its tendencies? What other attitudes does it, by its nature, and also historically, tend to produce?

The skeptical method of Descartes's first Meditation is self-consciously Pyrrhonistic. That is to say, it is a method that has its earliest origins in the views of the Greek skeptic Pyrrho of Elis and its classic formulation in the *Outlines of Pyrrhonism* and other works of Sextus Empiricus.[2] Descartes does not, as anyone who has read the *Meditations* knows, end up in skepticism. That he ends up not a skeptic but a dogmatist has more often been taken as evidence that his commitment to the method of doubt is less than wholehearted than as evidence that systematic doubt leads to dogmatism, scientismic or Fideistic. But more about that shortly.

Descartes says in the first of his Meditations that, when he came to the realization that many of the opinions he had accepted in his early life were mistaken, he determined that the only way he would come to a true knowledge was by undertaking to "set aside all the opinions which I had previously accepted" (75) and to "start again from the very beginning," putting aside, as he says later (Meditation 2, 81), every belief in which he can "imagine the least doubt" and assenting only to propositions that he finds it impossible to doubt.[3] Now, in the early Meditations, we find sometimes the language of *doubt* and sometimes the language of *denial*. Early along he speaks of *abstaining* from belief in what is not entirely certain (75), and later he says that if he achieves no other result at least he will have the power in the end to "suspend judgment" (80). But then he also says that, to counterbalance the force of his longstanding habits of belief, it may not be enough to "consider that they are what they really are—that is, somewhat doubtful," that it might be better if he "deliberately took the opposite position" and deceived himself, "pretending for some time that all these opinions are entirely false and imaginary" (79).

There are, then, *two* quite different methods recommended in the first Meditation, a method of systematic doubt and a method of systematic denial. It would be a misreading of Descartes's intentions, however, to regard the method of denial as anything more than a propaedeutic. The method of systematic denial in Meditation 1 is on a level with the "evil genius" hypothesis; it is a device with a specific purpose. The real method of the first Meditation is a method of systematic *doubt*, not a method of systematic denial. Denial is, in the face of a program of systematic doubt, simply another form of affirmation; and negative propositions (that the sky, the air, the earth, are nothing but illusions, for example, or that God does not exist) are on an equal footing with affirmative ones, disallowed if unaccompanied by the appropriate credentials. Now it is probably unfair to accuse Booth of confusing doubt with denial and consequently with misrepresenting the skeptical method. On the other hand, it is perhaps fair to say that some readers of *Modern Dogma* might get the impression that its author attributes a method of *systematic denial* to Descartes, a kind of systematic metaphysical naysaying, a program of *disbelief* rather than one of *nonbelief*. This would, among other things, make the method look less plausible than it is, since disbelief (being itself a form of belief) carries a much heavier epistemic burden than nonbelief, the suspension of belief.

So the method of systematic doubt, in the hands of Descartes (or in the hands of later philosophers, for that matter) is not so negative as a careless reader of Booth's account might suspect. Furthermore, Descartes, like many of the classical skeptics whom it was his intent to refute, has a *positive* program, one that he can implement even if he cannot get beyond his skepticism. And that positive program is one that in a sense preserves a commitment to values (which is at least part of what Booth wants to do with his method of assent). In part 3 of the *Discourse on Method* ("Some Moral Rules Derived from the Method"), Descartes says that he decided in implementing his method that "while reason obliged me to be irresolute in my beliefs, there was no reason why I should be so in my actions" (18). He then sketches a "provisional morality," whose first principle is "to obey all the laws and customs of my country, constantly retaining the religion which I judged best . . . , and in all other matters to follow the most moderate and least excessive opinions to be found in the practices of the more judicious part of the community in which I would live" (18). The second principle is to act as resolutely on these principles as if he were certain of their correctness: "when we cannot determine the course which is certainly best, we must follow the one which is probably the best; and when we cannot determine even that, we must nevertheless select one and follow it thereafter as though it were certainly the best" (20).

These are not the words of a man left awash in the wake of the application of his method of systematic doubting; they constitute, in fact, a kind of affirmation. And they have their counterpart in the *truly* skeptical philosophies of late antiquity, as well as in the views of sophisticated skeptics of later periods (and even in the skeptical rhetoric of the old Sophistic). According to the reports left to us by Sextus Empiricus, Cicero, and others, Academic skeptics of the post-Aristotelian period, while denying that we can be certain about anything more than appearances, adopted a policy of "living with the appearances," some going so far as to judge that there is a kind of "reasonable justification" for taking some appearances more seriously than others and for choosing some courses of action and policies over others.[4] Sextus reports that the Academic skeptic Arcesilaus "says that one who suspends judgment about everything will regulate choice and avoidance and actions in general by 'the reasonable'; and that by proceeding in accordance with this criterion he will act rightly" and that Carneades found grounds for distinguishing "merely convincing" impressions or appearances from "undiverted impressions," which were to be taken more seriously, and those from the weightiest of all, "thoroughly explored" impressions (Long and Sedley 451, 453). The significance of these reports and others like them is that they are evidence of the tendency of systematic doubt, after having illegitimized assent, to legitimize another order of affirmation.

Whether skeptics are consistent in this is open to debate; but the point is that systematic doubt does not inevitably engender a rhetoric of negation (on either of the levels Booth is concerned about). Systematic doubt need not provide the basis or impetus for the dogmas of scientism or for irrationalism; it can as easily generate a logic or rhetoric of "appearances" (as something akin to it did in the older Sophists) or clear the way for a logic and rhetoric of probabilities (giving the impetus to works such as Joseph Butler's *Analogy of Religion* or Newman's *Grammar of Assent*). (It is historical, causal connections we are concerned with here, not logical entailments, because it is on the grounds of the former that Booth impugns the program of systematic doubt.) One might even argue for an identification of the "appearances" of Academic skepticism and those of Sophistic rhetoric, and even for a kinship of both of those with the kind of probabilistic rhetoric that we find in Butler (though I would not be so bold as to advance such a hypothesis).[5]

The general point is that an attitude or method of systematic doubt tends to have a loosening effect. Its natural tendency, I suggest, is toward legitimizing a logic and rhetoric of probabilities, in some form or other, despite its ostensible commitments to a standard of certainty. Its partial failure to do so in the case of Descartes is *his* failure rather than a failure of the method or attitude.

Nor does a method of skeptical doubt inevitably generate the kind of "metaphysical" nay-saying with which Booth is concerned in the last chapter of *Modern Dogma*. A kind of *optimism* was actually more typical of the Pyrrhonistic and Academic skeptics. It was their view that systematic doubt liberates the mind, that it is therapeutic, that it provides the basis for inner tranquility (*ataraxia*).[6] Its influence in modern philosophy has at least sometimes been in that same direction. Whose works in modern philosophy are more pervasively cheerful than those of Hume, for example (or those of Bertrand Russell, for that matter)?

The truth of the matter seems to be that systematic doubt leads nowhere in particular. Skepticism provides a pretext sometimes for scientism, sometimes for Fideism, sometimes for irrationalism, sometimes for a rhetoric of angst, sometimes for moral cynicism; but among its purest devotees, I have meant to suggest, it has, if anything, tended to generate affirmation more than denial, and to clear the decks for a rhetoric of probabilities. It has tended, that is, to undermine the antirhetorical rhetoric of certainties. The pervasive effect, and enduring value, of skeptical doubt has always been that it undermines dogmatism, even if it at the same time tends to undermine itself. "The skeptics from Sextus Empiricus to Montaigne, Bayle, Hume, and Santayana," writes Popkin, "have pointed out that the strength of skepticism lies not in whether it is tenable as a position but in the force of its arguments against the dogmatic claims of philosophers" ("Skepticism" 457).

Let us grant, however, that there are certain important matters, certain metaphysical questions, and certain questions of value that seem to demand some more solid foundation than can be provided by the skeptic's "living by the appearances," that seem to call for some more vigorous and sustained affirmation than the systematic doubter seems entitled to provide. How is such a foundation to be provided? In particular, can it be provided by the method of systematic assent that Booth wants to counterpoise to the method of systematic doubt? And what exactly *is* this method of systematic assent?

SYSTEMATIC ASSENT

In the introduction to *Modern Dogma,* Booth endorses the view that "the primary mental act of man is to assent to truth rather than to detect error" (xvi). This brings to mind James's claim, in *The Principles of Psychology,* that "all propositions, whether attributive or existential, are believed through the very fact of being conceived, unless they clash with other propositions believed at the same time" (290). Let us grant that assent is the primary mental act, that it is our nature to assent to whatever propositions confront us, until we have reason to do otherwise, that the habit—even the *act*—of dissenting *or* of suspending belief has to be acquired, and that dissent and even doubt are in some sense parasitic upon assent. But to say that it is our nature to assent and that we have to learn to doubt is not to say that we *ought* to assent unless, as Booth puts it, we "cannot not doubt" (111). So the question remains whether assent ought to, or even *can,* occupy the kind of methodological position that doubt occupies in the method we have been considering in the previous section.

Booth's suggestion (40) that we consider what would happen to our "moral and intellectual life" if we "reversed that formula" (of systematic doubt) is a real conceptual eye catcher, though its impact is diminished somewhat by qualifications he immediately adds. Before looking at the method as Booth actually develops it, however, I would like to consider what it would mean to employ a method of systematic assent that was truly the logical counterpart to the method of systematic doubt.

In the first place, we need to remind ourselves again that the method of systematic doubt is not a method of systematic denial. The logical opposite of a method of systematic denial would perhaps be a method of systematic assertion. Such a method (either of assent or of denial), purely considered, would be logically incoherent. In theory, at least, every proposition that confronts us as a possibility confronts us also, by implication, with its negation, the proposition that asserts that what it asserts is not the case. A real *unimpeded* procedure of systematic assent would yield exactly the same incoherent results as a real procedure of systematic denial, an assenting to both every proposition confronting us and to its negation as well. (Bear with me if I seem for a moment to be "logic-chopping"; the point is to get at the logic of Booth's proposal. I know very well that such a procedure is not what Professor Booth has in mind; but I want to discover the logic of what he does have in mind.) It would not do, I think, to suggest that it is only the *affirmative* propositions, as opposed to the *negative* ones, that are to be assented to in this method, unless we are equipped with a procedure for deciding which propositions are truly affirmative and which truly negative. While this might seem easy enough with respect to certain classes of propositions (even though it isn't), its difficulty becomes apparent in the case of the kinds of propositions that are mainly in question in *Modern Dogma*. "A man ought to covet his neighbor's wife." "We should always act only for our own interests." "Ugliness is better than beauty." Are these affirmations or negations?

The bare fact that a proposition is affirmative rather than negative (if we can even make that differentiation with confidence) does not in itself count either for it or against it, does not make it any more or any less likely to be true. Assertion is inseparable from denial. Every act of affirmation is at the same time an act of negation. To assert that p is to deny that *not-p,* and to deny that p is to assert that *not-p*. Distinguishing ps from *not-p*s, moreover, is notoriously problematic, especially with respect to questions of value. The relevance of all this to Booth's program is this: the question, at the earlier stages of his game, is not really a question about the difference between affirming and denying; it is more a question about the status of certain foundational beliefs, beliefs that have already provided the foundations for our thinking about matters of value, or beliefs Booth wants to use as foundations for certain kinds of "yea-saying." The way in which Booth wants to *qualify* his methodological recommendation, which we will look at shortly, should make it clear that a contrast between "yea" and "nay" is not the real issue; the real issue is one of *presumption*.

But, in any case, a method of systematic assent cannot be the logical counterpart of a method of systematic doubt. We can withhold assent from *both* a proposition and its negation; we cannot *yield* assent to both a proposition and its negation. A method of systematic doubt may be impracticable if taken too seriously, but at least it makes sense. At least it is not in itself logically incoherent. Let us turn now, though, to the proposed method of systematic assent as Booth actually describes it.

The first real characterization of the proposed method of assent in *Modern Dogma* is at the end of chapter 1, in a passage from which I quoted earlier:

> But I ask you to think a bit . . . about what would happen to your intellectual and moral life if you reversed that [the skeptical] formula, cultivating a benign acceptance—perhaps temporary and tentative, but real—of every belief that can pass two tests: you have no particular concrete grounds to doubt it (as distinct from the abstract principle to doubt what cannot be proved); and you have *good reason to think all men who understand the problem share your belief.* (40)

Now the caveat "perhaps temporary and tentative" significantly closes the gap, I think, between the kind of procedure Booth seems to have in mind and the skeptic's "living with the appearances." But it is the second of the two "tests" to which I particularly draw attention. What is the real character of this test, how is it to be applied, and what are the likely results? What will constitute good reasons for thinking that all persons who understand the problem share my belief? *Motivists* (proponents of the first of the five dogmas attacked in *Modern Dogma*) surely have good reason to think that all who understand the problem share their belief, since it is the way in which they conceive the problem of believing that gives rise to, which entails, motivism. A simpler procedure is this: Believe what all right-thinking people believe; by "right-thinking people" I mean people whose beliefs on the question at hand are correct. "It is reasonable," Booth says later (101, at the start of the book's most full-blown account of the method), "to grant (one *ought* to grant) some degree of credence to whatever qualified men and women agree on, *unless* one has specific and stronger reasons to disbelieve."

The qualification, "whatever *qualified* men and women agree on," is highly problematic. Booth openly acknowledges a "deliberate embrace of circularity" (101). Circularity indeed; these formulations encourage a kind of begging of the question with respect to philosophical doctrines. But, that problem aside for a moment, it is not at all clear that this is a method of assent any more than it is a method of dissent or of doubt. A consistent adherence to the policy will oblige us to follow qualified men and women in their disbeliefs and doubts as well. (That is to say, we will be obliged, unless we have specific and stronger reasons not to do so, to assent to their beliefs about what is false and what is doubtful.) It is misleading, I say again in this context, to speak here of a method of systematic assent. I understand the point of a kind of application of that terminology later in the book, when Booth wants to promote rhetorical optimism and cooperativeness; but I do not understand it at this earlier stage, when the point is to offer an alternative to the philosophical method of systematic doubt.

THE METHOD

Booth's method is neither truly *systematic* (in the relevant sense) nor truly a method of *assent*. But if it is not really a method of systematic assent, what kind of a method is it? Well, it seems to have two related aspects. On the one hand, it is an *ad verecundiam* method, a method in whose application we defer to authorities in matters of belief. On the other hand, it is a *conservative* method, a method weighted in favor of established beliefs. There is something to be said in favor of both of its aspects, although Booth's account of the first is problematic (partly for reasons already given, and partly on account of vagueness), and the relationship between the two is not very clearly established. It may be that qualified authorities are simply authorities who agree with the beliefs we already hold, in which case it is the conservatism of the method which really carries the weight. By virtue of both of its aspects, the method's application (by philosophers, at least) seems weighted in favor of some of the very dogmas under attack in *Modern Dogma*. But let me say more clearly what I mean by the claim that the method is really a method of conservation.

"Abstract commands to 'doubt pending proof'" are to be replaced in this method with "the ancient and natural command to 'assent pending disproof'" (101). But we have seen that the real issue is not whether to follow a policy of assenting as opposed to a policy of doubting. Perhaps we can distinguish two real issues. One is whether we ought (in "nonscientific" matters, let us say) to assent at all (and, if so, in what *sense* or how strongly we are entitled to assent). The other is the question of what propositions or what *sorts* of propositions we ought to assent to, at the ground level, so to speak, in the application of this method. As to the first, let me say only that Booth's claim that modern dogmatists (Russell, for example) have "sliced the world into two unequal parts, the tiny domain of the provable, about which nobody cares very much, and the great domain of 'all the rest,' in which anyone can believe or do what he pleases" (85) is a straw man (see also 91). Even the older skeptics tend to reject, at some level, so absolute a dichotomy, to say nothing of Descartes or Russell, each of whom clearly affirms that, among propositions that are susceptible to neither proof nor disproof, and among possible courses of action, some are more reasonable than others.[7]

What sorts of propositions is it that Booth wants to have assumed innocent until proven guilty? Well, the way he begins to put the method into operation (starting on 111) is strikingly reminiscent of the "common sense" philosophy of Thomas Reid, or of G. E. Moore in the twentieth century. He runs through a series of propositions he thinks we all know very well that we know (even if we sometimes say otherwise): "Men are characteristically users of language," "Sometimes we understand each other," "What an adult man or woman is, in all societies, is in a large degree what other men and women have created through symbolic exchange," "We characteristically *intend* to change our fellows by symbolic devices," and so on.[8] These propositions are not randomly selected; Booth is, as we guess pretty quickly, headed in a certain direction. But what recommends these propositions to us—or what exempts them from the *need* for a recommendation, we should say—is the fact that we and our fellows already believe that they are true or at least conduct our mutual affairs as if their truth were unquestionable. What Booth is suggesting is that there is a *presumption* in favor of such beliefs, that the burden of proof is on the person who questions them rather than on the person who assents to them, so that the very fact that we hold them, especially the fact that we hold them *collectively,* carries a certain amount of weight. Richard Whately's discussion of presumption in *The Elements of Rhetoric* comes to mind: "There is a presumption," says Whately, "in favor of every *existing* institution. Many of these . . . may be susceptible of alteration for the better; but still the 'Burden of Proof' lies with him who proposes an alteration; simply, on the ground that since a change is not a good in itself, he who demands a change should show cause for it" (114). Certain classes of propositions have a kind of "institutional" status from a commonsense philosopher's point of view. They cannot be abandoned, our attitudes toward them cannot even be significantly altered (from confidence to doubt, for example), without serious doxastic and pragmatic consequences. Reasonable cause *can* be shown, of course, for alterations in belief; but there is, according to this policy, a heavy burden of proof that falls on the person who questions existing epistemic institutions.[9]

I hope I have not distorted Booth's view by putting it in these terms. The heart of the matter is a kind of epistemic conservatism, for which I believe there is something to be said. This heart is not really a question about assent, systematic or otherwise. The actual *procedure* in *Modern Dogma* is to focus on a carefully chosen subset of moderately institutionalized propositions and to lead us from them toward a certain conception of human nature (man the "rhetorical animal").[10] A critique of that constructive program is beyond the scope of the present discussion. However, I would like to make two comments about it in closing. First, it is ironic that the strategy of *Modern Dogma* is remarkably Cartesian, as it consists in an attempt to sweep away old prejudices and to lay and build upon new foundations. Second, it is also an irony that something like the kind of principle of conservation that the "method of systematic assent" really boils down to is, after all, endorsed by the chief foil of *Modern Dogma,* Bertrand Russell, from whose hold Booth has perhaps not gotten as free as he would like. In *The Problems of Philosophy,* after having pointed out that the view of the solipsist "cannot be definitively refuted," and after having given probabilistic arguments for the "common-sense" view that there is a world of objects independent of us, Russell says the following:

> The argument which has led us to this conclusion is doubtless less strong than we could wish, but it is typical of many philosophical arguments, and it is therefore worth while to consider briefly its general character and validity. All knowledge, we find, must be built up upon our instinctive beliefs, and if these are rejected, nothing is left. . . .
>
> Philosophy should show us the hierarchy of our instinctive beliefs, beginning with those we hold most strongly, and presenting each as much isolated and as free from irrelevant additions as possible. It should take care to show that, in the form in which they are finally set forth, our instinctive beliefs do not clash, but form a harmonious system. There can never be any reason for rejecting one instinctive belief except that it clashes with others; thus, if they are found to harmonize, the whole system becomes worthy of our acceptance. . . .
>
> This function, at least, philosophy can perform. (25)

Notes

1. I feel compelled, as in some respects an unrepentant Russellian, to observe that Russell receives what has to strike some readers as rather shabby treatment in chapter 2, especially in what looks like an imagined dialogue between Booth and Russell, but which really consists in a run of text from the first chapter of Russell's *What I Believe* (1925) with a series of interruptions by Booth. As was observed long ago by Plato in the *Phaedrus,* a written text has the disadvantage of being unable to defend itself. One has to wonder whether Russell the man (who comes across as a fool in this little dialogue) would have done somewhat better in a face-to-face symbolic exchange.

2. The extant works of Sextus Empiricus are published in four volumes, trans. R. G. Bury, in the Loeb Classical Library. For a detailed treatment of the more immediate skeptical antecedents to Descartes, see Popkin, *History of Scepticism.*

3. All quotations from Descartes will be from the *Discourse on Method and Meditations,* trans. Laurence J. Lafleur.

4. See Long and Sedley, section 69, "Living Without Opinions."

5. There is a theme here that one might attempt to trace through a variety of sources. One might, for example, argue that Cicero's defense of *honestas* in *De finibus* and *De officiis* is a kind of philosophical argument from appearances. The argument strategy of those two works consists largely in presenting the reader with examples of virtue and vice, the case for virtue being left to rest most heavily on the reader's response (a kind of assenting, we might say) to the appearances. Arguably, it is at least in part the influence of Academic skepticism on his philosophical works that makes this sort of approach agreeable to Cicero. For a more detailed account of Cicero's method (though without an attempt to make connections with skeptical doubt or a doctrine of "appearances"), see my "Cicero's Use of Historical Examples in Moral Argument."

6. "The Greek skeptic," writes Nussbaum, "does not present himself as seeking an external justification for beliefs. He is seeking freedom from disturbance; and he wishes to attain this happy condition by suspending belief. The equal force of opposing beliefs achieves, for him, this effect" (481–82).

7. That Russell believes in and is committed to the giving of "good reasons" with respect to questions of value and matters of practice should be clear enough from his ethical and political writings. With respect to the supposed gap between this commitment and Russell's commitment to a method of doubt, one ought to attend to Russell's efforts at theorizing about morality. See Monroe, "Russell's Moral Theories." The Pears volume also contains a bibliography of Russell's ethical, social, and political writings.

8. Compare, for example, G. E. Moore's list of "truisms" in "A Defence of Common Sense."

9. My characterization of Booth's method is influenced somewhat by

Quine and Ullian, especially chap. 2, "Belief and Change of Belief," and chap. 6, "Hypothesis."

10. Among these propositions, some—such as the proposition that we are largely "created through symbolic exchange"—would have a strange ring indeed to ordinary people, as it is mainly among theorists of discourse that they are institutionalized.

Bibliography

Booth, Wayne C. *Modern Dogma and the Rhetoric of Assent*. Notre Dame, IN: U of Notre Dame P; Chicago: U of Chicago P, 1974.

Brinton, Alan. "Cicero's Use of Historical Examples in Moral Argument." *Philosophy and Rhetoric* 21 (1988): 169–84.

Descartes, René. *Discourse on Method and Meditations*. Trans. Laurence J. Lafleur. Indianapolis: Bobbs, 1960.

James, William. *The Principles of Psychology*. 1890. New York: Dover, 1950.

Long, A. A., and D. N. Sedley, eds. *Translations of the Principal Sources, with Philosophical Commentary*. Vol. 1 of *The Hellenistic Philosophers*. Cambridge: Cambridge UP, 1987.

Monroe, D. H. "Russell's Moral Theories." *Philosophy* 35 (1960). Rpt. in *Bertrand Russell: A Collection of Critical Essays*. Ed. David Pears. Garden City, NY: Anchor, 1972. 325–55.

Moore, G. E. "A Defence of Common Sense." *Contemporary British Philosophy*. Ed. J. H. Muirhead. 2nd ser. London: Macmillan, 1925. 193–223.

Nussbaum, Martha. *The Fragility of Goodness*. Cambridge: Cambridge UP, 1986.

Popkin, Richard H. *The History of Scepticism from Erasmus to Descartes*. New York: Humanities, 1964.

———. "Skepticism." *The Encyclopedia of Philosophy*. Ed. Paul Edwards. 1967. New York: Macmillan, 1972.

Quine, W. V., and Joseph Ullian. *The Web of Belief*. 2nd ed. New York: Random, 1978.

Russell, Bertrand. *The Problems of Philosophy*. 1912. Oxford: Oxford UP, 1959.

Sextus Empiricus. *Works*. Trans. R. G. Bury. 4 vols. Loeb Classical Library. Cambridge, MA: Harvard UP, 1933.

Whatley, Richard. *The Elements of Rhetoric*. 1828. Carbondale: Southern Illinois UP, 1963.

15

Rhetoric without Sophistry: Wayne Booth and the Rhetoric of Inquiry

JAMES B. MCOMBER

JUDGING FROM SOME of his more offhand remarks, Wayne Booth has had uneven relations with the discipline of philosophy. As he introduces a group of essays in *Now Don't Try to Reason with Me,* for example, he expresses a general commitment to the spirit of reasonableness he finds in eighteenth-century philosophy. But he seems less generous toward some of the more recent voices. One of these, he tells us, suggested that Booth's own attempts at philosophy are "a shameless form of revenge on modern philosophy" (79). In *Modern Dogma and the Rhetoric of Assent,* clearly his most philosophical book, Booth gives the impression that he knows philosophers would find his arguments an easy target: "[T]hey know how much could be said about many of the questions I seem to settle with a twist of the wrist." Lest we take this as good reason to leave his book behind and turn to the true philosophers, he adds, "But it is part of my point that modern philosophy—at least until the last two decades—has saddled us with standards of truth under which no man can live" (xii).

We could write two different stories about Booth's attitude toward philosophy based on these sparse comments. On the one hand, we might portray him as a philosophical conservative who longs for the times when philosophy was relevant to everyday concerns and when even the most important philosophical works were accessible to the lay reader. On the other hand, we could use these same remarks to make Booth into something a little more trendy: an antiphilosopher. He seems to want to rescue academic argument from the logic-chopping his imaginary philosophical opponents would use against his own ideas. If we wanted to extend this image, we might say that in denouncing the "saddle" of rigorous standards of truth, Booth questions the philosopher's right to stand in judgment over the argumentative practices of other disciplines. This image, in short, might portray Booth as an opponent of what Richard Rorty calls "foundationalism."

While I suspect that Booth himself feels more comfortable with the first image, in this chapter I examine the antiphilosophical potential of Booth's writings. The reason for my choice should be apparent to anyone familiar with the body of research and argument now called "the rhetoric of inquiry." Booth's antimodernism already has been enlisted in the service of a project that seeks both to set aside formal epistemology and to reconstruct academic inquiry with rhetorical self-consciousness. Economist Donald McCloskey, for example, lets Booth and not Aristotle define rhetoric in *The Rhetoric of Economics* (29). And while he does not rely on Booth for his antiphilosophy, McCloskey certainly makes it clear that for him, promoting rhetorical thinking about science requires dethronement of the epistemologist: "The philosopher undertakes to second-guess the scientific community.... Such claims from the easy chair are hard to take seriously" (20). Elsewhere in the literature on the rhetoric of inquiry, Booth's name turns up alongside such famous antiphilosophers as Nietzsche, Wittgenstein, and of course Rorty (Nelson and Megill; Nelson, Megill, and McCloskey 3–18).

Given their goal of understanding the rhetorical dimension of inquiry, it is hardly surprising to find McCloskey and others citing Booth as an authority on the weaknesses of scientific epistemology. At least in the respects that he resists positivism, behaviorism, systematic doubt, the is–ought distinction, and other dogmas of modernism, Booth belongs with the antiphilosophers. But to what extent is Booth a participant with the more strident among them? And if he is not, what differences in Booth's approach to the rhetoric of inquiry might have significance for that line of scholarship? To answer these questions, it will help to have a good example of an antiphilosopher to compare with Booth. Simply because of his popularity among rhetoricians of inquiry and his unequivocal opposition to systematic philosophy, Richard Rorty makes an obvious choice (Nelson and Megill 26; see also Lyne 67). I will therefore explore some of Booth's antimodernist arguments in relation to Rorty's. My exploration will not make any new contentions about antiphilosophy; that discipline seems to be thriving quite well enough. I hope instead to use this comparison to provide some suggestions about how to say that inquiry is rhetorical without saying it is the worst sort of sophistry, or what Booth would call "the art of winning." I am in search, then, of a rhetoric of inquiry that is also an ethic of inquiry.

Readers of *Modern Dogma* and *Critical Understanding* can see plainly enough that Booth rejects certain philosophical ideas popular in this century. We know, for example, that Booth has little regard for Bertrand Russell's brand of modernism (*Modern Dogma,* chap. 2). But to say that he dislikes certain philosophers or their ideas is not to say that Booth altogether rejects the philosophical impulse, however defined. Rorty, on the other hand, seems committed to just such a rejection:

> People have, oddly enough, found something interesting to say about the essence of Force and the definition of "number." They might have found something interesting to say about the essence of Truth. But in fact they haven't. The history of attempts to do so, and of criticism of those attempts, is roughly coextensive with the history of that literary genre we call "philosophy"—a genre founded by Plato. So pragmatists [such as Rorty] see the Platonic tradition as having outlived its usefulness. (*Consequences* xiv)

It is difficult to imagine Booth ever entertaining such a sweeping dismissal. In what sense, then, can I even begin to compare Booth and Rorty for their antiphilosophical inclinations?

First, whatever generalizations Rorty may make about the whole gamut of Western philosophy, he does not intend to denounce everything that we call philosophy, and he does not anticipate the closing of philosophy departments. His enemy is Philosophy with a capital "P," defined as the discipline that seeks to "underwrite or debunk claims to knowledge," and more generally as literature that "proceeds on the assumption that all contributions to a given discourse are commensurable" (*Mirror* 3, 316). He invokes a great many philosophers, including many who make their livings in contemporary philosophy departments, to earn his antiphilosophical conclusions. By repeated appeal to his heroes—Dewey, Heidegger, and the later Wittgenstein—he further refines his concept of Philosophy. What really bothers him, it seems, is the attempt to make philosophy "systematic." In Rorty's view philosophy can still play an "edifying" role by constantly reacting against "the latest claim that such-and-such a discipline has at last made the nature of human knowledge so clear that reason will now spread throughout the rest of human activity" (*Mirror* 367).

So Rorty's antiphilosophy turns out to be a reaction against a particular kind of philosophy and the ambition that gives rise to it. When Rorty questions this "foundationalist" conception of philosophy in these more limited senses, he seems to have entered territory familiar to Wayne Booth. In *Critical Understanding,* Booth tries to find a pluralistic approach to critical argument. His concerns are largely with modes of literary criticism, but with just a little broadening, they come to resemble some of Rorty's rejections. Booth, for example, questions any form of critical "monism," or the view that there is one true critical conclusion to draw about a literary work (12–17). Rorty's rejection of foundationalism seems to be based on the same suspicion of final pronouncements, except that he rejects any claim to final truth in any domain.

Yet perhaps at this point the similarity between these two writers must end. As I suggested, Rorty rejects not just any claim to finality in matters of truth, but any claim to "systematicity." For Rorty, procedural rationality is inherently problematic (Nelson, Megill, and McCloskey 40). He would prefer to support philosophies precisely to the extent they mock any pretension to formulate recipes for reaching truth—or as he would put it, to the extent they "edify." At first glance, Booth's resistance to various modernist philosophies arrives at very different conclusions. Booth would replace one kind of systematicity with another: an exchange of systematic *doubt* for systematic *assent.* Would all of Rorty's dismissals of systematic philosophy apply equally to the procedures of systematic assent?

Again, however, a closer look at these two positions reveals their resemblance. Booth defines *systematic doubt* as "assent pending disproof" in deliberate contrast to the Cartesian and modernist formula of doubt pending proof (*Modern Dogma* 101). But when he discusses systematic doubt in detail, it becomes more than a mirror image of the modernist formula. The traditional conception made doubt an individual affair. Booth deliberately and consistently replaces the modernists' "I" with "we": "Instead of making doubt primary, let us see what happens if *we* know whatever *we* can agree together that *we* have no good reason to doubt, whether or not *we* can apply other more formal tests of doubt" (*Modern Dogma* 106, emphasis added). This simple change in pronoun has some important consequences. Once the process of assent becomes communal, it also becomes considerably more susceptible to the charge that it lacks the kind of systematicity Rorty objects to. Indeed, at such a formulation of the essence of knowing, Booth's imaginary philosophical opponents might assume that he *has* settled some very important questions with a twist of the wrist. Until we have reached some conclusions about who "we" are, we cannot say much about the kind of knowledge systematic assent will get us.

I will let Booth answer the obvious question about what he means by "we" in a moment. First I must note the important sense in which the notion of communal assent pending disproof converges with Rorty's ideas about the attainment of truth. Rorty is famous—perhaps notorious—for adopting an unrepentantly local and communal notion of truth: "[T]here is nothing to be said about either truth or rationality apart from descriptions of the familiar procedures of justification which a given society—*ours*—uses in one or another area of inquiry" (Nelson, Megill, and McCloskey 42). In this way truth-seeking becomes nothing more than a matter of letting academic conversations proceed with the hope of intersubjective agreement, and the only universal value to sustain in inquiry is the desire to keep the conversation going: "The application of such honorifics as 'objective' and 'cognitive' is never anything more than an expression of the presence of, or the hope for, agreement among inquirers" (*Mirror* 335).

Booth does not make any of these "nothing more than" arguments about the nature of truth. Indeed, he makes a point of avoiding the latent foundationalism that inheres in Rorty's embrace of consensus and conversation (*Critical Understanding* 25–26; *Modern Dogma* 99). Yet both Booth and Rorty are asking us to show a respect for honestly obtained consensus that their modernist predecessors either ignored or explicitly rejected. As a matter of everyday scholarly practice the need for consensus is difficult to challenge. Even philosophers with a distinctly individualistic notion of how truth is acquired tried to persuade their colleagues that their view of truth was correct. Then why not celebrate the virtues of tolerance, honesty, and willingness to listen that make conversation and consensus possible? Booth and Rorty want us to pay more than lip service to these simple virtues, and in this way they both authorize attention to the rhetorical practices on which scholarly inquiry depends.

Up to this point I have stressed the senses in which Rorty's attacks on foundationalism and Booth's resistance to critical monism and the dogmas of modernism resemble one another. We have seen that they both want to challenge any claims to finality and systematicity in matters of scholarly justification. They both authorize careful attention to scholarly consensus as well. But I have not attended to the arguments Booth and Rorty adduce in support of these notions. Critical differences between the two become apparent as soon as one turns away from their conclusions and begins to ask how they arrive at them.

Several strategies recur in Rorty's meticulous arguments against foundationalist philosophy. Overall, he relies on a version of Occam's razor: we can do all the work of scholarly justification we need to do without appealing to some immutable epistemological standards. In evidence for this, he notes that in spite of the failure of philosophers to agree on such standards, the practices of justification have continued anyway. In themselves, these strategies are not greatly different from anything Booth might use. But to apply these arguments, Rorty traces a path through the history of philosophy that begins with what he calls "the invention of the mind" in the seventeenth century. According to Rorty, a great mistake of modern philosophy was Descartes's decision to single out the mind as the special ontological realm where thought takes place. Once philosophers came to believe in such a nonspatial substance, they had to theorize its relations with the material in some way. The results were a preoccupation with that metaphysical relationship, a skepticism about the existence of other minds, and a host of other philosophical pseudoproblems cleared up hundreds of years later by Wittgenstein, Quine, and their followers (*Mirror* 17–127).

Rorty would prefer to do away with the notion of "mind" as an inner eye requiring a special theory of inner representation. Only once philosophers have stopped worrying about this "Glassy Essence" can they begin to see the problem of justification for what it is: a problem of "what our peers will, *ceteris paribus,* let us get away with saying" (*Mirror* 176). Rorty anticipates the obvious objection to this elimination of the concept of mind. He knows that for many, the notion of "self" or "personhood" is intimately connected to mentality. Without any conception of mind, so the argument runs, human beings lose their unique right to the respect of their fellows. But Rorty contends that the connection between mentality and personhood is a crucial mistake, perhaps even a historical accident. Once the notions of consciousness and reason are separated historically, "then personhood can be seen for what I claim it is—a matter of decision rather than knowledge, an acceptance of another being into fellowship rather than a recognition of a common essence" (*Mirror* 37).

At many points these arguments stand deeply at odds with Booth's whole approach to problems of rational justification. For Booth, the impulse to question modernist epistemology comes from its disastrous consequences for contemporary rhetoric. He finds that when systematically applied, the demand for rigorous doubt pending proof leaves arguers affirming truths at one another; again, rhetoric becomes "the art of winning" (*Modern Dogma* xi). When Rorty writes that truth is nothing more than "what our peers will . . . let us *get away with* saying," he seems to invite a view of rhetoric little different from the one Booth's whole effort sets out to overturn. One of the lessons of Rorty, then, is that even a dramatic and thorough rejection of constraining epistemologies is not enough to solve the rhetorical problems they have created. A winning argument against logical positivism, for example, does not guarantee a rosy future for practical reason, even though strict logical positivism inhibits the development of practical reason.

But there is another respect in which Booth's argument diverges from Rorty's. Booth depends heavily on the integrity and independence of the mind in both the premises and conclusion of his arguments for a responsible rhetoric of assent. Indeed, it often seems that Booth assumes the same interdependence of "mind" and "self" that Rorty so carefully dissolves. *Modern Dogma*'s opening question, "When should I change my mind?" surely presupposes that there is something to the notion of mind that is worth inquiring about. This something cannot be understood merely as a collection of dispositions toward certain behaviors, as Booth's frequent criticisms of behaviorism make clear (*Modern Dogma* 114; *Critical Understanding* 112, 262). Once *Modern Dogma* arrives at the concept of systematic assent as a guiding rhetorical principle, Booth first applies that principle to the mind itself. Among other things, he discovers that human beings do have the capacity to understand each other, that they do possess intentions, and that they are capable of inferring the intentions of their fellows. Throughout this discussion, Booth makes no distinctions between the mind and the self (111–25).

Thus, on this question of the nature of mind and its relationship to personhood, the differences between Booth and Rorty are so great that to accept the arguments of one in any degree precludes the acceptance of the arguments of the other. If we agree with Rorty that the path away from foundationalism requires abandoning the belief in the mind's intimate connection to personhood, then all of Booth's arguments about the changing of minds become unintelligible. If, on the other hand, we agree with Booth that abandoning the dogmas of modernism requires a fresh respect for the integrity of the mind and the self, the first step of

Rorty's complex argument becomes equally unintelligible and perhaps reprehensible.

Of course, I will choose the latter path. I have already suggested the problem with a rhetoric of inquiry based on Rorty's reduction of knowledge and truth to a matter of victory in argument. That problem is partly the one that prompted Booth to write *Modern Dogma* in the first place. Its cause is similar as well, for under the banner of "epistemological behaviorism," Rorty dismisses all claims for the philosophical importance of the concept of "mind" (*Mirror* 98–99). But no doubt Rorty would say that anyone who accepted Booth's story on this basis begs the question. Rorty is arguing that we can have respect for persons without recognizing a common essence, the mind, lying behind each of their utterances. Surely our peers will *not* let us get away with arguments that in some way grossly neglect personhood. So what have we to worry about in saying that truth is what we can persuade people to believe?

Answering Rorty on this point will require something more than the Booth I have already discussed. Specifically, the answer must show that in giving up our notions about the mind we are giving up something of vital importance in spite of the failure of modern philosophy to reach any final conclusions about what the mind is. And, because the answer cannot rely simply on what this or that community or culture finds persuasive (for that would be Rorty's point all over again), it must aspire to some degree of transcendence, perhaps even a latent "foundational" status. Finally, any well-rounded answer to Rorty must show concretely that it can do a better job of promoting respect for personhood than any purely consensual notion of truth.

Booth has more than fulfilled these apparently tremendous requirements. He does so in a way that Rorty never appears to anticipate, even though parts of the argument are not unique to Booth. The argument begins where Rorty leaves off—with the practical necessities of striving for and living with consensus in all human affairs. From *the fact that* all of us try to persuade each other to live and think similarly Booth infers the necessity of doing so. And from this necessity it is but a short step to the conclusion that persons and minds are essentially a matter of the persuasions they engage in and respond to: "What is a 'mind' and what is a 'self' in this rhetorical view? It is *essentially* rhetorical, symbol exchanging, a social product in process of changing through interaction, sharing values with other selves. Even when thinking privately, 'I' can never escape the other selves which I have taken in to make 'myself,' and my thought will thus always be a dialogue" (*Modern Dogma* 126). Here Booth begins to reply to that important question about who we are that I left dangling. At least as far as answering Rorty is concerned, the important point about this definition is not that it makes statements about what is essential to being human, although Rorty would probably object to that. Its significance lies in its constitution of a mind and a self that ought to be responsible for their persuasion precisely because they are partially remade in their attempts to shape other minds and other selves: "But if all men [and women] make each other in symbolic interchange, then by implication they *should* make each other, and it is an inescapable value in their lives that it is good to do it well—whatever that will mean—and bad to do it badly" (*Modern Dogma* 137). On this view, the reason rhetoric should not degenerate into the art of winning is that while mere victory might make others into what the rhetor wants, by itself it does not guarantee that it will help remake *rhetors themselves* into that same image.

To see the importance of this self-actualization for real academic arguments, it will be helpful to consider a rhetor who tries mightily to disregard it. Philosopher of science Paul Feyerabend, another resource for the rhetoric of inquiry, also argues against the traditional notions of formulaic rationality. One of his favorite strategies is to adopt his opponents' beliefs as an important resource for persuading them. For example, he challenges his opponents to be consistent, even though he does not recognize any problem with his own inconsistencies. In reply to the obvious criticisms of this tactic, he announces, "Some readers [of *Against Method*] objected that though I do not seem to mind inconsistencies I still present them as parts of my argument against standard views of rationality. I reply that I assume my readers to be rationalists. If they are not, then there is no need for them to read the book" (14). Elsewhere he explains that the mistake of these critics is to assume that an argument reflects the commitments of the arguer: "An argument is not a confession, it is an instrument designed to make an opponent change his [or her] mind. The existence of arguments of a certain type in a book may permit the reader to infer what the author regards as effective persuasion, it does not permit him [or her] to infer what the author thinks is true" (28).

With this stark theory of the purposes of rhetoric Feyerabend permits the construction of a clear line between Booth and Rorty, and he also reveals where Booth's notion of "the self as a field of selves" can have an important application. Clearly, Rorty could have very little to say against Feyerabend's strategy. Possibly he would say that Feyerabend's own use of inconsistency does not avail itself of the practices of justification endorsed in his own scholarly community—if indeed that audience of "rationalists" he addresses *is* Feyerabend's scholarly community. But to the extent that Feyerabend's audience lets him "get away with" his appeals to their inconsistencies, what challenge could Rorty raise?

Booth, on the other hand, would probably object to Feyerabend in the strongest of terms. Feyerabend's rhetorical appeals make Feyerabend, just as they hope to remake his opponents. What sort of Feyerabend comes into existence when he rebukes the rationalists for their inconsistencies while tolerating his own? Surely not one who hopes to engage in mutual inquiry, who would be as open to the persuasion of his fellows as he appears to want his opponents to be. Feyerabend probably would respond that respect for mutual inquiry and the constitution of a community of inquirers was never his *intention* anyway. But at this point we come to the bottom line of Booth's argument, indeed the bottom line of many of Booth's arguments. Feyerabend attempts to persuade his opponents. Booth has argued that the mere presence—or perhaps omnipresence—of attempts to persuade sets in motion a chain of inference leading to the conclusion that persuaders ought to attend carefully to the kinds of persons they make of themselves and their fellows as they inquire together. Thus even as Feyerabend tries to argue with his opponents he is *already* illustrating the importance of building a community of inquirers. Booth clinches this point in one of the more memorable sentences of *Modern Dogma:* "If a committed doubter says to us that he [or she] will not accept the valued fact of [our] rhetorical nature, we see now that he [or she] cannot avoid illustrating it as he [or she] tries to argue against it: we discuss our doubt together, therefore *we are*" (138). No doubt this argument also would not pacify Feyerabend. Indeed, as he sees no harm in his own inconsistencies he might simply deny the intention to persuade his opponents, even though he flatly states that effective persuasion is the proper goal of argument. But, as Booth says, once the objections reached this level of absurdity, "we may well continue to worry . . . about the intellectual climate that can make his kind of intellectual game seem less in need of defense than our own" (*Modern Dogma* 138). But what about that notion of "mind" that is so crucial to the differences between the arguments of Rorty and Booth? Notice that the force of these criticisms of Feyerabend depends on some degree of *continuity of consciousness* beyond the effects of Feyerabend's individual pronouncements on their readers. Once Feyerabend makes himself and his readers in the rhetorical process, then his opponents earn the right to question his inconsistencies because they have inferred his intentions and have assumed they live beyond his words. Without the ability to raise such challenges, of course, there would be no possibility that Feyerabend and his opponents could continue their conversation with any hope of agreement.

I have argued, in short, that while Rorty separates the "acceptance of another being into fellowship" from the "recognition of a common essence" of humanity, Booth gives us good reason to see such acceptance *as* an essential constituent of humanity. Without such a recognition, we lose the ability to make a certain kind of argument. This argument allows us to reason from the fact of our persuasion to the requirement that we do it with a respect for the kind of community our persuasion builds. While Rorty worries about "keeping the conversation going," his own arguments against the philosophical importance of the concept of mind prevent him from articulating any good reasons to be so concerned.

These differences have important consequences for the rhetoric of inquiry. That discipline has justified itself partly as an attempt to promote rhetorical self-consciousness among scholars (Nelson, Megill, and McCloskey ix; Bazerman). From Booth's standpoint, such rhetorical self-consciousness has an inescapably moral dimension: we build ourselves and our scholarly communities through our persuasion, and thus we have the responsibility to examine our own persuasion if only to find out about the sorts of people we are making of ourselves. That concern does not reinstate any particular formal system of inquiry, nor does it plunge us again into vexing and possibly insoluble philosophical problems of the sort Rorty dismisses. But it does allow us to recognize that some scholarly arguments, like Feyerabend's, inhibit the possibility of mutual inquiry. For this reason I would recommend Booth over Rorty as a rhetorician of inquiry who both attacks the foundationalist or modernist project and who reveals what *more* one can do with a rhetorical perspective on inquiry.

Bibliography

Bazerman, Charles. *Shaping Written Knowledge: The Genre and Activity of the Experimental Article in Science.* Madison: U of Wisconsin P, 1988.

Booth, Wayne C. *Critical Understanding: The Powers and Limits of Pluralism.* Chicago: U of Chicago P, 1979.

———. *Modern Dogma and the Rhetoric of Assent.* Chicago: U of Chicago P, 1974.

———. *Now Don't Try to Reason with Me: Essays and Ironies for a Credulous Age.* Chicago: U of Chicago P, 1970.

Feyerabend, Paul. *Science in a Free Society.* London: Verso, 1982.

Lyne, John. "Rhetorics of Inquiry." *Quarterly Journal of Speech* 71 (1985): 65–73.

McCloskey, Donald N. *The Rhetoric of Economics.* Madison: U of Wisconsin P, 1985.

Nelson, John S., and Allan Megill. "Rhetoric of Inquiry: Projects and Prospects." *Quarterly Journal of Speech* 72 (1986): 20–37.

Nelson, John S., Allan Megill, and Donald N. McCloskey, eds. *The Rhetoric of the Human Sciences: Language and Argument in Scholarship and Public Affairs.* Madison: U of Wisconsin P, 1987.

Rorty, Richard. *Consequences of Pragmatism (Essays 1972–1980).* Minneapolis: U of Minnesota P, 1982.

———. *Philosophy and the Mirror of Nature.* Princeton: Princeton UP, 1979.

Afterword

Let Us All Mount Our Good Chargers, Whatever Their Names, and Gallop Off Joyfully in All Directions, a Mysteriously United Company Serving the Empress of All the Sciences, Rhetoric

WAYNE BOOTH

"The crisis for all honest students of rhetoric comes when they realize that they know too much about too many things about which they know too little."
DIONYSIUS OF HALICARNASUS

"It is good to have friends because they can praise you when it would not be decent to praise yourself."
EUGENE GARVER

I CAN'T THINK of any writing assignment tougher than this one—except perhaps trying to draft a preface when you feel that a book is not really finished. The plaguey task here is to keep focused on the true *point* of such a book as this.

I'd love to be able to claim that none of the diverse selves in the chorus that Jost, McOmber, and others describe could be tempted to see that point as the exclusive celebration of "our" work or the correction of careless or hostile misrepresentations. The unsurprising fact is that among my chorus of selves there is a rather insistent deep bass who keeps his *Who's Who* entry up to date, who on rare occasions has even signed a letter of recommendation as "Distinguished Service Professor of English and Ideas and Methods Emeritus," and who cares far too much about being attended to. This self gets angry or depressed when people misread him, and he is already demanding a voice here. But because to give him his way would be to deflect us from our true business, I'll try very hard to ban him from our company.

To say as much of course implies that there is another self who feels some contempt for what I—we, the other selves—like to call DISTSERPROF: we like to mock him and all others who see the world as little more than a status-race. Indeed, we—that is to say, the I that is *above* all such stuff—recently wrote an utterly sincere satire—so far rejected by only two journals—against the growing practice of citation-counting—the very thing that DISTSERPROF might be guilty of.

> DISTSERPROF: Oh, come off it. You know you think that our satire is better than just "utterly sincere." Actually it's brilliant, not to say devastating. And while we're at it, surely we should mention that hilarious, published, but sadly neglected satire of ours directed against the national sport of image-building, The Art of Deliberalizing. And while I have the floor, surely we should . . .

That's enough of that. Just keep out of this, while we go about our serious work. As James Stephens once exclaimed to his unruly phallus, "Down, wanton, down!" I don't want to hear any more from you or from any of the others I sense clamoring for entry here. I promise that if I come to feel that you have anything really to say for yourself I may, just may, give you a chance later on.

> IGNORAMUSWB: As the only really honest one among those voices, can I just point out that we are not even sure it was James Stephens; we surely ought to be careful here throughout not to disguise our immense ignorance . . .

Don't you see what you're both doing? You're spoiling the true point. No more, please!

Every alert student of rhetoric must be plagued at times by St. Paul's kind of self-laceration: "I have left undone those things which I ought to have done, and I have done those things which I ought not to have done, and there is no [rhetorical] health in me." Reading through these essays I've been struck not so much by what we students of rhetoric have achieved, since "the great revival," as by what a wonderful variety of openings now face us. So, with rhetoric and its study fully legitimated in the academy, I would like now to imagine the totally unlikely appointment, in the year 2014, of a carefully selected international Board for Rhetorical Inquiry in General, twenty scholars authorized to make unlimited grants to their rhetorical brothers and sisters, using the essays in this book as one major source of topics, but adding, with the characteristic *bricolage* of rhetoricians, whatever else falls into their hands.

The Board will begin with the task of defining rhetoric, and it will find, if it prove honest, that it must support studies of *all* human discourse. Nothing anyone says about anything, even the weird result when two is added to two, can be ruled out: we live, as Jost has shown better than I have ever done, *in* our topics—neither in discursive Pandaemonia nor in a utopia but in a polytopia. Every utterance expresses not just the speaker's character but also the speaker's culture, including that culture's assumptions about what can be said and what should or should not be said. Even if Board members were to think, mistakenly, of our subject as the "mere" act of persuading, every utterance could be shoehorned into their domain.

The point about ubiquity will become more telling when the Board learns to move "upward" from persuasion in their definition to make rhetoric include the whole art, or faculty, of discovering what are good reasons, reasons capable of changing the thought and behavior not only of rhetors' hearers but also of rhetors themselves. That definition will naturally lead them on "upwards" to the heights where the hermeneuticists and theologians dwell (rhetoricians all), finally arriving at the peak, the comparative study of rhetorics—what I've recently been trying, rather unsuccessfully, to get people to call "rhetorology." And that will in turn lead them to see their conflicts and irresolutions and resolutions as implying that ultimate Rhetor, master of mystery and silence, who answers, when we ask "who are you?" with the enigmatical, "I am that I am."

With such properly universalized definitions (unargued here), the Board will quickly see that it cannot organize its allocations according to current academic disciplines. Name any field and you will almost certainly find not only laborers who call themselves students of rhetoric— the "revival" is in that sense demonstrable simply by citation counting.

You will also find under other rubrics innumerable projects that can only be effectively pursued using methods that only a full attention to rhetorical practice will support.

Naturally, every Board member will at times feel a sense of panic at the discovery that the diverse efforts to build a coherent field of rhetorical study prove just as confusing, just as difficult to interrelate, as the ultimate values they seek to serve. One can hope that after considerable debate they will deal with that panic by suppressing the impulse to precision and finality, and simply agree that their problems fall, loosely, loosely, under the three master headings that have outranked all others in the history of philosophy, of religion, and—of rhetoric:[1]

> *Goodness:* how rhetorical study can improve the world or the souls that inhabit it;
>
> *Truth:* how it can further the pursuit of genuine knowledge;
>
> *Beauty:* how it can assist artists in their creation of alternative, "better worlds," and enable re-creators to embrace and appraise such worlds.

The Board will discover that every applicant has a strong tendency to elevate one or another of these three to become architectonic—the emperor of the sciences. And they will soon find themselves in deep controversy over which of the three is in charge, as the one true and proper generator of the ultimate rhetorology.

What is more confusing, they will find that every applicant they deal with seems committed to one of two absolutely contradictory positions: (1) In the long run, "in principle," given sufficient thought and time for discussion, all such battles about the primacy of goodness, or of truth, or of beauty, or about the primacy of particular goods, or of particular truth-systems, or of particular standards of beauty, can be resolved into general agreement: that's what I—we—once firmly believed, and it seems to be the claim of the study by Callaghan and Dobyns here; (2) in both the long and short run, "in principle," we must accept the ultimate and absolute "incommensurability" of some "values," some goods: that's what many modern thinkers, such as Isaiah Berlin and Bernard Williams, have been arguing. For them, although many controversies can be resolved through the use of a powerful rhetorology that probes to the deepest levels underlying conflicts, some human goods are in permanent and irreconcilable conflict.

Of this second group, some will claim that the incommensurability demonstrates the ultimate irrationality of the universe; others, I among them, will claim that it is a blessed gift of life itself. We embrace the condition of being inherently limited, unable as human beings to reduce everything to some supreme harmony. The story of the tower of Babel carries a deeper message than is usually recognized: as creatures exercising freedom in manifold and unpredictable patterns, we cannot expect ever to achieve full agreement about any *one* One as a supreme Good. To have been banned from God's perspective on Her/His created multiplicities was to have been invited into meaningful debate and inquiry; if instead we had been granted unanimity, all values harmonized, ordered under any one of them, we would have lost one of the greatest gifts of human life itself.

Such a position need not diminish our passion for achieving understanding, especially when the alternative to understanding seems to be violence. What the Board must support is those studies that seek to discover just what kinds of encounter avert violence through an understanding of difference and what kinds lead to violence by insisting on an impossible harmony. When should we in effect lock controversialists up in a closed room pending verdict or compromise, and when should we not? What conditions allow the achievements that the jury system manages, at its best, or that President Carter and his team managed at Camp David? What kind simply escalate conflict? To insist that agreement, even loving agreement, is the ultimate purpose of discussion, or of life itself, would in fact destroy life as we value it—and love as we value it would die. Thus, though McOmber is right to say that my rhetoric of assent need not raise all the vexing philosophical problems of the kind that Rorty dismisses, it does plunge us into an eternally inexhaustible supply.

Anyway—as G. K. Chesterton taught everyone to say when a transition is weak—here at last is my memo to that Board, "A Rhetorologist's Agenda, 2014."

RHETORIC AND "GOODNESS," OR IMPROVING THE WORLD

Most rhetoricians have, like me, elevated political or ethical or social effect over the other two grand values—though the most penetrating ones, like Cicero, Quintilian, Kenneth Burke, and so on, have recognized that Goodness can't be achieved without Beauty and Truth, and have found ways to embrace them within their "practical" schemes.

What does this world of practice most need from students of rhetoric?

Studies of Pluralism, Politics, and the Rhetoric of Assent

Foley, Antczak, Garver, and McCloskey suggest or imply that what we *most* need are studies of the kind that grapple with political or institutional problems in a way that I have only rarely even attempted. I agree. My most overt missionary work, from the time when I was literally a missionary for the Mormon church on, has largely been centered, as they claim, on how persons, characters, and selves, real or literary, are made and improved or debased by rhetoric. In the hierarchy of goods served or harmed by rhetoric, the quality of rhetors and their hearers has indeed been my center. A given utterance (whether a one-word exclamation or a five-volume novel) affects, or is intended to affect, or is likely to affect, any person "taking it in." My emphasis has most of the time thus been one-on-one, and on how various "virtues" are strengthened when the right one meets the right one rightly. Though always in theory believing that politics is more fundamental than ethics (Aristotle is right: "You cannot create a fully good 'man' in a genuinely bad state"), I've done far too little with the rhetorical side of larger political conflicts and influences.

Especially important for our Board, then, is the question of whether a given kind of pluralistic rhetoric implicates a given politics. They should fund someone to work through the widespread charge that a pluralistic ethics like mine is always a covert power play, an effort to reduce all radical and controversial views to an easily accommodated range of possibilities that can be exhibited safely on the pluralist's chart, thus "conserving" the established and disempowering everybody else.

The grantee would obviously get Phelan and Foley together to talk it out. Phelan agrees with Foley that every pluralist's discourse is indeed political in one sense (because it "privileges" pluralism over any specific political claim to do the whole job). But he then argues that discourse need not be thought of as *only* political. To think of it as such is to impoverish our sense of what "conversation" can accomplish.

I think Phelan's argument will be hard to answer, if not impossible. Is it not puzzling that strong arguments like his, of which we have quite a few by now, seem to be ignored by those for whom everything is politics?

At the same time I have to agree with Brinton, whose critique I wish I could have read before *Modern Dogma* was sent to the printer, that my particular version of a rhetoric of assent, with all its professions of pluralism, is indeed in one strong sense conservative: it rejects any habitual "innovationism" that values change for its own sake. As Brinton puts it, it gives "presumptive" power to institutions and beliefs as they are inherited or imbibed, putting the burden of proof on those of us who would change them.

Such a stance is not conservative in the sense of being right-wing. Many of the institutional forces that have constituted me from birth on seem to me quite indefensible. I feel especially threatened these days by the consumer capitalism that most of us are largely mired in, and that the simplifiers tout as having "won against Communism." But since we inevitably "are" (that is, are constituted to some degree as) both what we would criticize and the techniques of criticism that we have inherited from institutions, we should be sure of our grounds when we attack them: we should not doubt everything we cannot prove, but assent to everything that we have no good reason to doubt.

I would still hold to that conserving line, while continuing with my fumbling attacks on the grotesque ravages committed by what some people call capitalism. The rhetoric of assent may be conservative, then, but in itself it need not lead any more strongly to my enthusiasm for (most parts of) Edmund Burke's *Reflections* than it does to my passionate belief that capital punishment is a terrible practice that must finally be abolished.

Still, Brinton is right to claim that if anything like a systematic rhetoric of assent is to survive, it will require extensions and somewhat more philosophically sophisticated articulations than I managed in *Modern Dogma* and have touched on here and there since. I'll return to this point when I get to Truth itself.

Studies of Fictions Overtly Political

The Board should approve, as Foley suggests, more studies of how particular fictions perform their reinforcement or questioning of political institutions and social structures; similarly, we should have more careful rhetorical studies of the works that Foley blames me for neglecting. So I must say a bit more about Foley's critique, which is to me the most challenging of the claims, in and out of this volume, that ethical critics fail to do justice to the claims of politics.

Her piece is challenging partly because she has labored to understand my work before criticizing it—not a fashionable practice these days. And she is right to complain that *Company* pays skimpy attention to various minority and protest literatures and critical theories. As I look at *Company* under her tutelage, I do wish that I had addressed more fully the ethical power of works like Morrison's *Beloved* or Silko's *Ceremony*. And she is right to call for studies of works in which the political import is more explicit, even blatant, and the classical status as literary form less obvious. She has forced me to wonder just why, given how much of my reading time is spent precisely with works of the nonestablished or anti-establishment kind, did I address no one of them at length.

It is certainly not, as she suggests, that I don't recognize the crucial importance, especially in America today, of any literary work that genuinely startles complacent readers into assuming "more egalitarian attitudes (anti-racist, anti-sexist, anti-elitist) than they might already espouse: of any work in which "the writer may be the principal 'ethical critic,'" and the would-be emancipated reader becomes "chastened . . . indignant, even resentful" (142). *Company* stressed—though with insufficient examples—that such challenges are one of the chief values of narrative. I would still want to insist that such chastening is often performed even more powerfully by a deeply probing classic—even a classic that on its surface might seem to be written within the same culture as the reader's—than by a passionate contemporary work that *claims* to shatter but that really just duplicates would-be shattering experiences already comfortably accommodated by the reader or spectator.[2] As Marx claimed, the highly conservative Balzac, with his painstaking reports of just how bourgeois capitalism worked, did more for the cause than any number of aggressively "progressive" arguments could do.

What's more, Foley does have too firm a notion of just what sort of jolt *all* readers need; she somehow knows that they all need a jolt in the direction of her particular politics. Though my confused politics are closer to hers than to the views of most of her opponents, what the Board should support are studies of how fictions can jolt readers *alive*. I quite agree that in America today, and quite probably in 2014, most middle-class readers need to be jolted from a complacent assumption that the market economy will save the world singlehandedly, and that everything about socialism, including its demand that we take responsibility for the welfare of others, has been discredited. But is that what readers in Moscow most needed, say, in 1960? The politics of fiction turns out to be as complicated, as bound to circumstance and human variety, as the ethics of fiction. A major value of *some* classics is their capacity to jolt political dogmatists. Every Marxist and in fact every socialist I have known, including Foley (and myself when I thought I was an atheistic socialist) needs the jolt that can result from a genuine engagement with any one of the great philosophies or theologies or religiously oriented fictions. If Foley, who really knows how to dig in, would ever settle into as sympathetic a reading of Augustine or Aquinas or Tolstoy's *Resurrection* or Mauriac's *Knot of Vipers* as she has given Marx, she would be *jolted*. I can't predict where she would come out, but she would no longer be her present kind of Marxist, or an "ist" of any kind, a bit too readily relying on one political perspective. (We know that she'll reply that she's read these greats—but just "reading" is not quite the kind of digging in that I have in mind.)

This does not mean that we can afford to neglect the ethical and political deficiencies, minor or major, of established works. Of those authors I dwelt on, Rabelais, Lawrence, Austen, and Twain, Austen is the only one who came off largely exonerated. The others survived as powerful and enduring literary friends, but only because they are redeemed by various qualities we readers always will need. They are not cleansed of their ethical faults, most of which do count for Foley as in some sense political: Rabelais's and Lawrence's sexism; Twain's optimistic racial liberalism, misleadingly comfortable to his predominantly white readers; Lawrence's forays into totalitarianism and anti-semitism). The purpose of choosing such classics rather than contemporary works was precisely to convince readers who were inclined to resist ideological criticism (of Foley's kind, say) that the narratives they love ought not to be swallowed uncritically just because they are seen *as classics;* in other words, my purpose would place me at least in part on Foley's side here.

Indeed I am puzzled by her suggestion that I would take the side of the canonists against the anti-canonists. I can only hope that when she sees Thomas's development here of my thoroughly political article on Hirsch's cultural literacy proposals, and of what Thomas rightly sees as the implications of my way of dwelling with the classics, she will want to change the line of her critique: not my neglect of politics, but perhaps my mistaken way of going about it.

Anyhow, my choice of the four established authors resulted from my reading of the critical audience in 1988—is that not a political, or at least an institutional, choice? I had no sense that feminists, or black aestheticians, or Marxists, needed to be persuaded that narratives should be subject to an ideological critique. The resisters are those who, while rightly insisting that most classics are classics for sound reasons, cannot see that the very power conferred by classical status cries out for a critical analysis of what that power can do to us as readers.

It is clear that our scene is still full of such resisters. Even those who were ostensibly convinced of our case, even those who claimed to agree that in my special sense "all fictions are didactic" (*Company* 13, 151–53), still often deny that an ethical fault in a novel can be legitimately taken as a "literary" or "aesthetic" fault. Perhaps in twenty years all such will have been converted, though I doubt it, especially when I see how widespread are "aestheticist" current attacks on what is called "political correctness." In any case, I'm not worried about the classics holding their own in the various battles. What should worry the Board is any temptation to take any established classic (or traditional educational view) as above ethical criticism.

The readers I wanted most to reach were of two kinds: those we have just described, readers who were not already converted to the relevance of ideological substractions when dealing with a classic, and those who were already too strongly converted to the pat application of narrow moral or political criteria in dealing with any work, classic or modern. If I had done a full ethical treatment on *Our Nig,* say, as Foley recommends, I would in fact have found just as much to question as I found in *Huck Finn*—but to what end? Every reader who is ever likely to read *Our Nig* will see it immediately and without question as inviting political and ethical questions: it is in effect *about* its own quite open protest. *Huck Finn,* in contrast, has too often been treated as above the battle.

Finally, if Foley had addressed *Modern Dogma* or some of the essays in *Now Don't Try to Reason with Me* and *The Vocation of a Teacher* her case about the neglect of politics would have been more difficult to make. Or if she'd given a careful reading to Antczak's essay here . . .

Ohmigod! What happened? Where was I? Oh, yes, the conspectus for the Board. How did I allow DISTSERPROF to take over like that? Will Foley see that for me to get distracted into petty personal speculation about her actually is a compliment?

Rhetoric and Morality

As rhetoricians have always claimed, all good rhetorical inquiry is embedded in moral questions—provided we use the broader definitions of "morality" to include not just moral demands but what I mean by ethical matters: the creation, improvement, or debasement of persons. So I can only say to the Board here, go read Aristotle's *Rhetoric* again, and then his *Politics* and *Ethics,* and put 'em all together with the GOOD on top, and you'll be ready to make your grants.

Studies of Rhetoric and Teaching

All teaching is—as every reader will by now expect me to say—rhetorical, in our definition, which by no means suggests that a teacher must be merely preaching or indoctrinating. The Board should not just read but *study* Thomas's answer to Hirsch here.

They should also give more support to studies of the best rhetoric for teaching the best rhetoric. Rhetoric as mere persuasion can be taught pretty well by lecturing persuasively, and thus *demonstrating* good persuasive techniques. But rhetoric as inquiry, rhetoric as the dialogical path to mutual understanding, rhetoric as the training of active, growing rather than passive, meandering minds—that rhetoric cannot be taught by even the cleverest of lecturers; it is learned in discussion, in the give-and-take that only a skilled discussion leader can elicit from a fairly small class. Many of us have made this claim again and again, while observing, in anguish, a national increase in class sizes and a growing dependence on clever lecturing—often in mechanical reproduction. Is it not possible that some careful statistical studies of just how little real improvement in *thinking* results from most so-called teaching (including of course inept discussion methods) would lead a statistics-besotted nation to pay attention to what we really need?

For about fifteen years I've been contemplating a book on the uses and abuses of classroom discussion, what Bialostosky might call the struggle for "genuine dialogics." The book just doesn't get written; the tapes recording successes and failures sit in the drawer unattended. The trouble is partly that most of the advice I try to extract from my experience sounds, when put into a book, frozen and uninventive, or self-dramatizing. Perhaps I can hope that by the time the Board gets to work, Homer Goldberg's promised book on the subject will be available, and that other scholars will be clamoring for support for similar studies.

Meanwhile I have a totally unrealistic fantasy of the one stroke that would, without waiting for further study, "save" American education: some grand philanthropist, some Ross-Perot-grown-wise, will announce massive grants available to any college or school district that will promise (with appropriate legal guarantees) to spend the money on one stroke only: cutting by half the enrollment in all courses that are devoted to improving thought through improving writing—that is, to "rhetoric." If this fanciful "Perot" himself (must it be a male?) wants to make doubly sure of success, he will decide to require that every institution receiving the grant install mechanical silencers at every teacher's desk, set to send an electric shock through the teacher's bottom whenever he or she talks longer than eight-and-a-half minutes at a stretch.

Studies of How the "Rhetoric of Assent" Applies to Particular Issues Beyond My Ken

Just as the ethics and politics of fictions need to be extended to a far broader range of texts than I have even dreamed of, so I would like to see the notions of *Modern Dogma* developed, as McOmber implies, into political and moral areas I've scanted. My hints at just what a genuine "presumptive" rhetoric would lead to are feeble compared with what we need, both in developing methods of argument and analysis and in making public arguments ourselves.

McCloskey's essay here is a fine start on how a rhetoric of assent could uncover, discipline by discipline, the largely silent ethical and political foundations of scholars at work. We need more studies that plunge us into the precise rhetorical complexities of special issues, studies like Antczak's exploration of Martin Luther King's rhetoric of non-violence. Far too many studies of particular debates fail, as my book did, to give a sufficiently sustained probing of how sheer faith (not unthinking at all and even systematic in the sense of critical, but privileged nonetheless) is depended on by every effort to engage in that controversy.

Studies of Why Mutual Understanding Is Itself a Good

Our Board must grapple with the radical difference between rhetorics that elevate the mere enlivening of a scene through controversy and those like mine that, while not rejecting the importance of sustaining vitality (*Critical Understanding*), would subordinate it to understanding: the intellectual equivalent of love. Not mere winning, and certainly not mere goading, but a genuine *joining* is what rhetoric should be about. Because joining need not entail agreeing, some devotees of mere vitality have rejected the very notion of finding an interpretive stopping point— the point, for example, when a reader or listener knows without question that an ironic reverse is intended. Is not the whole purpose of interpretation to keep going, to find one's very own reading, something to say that nobody else would think of saying, because it violates the "obvious" intention of the text?

Studies of both the ethics and the politics of these would-be disrupters should be related to the "goods" of community that are touted by us devotees of stabler ironies. Perhaps all one can hope for from the Board, though, is that they will be smart enough to reject projects that consist of the sort of pretentious padding I mocked in "The Empire of Irony"—the mere packing in of fashionable words in the "irony family." In a world that exhibits, as I say there, an average of three "ironically"s per article or chapter, surely we need more examples of meticulous deciphering based on careful theory about what is being deciphered. If "*everything* is ironic," nothing really is, and nobody can hope to possess that greatest of goods, human understanding.

RHETORIC AND "THE BEAUTIFUL," OR, "HOW BEAUTY BECOMES A GOOD"

The Rhetoric of Craft

The Board will want to fund an unlimited number of "rhetorics of" arts other than fiction: of drama, of every variety of poetry, painting or sculpture; of classical or rock music; of such-and-such an artistic period; of cartoon strips; of videos; and so on.[3] They should seek out critics who are willing to attempt not just piecemeal notations but full-scale inquiry into how different makers manage to induce their receivers to join the implicit worlds underlying (or overlaying) the radically different stories told by the different works.

Some projects worth funding will perhaps be described as *sciences* of fiction, not rhetorics: technical studies that show the strokes, the *how*, but don't ask sharply why the strokes are there. (Gérard Genette's procedure in *Narrative Discourse* could be a model for anyone working on the "how.") Needed even more, however, are studies that, while embracing anything that scientific probing can teach about the how of things, dwell on the question "why?" As Rabinowitz proceeds with music here and in his forthcoming book, so might students of every conceivable art or craft help the artists themselves to become better makers.

Such studies will naturally meet head-on any claims, if they are still around in 2014, that there are no *real* distinctions of better and worse in matters of art. One would think that the patent absurdity of such claims would long since have extinguished them. Every journal publishing such ostensibly "democratic" or "post-modernist" levelings exhibits on almost every page evidence that the asserters do not believe what they say. Somehow the assertions continue, and efforts to unmask the absurdity, like mine in *The Company We Keep* or Francis-Noël Thomas's in *The Writer Writing,* are never met *as argument,* only dismissed as elitist.

Studying with full attention and a fully open mind the rhetoric of various instances of a given art, no post-modernist, however freewheeling, could continue to say that value judgments are totally contingent or relative. It is in the details of structure and style that one finds overwhelming evidence that some rhetoricians, including those we call artists, are better than others, when judged on any scale except patently arbitrary ones that come into play when we say such things as: "'Ride-a-cock-horse' is better than *King Lear*—for two-year-olds" or "A whistled version of a bugle call will mean more, as a work of art, than *Oedipus Rex* means—to a dog.")

The Ethics of Craft, or *One of Many Places Where Beauty and Goodness Meet*

Here we meet not just the "How" and the "Why" but the "Ought." Having been instructed by the authors in this book, the Board will assume that any invitation to enter any alternative artistic world invites ethical appraisal: my ethos (my character, my psyche, my soul—the terms are by no means identical but they overlap, and they all fit my case) is changed—at a minimum for the duration of any artistic experience, but often enough also after "real life" is rejoined. It is rendered deeper or more shallow, muddier or more vital and down to earth; broader or narrower, more flabbily unfocused or more finely organized; morally improved or corrupted; more or less bigoted, inhibited, alert to injustice—any adjective for any human quality can be added here.

Every change will occur on disputed territory, but the changes are real, and I am puzzled about why so few critics, even now, seem willing to talk about them, professionally and openly: they all in fact have been changed by fictions, and the changes are reflected in their work. But they usually don't "theorize" ethical evaluation in the ways underlined here by Johnstone, in her honest and revealing struggle with the vicious Genet, or by Shapiro, in grappling with the quite different test presented by Wiesel and the Holocaust, or by McCloskey in revealing the ethics of economists' stories, or by Rabinowitz, in uncovering the powers of opera and stories about it.

Fortunately more and more critics have been addressing ethical questions. These too often avoid technical and formal talk about the quality of a total experience, in all its detailed articulations. Too many of them rely on the sort of judgment that would have resulted if Johnstone had said in her piece here, "Genet's books clearly advocate vicious behavior—therefore they are worthless or harmful, for all readers on all occasions." May the Board heed our call and fund those who are willing to plunge into the threatening difficulties that underlie moral surfaces.

The word "threatening" leads to one more recommendation, before we leave the subject of rhetoricians as beauticians. The subjects writers choose can be threatening not just intellectually but quite personally to the writers themselves: they are sometimes blessed, sometimes harmed, and sometimes even destroyed by living with their subjects. If the Board cares about the ethics of narration at all, it will fund ethical inquiry into fictional, biographical, and autobiographical writing as it affects those who write it. James Gleick has recently reported—explaining why he will never do another biography—just how much his own behavior was changed by spending five years working on his biography of Richard Feynman: "I wasn't prepared for what happens to your psyche when you spend that long tunnelling . . . into someone else's life . . . One gets taken over by this other person to the extent that I would sometimes be getting dressed . . . and I would think, Well, what would my subject wear?"[4]

I offer the Board a title for the first of such studies—*Lives Changed by 'Lives'*—without even requesting a grant for my friends or heirs.

RHETORIC AND TRUTH

Studies of Pluralism and Relativism

The quarrel-ridden marriage of rhetoric and truth, or of what we might call philo-logos and philo-sophy, is going to give our Board a lot of trouble. Do we need more philosophers' claims that truth gets ignored by rhetoricians, all of whom are Sophists?

The conflict of Booth and Rorty with philosophers of various kinds, as carefully traced by McOmber, like the conflict with Bertrand Russell and Descartes that Brinton attributes to one "Professor Booth" (close kin to DISTSERPROF), is almost certainly one of those essentially contested matters that, like the ancient battle between poetry and philosophy, will always produce incommensurables: you can't grant total allegiance to the God of successful practical discourse and at the same time honor the God of truth.

Brinton's critique is just the kind that any honest author ought to take seriously. He teaches us a lot about just how much rhetoric of assent has been practiced by some whom I earlier blamed as excessive doubters.

He and I agree that for practical purposes the question of truth boils down to the question of just what kinds of argument offer good reasons for changing one's mind. Like most philosophers since Kant, he wants good reasons to be subjected to a systematic doubt, and then rejected if they cannot offer hard proof for themselves; all my selves, except IGNORAMUSWB, believe that such privileging of doubt will finally destroy even the best of our reasons—in all of the matters that matter most to us.

I agree that what I called systematic assent is not systematic in any sense that would be recognized by Brinton's philosophical schools: I should perhaps have used a different adjective: "persistent," or "habitual," or "privileged." The point was to *privilege* assent, or as Brinton puts it, to show that our assent to what we know already puts the burden of proof on doubt. Our "common sense"—that is, whatever our deepest intuitions tell us is true—should be assented to *unless* and *until* we are presented with reasons to doubt, reasons that seem stronger than the reasons to assent. Such a view could never be systematic in the way that analytical philosophers try to be systematic; as Brinton says, the problems of determining, in theory, just which "intuitive" or communal assents to assent to are immense. But these new problems do not leave us, like the problems a habitual doubter faces when forced to make practical choices, convinced that all of our reasons for choice are a bit shameful. And McOmber is right to distinguish my problems from those raised by Rorty's or Feyerabend's kinds of rootless freewheeling.

I do wish that my rhetoric of assent had been less catch-as-catch-can. Further work like McOmber's would show that such a rhetoric need not lead, as Brinton claims, to "exactly the same incoherent results as a real procedure of systematic denial" (p. 259). Systematic denial leads, as he says, nowhere—or as I would say rather, to Nowhere: it leaves us without a leg to stand on, and, as all of the great pursuers of where it leads have shown (Descartes, Hume, Santayana . . .), it leaves the doubter forced to find some way out of nothingness: either to total silence (often that has meant suicide), or to the employment, more or less shamefacedly, of the methods the unsystematic folk have been practicing all the while. Is that not where the most influential of recent skeptics, Jacques Derrida, tells us we are forced to return, relying on the very language with which he has conducted his annihilations and deferrals?

Brinton shows that Bertrand Russell, one of whose three major personae I used as whipping boy in *Modern Dogma,* readily assented in many of his works to forms of reasoning that resemble what I call the rhetoric of assent. Almost all professional philosophers who've seen my little gambit have, like Brinton, resented it as if it were an effort to deny Russell's greatness, which it is not. My claim was only that Russell, taught by philosophical history and his own failed attempts to believe that values could not be "proved," was always plagued, sometimes even tortured, by the belief that when he turned to "probabilistic" or "everyday" reasoning (of the kind quoted in Brinton's conclusion) he was in effect betraying his own standards of rationality. He also believed, as the quotation shows, that unless we could harmonize all our instinctive beliefs, they have no intellectual standing.

Still, Brinton's concluding quotation from Russell could almost make an epigraph for *Modern Dogma,* which was only one of many attempts, neither "modern" nor "post-modern," back beyond Shaftesbury and Bishop Berkeley and the Bacon uncovered in Garver's fine digging here, and on back to Cicero, to claim full intellectual respectability for a communal pursuit of where our *sensus communis* leads.

The battle between the apodeictic and the just plain reasonable will inevitably continue, perhaps forever, regardless of the cogency of anyone's rhetoric of assent. I do hope that professional philosophers, as they continue their work in rehabilitating what they call informal logic and rediscovering the relevance of the basic virtues to philosophizing,[5] will begin to incorporate the work of traditional rhetorical theories, supplemented nicely by the current discoveries of just how "rhetorical" was the work of the great Wittgenstein.

Studies of Metaphors as the Key to All the Mythologies

The Board should study Richter's piece carefully, not for what it says about me but for what it says about how to analyze metaphors. It is true that much of his method in exploring me is implicit in the teaching of that recent grand invasion of French rhetoricians (raiding under other banners, of course). Close attention to an author's or movement's metaphors, and especially their macro-metaphors (or metaphorical "worlds" that I grappled with in *Company*) is one of the three best paths to full understanding of any rhetorical practice (the other two, which after full probing tend to merge with metaphor, are—as everyone still with us "here" knows—*invention,* as dealt with by Jost working on the topics, and *arrangement:* the choice of hierarchies, whether vertical (as in Burke's *Rhetoric of Religion*) or horizontal (as in the long history of advice about how best to organize a speech).

The fashionable study of metaphors under the "rhetoric of suspicion," in the search for a foreordained and inherently disempowered incoherence (or, as with some French feminists, an inherent drive for patriarchal dominance) is radically different from Richter's practice, which would suggest for our masthead the slogan: Metaphors are inherently constructive, not deconstructive.

Studies of the Rhetoric of Silence

Board members: Read Garver. Read him again, then go read Bacon. Fund studies of silence, of What Goes Without Saying. This piece of Garver's is original.

Studies of Dialectic, Dialogics, Pluralism, and the Threat of Relativism

Among the essentially contested, eternally irresolvable conflicts the Board must face are two that, as Bialostosky shows, Bakhtin and I wrestle with. (1) How can we interrelate or choose among our dialogics or pluralisms? (2) How can we harmonize our dialogics or pluralisms with the demands of practical decisions in the world?—or even better, make use of them, a problem Phelan addresses.

(1) If the Board does its work properly, it will take massive steps to break down the isolation among various universalist "specialists in generalities." It will fund lots of studies like Bialostosky's. And it will work to persuade every field in which specialists make a claim, in principle, to "cover everything," to appoint at least one rhetorologist to serve as reconnaissance and liaison officer to the other groups: "cognitive science," linguistics, structuralism, deconstruction, "informal logic," "critical thinking," and so on. A lot of wasted efforts at refutation could thus be avoided.

(2) The charge of relativism—or its genuine threat—will not go away. The Board should plan to fund Phelan (after all, he'll still be perking in 2014) and others like him, to continue the search for persuasive routes through the Scylla of dogmatism and the Charybdis of skepticism. We can be sure that dogmatists will continue to label efforts like ours as utterly relativistic, and that utter relativists will continue to show (as would be easy to show about Bakhtin), that we are in fact "not total pluralists" but actually committed to certain "values" (in my other terms, "assentings") that remain finally—in our sense of the word—indubitable.

The Board need not feel uncomfortable about this unresolved battle about and among pluralisms: it is both the case that no statement is true except as relative to other statements, and that there are genuine (though multiple) standards of taste, of moral judgments, and of truth. And this means that there are many assertions about such matters that have to be rejected by anyone who thinks hard about them.[6]

Studies of Rhetoric and Religion

If they do things right, the Board must spend a good share of their unlimited budget on the rhetoric of religion. The whole enterprise of criticism, and particularly of rhetorical criticism, is pointless unless it has a point—to return to the key word of my opening paragraph. And to me it has become increasingly obvious that to claim a *point* to any human activity is to see it in one or another cosmic perspective, leading to the kind of inquiry Shapiro exhibits here. Everything we do, if it has a point, can be shown to relate to some notion of a cosmos that, however "chaotic," validates its making. A real point is a point that matters, and to matter, unless one thinks of mattering as only private, personal, and hence entirely relativized, is to matter in some scheme, or world, or pattern, or dimension of reality, larger than any one person's vision.

Such a claim seems self-evident once one sees it clearly—as Anselm said of his ontological proof. The steps to its self-evidency, however, are difficult and manifold. In other words, the field/fields of rhetoric require the Board to fund lots of hard argument about religion—lots of theological study, most of it under different names. Let us hope that many will follow Shapiro and Jost here in pursuing leads that have been largely mere assertions or wonderings.

In "Are Rhetoric and Religion Permanently Wedded?" I argue that "the student of rhetoric will be led, inescapably led provided that he or she pushes the inquiry with full rigor, to religion"—not just, with

Kenneth Burke, to religious language but to religious belief itself. I can't argue that case here, but I do hope that the Board will fund studies of the entire history of religious rhetoric, and rhetorics of religion, to demonstrate, in the languages of diverse schools, just why rhetorical inquiry and religious belief of *some* kind are inseparable.

Studies of the Rhetoric of "Secular Religions"

The Board should also pursue just how this or that current social movement or academic discipline might be treated as a "secular religion," since it claims to provide the grounding for legitimate point-making that any true religion must provide. Our confusing culture provides innumerable claimants who offer some sort of "cosmos," some picture of the whole of things that legitimates, or commands, certain forms of behavior. When cosmologists, artificial intelligence enthusiasts, psychologists, deconstructionists, rational choice theorists, economists claim to offer us *the* picture of the world and our place in it, and when they then rehearse, often unwittingly, the topics that traditionally belonged to religion, it should be obvious that students of rhetoric are called on to attempt some high-powered translating and evaluating. We can be sure that between now and 2014 other secular religions will rise, claiming at last to tell us just what the world is made of and just what the making demands of us.

These secular religions usually do not put their Thirty-Nine Articles up front, but they exhibit kinds of devotion and expression that traditionally marked religious devotion and inquiry. Be generous, oh, Board, in funding those rhetorologists who engage in comparing the strengths and weaknesses of our many secular religions. And while you're at it, you should fund unlimited studies of how conversion stories work and what they reveal—both conversions to "real" religions and to the secular religions that pretend to be freed of religion.

To talk of religion leads us inevitably back to systematic assent, and to my lament about how few critics are really pursuing a full rhetoric of inquiry. Assent is in the air all right, if we mean by it only the habit of saying yes to whatever doctrine happens to seem appealing or provides temporarily the line of least resistance or most plausibly profitable results. But though by systematic assent I did not mean to suggest the kind of systematic philosophising that Brinton rebukes me for failing to achieve, I did mean something more than the blind unmethodical faith that McOmber sees in Feyerabend and that he helpfully distinguishes from the faith that I had in mind.

Studies of the "Self," of Just Who "We" Are as We Engage with One Another in our Rhetoric

Having done a fair job of suppressing a chorus of voices who could have made this a decidedly silly response, I must urge in conclusion that the Board fund . . .

DISTSERPROF: The only proper summary here will be about US: pull us together, man. You can't deny that the five of us (no doubt along with others that we scarcely acknowledge) live together daily, happily united under my tutelage and without too many hours spent in quarreling. Let's make the point of this response, and thus of this book, what I've wanted it to be all along, an intellectual triumph . . .

THE "I" OF THIS RESPONSE: But if we do that we'll be not elevating but lowering ourselves to your competitive world, not only making US the center, as we should not be, but pretending to a clear harmony that would be a downright lie. I'm sure that we should maintain my tone—not that of a defensive, pedantic fool like you but of one who is calmly, open-mindedly inquiring . . .

DISTSERPROF: Nonsense! If we really want that Board to fund—but let's drop the weak fantasy about what they might do in 2014 and come down to earth here and now: if we really want any reader to undertake studies of why and how the self is always a rhetorical society, and of what to do about our quarrel with individualism, we MUST end on this problem of voices. And in doing so we could unify our two points and impress everybody with . . .

Oh, all right, let's give it a try. But we simply must drop that cruddy effort to defend on every point . . .

In fact, knowing the rebellious voices as I do, I must advise all high-minded folks just to skip now to page 306. You'd just be annoyed by the next few pages.

Let's see now . . .

DISTSERPROF: This whole piece has been much too polite. You've simply silenced me at many points where it would have been highly appropriate to complain about the grotesque distortions our work has been subjected to. You're always going around quoting Aristotle, and any other polyanna you can find, such as Anatole France's M. Bergeret on the Dreyfus affair, claiming that since truth has a natural power to endure, a power that error lacks, we should not worry about petty misunderstandings. Maybe. But that's true about truth, at best, only in the long run. Truth has that power only when someone like us has the guts to ...

IGNORAMUSWB (henceforth IWB for short): Darn it, we just don't KNOW enough, any one of us or all together, to accomplish what we're trying to do here. We have read not a single classical rhetorician in the original language. We can't keep up with the journals, not even those explicitly in our ...

TRUTHGOODNESSBEAUTYWB (Henceforth TGBWB for short): I must insist, once and for all, that I deplore interruptions from either of these rebels. On the one hand, DISTSERPROF's ego-stroking-and-protecting stuff provides a wonderful opening for those who would like to whip us by practicing "motivism"—reducing everything we've done to our motives. On the other, we are really doomed if we must follow IWB, and confess to every yawning gap in our knowledge. Are you ALL going to claim that I am not the most important one of us, as I speak here for Truth, Goodness, and Beauty? Are you really going to let our readers think that we are speaking for anything other than those three supreme goals, which as I've said everyone from ... ?

THE "I" OF THIS RESPONSE ("I" for short): I don't know yet. I feel thrown off balance by all this nattering, especially the boasting of DISTSERPROF. My only comfort, as I have expunged his pontifications from a first, second, and third draft, is that I have never yet encountered any member of our citation-counting, prize-seeking culture who was completely beyond all petty defenses of ego, completely freed of all fear of being discovered as a fraud. Even those who work hard to appear above the battle turn out, when we get a chance to see their diaries or letters, to have spent too much of their time cursing or correcting reviewers, or lamenting the prizes awarded to others, or nagging their publishers about inadequate publicity.

How sad it is to read the self-absorbed laments of aging celebrities angry about being neglected, or echoing Heidegger's (possibly apocryphal) deathbed lament: "Only one reader ever understood me—and even he didn't understand me." A recent biography of Philip Larkin reveals, among many other Larkins, one who convinced his public, including me, that he was not just indifferent to fame but contemptuous of it, above the battle, wise, mature. All the while he was living intimately with another Larkin, a would-be distinguished professor of poetry, as it were, who never turned down an offered honorary degree or invitation for a public reading; he was miserable and furious when criticized.[7] Another example: Derrida's reputation is being slightly tarnished, in my view, by his spending so much time, in journal after journal, worrying the bones of fame. "What he seems to be saying," one friend said, "is that everyone is plain stupid not to grasp the importance of his utterly clear, straightforward, unambiguous, undeferred meanings."[8] I just don't want us to sound like Karl Popper in his later years . . .

A CHILD'S VOICE, WHINING: What IS truth, anyway? Who cares about it? Why doesn't anybody pay attention to ME? It's not truth we should care about but getting people to love us, unconditionally. I never get the love we deserve. I'm always . . .

TGBWB: Ohmigod! We're surely not going to let that one in, that WHINER, that eternal *Id* who never grows up. I say "Ban him!" He predates, and radically corrupts or misrepresents, all the rest of us . . .

WHINER: Well, I should have at least this one chance, and I want to complain about . . .

DISTSERPROF: *Tais-toi!* You're embarrassing all of us. The point is not to be loved but to get credit for the truths of Booth, as straightened out in the public mind by me, and . . .

"I": I'm taking over here, for now. We've already spent far too long on this family quarrel. Do I have to say again that the point of a volume like this should be to invite our readers to join the field of inquiry that has been the most interesting and important of all fields, from ancient times to the present? We should be thinking about how one struggler's unfinished and inevitably inharmonious and vulnerable projects could help him and others improve our study of rhetoric and thus our chances of understanding one another—and thus help us all to turn from physical violence, first at least to bloodless logomachy, and then hopefully[9] from logomachy to serious debate, and then from debate to dialogue, and then on, even perhaps to achieve the dialogics that Don Bialostosky derives from Bakhtin? And—to complicate the case—how can we develop, as part of that ultimately practical project, a philosophy of comparative rhetorics, what DISTSERPROF insists—perhaps justifiably—that we call a "rhetorology," one that would adequately "theorize," though never "finalize," the whole of humankind's communicative endeavors? There's our proper summary and . . .

DISTSERPROF: If that's our only kind of point, we'll lose this chance, probably the last we'll ever have, to set the world straight—to choose only one example from this book—about how Bialostosky misleads readers by writing as if, in *Critical Understanding,* we ourselves embrace the battle metaphors we use in deploring the world's way of handling conflict. Are you going to let even your friends' misreadings go uncorrected?

"I": Yes, certainly I am. What YOU will choose to do is another matter. But you know as well as I do, arrogant one, that Aristotle's picture of the magnanimous man is one of my, and I would wish "our," many ideals. What would he think of your way of thinking, foul lackey of Lucifer that you are? Yes, indeed, I've changed my mind, we're going to rule out petty cavils, including this conversation, leaving nothing but pure, disinterested inquiry. Only thus can we maintain our "hypocrisy upward" as generous-spirited, disinterested inquirers.

IWB: It makes me feel embarrassed when you refer to Aristotle when we don't even know any Greek . . .

DISTSERPROF: Well, I certainly agree that you should cut all the dissenting voices—except mine. Do you really believe that our readers, or even Bialostosky himself, will see what a powerful challenge all this open-spirited dialogue gives to his critique?

And speaking of what makes us vulnerable, take as one sad example your invention of that silly Board for Rhetorical Inquiry in General. Don't you see that your enemies will immediately spot that the acronym is BORING? Why not—if you insist on the sort of game-playing that besmirches our ethos—why not something safe, like POROI, echoing that outfit at The University of Iowa that McCloskey and Antczak are running? Or RUN, for Rhetoric-Universal, or UNIRHET, or even something that will resist mockery, like RFA (Rhetoric For All), or simply UR, for Universal Rhetoric?

And while I've got the floor, I have to say that you exaggerate how fully we're legitimated by widespread recognition of rhetorical studies. Why not acknowledge the plight "rhetoric" is in—precisely the plight it has been in since at least the time of Plato's attack on the Sophists? You talk as if our study, as distinct from persuasive practice, were triumphing, but it's not. Worried about where we stand, I've just done a quick survey of the listed titles and ads in *The London Review of Books* for April 8, 1993, *The New York Review of Books* for April 22, and *The Times Literary Supplement* for April 2. The word "rhetoric" occurs not even once in all those titles! Looking back a bit, and "rising" to the quarterlies, in the one issue of *Critical Inquiry* that I happen to have with me in London I find at last, among all the titles, all the advertisements, and the index of the entire 1992 volume, one appearance of "rhetoric"—and that in a subtitle! One appearance only! I about gave up. But then, reading casually in a movie review by Terrence Rafferty in *The New Yorker,* what do I find? "Lucille heads off to college, which, in the rhetoric of growing-up stories, means she'll be fine." Does that sound as if Rafferty were au courant in rhetorical studies? Meanwhile President Clinton is quoted using the word "rhetoric" twice in one speech, in exactly the sense we've been fighting against all our lives. If "rhetoric" is still languishing, what about its half-synonyms that are popular? I've made a long list...

"I": Sorry, but I'm cutting two pages of your so-called research, and I want to insist...

ALL THE OTHER VOICES TRY TO INTERRUPT, BUT DISTSERPROF SHOUTS LOUDEST: What I want to insist on is that you make far too little of the misunderstandings even your friends exhibit of your conception of rhetorical studies. Are you just listening to WHINER when you tread so lightly on Garver and Bialostosky, both of whom saddle our later views with earlier talk that made mere persuasion too central? If they had taken the pains that Richter takes to trace a development, they would not have frozen us into relatively authoritarian poses. And while I'm at it, surely we must tell the world that Garver's fine original essay on Bacon, on "What Everybody Knows," and on the uses of silence, understates (while politely acknowledging) just how much we have recently done with the rhetoric of silence!

AGAIN THE CHORUS TRIES TO INTERVENE, UNSUCCESSFULLY: And why not reveal the absolute scandal in the world's neglect of our admirably few and tastefully chosen neologisms? I'm pleased that you managed to bring in "rhetorology" without too much apology, but you really ought to flaunt it, man! It's true that some people find it absurdly ugly on first encounter, but so was "socio-logy" when it first appeared. "Bio-logy" was unheard of until early in the nineteenth century. And surely "theo-logy" offended many when it first offered to take over all talk about God. You know perfectly well that our rhetorology is a more useful term than Kenneth Burke's "logo-logy," because, though his term was useful for his study of "The Rhetoric of Religion," it is too narrow for our purposes: it covers only comparative religious languages. Rhetorology covers the theoretical interrelationships of all rhetorics about anything. That would be clear to everybody by now, if you weren't such a pussyfooter...

WHINER: Who cares about all that? I care a lot more about the nasty, silly attacks we've been subjected to. For example, we absolutely must get in here a reference to our annihilating and witty response to S****** F****'s mutilation of *A Rhetoric of Irony*;[10] it has been largely ignored, perhaps because our ironies against him were just too subtle. F*** himself has shrewdly ignored it, reprinting his own inane and uninformed attack without mentioning our refutation. Get in there and gut F*** again, once and for all . . .

DISTSERPROF: As for me, that is the ONLY one of WHINER's points worth preserving. It's important to include such evidence that will counter the misconception of friends like Callaghan and Dobyns who, careful as they are, seem to say that we say that everybody should "argue to agree," as if like Habermas we thought all reasonable arguers would agree if given enough time. Though we did once believe that, we no longer see ultimate harmony as either possible or desireable, especially with careless folk like F***. Look again at what I said earlier and . . .

CHORUS: But . . .

DISTSERPROF: But me no buts. The question of easy or final agreement brings up the question of politics. You have been much too polite with those who accuse us of ignoring it. You could at least mention the range of our actual explicit wrestlings with politics—for example our recent defense of Amnesty International's program, "Does Amnesty Have a Leg to Stand on?" with its extended refutation of the very notion of an isolated, in-dividual distinguishable from his or her political or social surroundings, what we are now calling "philiations"—another neologism the world is neglecting!

Why not refer to your many anticapitalist digs, especially in that unpublished speech you gave in Moscow, arguing that the very principles of free speech we all depend on are now seriously threatened by the control over "speech"—that is, over the media—exercised by commercial exploiters? You've said a lot about the increasing debasement of our lives, especially in the direction of legitimated violence, sexual and otherwise, committed by the exploiters. And why not mention that idea of ours about a special "education" tax on all who make fortunes by miseducating us, in "An Arrogant Proposal" and "Self-Making in Imaginative Art"?

And how about that unpublished talk, "The Crazy Canon Controversy", different versions delivered at half-a-dozen campuses as an effort to see behind the false issue of pro-anti-classics? Besides, we could show that some reviewers of *Company* have accused us of selling out to various current political movements that question the canon and thus of politicizing criticism.

IWB: I'm so embarrassed I could die. You're both concealing the fact that we haven't read more than a fraction of what would be important to any one of these matters. We have scores of unread books on our shelves, to say nothing of those we should have bought to put on those shelves, read or unread. Are you really willing to imply that in any sense we "keep up" on what is going on in ANY of this stuff? We don't, even in fields that travel under the word "rhetoric." Why don't you throw in the towel? We'll never know enough to do the response we're attempting here . . .

DISTSERPROF: Well, we surely know enough to complain about "I" 's not even mentioning the current neglect of formal and technical literary questions, or our recent defense of the *Poetics*. Even the friendly authors in this book don't often look at any one work with the kind of loving attention to detail that . . .

TGBWB: Doesn't it shock you more to have us ignore the whole question of philosophical truth. You write as if Brinton's penetrating critique doesn't deserve a respectful demolition. You . . .

DISTSERPROF: What we should do is just point out that if Brinton would only admit the influence of his upbringing as an analytical philosopher, he would see that his response to certain kinds of philosophy and to our questioning of Russell's coherence were foreordained. Move in there and do some punching for a change. For example, he seems to suggest that we are ignorant of Descartes's constructive side. Well, dang it all, I once even reported in print how much trouble I had trying to teach students of Descartes to respect his—to me—persuasive proof for the existence of God. . . .

And while I'm at it, I have to say that it really burns me to see how lightly you deal with those French raiders. Here's our one chance to insist that they've been getting credit, because of their fancy Greek vocabulary, for a lot that we said earlier, and for even more that Richard McKeon and Kenneth Burke said more forcefully. And they are so awfully reductive: beneath their fancy surfaces there is a reduction of rhetoric almost as maiming as what Renaissance writers did when they turned the whole thing into lists of figures. By the way, on "listings," see Jost: he's good on their use and abuse—and you don't even mention it.

As for pluralism, which you hardly touch on, at the very least you could refer the Board to our essay in the *Encyclopedia of Poetics* and the recent answer to Nussbaum, "On Relocating Ethical Criticism."

CONCLUSION I

Who, then, *is* the WB who, like everyone else in the world, exhibits, for all who look closely, unlimited multiplicity? If Jost's "topics" won't *quite* hold him together, will *anything*?

The question would seem a strange one in most historical periods, because until modern times nobody was troubled by the search for unique *identity:* it was enough to be simply a person practicing a variety of roles—not an identity at all, but a character employing "hypocrisy upward" in an effort to do or be better. It is the history of in-dividualism, with all its triumphs and woes, that wills upon us this strange desire to get our act together. Today, instead of just doing what needs to be done, we all struggle to find someone *inside,* someone already made and waiting to be discovered, the *real me.*[11]

I find all the unity I need in the simple continuation of the very drama among my selves that I have reflected here—one that is, like yours, oh, reader, far richer than my little game could hope to reflect. That continuation builds a story-line with a unique pattern of more or less untrustworthy but precious memories. We all plot out a little life-story, a play that contains many "plays-within-the-play." Much of the story, like the stories of heroes in drama, is beyond our control, even on the rare occasions when our various characters act in harmony. But if we are born lucky we are able to plot a good deal of it. Uniqueness is no longer a problem for us because nobody else's plot is exactly like "mine," "ours." In that sense, and that sense only, "I" am an "individual." Just about everything I'm made of can be found in other people—both the defensible and the indefensible parts.

As a rhetorical society, throwing my various roles into dialogue with one another, I find that many modern and post-modern anxieties simply evaporate. It is true that DISTSERPROF can still become very anxious indeed about doing an adequate response to essays as diverse and challenging as these; he fears that we are in danger of ending a career with a whimper instead of a bang. IWB can, especially in the late afternoon, panic because of how little we know about all this. WHIMPER can whimper about not getting enough loving admiration. TGBWB can pretend to a clearer and fuller conspectus than he has a right to, and "I" could wish that most of their deflections would just not occur. But as soon as we call them together they demonstrate the essentially comic *point* of it all. The comedy is by no means in itself divine, but once they start laughing together at one another, the life-story can continue vigorously—sometimes even happily—without much worry about whether it/we/they are modern, post-modern, or simply guilty of radical traditionalism.

CONCLUSION 2

I simply cannot accept that conclusion, which sucks us back into the very "point" I rejected in my opening paragraphs. The true point of all this is to give the best possible boost to humane studies, conceived as studies of how to improve our inquiry into how we inquire together. To deflect us back to the effort to pull various Wayne Booths together is exactly the wrong way to go about that task. When things seem, as always, to be falling apart, surely we should not encourage the world to see each self as in any way a fiction. Surely we should . . .

Notes

1. For Plato, truth, goodness, and beauty; for Aristotle, inquiry into three kinds of activities and problems: theoretical, practical, and productive (the arts and crafts); for Kant, the three Critiques; and so on.

2. Yes, I am thinking of a specific work here, one that recently bored me while in effect claiming to startle: Joe Orton's *What the Butler Saw*. The anti-institutional clichés of 1960s revolt, turned into a skilfully constructed farce, do not undermine the destructive complacencies of American theatergoers in 1991, whatever their political views. But then I suppose that Foley could admit, without hurting her case, that the play does not offer the kind of "political" challenge she would hope for.

3. Discursive, non-narrative prose, the kind most often treated by traditional rhetoricians, will still deserve funding, though it has been somewhat better served than the arts have been. See, for example, Antczak's piece in this volume and his book, *Thought and Character: the Rhetoric of Democratic Education* (Ames, IA, 1985); Gary Saul Morson's emerging works on what he calls "Prosaics"; and indeed a long history of rhetorics of "rhetoric," "rhetorologies." But I don't know of anyone who has come close to exhausting our needs.

4. *The New Yorker* 29 March 1993: 41.

5. For a sign of just how much of a return to the "virtues" recent philosophers have been showing, see the *Times Literary Supplement* for 18 June 1993.

6. Many current philosophers have embraced incommensurability theories that are not utterly relativistic. For a recent example see Isaiah Berlin, *The*

Crooked Timber of Humanity: Chapters in the History of Ideas, ed. Henry Hardy (New York: Knopf, 1991).

7. Andrew Motion, *Philip Larkin: A Writer's Life* (London: Faber, 1993).

8. See the series of letters, pro and con, in the *New York Review of Books* through the spring of 1993.

9. For a defense of "hopefully" in this absolute construction, see the third edition of *The American Heritage Dictionary of the English Language.*

10. See my "A New Strategy for Establishing a Truly Democratic Criticism."

11. The best critique I know of this mistaken direction of the quest for authenticity is that of Charles Taylor, in *Sources of the Self* (Cambridge: Harvard UP, 1989), and, in somewhat more "popular" form, in *The Ethics of Authenticity,* same press, 1992.

Bibliography

Booth, Wayne C. "An Arrogant Proposal: A New Use for the Dyshumanities." *Profession* 77.1 (1977): 1–6.

———. *The Company We Keep: An Ethics of Fiction.* Berkeley: U of California P, 1988.

———. "The Company We Keep: Self-Making in Imaginative Art, Old and New." *Daedalus* 111 (1982): 33–59.

———. *Critical Understanding: The Powers and Limits of Pluralism.* Chicago: U of Chicago P, 1979.

———. "The Empire of Irony." *Georgia Review* 37 (1983): 719–37.

———. "Individualism and the Mystery of the Social Self; or, Does Amnesty Have a Leg to Stand On?" *Freedom and Interpretation: The Oxford Amnesty Lectures 1992.* Ed. Barbara Johnson. New York: Basic, 1993. 69–102.

———. "A New Strategy for Establishing a Truly Democratic Criticism." *Daedalus* 12 (1983): 193–214.

———. "On Relocating Ethical Criticism." *Explanation and Value in the Arts.* Ed. Salim Kemal and Ivan Gaskell. Cambridge: Cambridge UP, 1993. 71–93.

———. "Pluralism." *The Encyclopedia of Poetry and Poetics.* Princeton: Princeton UP, 1991.

———. "The *Poetics* for a Practicing Critic." *Essays on Aristotle's Poetics.* Ed. Amelie Oksenberg Rorty. Oxford: Princeton UP, 1992. 387–408.

———. "Rhetoric and Religion: Are They Essentially Wedded?" *Radical Pluralism and Truth.* Ed. Werner G. Jeanrond and Jennifer L. Rike. New York: Crossroad, 1991. 62–80.

Thomas, Francis-Noël. *The Writer Writing.* Princeton: Princeton UP, 1993.

BIBLIOGRAPHY: WAYNE C. BOOTH

Compiled by Lee Artz

WORKS BY WAYNE BOOTH

BOOKS

The Rhetoric of Fiction. Chicago: U of Chicago P, 1961; 2nd ed., 1983.
The Knowledge Most Worth Having. Ed. Wayne C. Booth. Chicago: U of Chicago P, 1967.
Now Don't Try to Reason with Me: Essays and Ironies for a Credulous Age. Chicago: U of Chicago P, 1970.
Modern Dogma and the Rhetoric of Assent. Notre Dame: U of Notre Dame P, 1974.
A Rhetoric of Irony. Chicago: U of Chicago P, 1974.
Critical Understanding: The Powers and Limits of Pluralism. Chicago: U of Chicago P, 1979.
The Harper and Row Reader. With Marshall W. Gregory. New York: Harper and Row, 1984; 2nd ed., 1988.
The Harper and Row Rhetoric: Writing as Thinking, Thinking as Writing. With Marshall W. Gregory. New York: Harper and Row, 1987; 2nd ed., 1991.
The Company We Keep: An Ethics of Fiction. Berkeley: U of California P, 1988.
The Vocation of a Teacher: Rhetorical Occasions, 1967–1988. Chicago: U of Chicago P, 1989.

ARTICLES

"The Mormon Liberal." *Chicago Jewish Forum* Spring 1944: 192–96. (Written under the pseudonym George Chipman.)
"Notes toward a Definition of Synaestheticology." *Furioso* 4.3 (1949): 61–65.
"*Tristram Shandy* and Its Precursors: The Self-Conscious Narrator." Diss. U of Chicago, 1950.
"Did Sterne Complete *Tristram Shandy?*" *Modern Philology* 48 (1951): 172–83.
"Farkism and Hyperyorkism." *Furioso* 6.3 (1951): 41–44.
"Macbeth as Tragic Hero." *Journal of General Education* 6 (1951): 17–25. Rev. as "Shakespeare's Tragic Villain." *Shakespeare's Tragedies: An Anthology of Modern Criticism.* Ed. Laurence Lerner. Harmondsworth: Penguin, 1963. 180–90.

"Reading and Writing on Human Values." With Ralph M. Sargent. *Journal of General Education* 5 (1951): 245–53.

"Thomas Mann and Eighteenth-Century Comic Fiction." *Furioso* 6.1 (1951): 25–36.

"Reflections of a Young Teacher." *Journal of General Education* 7 (1952): 9–16. (Written under the pseudonym D. Phillips.)

"The Self-Conscious Narrator in Comic Fiction before *Tristram Shandy*." *PMLA* 67 (1952): 163–85.

"Dawn, Delight, Dew, Dove." *College English* 15 (1953): 171–76.

"The Morley Boswell." *Chicago Review* 7.3 (1953): 36–46.

"A Brush in Pasadena." *Progressive* October 1954: 25–26.

"Farkism and Hyperyorkism, Part II." *Western Humanities Review* 8 (1954): 15–18.

"The Utilization of Methodological Consciousness." *College English* 16 (1955): 373–75.

"Imaginative Literature Is Indispensable." *College Composition and Communication* 7 (1956): 35–38.

"Knowledge and Opinion: An Address to College Seniors." *Journal of General Education* 10 (1957): 17–23.

"Dangers of 'a Practical Education.'" *Listener*, 4 Apr. 1957: 550–52.

"The Two Worlds in the Fiction of Wright Morris." *Sewanee Review* 65 (1957): 375–99.

"Straw Men and the Life of Criticism." *Western Humanities Review* 12 (1958): 81–86.

"Elevators, Trains and the Dippler Effect." *Earlham Review* 2.3 (1959): 18–20. Rpt. as "Einstein, Elevators, the Fourth Dimension, and the Dippler Effect (A Humanities Professor Who Keeps-Up-On-Things Lectures on Recent Developments in Space)." *Carleton Miscellany* 1.1 (1960): 65–70. And as "A Humanities Professor Translates Einstein For Us." *Delos* 1.1 (1988): 139–42.

"The Myth of Beuth: Plato on Teaching Machines." *Earlham Review* 3.2 (1959): 17–19.

"The Art of Sinking in Prose, by Professor John R. Buthnot, Ph.D." *Carleton Miscellany* 1.4 (1960): 102–8. "The Art of Sinking in Prose (Chapter Two)." *Carleton Miscellany* 2.1 (1961): 121–26. "The Art of Sinking in Prose (continued), by Professor John R. Buthnot, Ph.D." *Carleton Miscellany* 3.2 (1962): 3, 5–7, 127–28.

"The Golden Rule Revisited: A Sermon to One Hundred and Twenty-Two Sinful Seniors Being Graduated into a Sinful Society." Baccalaureate address, Earlham College, 1960.

"*Lady Chatterley's Lover* and the Tachistoscope." *Carleton Miscellany* 1.2 (1960): 41–47.

"Another True Moment in American History." *Carleton Miscellany* 2.2 (1961): 68–69.

"Distance and Point-of-View: An Essay in Classification." *Essays in Criticism* 11 (1961): 60–79.

"The First Full Professor of Ironology in the World." *Carleton Miscellany* 2.2 (1961): 60–67.

"Point of View and the Control of Distance in *Emma*." *Nineteenth-Century Fiction* 16 (1961): 95–116.

"From Domes of Pleasure and Displeasure: La Douche." *Carleton Miscellany* 3.1 (1962): 81–85.

"The Shaping of Prophesy: Craft and Idea in the Novels of Wright Morris." *American Scholar* 31 (1962): 608–26.

"The Worst Thing That Can Happen to a Man." Address delivered at Senior Recognition convocation, Earlham College, 1962.

"Boring from Within: The Art of the Freshman Essay." *Occasional Essays in the Humanities from The University of Chicago*. Chicago: Division of Humanities, U of Chicago, n.d.

"Interrelationships of Reading and Writing." *Reading and the Language Arts: Proceedings of the Annual Conference on Reading Held at The University of Chicago, 1963*. Ed. H. Alan Robinson. Chicago: U of Chicago P, 1963. 113–22.

"The Northfield Times Book Review." *Carleton Miscellany* 4.1 (1963): 91–96.

"The Rhetorical Stance." *College Composition and Communication* 14 (1963): 139–45.

"'What's Wrong with *The New York Times Book Review*' by One Who Has Written One Thousand Words for It." From "What to Do With or About *The New York Times Book Review*: A Symposium." *Carleton Miscellany* 4.1 (1963): 65–66.

"Censorship and the Values of Fiction." *English Journal* 53 (1964): 155–64. Rpt. in *Celebrating Censored Books*. Ed. Nicholas J. Karolides and Lee Burress. Racine: Wisconsin Council of Teachers of English, 1985. 21–26.

"Letter from Africa." *Carleton Miscellany* 5.1 (1964): 89–96.

"Department of American." Ed. Wayne Booth. *Carleton Miscellany* 5.4 (1964): 122–29. Rpt. in *Delos* 3.1 (1990): 103–7.

"Motivation in the Teaching of Composition." *English Teaching in South Africa: Papers of the Conference of Teachers of English Organized at the Request of the Headmasters' Conference by the Grahamstown Private Schools*. Grahamstown, S.A.: Grahamstown Publications, 1964. 105–20. Also "The Teaching of English in South Africa." 261–88. And "Teaching the Novel." 208–27.

"The Revival of Rhetoric." *PMLA* 80.2 (1965): 8–12.

"The Undergraduate Program in the College Teaching of English." *College English* 26 (Dec. 1964): 198–229.

"College Education for What?" *NEA Journal* Dec. 1965: 14–16.
"Concerning the Liberal Arts." *North Central Association Quarterly* 40. 2 (1965): 194–200.
"Mr. Gradgrind, 1965." Speech at commencement convocation, University of Chicago, winter 1965. *University of Chicago Magazine* May 1965: 4–7.
"Salvation Justified." *University of Chicago Magazine* Mar. 1965: 16–17.
"The New College." *University of Chicago Magazine* Nov. 1965: 9–13.
"Rear Guard or Avant-Garde: The Schizoid Professor." *The Little Magazine and Contemporary Literature: A Symposium Held at the Library of Congress, 2 and 3 April 1965*. New York: Modern Language Association. 78–85.
"The University and Public Issues." Lecture delivered at an open meeting sponsored by students at the University of Chicago, fall 1965.
"The Use of Criticism in the Teaching of Literature." *College English* 27 (1965): 1–13.
"The College as Church: or, Screwtape Revived." Address given to a conference of the Danforth Associates at Estes Park, Colorado, August 1966. *Earlham Review* (Summer 1967).
"What Knowledge Is Most Worth Having?" Speech given to the College of St. Catherine's faculty, 24 Feb. 1966, and at the conference of that title, University of Chicago, January 1966 (the 75th Anniversary Alumni Conference on the College). Rev. version in *University of Chicago Magazine* Apr. 1966: 11–13.
"Introduction." *The Idea of the Humanities*. By R. S. Crane. Vol. 1. Chicago: U of Chicago P, 1967. xiii–xxii.
"'Now Don't Try to Reason with Me': Rhetoric Today, Left, Right, and Center." *Carleton Miscellany* 8.4 (1967): 10–30. Rpt. in *University of Chicago Magazine* Nov. 1967: 12–15 (part 1); Dec. 1967: 17–21 (part 2).
"The College as Church: Or, Screwtape Revised." *Earlham Review* 2.1 (Summer 1967): 12–24.
"'Fielding' in *Tom Jones*." *Twentieth Century Interpretations of* Tom Jones. Englewood Cliffs, NJ: Prentice-Hall, 1968. 94–96.
"The Problem of Distance in *A Portrait of the Artist*." *A Portrait of the Artist as a Young Man*. By James Joyce. Ed. Chester G. Anderson. New York: Viking, 1968. 455–67.
"Who Killed Liberal Education?" Address delivered to the undergraduate Liberal Arts Conference at the University of Chicago, April 1968. Printed in abridged form as "The Luxury of Liberal Learning." *Graduate Comment* 11 (1968): 255–69. And in *The Relevant College: Addresses Delivered at The University of Chicago*. Chicago: The College, U of Chicago, 1968. 3–14.
"*The Rhetoric of Fiction* and the Poetics of Fictions." *Novel* 1 (Winter 1968): 105–17. Rpt. in *Towards a Poetics of Fiction: Essays from* Novel: A Forum

on Fiction, *1967–1976*. Ed. Mark Spilka. Bloomington: Indiana UP, 1977. 77–89.

"Who Should Go to College." *University of Chicago Round Table,* no. 8 (1968): 3–18.

"The Author of the Single Standard." Convocation Sunday sermon, Rockefeller Chapel, University of Chicago, May 1969.

"The Compleat Equivocator: or, How the Dean Entered with Unqualified Sympathy into Many Different and Utterly Contradictory Intellectual Positions and Emerged Smelling Like a Rose." Opening address for the Festival of the Arts at the University of Chicago, May 1969.

"Introduction." *Robert Liddell on the Novel.* By Robert Liddell. Chicago: U Chicago P, 1969. xiii–xx.

"The Power to Be a University." Lecture delivered at a conference of Danforth Associates and students at the University of Chicago, August 1969. *University of Chicago Magazine* Jan.–Feb. 1971: 2–9.

"The Uncritical American: or, Nobody's from Missouri Any More." Address given to teachers of English, Asilomar, CA, 1969. Rev. version in *Midway* Spring 1970: 3–14.

"White v. Thompson." Letter. *College Journal* 12 (1974): 55.

"Centre of All Intellectual Development." From "English: More Than Just a Subject," an overview of the International Conference on Teaching and Learning English, York, July 1971. *Times Educational Supplement* 26 Nov. 1971: 4.

"The Liberation of Minds: The Ancient Theme Revisited." *Earlham Review* 3.2–3 (1971): 43–81.

Rev. of *Now Don't Try To Reason with Me: Essays and Ironies for a Credulous Age. Carleton Miscellany* 12.1 (1971–72): 125–29.

"The Scope of Rhetoric Today: A Polemical Excursion." *The Prospect of Rhetoric.* Ed. Lloyd F. Bitzer and Edwin Black. Englewood Cliffs, NJ: Prentice-Hall, 1971. 93–114.

"Why Don't You Do It My Way? or, An Arrogant Stitch in *Time.*" *University of Chicago Magazine* July–Oct. 1971: 15–19. Rpt. in abridged form as "Facts and Values in Journalism." *Dialogue* 5.2 (1972): 69–72.

"The Meeting of Minds." *College Composition and Communication* 23 (1972): 242–50. Address to the annual CCCC luncheon, 26 Nov. 1971, during the NCTE convention, Las Vegas, NV.

"Teaching Literary Criticism, 1971." *Bulletin of the Midwest Modern Language Association* 5.1 (1972): 1–10. Paper delivered at the opening general session on Criticism and Teaching, 1971 MMLA Meeting, 4 Nov. Detroit, MI.

"Knowing in Ceremony." Address at the University of Chicago Special Convocation rededicating new quarters for the College, 26 Oct. 1973. *University of Chicago Record* Feb. 1974: 35–39.

"Bandwagon, Relevance, and the Rhetoric of Assent." *University of Chicago Magazine* Winter 1974: 20–23.

"Kenneth Burke's Way of Knowing." *Critical Inquiry* 1 (1974): 1–22.

"Sieves and Sewers: The Open Mind and the University." 349th convocation address. *University of Chicago Record* Sept. 1974: 144–48.

"Irony and Pity Once Again: *Thaïs* Revisited." *Critical Inquiry* 2 (1975): 327–44. Rpt. as "Introduction." *Thaïs*. By Anatole France. Trans. Basia Gulati. Chicago: U of Chicago P, 1976. 1–24.

"Rescue Regenstein." *Chicago Maroon* 30 May 1975: 5. Rpt. in *University of Chicago Record* 10 (1976): 5–6.

"M. H. Abrams: Historian as Critic, Critic as Pluralist." *Critical Inquiry* 2 (1976): 411–45.

"The Modern Novella." Letter. *Times Literary Supplement* 3 Sept. 1976: 1078.

" 'The Self-Portraiture of Genius': *The Citizen of the World* and Critical Method." *Modern Philology* 73.4, part 2 (1976): S85–S96.

"The Good Teacher as Threat." Address at reunion of Quantrell Prize winners, spring 1977.

"The Writing of Organic Fiction; A Conversation: Wright Morris and Wayne Booth." *Critical Inquiry* 3 (1976): 387–404. Rpt. in *Conversations with Wright Morris: Critical Views and Responses*. Ed. Robert E. Knoll. Lincoln: U of Nebraska P, 1977. 74–100.

"An Arrogant Proposal: A New Use for the Dyshumanities." *Profession 77*. New York: Modern Language Association, 1977. 1–6. Rpt. in *ADE Bulletin* 54 (Sept. 1977): 6–11. And in *ADFL Bulletin* 9.1 (1977): 5–10.

"How Can I Develop a Love for Great Literature?" In "I Have a Question." *Ensign* (Salt Lake City) December 1977: 25.

"Form in *The Works of Love*." *Conversations with Wright Morris: Critical Views and Responses*. Ed. Robert E. Knoll. Lincoln: U of Nebraska P, 1977. 35–73.

"For the Authors." In "In Defense of Authors and Readers." Ed. Edward Bloom. *Novel* 11 (1977): 6–17.

" 'Preserving the Exemplar': or, How Not to Dig Our Own Graves." Part 1 of "The Limits of Pluralism," a critics' exchange. *Critical Inquiry* 3.3 (1977): 407–23.

"Notes and Exchanges," *Critical Inquiry* 4 (1977): 203–5.

"Occam's Razor O. K." Letter. *American Bar Association Journal* 63 (1977): 296.

"Three Functions of Reviewing at the Present Time." *Bulletin of the Midwest Modern Language Association* 11.1 (1978): 2–12. Rpt. in *The Horizon of Literature*. Ed. Paul Hernadi. Lincoln: U of Nebraska P, 1982. 261–81.

"Metaphor as Rhetoric: The Problem of Evaluation." *Critical Inquiry* 5.1 (1978): 49–72. Also "Ten Literal 'Theses,' " Part 4 of "Afterthoughts on Metaphor," in the same number, 175–76.

"The Pleasures and Pitfalls of Irony: or, Why Don't You Say What You

Mean?" *Rhetoric, Philosophy, and Literature: An Exploration.* Ed. Don M. Burks. West Lafayette, IN: Purdue UP, 1978. 1–13.

"Re-Viewing Reviews: Letters by Susan Suleiman and Wayne Booth." *Bulletin of the Midwest Modern Language Association* 12 (Spring 1979): 43–52.

"Art and the Church: or 'The Truths of Smoother.'" *Dialogue: A Journal of Mormon Thought* 13.4 (1980): 9–25. Speech delivered at the Brigham Young University Humanities Symposium, 1980.

"'The Way I Loved George Eliot': Friendship with Books, a Neglected Critical Metaphor." *Kenyon Review* n.s. 2 (Spring 1980): 4–27.

"Interview: Wolfgang Iser." *Diacritics* 10.2 (1980): 57–74.

"Religion versus Art: Can the Ancient Conflict Be Resolved?" *Arts and Inspiration: Mormon Perspectives.* Ed. Steven P. Sondrup. Provo, UT: Brigham Young UP, 1980. 26–34.

"Selections from Susan Dunham's *Cass Andor, or Nihilism: The Last Anti-Novel.*" Ed. W. Clayson Booth. *Chicago Review* 32.1 (1980): 49–88. Excerpt from an unfinished novel.

"Is There Any Knowledge a *Woman* Must Have?" Speech delivered to undergraduates of the University of Chicago at the invitation of the Liberal Arts Forum, December 1980.

"Critical Understanding." Letter. *Times Literary Supplement* 25 Apr. 1980: 468.

"Do Reasons Matter in Criticism? Or, Many Meanings, Many Modes." *Bulletin of the Midwest Modern Language Association* 14.1 (1981): 3–23. Rev. version of keynote address at the 1980 MMLA meeting.

"A Report on the Failure of Idecom." *College English* 43 (Feb. 1981): 111–21.

"Criticulture: Or, Why We Need at Least Three Criticisms at the Present Time." *What Is Criticism?* Ed. Paul Hernadi. Bloomington: Indiana UP, 1981. 162–76.

"History as Metaphor: Or, Is M. H. Abrams a Mirror, or a Lamp, or a Fountain, or . . . ?" *High Romantic Argument: Essays for M. H. Abrams.* Ed. Lawrence Lipking. Ithaca: Cornell U P, 1981. 79–105. First delivered at a symposium sponsored by the Society for the Humanities, Cornell University, Apr. 1978.

"The Scholar in Society." *Introduction to Scholarship in Modern Languages and Literatures.* Ed. Joseph Gibaldi. New York: Modern Language Association, 1981. 116–43.

"A Cheap, Efficient, Challenging, Sure-Fire and Obvious Device for Combatting a Major Scandal in Higher Education Today." *Writing Program Administration* 5.1 (1981): 35–39.

"The Common Aims That Divide Us; Or, Is There a 'Profession 1981'?" *ADE Bulletin* 69 (1981): 1–5. Rpt. in *Profession 81.* New York: Modern Language Association, 1981. 13–17.

"Letters to Smoother." In *Letters to Smoother, etc. . . .* Ed. Joy C. Ross and Steven C. Walker. Proceedings of the 1980 Brigham Young University

Symposium on the Humanities. Provo: Brigham Young UP, [1981]. 3–20. Partly rpt. as "Art and the Church: or 'The Truths of Smoother." *Dialogue* 13 (Winter 1980): 9–25. And as "Art and the Church: Question and Answer Sessions with Wayne C. Booth." *Literature and Belief* 1 (1981): 19–37.

"Mere Rhetoric, Rhetoric, and the Search for Common Learning." *Common Learning: A Carnegie Colloquium on General Education.* Washington, D.C.: Carnegie Foundation for the Advancement of Teaching, 1981. 22–55.

"Freedom of Interpretation: Bakhtin and the Challenge of Feminist Criticism." *Critical Inquiry* 9.1 (1982): 45–76.

"Interview." Conducted by Mary Frances Hopkins. *Literature in Performance* 2.2 (1982): 46–63.

"M. H. Abrams." Honorary degree presentation, University of Chicago, 27 May 1982.

"Rhetoric, Mere Rhetoric, and Reality: Or, My Basics Are More Basic Than Your Basics." *The English Curriculum under Fire: What Are the Real Basics?* Ed. George Hillocks, Jr. Urbana, IL: National Council of Teachers of English, 1982.

"The Company We Keep: Self-Making in Imaginative Art, Old and New." *Daedalus* 111 (Fall 1982): 33–59. Rpt. in *The Pushcart Prize, VIII: Best of the Small Presses.* Ed. Bill Henderson. Wainscott, NY, 1983. 57–95.

"Between Two Generations: The Heritage of the Chicago School." *Profession 82.* New York: Modern Language Association, 1982. 19–26.

"A New Strategy for Establishing a Truly Democratic Criticism." *Daedalus* 112 (Winter 1983): 193–214. Rpt. in *Reading in the 1980s.* Ed. Stephen Graubard. New York: Bowker, 1983. 193–214.

"Arts and Scandals 1982." *PMLA* 98 (May 1983): 312–22. Presidential Address at 1982 meeting of Modern Language Association.

"Renewing the Medium of Renewal: Some Notes on the Anxieties of Innovation." *Innovation/Renovation: New Perspectives on the Humanities.* Ed. Ihab Hassan and Sally Hassan. Madison: U of Wisconsin P, 1983. 131–59.

"Rhetorical Critics Old and New: The Case of Gérard Genette." *Reconstructing Literature.* Ed. Laurence Lerner. Oxford: Blackwell, 1983. 123–41.

"'LITCOMP': Some Rhetoric Addressed to Cryptorhetoricians about a Rhetorical Solution to a Rhetorical Problem." *Composition and Literature: Bridging the Gap.* Ed. Winifred Bryan Horner. Chicago: U of Chicago P, 1983. 57–80.

"The Empire of Irony." *Georgia Review* 37 (Winter 1983): 719–37.

"Corruptions of Rhetoric in *1984* and 1984." *Chicago Tribune* 27 Oct. 1983, education suppl.: 5.

"Emma, *Emma,* and the Question of Feminism." *Persuasions: Journal of the Jane Austen Society of North America* 5 (16 Dec. 1983): 29–40.

"Let's Be Practical: An Imaginary Talk by a Staleperson to This Year's Entering Class of Freshpersons." *Florida Review* 12 (Winter 1984): 1–10.
"Catching the Overflow." *College English* 46 (Feb. 1984): 140–42.
"What Do We Mean When We Talk about Irony?" *Harper's Magazine* May 1984: 11–12.
"Communal Affirmation." *Kettering Review* Fall 1984: 42–45.
"Introduction." *Problems of Dostoevsky's Poetics*. By Mikhail Bakhtin. Ed. and trans. Caryl Emerson. Minneapolis: U of Minnesota P, 1984. xiii–xxvii.
"What Is Not Old about the New Critics." *Humanities* 6.2 (1985): 7–8.
"Memoir: Richard McKeon." *University of Chicago Record* 7 June 1985: 10–11.
"Reply to Richard Berrong." *Critical Inquiry* 11.4 (1985): 697–701.
"Systematic Wonder: The Rhetoric of Secular Religions." *Journal of the American Academy of Religion* 53.3 (1985): 677–702.
"Pluralism in the Classroom." *Critical Inquiry* 12.3 (1986): 468–79.
"The Idea of a *Uni*versity as Seen By a Rhetorician." 1987 Ryerson Lecture. Chicago: U of Chicago P, April 1987. Rpt. in *University of Chicago Record* 13 Oct. 1988: 2–6.
"Reversing the Downward Spiral: Or, What Is the Graduate Program *For?*" *Profession 87*. New York: Modern Language Association, 1987. 36–39. Rpt. in *The Future of Doctoral Studies in English*. Ed. Andrea Lunsford, Helene Moglen, and James F. Slevin. New York: Modern Language Association, 1989. 3–8.
"The Don't Tell Mentality." Letter, with J. G. Turner. *American Journal of Nursing* 10 (1987): 1281.
"Why Ethical Criticism Fell on Hard Times." *Ethics* 98 (Jan. 1988): 278–93.
"Enduring Interest Puts a True Classic on the List." *Christian Science Monitor* 22 Apr. 1988: B6.
"Cultural Literacy and Liberal Learning: An Open Letter to E. D. Hirsch, Jr." *Change* 20.4 (1988): 10–21.
"Introduction to 'Just Because You Cannot Read—Does Not Mean You Are Dumb.'" *University of Chicago Magazine* Winter 1989: 18–21.
"Are Narrative Choices Subject to Ethical Criticism?" *Reading Narrative: Form, Ethics, Ideology*. Ed. James Phelan. Columbus: Ohio State UP, 1989. 57–78.
"Confessions of a Lukewarm Lawrentian." *The Challenge of D. H. Lawrence*. Ed. Michael Squires and Keith Cushman. Madison: U of Wisconsin P, 1990. Keynote address, 1985 Annual Meeting of the D. H. Lawrence Society, Tufts University.
"A Reply to Mr. Kimball." *American Journal of Education* 98 (May 1990): 270–73.
The Art of Deliberalizing: A Handbook for True Professionals. Washington, D.C.: Association of American Colleges, 1990. 13 pp. Keynote address, 76th An-

nual Meeting of the Association of American Colleges, 10–13 Jan. 1990, San Francisco.

REVIEWS

Review of *The Unsentimental Journey of Laurence Sterne*, by Ernest Nevin Dilworth. *Modern Philology* 46 (1949): 280–82.
"A Flouting of Liberal Gods." Review of *Liberties of the Mind*, by Charles Morgan. *New Leader* 17 Dec. 1951: 23.
Review of *Tristram Shandy's World: Sterne's Philosophical Rhetoric*, by John Traugott. *Modern Philology* 53 (1955): 138–41.
Review of *An Experiment in Fiction*, by C. S. Lewis. *English Fiction in Transition* 5.1 (1962): 51–54.
"Professor Soby's Sabbatical." Review of *What a Way to Go*, by Wright Morris. *New York Times Book Review* 23 Sept. 1962: 4.
"The Transformation of Semantics." Review of *The Rhetoric of Religion: Studies in Logology*, by Kenneth Burke. *Modern Age* 6 (1962): 329–30.
"Anthologies of World Literature." Review of thirteen anthologies. *College English* 25 (1963): 50–56.
Review of *Jane Austen's Novels: The Fabric of Dialogue*, by Howard S. Babb. *Nineteenth-Century Fiction* 17 (1963): 395–99.
"Yes, But Are They Really Novels?" Review of six novels. *Yale Review*.
Review of *Cervantes's Theory of the Novel*, by E. C. Riley. *Modern Philology* 62 (1964): 163–65.
"Salvation Justified." Review of *Herzog*, by Saul Bellow. *Chicago Maroon Literary Review* 23 Oct. 1964: 1. Rpt. in *University of Chicago Magazine* Mar. 1965: 16–17.
Review of *One Day*, by Wright Morris. *Kenyon Review* 27 (1965): 569–70.
"Scare Trend Division—Campus Department." Review of *The Sheepskin Psychosis*, by John Keats. *Chicago Tribune Books Today* 16 May 1965: 12.
Review of *The Partial Critics*, by Lee T. Lemon. *College English* 27 (1966): 584.
"Over the Mountain, Another Mountain." Review of *A History of Modern Criticism, 1750–1950*, by René Wellek. *Book Week* 27 Feb. 1966: 3.
"The Organization and Methods of Inquiry." Review of *The Reforming of General Education*, by Daniel Bell. *Book Week* 22 May 1966: 5.
Review of *Satire and the Novel in Eighteenth-Century England*, by Ronald Paulson. *Philological Quarterly* 47 (1968): 340–42.
"The Words and Pictures of American Vision." Review of *God's Country and My People*, by Wright Morris. *Sun-Times* (Chicago) 18 Dec. 1968: 70.
Review of *Max Rafferty on Education*, by Max Rafferty. *English Journal* 58 (1969): 450–52.
Review of *Middlemarch: Critical Approaches to the Novel*, by Barbara Hardy. *Nineteenth-Century Fiction* 23 (1969): 478–81.

"Storytelling and Creative Drama." Review of D. W. Chambers. *Peabody Journal of English* 47 (1970): 364–65.

"My Granpa's Scalp." Review of Wright Morris. *Nation* 23 Mar. 1970: 344–45.

"A Divided Message for a Badly Divided America." Review of *The Time Has Come,* by K. Ross Toole. *Sun-Times* (Chicago) 21 Mar. 1971: 19.

"Loathing and Ignorance on the Campaign Trail: 1972." Review of *The Making of the President 1972,* by Theodore H. White, and *Fear and Loathing: On the Campaign Trail '72,* by Hunter S. Thompson. *Columbia Journalism Review* Nov.–Dec. 1973: 7–12.

Review of *Some Words of Jane Austen,* by Stuart Tave. *Wordsworth Circle* 6 (1975): 133–36.

"Seventeen Types of Incongruity." Review of *The Uses of Division,* by John Bayley. *Times Literary Supplement* 23 July 1976: 914–15.

Review of *Tellers and Listeners: The Narrative Imagination,* by Barbara Hardy. *Modern Language Review* 73 (1978): 144–51.

"Works of Love in Nebraska." Review of *Plains Song: For Female Voices,* by Wright Morris. *London Review of Books* 22 May–4 June 1980: 16–18.

"Becoming Dangerous Again." Response, with others, to Christopher Clausen's *The Place of Poetry. Georgia Review* 35 (Winter 1981): 752–56.

Review of *Metaphors We Live By,* by George Lakoff and Mark Johnson. *Ethics* 93 (Apr. 1983): 619–21.

Review of *R. S. Crane: An Annotated Bibliography,* by John C. Sherwood. *AEB: Analytical and Enumerative Bibliography* 1.3 (1987): 184–89.

Review of *Henry James and the Woman Business,* by Alfred Habegger. *New York Times Book Review* 24 Sept. 1989: 54–55.

WORKS ABOUT WAYNE BOOTH

REVIEWS

The Rhetoric of Fiction

Stegner, Wallace. "An Indispensable Book." *American Scholar* 31 (1961): 464–8.

Beebe, Maurice. "Through a Glass Darkly." *Modern Fiction Studies* 7 (1961): 373–74.

Lodge, D. *Modern Language Review* 57 (1962): 580.

McKillop, Alan D. "Wayne C. Booth: *The Rhetoric of Fiction.*" *Modern Philology* 60 (1962): 295.

Roberts, Mark. "Means to Ends in the Novel." *Essays in Criticism* 12 (1962): 322.

Wright, Andrew. "Man in Charge." *Kenyon Review* 24 (1962): 566.

Long, Maxine M. "Too Good to Miss." *English Journal* Oct. 1981: 67–68.

Schwarz, Daniel R. "Reality as Moral Activity." *Sewanee Review* 93 (1985): 480–85.

The Knowledge Most Worth Having

Cornog, William H. "An Open-Ended Question." *Virginia Quarterly Review* 43 (1967): 489.

Now Don't Try to Reason with Me

Carleton Miscellany 12.3 (1971): 125–28.
Benson, Thomas W. *Quarterly Journal of Speech* 58 (1972): 108.

A Rhetoric of Irony

Campbell, Paul Newell. *Quarterly Journal of Speech* 60 (1974): 511.
Donoghue, Denis. "Between Fact and Value." *Times Literary Supplement* 6 Dec. 1974: 1358–59.
Buffington, Robert. "Rhetoric and Post-Modernism." *Sewanee Review* 83 (1975): R34–40.
Empson, William. "The Voice of the Underdog." *New York Review of Books* 12 Jun. 1975: 37–39.
Gibson, Walker. *College English* 37 (1975): 99–101.
Iseminger, Gary. "The First Textbook of Ironology in the World." *Carleton Miscellany* 15.2 (1975): 137–40.
McFadden, George. *Journal of Aesthetic and Art Criticism* 33 (1975): 361–63.
Cigman, Gloria. *Review of English Studies* 27 (1976): 361–63.
Stevick, Philip. *Comparative Literature* 28 (1976): 277–79.

Modern Dogma and the Rhetoric of Assent

Burgess, Parke C. *Quarterly Journal of Speech* 61 (1975): 459–62.
Iseminger, Gary. "Reconstituting the Community of Believers." *Carleton Miscellany* 15.1 (1975): 145–48.
Towne, Robert. *Journal of Aesthetic and Art Criticism* 34 (1975): 90–92.

Critical Understanding

Balthrop, V. William, and Beverly Whitaker Long. "Yes, But . . . Voices in Current Literary Criticism." *Quarterly Journal of Speech* 66 (1980): 211–13.
Clark, Walter H., Jr. *Journal of Aesthetic and Art Criticism* 38 (1980): 331–33.
Fischer, Michael. "Is Literature Worth Discussing?" *Georgia Review* 34 (1980): 678–81.
Peckham, Morse. *Journal of English and Germanic Philology* 79 (1980): 429–31.
Yoos, George E. *Quarterly Journal of Speech* 68 (1982): 214–16.
Preston, John. *Modern Language Review* 78 (1983): 631–32.

The Company We Keep

Bawer, Bruce. *American Scholar* 58 (1989): 610–12.
Broyard, Anatole. "A Fiction User's Manual." *New York Times Book Review* 22 Jan. 1989: 3+.

Nemoianu, Virgil. *Modern Language Notes* 104 (1989): 1178–80.
Spilka, Mark. *America* 3 Jun. 1989: 538–40.

The Vocation of a Teacher

Pinsker, Sanford. "After Such Knowledge, What Forgiveness?: The Rise of Ethical Criticism." *Georgia Review* 43 (1989): 395–405.

The Harper and Row Rhetoric

Olive, Barbara. *College Composition and Communication* 39 (1988): 366–67.

ARTICLES

Kummer, C. "Wayne C. Booth and the Implicit Author of Voyage." *Australian Journal of French Studies* 13 (1976): 18–24.
Jakobsen, A. L. "Critique of Wayne C. Booth and the Rhetoric of Irony." *Orbis Litterarum* 32 (1977): 173–95.
Handy, B. "Tellers and Listeners: Narrative Imagination." *Modern Language Review* 73 (1978): 144–51.
Lang, Candace D. "Irony/Humor: Assessing French and American Critical Trends." *Boundary 2* 10 (1982): 271–302.
Kaufer, David S., and Christine M. Neuwirth. "Contrasts between Ironic and Metaphoric Understanding: An Elaboration of Booth's Observations." *Western Journal of Speech Communication* 47 (1983): 75–83.
Phelan, James. "Data, Danda, and Disagreement." *Diacritics* 13.2 (1983): 39–50.
Berrong, R. M. "Finding Anti-Feminism in Rabelais, or a Response to Wayne Booth's Call for Ethical Criticism." *Critical Inquiry* 11 (1985): 687–96.
Bialostosky, Donald H. "Booth's Rhetoric, Bakhtin's Dialogics and the Future of Novel Criticism." *Novel* 18 (1985): 209–16, 223–26.
Bator, Paul G. "The 'Good Reasons Movement': A 'Confounding' of Dialectic and Rhetoric?" *Philosophy and Rhetoric* 21 (1988): 38–47.
Leitch, Vincent B. "Taboo and Critique: Literary Criticism and Ethics." *ADE Bulletin* Fall 1988: 46–52.
Chatman, Seymour. "The 'Rhetoric of Fiction.'" *Reading Narrative: Form, Ethics, Ideology.* Ed. James Phelan. Columbus: Ohio State UP, 1989. 40–56.

DISSERTATIONS

Valley, Philip Joseph. "The Relationship between Critical Flexibility and Interdisciplinary Study of the Arts." *DAI* 46 (1985): 2185A. New York U.
Rooney, Ellen F. "At the 'Limits of Pluralism': Constructing the Problematic of American Literary Theory." *DAI* 47 (1986): 1718A. Johns Hopkins U.

Haun-Montiel, Margaret E. "Twentieth-Century Neo-Aristotelian Criticism: Five Theorists (Lane Cooper, R. S. Crane, Elder Olson, Wayne C. Booth, Ralph W. Rader)." *DAI* 48 (1987): 924A. U of Miami.

Kraemer, Donald J., Jr. "Creating and Controlling Plurality: A Critique of Some Attempts to Unify the Profession of Literary Studies." *DAI* 49 (1988): 3712A. U of Oregon.

CONTRIBUTORS

FREDERICK J. ANTCZAK is associate professor and chair of the Department of Rhetoric at the University of Iowa. His book *Thought and Character* won a Phi Beta Kappa book award, and among his other honors was a Thomas Jefferson teaching award at the University of Virginia. He studies and teaches about rhetoric's relation to the development of character, and about the standing accorded to rhetoric and character in liberal polity.

LEE ARTZ (Ph.D., University of Iowa, 1990) is assistant professor and chair of the Social Justice Task Force in the Department of Communication at Loyola University, Chicago. A former high school teacher, machinist, and union activist, his research interests include cultural studies, participatory communication, and communication and social change.

DON H. BIALOSTOSKY teaches rhetoric at Penn State University. He has published *Making Tales: The Poetics of Wordsworth's Narrative Experiments* and *Wordsworth, Dialogics, and the Practice of Criticism*. His dialogue with Wayne Booth began his first year of college, intensified in graduate study, and continues in his "own" critical voice.

ALAN BRINTON, professor of philosophy at Boise State University, received his Ph.D. from the University of Minnesota in 1974. He has published widely on rhetoric and philosophy in journals such as *Philosophy and Rhetoric, Rhetorica,* the *Quarterly Journal of Speech, Philosophical Quarterly, Informal Logic, Argumentation,* and the *History of Philosophy Quarterly*.

PATSY CALLAGHAN, a professor of English at Central Washington University, teaches rhetoric, writing, English education, and world literature. Her recent publications and presentations focus on the rhetoric of reading. Frequently she finds reasons to read and write with Ann Dobyns, with whom she is currently completing a text for introductory literature courses.

ANN DOBYNS completed her Ph.D. at the University of Oregon in 1983 and is now associate professor of English at John Carroll University in Cleveland, Ohio, where she teaches medieval literature. Her publications include *The Voices of Romance: Studies in Dialogue and Character* (1989), as well as "Interpretation as a Rhetorical Act," cowritten with Patsy Callaghan. She is at work, also with Patsy Callaghan, on a textbook, "The Reader's Companion: Thinking, Talking and Writing about Literature."

BARBARA FOLEY is associate professor of English at Rutgers University, Newark Campus. She has written articles on Marxist criticism, African American literature, and literary theory and has authored two books: *Telling the Truth: The Theory and Practice of Documentary Fiction* and *Radical Representations: Politics and Form in U.S. Proletarian Fiction, 1929–1941*.

EUGENE GARVER holds the McNeely Chair in Thinking at Saint John's University. He is author of *Machiavelli and the History of Prudence* (1987), and *Aristotle's Rhetoric: An Art of Character* (1994). He once took a course from Wayne Booth on Aristotle's *Rhetoric*.

MONICA JOHNSTONE is assistant professor of writing and media at Loyola College in Maryland, where she teaches composition, rhetoric, speaking, and playwriting. She has published articles on rhetoric and teaching, opinion and travel essays for various newspapers, and is working on a book on Lanford Wilson.

WALTER JOST is associate professor of rhetoric and communication studies at the University of Virginia. He is the author of *Rhetorical Thought in John Henry Newman* (1989) and editor, with Michael Hyde, of *Rhetoric and Hermeneutics in Our Time* (forthcoming). He is now completing a book on rhetoric and hermeneutics in the poetry of Robert Frost.

DONALD N. MCCLOSKEY is John F. Murray Professor of Economics and professor of history at the University of Iowa. He has written on British economic history, and in recent years on the literary element in economics. In this vein he has written *The Rhetoric of Economics* (1985), *If You're So Smart: The Narrative of Economic Expertise* (1990), and *Knowledge and Persuasion in Economics* (1994).

JAMES B. MCOMBER is assistant professor of communication/theatre at Central College in Pella, Iowa. He conducts research in the rhetoric of inquiry, the ethics of rhetoric, and the relationship between rhetorical theory and psychoanalysis.

JAMES PHELAN practices pluralism at Ohio State University, where he teaches courses in the novel, critical theory, and narrative theory. The editor of *Narrative*, the journal of the Society for the Study of Narrative Literature, his most recent books are *Understanding Narrative,* edited with Peter J. Rabinowitz, and *Beyond the Tenure Track: Fifteen Months in the Life of an English Professor.*

PETER J. RABINOWITZ, who divides his time between music and narrative theory, is the author of *Before Reading: Narrative Conventions and the Politics of Interpretation* (1987) and coeditor, with James Phelan, of *Understanding Narrative* (1994). A professor of comparative literature at Hamilton College, he is also an active music critic and a contributing editor of *Fanfare.*

DAVID RICHTER, who studied with Wayne Booth at the University of Chicago in the 1960s, is professor of English and director of graduate studies at Queens College in New York. He is the author of *Fable's End* (1975), *The Critical Tradition* (1989), *Falling into Theory* (1994), and is currently completing *The Progress of Romance: The Gothic Novel and Literary Historiography.*

SUSAN E. SHAPIRO is assistant professor in the Department of Religion of Columbia University where she teaches Jewish thought and philosophy of religion. Her areas of research are post-Holocaust thought (her book *Recovering the Sacred: Hermeneutics and Theology after the Holocaust* is forthcoming), the role of rhetorics of body and gender in (Jewish) philosophy, and the philosophical imagination of the Jew as uncanny other in the discourses of the modern nation-state.

FRANCIS-NOËL THOMAS, professor and chair of the Department of Humanities, Truman College, is the author of *The Writer Writing: Philosophic Acts in Literature* (1992) and—with Mark Turner—*Clear and Simple as the Truth: Writing Classic Prose* (1994).

WAYNE C. BOOTH—The various Booths whom readers have met here and will meet in his reply have consulted together, at length, and have decided that this volume already contains too much about him. They therefore refuse the editor's request for a short biographical note. Needless to say, the vote was not unanimous.

INDEX

Abrams, M. H., 6, 100, 112–13
  The Mirror and the Lamp, 107
ad hominem argument, 42, 51
The Adventures of Huckleberry Finn
  (Twain), 9, 138, 142–43, 147,
  151n, 290
ad verecundiam argument, 261
After Virtue (MacIntyre), 66
agency, and ethical criticism, 161
Aids to Reflection (Coleridge), 36
Ajax Kitchen Cleanser, 190
American Fork, Utah, 2, 44, 51
Amnesty International, 304
Annunciation, the, 40, 51
Antczak, Frederick J., 284, 290, 302, 307n
antifoundationalism, 267–71
arguing to agree, 240–41, 282, 304
  and purpose of rhetoric, 290
Aristotle, 20, 22, 23, 25, 34, 35, 36, 205,
  215, 220, 234n, 289, 302, 305
  Gryllus, 34
  Nichomachean Ethics, 36, 289
  contrasted with Nietzsche, 66
  Politics, 289
  preference of character over knowledge, 217
  Rhetoric, 23, 34, 289
Arnold, Matthew, 189
Art of Growing Older, The, 8
assent, 5, 6
  as inseparable from denial, 259
  logical limits on yielding, 260
assent, systematic, 253–65, 294
Auden, W. H., 96
Augustine, Saint, 287
Austen, Jane, 9, 40, 44, 48, 51, 123,
  140, 201

Emma, 61, 137, 143–44, 147, 148
Mansfield Park, 47, 51
Pride and Prejudice, 40, 46, 47, 50,
  51, 120
Austin, J. L., 172
Austrian economists, 204

Babbitt, Milton, 169, 170
Bach, Johann Sebastian, 169
Bacon, Francis, 10, 13, 35, 295
  The Advancement of Learning, 215,
  220, 221
  De Augmentis, 225
  Essays, 35, 218, 211–36
  The New Organon, 221
Bakhtin, Mikhail, 10, 11, 88–103, 301
  and carnivalization of language,
  92, 109
  and the Dostoevskyan novel, 92–93
  influence of, on *The Company We
  Keep*, 114
  relativism of, 92, 297
Balzac, Honoré de, 286
Barber of Seville, The (Rossini), 181
Barry, Brian, 194
Barthes, Roland, 112, 125
  "The Grain of the Voice," 177–78
battle metaphors, 100–101, 301–2
Becker, Gary, 190–91
Beethoven, Ludwig van, 167, 169, 178
Beloved (Morrison), 140, 286
Bentham, Jeremy, 204
Berkeley, George (Bishop), 295
Berlin, Isaiah, 282, 307n
Bernstein, Leonard, 178
Bernstein, Richard, 37n
Berry, duchy of, 40, 51, 52

Bialostosky, Don, 11, 289, 296, 301–2, 303
Black, Edwin, 162n
Blaug, Mark, 195
Booth, Wayne C.
   as antifoundationalist, 267, 270
   as antimodernist, 267–68
   as antiphilosopher, 266
      compared with Rorty, 268–76
   as apolitical, 12
   The Art of Growing Older, 8
   and assent
      communal concept of, compared with Rorty's notion of truth, 270
      systematic, 294
   and Bahktin's dialogism, 88–103, 108, 114
   battle metaphors of, in *Critical Understanding,* 100–101, 301–2
   and character, 20–36
   and the classics, 145
   The Company We Keep, 1, 8, 12, 59, 62, 96, 111, 113–14, 168, 173, 194, 195, 197, 205, 217, 218, 229n, 234n, 239, 245, 286, 292, 304
      intended critical audience of, 288
      and politics of ethics, 135–49
   conservatism of method of, 261, 263, 284
   and Crane's dialectical pluralism, 98–100, 108
   Critical Understanding, 6, 7, 31, 61, 94, 96, 99, 100–101, 104–5, 111–14, 119, 132, 170, 194, 195, 234n, 239, 252, 269, 270, 272, 290
   definition of rhetoric of, 25
   early career of, 2–3
   and ethics
      depoliticization of, 145
      as nonconsequentialist, 155
      as reflexive and reciprocal, 155–56
   as generalist, 19
   Harper and Row textbooks (with Gregory), 246–47, 248–49
   "Hippocratic Oath for the Pluralist," 194
   The Knowledge Most Worth Having, 7
   as liberal educator, 26–33
   Modern Dogma and the Rhetoric of Assent, 5, 8, 13, 154, 168, 170, 173, 178, 183n, 192, 239–44, 246, 248, 253–63, 266, 269, 270, 272, 273, 285, 288, 290, 295
      as Cartesian in procedure, 263
   and monism, resistance to, 268
   accused of monologism, 92–93
   and narrative pluralism, as a lesson for economics, 205–6
   Now Don't Try to Reason with Me, 7, 239, 266, 288
   public and administrative roles of, 11–12, 19
   and purpose of rhetoric, 290–91
   and respect for persons, compared with Rorty, 273–76
   The Rhetoric of Fiction, 2, 3, 4, 5, 7, 9, 13, 14, 29, 59, 61, 91, 92, 95, 96, 115, 135, 138, 168, 211, 212, 214, 231n, 239
   "*The Rhetoric of Fiction* and the Poetics of Fictions," 104–7
   A Rhetoric of Irony, 5, 27, 109, 135, 169, 239, 303
   and teachers, 10, 41, 43, 53
   on teaching fourth graders, 54n, 62
   "Three Functions of Reviewing at the Present Time," 104, 107
   compared to Vinogradov, 91
   The Vocation of a Teacher, 1, 7, 9, 21, 35, 52, 61, 288
Borland, Leonard, 178, 179, 180
Bourges, 40, 51, 52
Bourgh, Lady Catherine de, 47
Bradley, A. C., 106
Brigham Young University, 2
Bringing Up Father (McManus), 174
Brinton, Alan, 13, 285, 294, 295, 305
Brontë, Charlotte, *Jane Eyre,* 128–30

Index

Brontë, Emily, 123
Brooks, Peter, 193
Buber, Martin, *I and Thou*, 35
Buffalo, N.Y., 44, 51
Burke, Kenneth, 6, 21, 27, 59, 100, 108,
    112, 113, 132, 133n, 150, 283, 296,
    298, 303, 305
    and holoscopic pluralism, 115n
Bush, George, 250
Butler, Joseph, 257

Cain, James M., 167–86
    The Butterfly, 168
    Love's Lovely Counterfeit, 168
    Mildred Pierce, 176
    The Moth, 179
    Past All Dishonor, 179
    The Postman Always Rings Twice, 167
    Serenade, 168, 177, 178–81
Callaghan, Patsy, 13, 282, 304
Callas, Maria, 184n
Camp David, 283
Capital (Marx), 147
capitalism, 200–201, 285
capital punishment, economic argument
    concerning, 190–91
Carmen (Bizet), 174
Carpentier, Georges, 180
Carter, Jimmy, 283
Cato the Censor, 233n
Cather, Willa, 175
Cavell, Stanley, 233n
Celan, Paul, 71
Ceremony (Silko), 286
Chall Curve, 41, 48, 51
Champaigne, Philippe de, 44, 51
Chandler, Raymond, 168
character, 13
    as center of Booth's concerns, 20
Chesterton, G. K., 283
Chicago, University of, 2, 11, 31
    Chicago school of critics, 2, 3, 4, 91,
        135–37, 150n

and Longinus as alternative to
    Aristotle, 94
as monologic, 11
Churban, 84n
Christensen, P. A., x, 2
Christian Century (journal), 159
Cicero, 2, 7, 31, 34, 35, 37n, 256, 264n,
    283, 295
    De officiis, 36
    De oratore, 27
Clément, Catherine, 177, 180, 184
Clinton, Bill, 250, 303
Coase, Ronald, 206
Cobb, Ty, 180
coduction, 67, 71
coherence, as a Boothian term, 6
Coleridge, Samuel, 36, 99
Color Purple, The (Walker), 140
community, rhetorical, 242–44
Company We Keep, The, 1, 8, 12, 59, 62,
    96, 111, 113, 168, 173, 194, 197, 205,
    217, 218, 229n, 234n, 239, 245, 286,
    292, 304
    intended critical audience of, 288
    and the relation of ethics to politics,
        135–49
comprehensiveness, as a Boothian term, 6
Comstock, Gary, 3, 4
Concluding Unscientific Postscript (Kierkegaard), 36
Conley, Thomas, 8
Conrad, Joseph, 146
constatives, 172
correspondence, as a Boothian term, 6
Crane, R. S., x, 2, 6, 113, 120, 132, 133n,
    136, 138
    and dialectical pluralism, 98–100, 105
    *The Languages of Criticism and the
        Structure of Poetry*, 100
Critical Understanding, 6, 7, 31, 61, 94, 96,
    99, 100–101, 104–5, 111, 112, 113,
    119, 132, 194, 234n, 239, 252, 269,
    270, 272, 290
Crito (Plato), 109

Crush Collision March (Joplin), 173
Cultural Literacy (Hirsch), 41, 45
culture of criticism, 88
cummings, e. e., 136, 145
Cuomo, Mario, 247

Defoe, Daniel, 201–3
Dempsey, Jack, 180
De officiis (Cicero), 36
De oratore (Cicero), 27
DeQuincey, Thomas, 37n, 38n
Derrida, Jacques, 65, 295, 301
　and the debate with Searle, 230n
Descartes, René, 13, 262, 293, 295, 305
　Discourse on Method, 256
　invention of the mind, 271
　Meditations, 254–55
　and systematic doubt, 253, 254–58
Dewey, John, 21, 36n, 158, 229n
　as antiphilosopher, 268
dialectic, 89
dialogic criticism, 88, 89, 94
dialogics, 11, 301
Dickens, Charles, 146, 201
Dickinson, Emily, 123
Dictionary of Literary Biography, 1, 36
Dobyns, Ann, 13, 282, 304
Don Giovanni (Mozart), 167, 179
Dostoevsky, Fyodor, 112
doubt
　systematic, 253, 254–58, 269
　loosening effect of, 257
Douglass, Frederick, 142–43, 148

Eagleton, Terry, 37n
Earlham College, 2
Eatwell, John, 191
Eco, Umberto, 112
economics
　Aristotelian *ethos* of, 12–13, 204–5
　and ethics, 12, 187–210
　as fiction, 193
　and pluralism, 205
economic Platonism, 207–8

Ehrlich, Isaac, 190
Emerson, Caryl, 94
Emma (Austen), 61, 137, 143–44, 146, 148
emotivism, 196
Empson, William, 108
ethical argument, 13
ethical criticism, 8, 146
　agency of, 161
ethics, 4
　and economics, 187–210
　as heuristic, 10
　of narration, 293
　and politics, 135–49
ethos
　of economics, 12–13, 204–5
　of rhetoric, 155

Fauset, Jessie Redmond, 144
Federalist Papers, The, 35
feminist criticism, 8, 11, 12, 146
Feyerabend, Paul, 274–76, 294
Figaro (Mozart), 181
Finn, Chester, 53
Fish, Stanley, 195, 218, 221, 229n, 230n, 231n
Fisher, Walter, 162n
Flaubert, Gustave, 48, 51, 52
flexible response, strategic doctrine of, 44, 52
Foley, Barbara, 12, 284, 285–88
Foucault, Michel, 85n
Franklin, Ben, 198
friendship, 8
　as ground for communication, 75
　as resistance to dehumanization, 82
　narratological, 71, 79
　risk of, 86n
Frye, Northrop, 207

Gadamer, H. G., on tact, 227n
Galileo, 9
Gandhi, Mohandas, as influence on Martin Luther King, 160
Gargantua and Pantagruel (Rabelais), 138

Garver, Eugene, 13, 284, 295, 296, 303
Gates of the Forest, The (Wiesel), 73
Geertz, Clifford, 36
Genet, Jean, 11, 60, 293
   Derrida's critique of, 65
   as Nietzschean, 68
   Sartre's defense of, 63
   A Thief's Journal, 65
Giddings, Luther, x, 2
Gilbert, Sandra, 12, 120, 122–25, 126, 128–32
Gilles (La Rochelle), 111–12
Gleick, James, 293
Goldberg, Homer, 289
goods, incommensurability of, 204–5, 282, 283
Graff, Gerald, 35, 37n, 192
Grammar of Assent (Newman), 257
Grammar of Science, The (Pearson), 189
Greene, Thomas, 229n
Gregory, Marshall W., 246–47
Grimaldi, William, 37n
Gubar, Susan, 12, 120, 122–25, 126, 128–32

Habermas, Jürgen, 304
Hairston, Maxine, 246–47
Halachah, 83, 86n
Hammett, Dashiell, 168
Hartman, Geoffrey, 88, 89, 96
Hauerwas, Stanley, 36n
Haverford College, 2
Hayworth, Rita, 174
Heidegger, Martin
   as antiphilosopher, 268
   as influence on Martin Luther King, 159
   last words of, 300
Heinzelman, Kurt, 187
Henderson, W. J., 169
Hermogenes, 34
heteroglossia, 104, 112
   authentic, 97
   rhetoric as inauthentic, 91

Hexter, J. H., 218–19, 193
Higgins, Henry, 49, 50, 52
Hill, Anita, 250
Hirsch, E. D., Jr., 287, 289
   and concept of cultural literacy, 40–55
   influence of, on administrators, 40–41, 43–44, 52
   Cultural Literacy, 40, 41, 45
Holocaust, 11, 84n, 293
   and narrative discourse, 71–86
Homo economicus, 197, 198
   in literature, 201–3
   as company, 195, 197, 203
Horkheimer, Max, 216
House of Mirth, The (Wharton), 146
Howdy Doody, 45, 51
Hume, David, 258, 295
   optimism of, 257
Huxley, Thomas, 189

I and Thou (Buber), 35
Iowa, University of, 302
irony
   as interaction between people, 5
   as source of knowledge, 28
   stable and unstable, 5, 28
   as *topos,* 29
Ives, Charles, 181

Jabès, Edmond, 71
James, William, 194
   The Principles of Psychology, 258
Jane Eyre (C. Brontë), 128–30
Jaspers, Karl, as influence on Martin Luther King, 159
Jaws (Peter Benchley), 140
Jevons, William Stanley, 189
   Theory of Political Economy, 187
Johnson, Samuel, 35, 51, 218
Johnstone, Henry, 59, 68
   rule of bilateral argument of, 63
Johnstone, Monica, 10–11, 292, 293
Jonsen, Albert, 205
Joplin, Scott, 170, 173

Jost, Walter, 10, 279, 305, 306
Joyce, James, 140, 146
justice, as a value of pluralism, 7, 11, 113

Kant, Immanuel, 232n, 293
Kelvin, Lord (William Thompson), 189
ken of discourse, 157
Keynes, John Maynard, 207
Kierkegaard, Søren, 21
  as influence on Martin Luther
    King, 159
  Concluding Scientific Postscript, 36
Killham, John, 105–6, 112, 115n
King, Dr. Martin Luther, Jr., 12
  and Gandhi's *satyagraha,* 160
  "Pilgrimage to Nonviolence," 158–63
  Stride Toward Freedom, 158
  as torn between liberalism and fundamentalism, 159
Kissinger, Henry, 197
Knights, L. C., 106
Knopf, Alfred, 169
Knowledge Most Worth Having, The, 7
Kolb, Gwin, 42
Kolodin, Irving, 179
Krenek, Ernst, 170

labor theory of value, 204
Lang, Paul Henry, 171, 183n
Lanham, Richard, 232n
Larkin, Philip, 300
La Rochelle, Drieu, 111
Lawrence, D. H., 9, 140, 146, 287
learning, purposes of, 42–46, 49–50, 53
Leff, Michael, 33, 37n, 38n
Lentricchia, Frank, 37n
Lerner, Alan Jay, 49, 51
Levenson, Michael, 60, 67
Levinson, Stephen, 229n
Levy, F. J., 228n
liberal education, 20, 21, 22, 26
Lillo, George, 198
logomachy, 6
Longinus, 94–95

Lovibond, Sabina, 228n

Macauley, Thomas Babington, 199
Machiavelli, Niccolò, 35
MacIntyre, Alasdair, 38n, 59, 66–68, 196, 204, 228n
  After Virtue, 66–67
Madame Bovary (Flaubert), 48, 51
Madden, David, 168
Magnificat, The (Bach), 40, 51
Mailloux, Steven, 37n
Mansfield Park (Austen), 47, 51
Marshall, Alfred, 189, 207
Marx, Karl, 147, 148, 192, 286
Marxist criticism, 8, 11, 146
Mayer, Leonard, 169
McCloskey, Donald, 12, 284, 293
  and POROI, 302
  The Rhetoric of Economics, 267
McDaniel, Hattie, 45, 51, 52
McKeon, Richard, x, 2, 27, 105, 132
  and meroscopic pluralism, 107
McManus, George, 174
McOmber, James, 14, 279, 283, 293, 294
Michelangelo, 44, 51
Mildred Pierce (Cain), 176
Mill, John Stuart, 188
  Principles of Political Economy, 187
Miller, Carolyn, 24
Miller, J. Hillis
  and teaching fourth graders, 54n
  and uncanny critics, 110
Modern Dogma and the Rhetoric of Assent, 5, 8, 13, 150, 168, 178, 183, 192, 239–44, 246, 248, 253–63, 266, 269, 270, 272, 273–74, 285, 288, 290, 295
  as Cartesian in procedure, 263
Moi, Toril, critique of Gilbert and Gubar of, 12, 120, 124–28, 132
monologism, 92
Montague, F. C., 187
Montaigne, Michel, 50, 51, 258
Moore, G. E., 262
More, Thomas, 35, 218, 247

Morrison, Toni, 140, 291
Morson, Gary Saul, 307n
Moses, Paul, 9, 138, 148
Moth, The (Cain), 179
motivism, 192
motivists, 260
Mozart, Wolfgang Amadeus, 167, 169, 181, 182
  Don Giovanni, 167, 179
  Figaro, 181
music, as rhetorical situation, 12
My Fair Lady (Lerner), 49, 51, 109

Narrative of the Life of an American Slave (Douglass), 142
Native Son (Richard Wright), 150
New Critics, 99
Newman, John Henry, 20, 23, 36, 37n, 257
Newton, Isaac, 195
Nichomachean Ethics (Aristotle), 36n
Niebuhr, Reinhold, as influence on Martin Luther King, 159
Nietzsche, Friedrich, 66–67, 159
  as antiphilosopher, 267
Notre Dame, University of, 239
Now Don't Try to Reason with Me, 7, 239, 266, 288
Nussbaum, Martha, 305

Occam's razor, 271
Olsen, Tillie, 140
Olson, Elder, x, 2, 99, 138
On Becoming a Person (Rogers), 36
Ong, Walter, 37n
opportunity costs, 202
Orton, Joe, 307n
Orwell, George, 119, 132
Our Nig (H. Wilson), 144, 288
"overstanding," 111

Paradise Lost (John Milton), 123
Pareto optimality, 189–90
Pascal, Blaise, 206

Past All Dishonor (Cain), 179
Pearson, Karl, 189
Peloponnesian War, The (Thucydides), 46, 50, 51
performatives, 172
Phantom of the Opera (Gaston Leroux), 177
Phelan, James, 4, 12, 36n, 113, 115n, 116n, 211, 284, 296, 297
Philosophy and the Mirror of Nature, 268, 272, 273
Piccolomini, Aeneas, 45, 51, 52
"Pilgrimage to Nonviolence" (King), 158–62
Plato, 234n
  Crito, 109
  Phaedrus, 264n
  The Republic, 42, 51, 89, 228n
  The Symposium, 178
Plum Bun (Fauset), 144
pluralism, 6, 14
  instrumental, 11, 105, 112
  holoscopic, 115n
  meroscopic, 107
  and politics, 120, 284
  and umbrella paradox, 113
  values of, 7, 113
Polanyi, Michael, 31
politics, and ethics, 135–49
polytopia, 30–33, 281
Popper, Karl, 301
POROI, 302
Postman Always Rings Twice, The (Cain), 167
Pound, Ezra, 140
Practical Criticism (Richards), 96
presumption, system of, 262
Pride and Prejudice (Austen), 46, 47, 50, 51, 120
Principles of Political Economy (Mill), 187
propriety, in Cicero, 38n
Pygmalion (Shaw), 49, 51
Pyrrhonistic skeptics, 254
  optimism of, 257

Querelle (Genet), 11, 60–61, 63–70
   solipsism of, 67
Quintilian, 23, 34, 35, 37n, 283

Rabelais, François, 9, 138, 140, 141, 148
Rabinowitz, Peter, 12, 286, 289, 292
   Before Reading, 175
Rader, Dotson, 60, 67
Rafferty, Terrence, 303
Ramus, Peter, 34
Rand, Ayn, 207
Rauschenbusch, Walter, as influence on Martin Luther King, 159
Rawls, John, 190
reading degree zero, 110–12
Reid, Thomas, 262
Reise, Jay, 170, 183n
religion, rhetorics of, 297
Republic, The (Plato), 42, 51, 89, 228n
Resurrection (Tolstoy), 287
rhetoric, as art or method, 20–21
Rhetoric of Fiction, The, 2, 3, 4, 5, 7, 9, 13, 14, 29, 59, 61, 91- 93, 95, 100, 115, 135, 138, 168, 211, 212, 214, 239
"*Rhetoric of Fiction* and the Poetics of Fictions, The,*"* 104–7
rhetoric of inquiry, 268, 274
Rhetoric of Irony, A, 5, 27, 109, 135, 239, 303
rhetorology, 303
Ricardo, David, 207
Richards, I. A., 96
Richter, David, 11, 295, 303
Rigoletto (Giuseppe Verdi), 178, 179
Robinson Crusoe (Daniel Defoe), 202–3
   as *Homo economicus*, 202
Robinson, Paul, 181, 182
Rogers, Carl, 36
Rorty, Richard, 36, 194, 283, 293, 294
   as antiphilosopher, compared with Booth, 268–76
   Philosophy and the Mirror of Nature, 268, 271
   and rejection of the mind, 271–73
   and respect for persons, 273–76

Rossi, Paolo, 231n, 233n
Rossini, Gioacchino, 181, 182
Ruskin, John, 188
Russell, Bertrand, 13, 14, 192, 262, 263, 264n, 268, 293, 295
   optimism of, 257

Sachs, Nelly, 71
Sachs, Sheldon, 150n
Said, Edward, 124, 125, 126
Saint-Etienne de Bourges, Cathedral of, 46
Samuelson, Paul, 207
Santayana, George, 192, 258, 295
Sartre, Jean-Paul, 63, 67, 159
satyagraha, 160
scarcity, 203
science, definition of, in English, 188
Schumpeter, Joseph, 196
Schwab, Joseph, 42, 43, 54
Searle, John R., 189
   and the debate with Derrida, 230n
Sen, Amartya, 190
Serenade (Cain), 167, 177, 178–81
Sextus Empiricus, 256, 258
Shaftesbury, third earl of (Anthony Ashley Cooper), 295
Shapiro, Susan, 11, 293, 297
Shaw, George Bernard, 49
Shelley, Mary, 123
Shoah, 71, 79–80, 84n
silence
   as ignoring/denying, 72, 74
   as tacit agreement, 213
Silko, Leslie M., 286
Sloane, Thomas O., 35, 38n
Smith, Adam, 187, 196, 206
   Wealth of Nations, as theory of selfishness, 201
Song of the Lark (Cather), 175, 177
Stephens, James, 280
Stevens, Wallace, 192, 206, 207
Strauss, Harold, 168
Streuver, Nancy, 37n
Stride Toward Freedom (King), 158

Stigler, George, 192
Suleiman, Susan, 109–12, 115n
Symposium, The (Plato), 178

tact, 227n
Taylor, Charles, 308n
Taylor, Cecil, 179
Taylor, General Maxwell, 44, 51, 52, 54n
Tell Me a Riddle (Olsen), 140
temporality, in narrative, 79
"text"
  as problematic term, 3
  as interaction, 8
Theory of Political Economy, The (Jevons), 187
Thermopylae, Battle of, 40, 51
Thief's Journal, A (Genet), 65
Thomas, Clarence, 250
Thomas, Francis-Noël, 10, 287, 289
  The Writer Writing, 292
Thomas Aquinas, Saint, 287
"Three Functions of Reviewing at the Present Time," 104, 107
Thucydides, 47, 51
Todorov, Tzvetan, 112, 190
Tolstoy, Leo, 287
topics, 22, 27, 99, 281
  as defining the rhetorician, 34
  formal/general and special/material, 10, 23, 24
Toulmin, Stephen, 205
Town Beyond the Wall, The (Wiesel), 74
Tracts for the Times (Newman), 36
Tres riches heures de Jehan, duc de Berry, Les, 46, 51
true fiction, 79–81
Trump, Donald, 199–200
Turing, Alan, 50, 52
Turing Test, 50
Twain, Mark, 9, 140, 150
  Adventures of Huckleberry Finn, 9, 138, 142–43, 147, 151n, 288

umbrella paradox, 113

understanding, as a value of pluralism, 7, 11, 113
University of Chicago. *See* Chicago, University of
University of Iowa, 302
University of Notre Dame, 239
utilitarians, as Platonists, 204
Utopia (More), 35, 218

van der Weyden, Rogier, 44, 51, 52
via negativa, 74
Vico, Giambattista, 21
Vienna Circle, 196
Vietnam War, 40, 44
Vinogradov, Victor, 90–93
vitality, 7, 11, 101, 113, 290
Vives, Juan, 21
Vocation of a Teacher, The, 1, 7, 9, 21, 35, 52, 61, 288

Walker, Alan, 170
Walker, Alice, 140
Watson, Walter, 115
Weaver, Richard, 59, 68
  and ethical criteria, 62
  Ethics of Rhetoric, 62
Wharton, Edith, 146
Whately, Richard, 262
Whigham, Frank, 228n, 229n, 230n
White, James Boyd, 162n
  Heracles' Bow, 229n
Whitney, Charles, 232n
Wicksell, Knut, 207
Wiesel, Elie, 11, 292
  and ethical criticism, 71–87
  The Gates of the Forest, 73
  indictment of God of, 83
  The Town Beyond the Wall, 74
  and true fiction, 79–81
Wilde, Oscar, 190
Williams, Bernard, 228, 282
Wilson, Edmund, 167
Wilson, Harriet, 144
Wittgenstein, Ludwig, 295
  as antiphilosopher, 267, 268

Writer Writing, The (F.-N. Thomas), 292
Wuthering Heights (E. Brontë), 123

Yeats, W. B., 140

Yoos, George, 68n
Young, Karl, x, 2